PRIMITIVE WORSHIP
& THE PRAYER BOOK

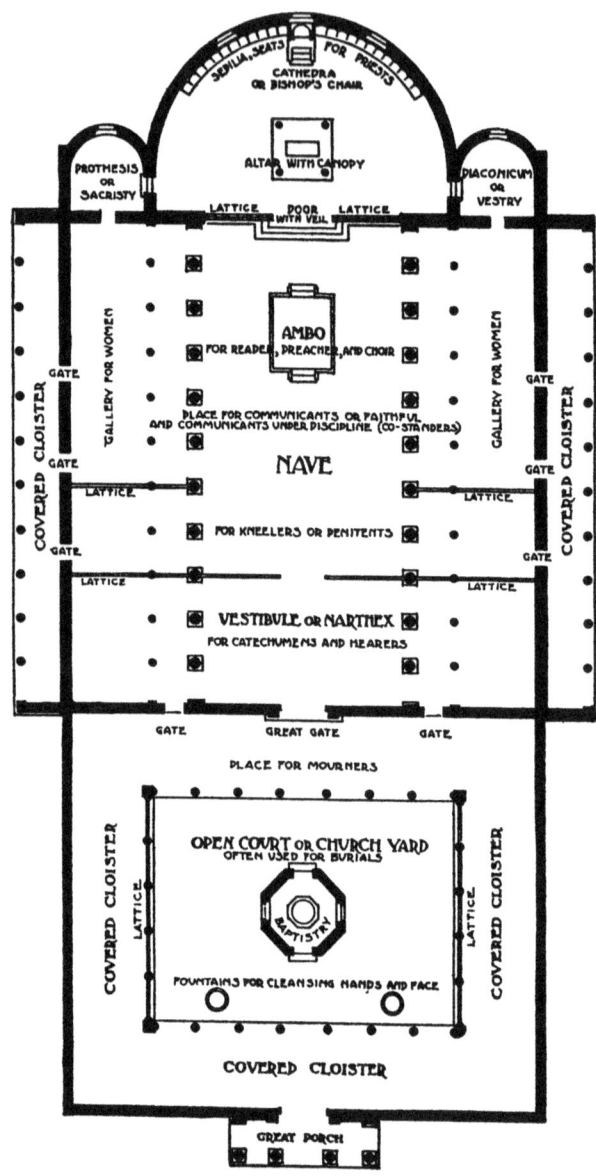

PLAN of a Church in the reign of Constantine, the first Christian Emperor (A.D. 306-337), as described by the historian Eusebius (A.D. 266-340), and other early Christian writers. The chief features are those of the Cathedral Church of Tyre, erected in A.D. 314. For further description see pages 40, 41, 42, 54, and 55.

PRIMITIVE WORSHIP & THE PRAYER BOOK

RATIONALE, HISTORY, AND DOCTRINE OF THE
ENGLISH, IRISH, SCOTTISH, AND AMERICAN BOOKS

BY

THE REV. WALKER GWYNNE, D.D.

AUTHOR OF "THE CHRISTIAN YEAR, ITS PURPOSE AND
ITS HISTORY," "THE GOSPEL IN THE CHURCH," etc.

WIPF & STOCK · Eugene, Oregon

Wipf and Stock Publishers
199 W 8th Ave, Suite 3
Eugene, OR 97401

Primitive Worship and the Prayer Book
Rationale, History, and Doctrine of the English, Irish,
Scottish, and American Books
By Gwynne, Walker
Softcover ISBN-13: 978-1-6667-3538-3
Hardcover ISBN-13: 978-1-6667-9240-9
eBook ISBN-13: 978-1-6667-9241-6
Publication date 9/28/2021
Previously published by Longmans, Green and Co., 1917

This edition is a scanned facsimile of
the original edition published in 1917.

TO THE BELOVED MEMORY OF
TWO BISHOPS OF THE HOLY CATHOLIC CHURCH
BOTH ORATORS, POETS, AND DEFENDERS OF THE FAITH

WILLIAM ALEXANDER
Archbishop of Armagh and Primate of All Ireland

ONE HUNDRED AND NINTH IN THE SUCCESSION OF THE
SEE OF S. PATRICK
WHOSE VOICE DID GREAT THINGS FOR THE CHURCH IN
PERILOUS TIMES
TO WHOM ALSO THE AUTHOR AS CHILD AND MAN OWES A
DEEP SPIRITUAL DEBT: AND

WILLIAM CROSWELL DOANE
First Bishop of Albany

FROM WHOM UNDER GOD HE RECEIVED THE SACRED ORDER
OF PRIESTHOOD AND MUCH BESIDES
THIS VOLUME ON THE BOOK OF THEIR DEVOTION AND
LOVING LOYALTY IS AFFECTIONATELY DEDICATED

PREFACE

AN apology may seem to be needed for another manual on Church Worship. It is evident, however, to any one who takes up the serious study of the Prayer Book, which, next to the English Bible, is the greatest classic in the language, that in almost every volume on the subject the rationale, and the authority of Holy Scripture and the Primitive Church have been assumed, or else almost wholly overlooked. Nevertheless, in the vast majority of cases, not only among converts to the Church's ways, but among intelligent laymen, Churchmen by tradition, the first and most important things to know are why we use a book of worship at all, and on what fundamental principles, apart from mere æsthetic or personal preference, the volume which we call the Book of Common Prayer, and "our incomparable Liturgy," is based.

It is greatly to the honor of the English Church that she has had so many and so able liturgical scholars who, for the last three centuries, have created a new field of theological study. The object of the present volume is to utilize this vast store of buried learning, so that the general reader, as well as teacher and candidate for Holy Orders, may have a book of modest dimensions that will give a bird's-eye view of the subject. To the student it may serve as an introduction to a more exact study later on of those treasures of devotion which, in all ages of the Church, and in many tongues, have been the censers on which have been laid the heart thoughts and petitions of martyrs and saints, and those myriads of unnamed servants of our Lord who are now with Him in Paradise.

PREFACE

In addition to tracing the origin and development of Christian worship to its present form for English-speaking people, the author has had one other object in view in the preparation of this volume. The Book of Common Prayer represents from age to age the living voice of the Church, the *Ecclesia docens*, as interpreting and witnessing to us "the mind of Christ," and the doctrine and practice of His Apostolic master builders. And so it is continually asked, What does the Prayer Book teach? or rather, What does the Church teach by means of her Prayer Book? Nevertheless it is true today, as it was true in 1823, when Bishop Brownell of Connecticut in the Preface to his "Family Prayer Book, with Commentary," etc., declared his "persuasion that many who habitually use the Book of Common Prayer have a very imperfect appreciation of the full import of its several Offices."

To make plain, then, what the Church teaches, from the words of her own formularies, from her traditional customs and ways, and her interpretation of Holy Scripture, is a most necessary object when discordant voices in diverse directions are claiming authority for their own ideas as to what the Church stands for, and *is*, or should be. "To the law and the testimony" in this authoritative volume, therefore, let our appeal be, in accordance with our Lord's command to "Hear the Church." *Lex orandi, lex credendi* is still her wise rule, and happily the teaching of her manual of devotion is so unmistakable, that it only needs a little painstaking examination to learn what this is on every matter of fundamental importance. "Church Doctrine Bible Truth" was the pithy title of a small but great book by Prebendary Sadler some fifty years ago, and the Church speaks here so clearly that a thoughtful writer can well say: "The honest and careful study of the Book has invariably led either to the adoption of its teaching, or to a desire

PREFACE ix

that the Book itself should be changed; a sufficiently plain admission by both parties that its meaning is clear, if men will only take the trouble to discover it."[1]

The preparation of the present book has grown out of circumstances similar to those which occasioned the writing of the companion volume on *The Christian Year: Its Purpose and its History*. The author was asked to teach the subject of Church Worship in the Newark Diocesan Training School, and he could find no manual adapted to the needs of his pupils. Of learned treatises there were abundance, and also of elementary books dealing in a very cursory way with the subject. But the learned treatises were dry and unattractive to all but liturgical students, and the others were lacking in fulness and breadth of treatment. The author can only appeal to the judgment of those for whom the book is primarily intended, and of that larger class of general readers to whom the subject may prove of interest, as to whether he has succeeded in his aim or not.

For the benefit of those who may desire to pursue their studies further, or to verify the positions taken in the book, he gives here the following list of helpful works in English:

Barry, Bp., *Teacher's Prayer Book;* Benton, *Catalogue of Prayer Books in the Collection of the Author* (Boston, U.S., 1910); Bingham, *Antiq.*, Books X–XV; Blunt, *Ann. Prayer Bk.*; Bright, *Ancient Collects;* Brightman, *The English Rite;* Burbidge, *Liturgies and Offices of the Church;* Cardwell, *History of Conferences;* Cyril, Saint, *Catechetical Lectures*, XXII, XXIII (Oxford, 1838); Daniel, *The Prayer Book, its History*, etc.; Dearmer, *Parson's Hand Book;* Dowden, *Studies in the Prayer Book*, and *The Workmanship of the Prayer Book;* Duchesne, *Christian Worship, its Origin and Evolution* (trans. of *Origines du culte chrétien*, London, S. P.C.K. 1912); Ffoulkes, *Prim. Consecration of Euch. Oblation;*

---
[1] J. S. B. Monsell, Preface to *Our New Vicar*.

PREFACE

Freeman, *Prin. Div. Ser.*; Frere, *Principles of Religious Ceremonial*, and *Some Principles of Lit. Reform* (see also Procter and Frere); Gasquet and Bishop, *Edward VI and the Book of Comm. Pr.*; Gummey, *The Consecration of the Eucharist*; Hammond, *Liturgies Eastern and Western*; Hart, *Book of Comm. Pr.* (American); Heurtley, *Harmonia Symbolica*; Hooker, *Ecc. Pol.*, Book V, chapters xxiii–lxxv; Legg, *Cranmer's Liturgical Projects*; L'Estrange, *Alliance of Divine Offices*; Linklater, *True Limits of Ritual in the Church*; Luckock, *Studies in the Pr. Bk.*, and *The Divine Liturgy*; McGarvey, *Liturgiae Americanae*; Maclean, *Early Christian Worship*; Maskell, *Ancient Liturgy of the Ch. of Eng.*, and *Monumenta Rit. Ecc. Anglicanae*; Moberly, *Ministerial Priesthood*; Neale, *Essays on Liturgiology*; Neale and Littledale, *Commentary on the Psalms* (Liturgical, Mystical, and Messianic), and *Translations of the Prim. Liturgies*; Palmer, *Origines Lit.*; Prayer Books, *First and Second of Edward VI.* (Everyman's Lib.); *Prayer Book Commentary* (S.P.C.K.); Procter and Frere, *New His. Bk. Comm. Pr.*, 1907; Pullan, *His. Bk. Com. Pr.*; Scudamore, *Notitia Euch.*; Staley, *Liturgical Studies*; Warren, *Lit. Ante-Nicene Church*, *Lit. of Celtic Church*, and *The Sarum Missal in English*; Wheatly, *Rational Illustration of Bk. Comm. Pr.*; Wordsworth and Littlehales, *The Old Service Books of the English Church* (1904).

The author would record his appreciation of helpful suggestions given him by the Right Rev. A. C. A. Hall, D.D., Bishop of Vermont, and of valuable assistance in the article on "Music in the Church" by the Rev. Charles Winfred Douglas, though without committing either of these friends to all that he has written. To Mr. H. H. Wheeler, Member of the American Institute of Architects, he is deeply indebted for his most painstaking work in drawing the ground-plan of a typical church of the early fourth century, based on the descriptions of the Church historian, Eusebius (A.D. 266–340), and other primitive writers.

SUMMIT, N.J , Lent, 1917

CONTENTS

PART I. — Rationale and History

CHAPTER   PAGE

I. — PRACTICAL REASONS FOR A LITURGY 3

"THE PRAYER BOOK" — MR. GLADSTONE AND "MANY IMPROVEMENTS." — BAXTER'S PRAYER BOOK MADE IN A FORTNIGHT — NECESSITY FOR A BOOK OF "COMMON" PRAYER. — CHANGE OF MIND AMONG DESCENDANTS OF PURITANS. — PROFESSOR HOPKINS ON A LITURGY FOR AMERICAN PRESBYTERIANS. — "THE BOOK OF COMMON WORSHIP" PUBLISHED IN 1906. — INCREASING OBSERVANCE OF THE CHRISTIAN YEAR — LITURGIC USAGE A HERITAGE FROM ISRAEL — NECESSARY FOR PROTECTION FROM IRREVERENCE, ECCENTRICITY, INCOMPETENCE, AND ERROR — HOW CONGREGATIONALISTS OR INDEPENDENTS, AND PRESBYTERIANS BECAME UNITARIANS. — DR. W. R. HUNTINGTON ON FORM AND CEREMONY.

II. — THE AUTHORITY OF OUR LORD AND THE HOLY SCRIPTURES FOR A LITURGY. 13

EVIDENCE OF THE OLD TESTAMENT, AND OF THE CHURCH OF ISRAEL IN THE TIME OF OUR LORD — HIS "CUSTOM" AS CHILD AND MAN. — DR EDERSHEIM ON THE SYNAGOGUE SERVICE IN NAZARETH, AND THE BURNING OF INCENSE IN THE TEMPLE. — OUR LORD'S PRECEPTS CONCERNING PRAYER.

III. — "THEY CONTINUED STEDFASTLY IN THE PRAYERS" 23

THE APOSTLES DEVOUT WORSHIPPERS IN SYNAGOGUE AND TEMPLE EVEN AFTER THE SETTING UP OF THE CHURCH — NO LACK OF MATERIAL FOR A CHRISTIAN LITURGY. — "COMMON PRAYER" IN ACTS IV. — ALLUSIONS TO CHRISTIAN WORSHIP. — PROBABLE

CONTENTS

CHAPTER   PAGE

Quotations from Early Christian Liturgy and Hymns, in the Epistles — No Full Account to be Expected in the New Testament. — Forms not in Themselves Prayers, but Vessels to be Filled with Prayer.

IV. — "They Continued Stedfastly in the Breaking of the Bread" 31

The Breaking of Bread the One Act of Worship Ordained by Christ. — Five Words Applied to the Sacrament in the New Testament. — 1. The Breaking of Bread. — 2. The Lord's Supper. — 3. The Eucharist. — 4. Holy Communion — 5 "Eulogia," or the Blessing. — A New Rite, but the Fulfilment of an Older One. — The Change Prepared for by Our Lord in S. John vi. — Instituted at the Last Passover, and with the Elements Employed there. — Becomes at Once the "Daily" Act of Worship in the Apostolic Church.

V. — Christian Worship in the First Three Centuries 40

All Worship in the First Three Centuries Gathers around the Holy Eucharist — The Altar or Holy Table. — The Temple and not the Synagogue the Model. — Canon Warren on the Character of the Synagogue. — Our Lord's Language at the Cleansing of the Temple — The Sacrificial Character of Christian Worship. — The Puritan Baxter on the Word Altar — The Evidence of the Younger Pliny, Justin Martyr, the Didache, or Doctrine of the Apostles, and of Clement of Rome. — Reasons for the Absence of Early Written Liturgies. — The Disciplina Arcani. — Reasons for Lack of References to Church Buildings. — Earliest Accounts in the Third and Fourth Centuries.

VI. — The Parent Liturgies 56

Little Development of Worship while the Church is under the Ban of the Empire. — In the Fourth Century Six Chief

CONTENTS xiii

CHAPTER PAGE
LITURGICAL TYPES — THE SYRIAN USED IN THE PATRIARCHATES OF JERUSALEM AND ANTIOCH — MANY REVISIONS AND ADAPTATIONS. — THOSE OF S. BASIL AND S CHRYSOSTOM MOST NOTED — SOURCES OF OUR KNOWLEDGE OF THE SYRIAN LITURGY. — THE CENTRAL PORTION OF THAT OF S. CHRYSOSTOM, AND PRAYER FOR THE FAITHFUL DEPARTED. — THE CHIEF DIVISIONS OF EVERY LITURGY — COMPARATIVE TABLE OF FOUR PARENT LITURGIES, SHOWING THEIR UNMISTAKABLE ORIGIN FROM A SINGLE SOURCE.

VII. — THE BRITISH AND IRISH LITURGIES 70
THE BRITISH CHURCH FULLY ORGANIZED IH THE FOURTH CENTURY — THE ANALOGY OF INDIA UNDER THE BRITISH, AND THE PHILIPPINES UNDER THE AMERICANS — TWO LANGUAGES, LATIN AND GAELIC, SPOKEN IN BRITAIN — THE BRITISH CHURCH INDEPENDENT OF ROME IN ORIGIN AND MISSION. — THE CHRISTIANIZING OF IRELAND BY S PATRICK IN THE FIFTH CENTURY, AND OF SCOTLAND BY S. COLUMBA IN THE SIXTH. — IRISH MISSIONS IN ENGLAND, THE CONTINENT, AND EVEN ICELAND. — CATHOLIC IN DOCTRINE, AND PRACTICE YET INDEPENDENT OF ROME. — SIGNS OF THE CLOSE CONNECTION WITH THE GALLICAN CHURCH, AND OF DIFFERENCE FROM THE ROMAN. — THE MILANESE AND THE SPANISH OR MOZARABIC LITURGIES.

VIII. — GROWTH OF THE ENGLISH LITURGY 82
THE MISSION OF AUGUSTINE IN CANTERBURY. — THE LITURGY HE PREPARED FOR HIS ANGLO-SAXON CONVERTS (601). — THE COUNCIL OF CLOVESHOO (747) ADOPTS A CANON REQUIRING THE ROMAN USE, BUT THE CELTIC RETAINS ITS HOLD — THE USE OF SCOTLAND TILL THE ELEVENTH CENTURY. — AT THE NORMAN CONQUEST (1066) MANY DIOCESAN "USES." — BISHOPS OSMUND AND GOODE AND THE USE OF SALISBURY OR SARUM. — DIVERSE USES TILL 1549 — FIRST ATTEMPT AT REFORM OF THE DAILY OFFICES IN 1516, AND FOR HOLY COMMUNION IN 1533. — CLOSE OF THE THIRD GREAT PERIOD IN THE HISTORY OF THE CHURCH OF ENGLAND. — DETERIORATION IN WORSHIP AND LIFE. — INFLUENCE OF NEW SCHOOLS AND COLLEGES

CONTENTS

CHAPTER	PAGE
IX. — THE BEGINNINGS OF REFORM	90

THE REFORMATION NO SUDDEN CATASTROPHE. — SPREAD OVER MORE THAN TWO HUNDRED YEARS (1450-1662). — STRONG PROTESTS AS EARLY AS THE ELEVENTH, TWELFTH, AND THIRTEENTH CENTURIES — COUNCIL OF CLARENDON (1164). — "MAGNA CHARTA" (1215). — NO "CHURCH OF ROME" EVER IN ENGLAND — STATUTES OF "PROVISORS" AND "PRAEMUNIRE." — ARCHDEACON (AFTERWARDS CARDINAL) MANNING ON THESE PROTESTS. — WORK AND CHARACTER OF WICLIFFE. — HIS TRANSLATION OF THE BIBLE. — THE DESTRUCTION AND ROBBERY OF THE MONASTERIES. — THE GOOD WORK OF CARDINAL WOLSEY — BEGINNINGS OF REFORMATION IN DOCTRINE. — THE USURPED AUTHORITY OF THE BISHOPS OF ROME REJECTED IN 1534 — PUBLICATION OF "THE GREAT BIBLE" IN 1539. — COMMITTEE OF REVISION APPOINTED IN 1543. — REVISED LITANY IN 1544 — HENRY VIII DIES IN 1547.

X. — THE FIRST REFORMED PRAYER BOOK	98

THE NEW BOOK NOT A "COMPILATION" — MANY REVISERS IN THE PAST. — THE CHIEF BOOKS OF WHICH THE BOOK IS A REVISION — WHY SO FEW OF THESE REMAIN — CAXTON THE FIRST ENGLISH PRINTER. — EDWARD VI ON THE THRONE. — DUKE OF SOMERSET "PROTECTOR." — SERVICE IN ENGLISH FOR COMMUNION IN 1548 — THE WHOLE BOOK IN 1549. — NO IRISH OR WELSH VERSION. — CONTENTS OF THE BOOK. — COMMUNION IN BOTH KINDS. — PALMER ON THIS. — RESTORATION OF THE INVOCATION. — THE ORDER OF THE SERVICE AND THE PRAYER OF CONSECRATION. — THE CHARACTER OF THE FIRST BOOK. — FOUR OBJECTS IN VIEW.

XI. — REACTION AND RESTORATION 1552-1662	109

RISE OF PURITANISM. — NEW COMMITTEE APPOINTED BUT ONLY BY THE COUNCIL OF STATE. — BOOK OF 1552 WITHOUT AUTHORITY FROM THE CHURCH — CHARACTER OF SOMERSET AND HIS ASSOCIATES — ROBBERY OF CHURCHES — DR MORGAN DIX ON THE SECOND PRAYER BOOK. — CHIEF CHANGES FOR THE

CONTENTS

CHAPTER — WORSE. — EDWARD DIES AND THE BOOK DIES WITH HIM. — OLD LATIN SERVICE RESTORED AND PERSECUTION FOLLOWS. — MARY DIES IN 1558. — NEW REVISION UNDER ELIZABETH. — COMPROMISE RETAINING SOME CHANGES OF 1552 — ELIZABETH DIES IN 1603. — UNDER JAMES I SOME CHANGES IN 1604. — BOOK PROHIBITED BY PURITAN PARLIAMENT IN 1645. — SAVOY CONFERENCE IN 1660. — THE PRESENT BOOK ADOPTED BY BOTH CONVOCATIONS IN 1661 — BY ENGLISH AND IRISH PARLIAMENTS IN 1662 AND 1666 — WAKEMAN ON THIS REVISION AND THE EJECTMENT OF NONCONFORMIST MINISTERS.

XII. — THE SCOTTISH, AMERICAN, AND IRISH REVISIONS 120

REVOLUTIONARY WORK OF THE SCOTTISH PARLIAMENT IN 1560. — "TULCHAN" BISHOPS. — EFFORTS IN THE NEXT HUNDRED YEARS TO RESTORE EPISCOPACY. — PRAYER BOOK OF 1637. — ITS USE IN EDINBURGH CATHEDRAL — EPISCOPACY ABOLISHED ONCE MORE. — UNDER CHARLES II EPISCOPACY AND LITURGY PARTIALLY RESTORED. — UNDER WILLIAM III AGAIN OVERTHROWN IN 1689. — PRESBYTERIANISM ESTABLISHED. — "THE CATHOLIC REMAINDER" OF EPISCOPALIANS UNDER PENAL LAWS. — REVISION OF THE SCOTTISH BOOK IN 1764. — CONSECRATION OF BISHOP SEABURY FOR AMERICAN CHURCH IN 1784. — THE AMERICAN REVISIONS OF 1789 AND 1892. — IRISH REVISION OF 1877. — INTRODUCTION OF "PROTESTANT EPISCOPAL" IN AMERICAN BOOK. — OBJECTIONS TO THE NOVEL TITLE. — GROWTH OF MOVEMENT FOR RESTORATION OF SCRIPTURAL NAME. — APPENDIX WITH COMPARISON OF PRAYERS OF CONSECRATION, AND GENEALOGY OF LITURGIES OF ANGLICAN COMMUNION.

CONTENTS

PART II. The Prayer Book and What it Teaches.

XIII. — THE HOLY COMMUNION. — THE PREPARATION OR PRO-ANAPHORA 135

THREE CLASSES OF SERVICE IN THE PRAYER BOOK. — 1. PUBLIC WORSHIP; 2 OCCASIONAL OFFICES FOR PRIESTS; 3. OCCASIONAL OFFICES FOR BISHOPS. — THE HOLY EUCHARIST AN ORDINARY, NOT EXTRAORDINARY, SERVICE — THE "LITURGY" PROPER A GREAT PREACHING SERVICE — THE ORDINARY OR PRO-ANAPHORA, AND THE CANON OR ANAPHORA. — "ANTE-COMMUNION." — TITLE OF THE OFFICE IN THE FIRST BOOK. — ORIGIN OF "MISSA," OR MASS — BETTER TITLE, HOLY EUCHARIST — RUBRICS CONCERNING THE "CURATE," "REPULSION," PLACE OF THE HOLY TABLE, "FAIR LINEN CLOTH," NORTH OR "RIGHT" SIDE. — THE LORD'S PRAYER, AND USE OF ITALICS AND CAPITALS. — TEN COMMANDMENTS.

XIV. — THE COLLECTS 145

COLLECTS, ETC., SHOW MIND OF THE CHURCH AS TO FREQUENCY OF CELEBRATION. — TRUE EVEN OF GOOD FRIDAY. — COLLECTS PECULIAR TO THE WEST. — THE SONNET OF DEVOTION. — ORIGIN OF THE WORD. — MOSTLY TRANSLATIONS FROM ANCIENT USE. — INVOCATION OF SAINTS — CRANMER AS A TRANSLATOR. — ADDITIONAL COLLECTS IN SCOTTISH AND AMERICAN BOOKS. — CANON BRIGHT AND LORD MACAULAY ON COLLECTS. — APPENDIX SHOWING ORIGINAL SOURCES, AND CLASSIFICATION FOR PRIVATE USE.

XV. — EPISTLES, GOSPELS, CREED, AND SERMON . . 154

MOST OF EPISTLES AND GOSPELS AS IN USE OF SARUM. — PRINCIPLE OF THEIR SELECTION — AT FIRST ONLY SELECTIONS FROM THE OLD TESTAMENT. — RETAINED IN ARMENIAN AND MILANESE LITURGIES — ORIGIN OF THE EPISTLES OR "APOSTLES." — SITTING AT THE EPISTLES, STANDING AT THE GOSPELS. — "GLORIA TIBI" — THE EUCHARISTIC CREED — ORIGIN OF THE "FILIOQUE." — BOWING AT THE SACRED NAME — THE SERMON, AND THE BIDDING PRAYER.

CONTENTS

XVI. — THE OFFERTORY, PRAYER FOR THE CHURCH, EXHORTATION, AND INVITATION 159

OFFERINGS FOR SUPPORT OF THE CHURCH AND CLERGY. — ORIGIN OF ENDOWMENTS — THE CHURCH OF ENGLAND NOT "STATE-PAID." — THE MIXED CHALICE. — UNLEAVENED BREAD. — "UNFERMENTED WINE." — THE CREDENCE. — "INDIVIDUAL CUPS." — PROTHESIS AND THE "GREAT ENTRANCE." — PRAYER FOR CHRIST'S CHURCH MILITANT. — COMMEMORATION OF AND PRAYER FOR THE FAITHFUL DEPARTED. — WITHDRAWAL OF COMMUNICANTS — THE EXHORTATION TO COMMUNION. — DIFFERENCE BETWEEN "NOTICE" AND "WARNING" — "YE THAT DO TRULY, ETC." — "KISS OF PEACE." — FALSE INTERPRETATION OF THE INVITATION AS APPLYING TO ALL PERSONS CONFIRMED OF UNCONFIRMED.

XVII. — CONFESSION, ABSOLUTION, COMFORTABLE WORDS 167

NO GENERAL CONFESSION IN ROMAN OR MEDIAEVAL ENGLISH LITURGY. — THE "CONFITEOR" ONLY FOR THE CELEBRANT AND HIS ASSISTANTS — THE USE OF AN UNKNOWN TONGUE PREVENTED A GENERAL CONFESSION. — PRIVATE OR "AURICULAR" CONFESSION. — VOLUNTARY IN THE PRIMITIVE CHURCH. — STILL VOLUNTARY IN ALL THE ORIENTAL CHURCHES — ABSOLUTION AND THE "MINISTRY OF RECONCILIATION" — THE COMFORTABLE WORDS — A FITTING CLOSE OF THE PREPARATION OR PRO-ANAPHORA.

XVIII. — THE CELEBRATION: ANAPHORA OR CANON 172

THE "SURSUM CORDA." — "SANCTUS" OR "TRISAGION." — PROPER PREFACES. — PREFACE FOR TRINITY SUNDAY. — PRAYER OF HUMBLE ACCESS. — PRAYER OF CONSECRATION IN ENGLISH BOOK LACKING IN INVOCATION. — L'ESTRANGE ON THE INCONSISTENCY OF THE REVISERS. — CORRECTED IN SCOTTISH AND AMERICAN BOOKS. — "THE CONTINUAL REMEMBRANCE." — THE "ANAMNESIS" IN THE PASSOVER AND THE SHEW BREAD. — THE MEMORIAL OF MELCHIZEDEC AND THE

CONTENTS

CHAPTER
Bow in the Cloud. — Hymn of Canon Bright. — "We" a Witness to the Priesthood of all the People. — But no Contradiction of the Ministerial Priesthood. — Liddon and Gore on "Sacerdotalism."

XIX. — Christ's Presence in the Holy Communion . . . 185
The Church has no Theory as to How. — Transubstantiation. — Article XXVIII and Pope Gelasius. — Consubstantiation and the Theory of Zwingli. — All Theories Equally Objectionable — Princess Elizabeth. — The Fact, and not the Manner of the Presence. — S. T. Coleridge and Hooker — A Good Test-Question. — Canon Scott Holland on the Central Act of Public Worship.

XX. — Communion and Post-Communion 191
Self-Examination. — Bishop C. Wordsworth, Bishop Kingdon, Dr. Pusey, and the Convocation of Canterbury on Fasting Reception — "Into the Hands." — Rule Taught by S. Cyril of Jerusalem. — Various Customs as to Administration. — "Communicate" — "Daily Bread" — "Gloria in Excelsis" — Consumption of Elements, and Ablutions. — Reserved Sacrament. — "Black Rubric."

XXI. — Daily Morning and Evening Prayer: Matins and Evensong 200
The Successor of the Daily Prayers of the Temple and Synagogue. — Preserved for the People only in the Anglican Communion. — The Rule as Early as the Third Century. — In the Fourth Century Increased and Elaborated. — Under the Influence of the Monasteries Developed into Seven. — Impracticable for Ordinary Use. — Matins and Evensong Formed from These on Definite Plan. — Sentences or "Capitula," Exhortation, Confession, etc. — Concerning Late-Comers. — Absence of Office Hymns.

CONTENTS

CHAPTER   PAGE
XXII. — THE PSALTER 208
PRAISE THE DOMINANT NOTE OF THE PSALMS. — THE "VENITE," OR INVITATORY. — OUR LORD'S USE OF THE PSALMS ON THE CROSS — ARCHBISHOP ALEXANDER AND S. AUGUSTINE ON THE PSALMS. — THE VALUE OF THEIR CONSTANT RECITATION. — THE "IMPRECATORY" PSALMS. — BISHOP BUTLER ON "RESENTMENT." — THE THEORY OF MOSES MENDELSSOHN, AND OTHERS. — PECULIARITY OF HEBREW POETRY FOR TRANSLATION. — LIDDON ON CRANMER. — PECULIARITY OF THE PRAYER BOOK TRANSLATION. — THE DESIRABLILTY AND NEED OF ENGLISH TITLES — VALUE OF ANTIPHONS. — THE ARRANGEMENT OF THE PSALMS FOR RECITATION — THE SCOTTISH PLAN. — METHODS OF SINGING. — HOOKER ON THE OBJECTIONS OF THE PURITANS. — *Appendix I.* SUGGESTED ENGLISH TITLES FOR THE PSALMS. — *Appendix II.* MUSIC IN THE CHURCH — DUPANLOUP AND DARWIN. — PLAIN SONG — COUNCIL OF TRENT. — PALESTRINA — "AUTHENTIC" AND "PLAGAL" MODES. — MERBECKE, TALLIS, AND ANGLICAN CHANTS. — METRICAL HYMNS AND PSALMS.

XXIII. — THE LESSONS AND CANTICLES 235
SCRIPTURE LESSONS IN THE MEDIÆVAL SERVICES VERY BRIEF. — PLAN OF READING OLD TESTAMENT ONCE EACH YEAR, AND THE NEW TWICE. — SOME PROPER LESSONS FIRST APPOINTED IN 1559. — CHANGES IN 1662. — IN USE IN AMERICA TILL 1789, IN ENGLAND TILL 1871. — THE "TE DEUM" A HYMNLIKE CREED. — THE "BENEDICITE." — S. AUGUSTINE AND COLERIDGE ON THE WITNESS OF NATURE TO GOD — "BENEDICTUS" AND "JUBILATE." — EVENSONG AND NOT VESPERS THE NAME IN THE ENGLISH BOOK. — THE "MAGNIFICAT." — ARCHBISHOP ALEXANDER ON ITS AGE, LIDDON ON ITS CHARACTER — "CANTATE DOMINO," "NUNC DIMITTIS," AND "DEUS MISEREATUR."

XXIV. — THE CREED 245
NOT THREE CREEDS. — NOT A COMPOSITION OF HUMAN REASON. — DIFFERENT FROM MODERN "CONFESSIONS" IN ITS SIMPLICITY. — THE KEY OF ALL INTELLECTUAL DIFFICULTIES. — A "FORM

CHAPTER   PAGE
OF SOUND WORDS" EXISTING BEFORE THE NEW TESTAMENT. — A NECESSITY STILL FOR ALL. — R. H. HUTTON ON THE VALUE OF THE CREED. — ITS USE BY AN AMERICAN ARCTIC EXPLORER, BY A LITTLE CHILD, BY CATHARINE CRAUFORD TAIT.

XXV. — THE THREE CREEDS 250

THE CREED A SUMMARY OF FACTS UNDISCOVERABLE BY HUMAN REASON — CHRIST THE GREAT CREED-MAKER — THE FORM OFTEN DIFFERED IN DIFFERENT DIOCESES. — THE SUBSTANCE ALWAYS THE SAME. — THAT OF AQUILEIA THE NORM OF THE WEST. — ITS ANCIENT PLACE AFTER PSALMS AND LESSONS. — THE NICENE CREED IN THE LITURGY. — WHY FORMERLY SAID SECRETLY — THE ORIGINAL OF THE NICENE PROBABLY THAT OF JERUSALEM AND CAESAREA. — ITS ADOPTION AT NICE. — THE ONLY QUESTION HOW BEST TO EXPRESS THE TRADITIONAL FAITH — THE ADDITIONS MADE AT CONSTANTINOPLE, EPHESUS, AND CHALCEDON. — THE "FILIOQUE," "AND FROM THE SON." — ARCHBISHOP ALEXANDER ON THE NICENE CREED — THE CREED OR HYMN OF S. ATHANASIUS — HILARY OR VICTRICIUS ITS PROBABLE AUTHOR — ACCEPTED AS A CREED ONLY IN THE THIRTEENTH CENTURY. — THE "DAMNATORY" CLAUSES. — KEBLE ON THIS CREED — WHEN USED IN THE ENGLISH BOOK — NOT PRINTED IN THE AMERICAN BOOK. — PRINTED BUT NOT REQUIRED FOR PUBLIC USE IN THE IRISH BOOK.

XXVI. — THE PRAYERS, LITANY, AND OCCASIONAL PRAYERS 261

THE "MUTUAL SALUTATION" AND VERSICLES — COLLECT FOR THE DAY. — OTHER PRAYERS — AMERICAN REVISIONS IN 1789 AND 1892 — THE LITANY OR ECTENE IN THE EAST AND WEST. — S. AUGUSTINE'S LITANY AT CANTERBURY. — HOOKER'S DEFENCE OF THE LITANY AGAINST THE PURITANS — "SUNG OR SAID" — IN FIVE DIVISIONS — "FROM SCHISMS" ONLY INTRODUCED IN 1661 AFTER THE PURITAN AND ROMAN SECTS FORMED IN 1568, 1570, 1572, AND 1633 — ALL PETITIONS BUT THREE ADDRESSED TO THE LORD JESUS. — THE AMERICAN CHANGES — OCCASIONAL PRAYERS, ETC. — NEED OF ADDITIONAL PRAYERS.

CONTENTS

CHAPTER   PAGE

XXVII. — ORNAMENTS OF THE CHURCH AND OF THE MINISTERS THEREOF 272

FEW RITUAL DIRECTIONS IN THE BOOK OF 1549 — THE "ORNAMENTS RUBRIC" ADOPTED IN 1559 TO CORRECT THE ABUSES OF THE PURITANS. — THE INTERPRETATION OF THE ENGLISH FINAL COURT OF APPEAL IN 1857 — THE FORCE OF THE ORNAMENTS RUBRIC IN THE AMERICAN CHURCH. — THE USE OF INCENSE AND LIGHTS.

XXVIII. — THE BAPTISMAL OFFICES 281

THE SARUM OFFICE VERY COMPLICATED. — THE SIGN OF THE CROSS. — PURITAN OBJECTIONS. — THE GOSPEL, AND THE RULE AS TO SPONSORS. — MODIFICATION IN THE AMERICAN CHURCH. — INFLUENCE OF ARCHBISHOP HERMANN'S REVISIONS — IMMERSION AND POURING BOTH ALLOWED — HISTORICAL AND GRAMMATICAL REASONS FOR POURING. — THE PROPER MINISTER — LAY BAPTISM — REGENERATION NOT CONVERSION — BAPTISM OF INFANTS. — BAPTISM OF ADULTS.

XXIX. — THE CATECHISM 295

INSTRUCTION OF CATECHUMENS IN THE PRIMITIVE CHURCH AND IN MEDIAEVAL ENGLAND — PRACTICAL NECESSITY FOR SUCH A GUIDE TO "FIRST PRINCIPLES" INSTEAD OF MERE BIBLE KNOWLEDGE. — THE LIVING CHURCH TO "TEACH," THE BIBLE TO GIVE "THE CERTAINTY" — THE BREVITY OF THE CATECHISM — ENLARGEMENT PROPOSED BY THE LOWER HOUSE OF CANTERBURY. — CATECHIZING "OPENLY IN THE CHURCH" SADLY NEGLECTED WITH GREAT LOSS — THE STILL MORE EXPLICIT DIRECTION BY CANON IN THE AMERICAN CHURCH.

XXX. — CONFIRMATION 303

THOUGH NOT A SACRAMENT "GENERALLY NECESSARY TO SALVATION," NEVERTHELESS "ORDAINED BY CHRIST HIMSELF." — POSSESSES "AN OUTWARD VISIBLE SIGN AND AN INWARD SPIRITUAL GRACE" — ONE OF SIX "PRINCIPLES OF CHRIST'S DOCTRINE." — CONFIRMATIONS IN SAMARIA AND EPHESUS — MANY ALLUSIONS TO CONFIRMATION AS "THE SEAL," "UNC-

xxii CONTENTS

CHAPTER PAGE
TION," "ANOINTING." — CONTINUOUS USE FROM THE BEGINNING. — THE TRUE PURPOSE AND EFFECT OF CONFIRMATION. — NOT MERELY "CONFIRMING" BUT "BEING CONFIRMED." — THE LAYMAN'S ORDINATION TO PRIESTHOOD. — THE MINISTER OF CONFIRMATION. — THE ORIENTAL RULE. — NONE TO BE ADMITTED TO HOLY COMMUNION UNLESS CONFIRMED, OR READY AND DESIROUS. — METHODS OF CONFIRMING. — AGE OF CANDIDATES.

XXXI. — SOLEMNIZATION OF MATRIMONY: MARRIAGE AND DIVORCE 318

VALID MARRIAGE NOT DEPENDENT ON SOLEMNIZATION. — A NATURAL UNION, "ONE FLESH," INDISSOLUBLE EXCEPT BY DEATH. — GRIEVOUSLY ABUSED AMONG THE JEWS. — THE DIVINE LAW RESTATED BY OUR LORD. — ONLY ONE GROUND FOR "PUTTING AWAY," NONE FOR REMARRIAGE. — THE BOND NOT BROKEN BY ADULTERY, BUT ONLY PROFANED. — S. PAUL'S INTERPRETATION OF CHRIST'S COMMAND — TESTIMONY OF THE APOSTOLIC FATHERS AND OF THE FIRST THREE CENTURIES. — THE CAUSE OF LOOSE IDEAS IN THE EASTERN CHURCH — THE STRICTNESS OF THE WEST, ESPECIALLY IN ENGLAND. — THE LOW TEACHING OF THE PROTESTANT LEADERS IN GERMANY, AND OF THE PURITANS IN ENGLAND. — THE FIRST DIVORCE COURT SET UP BY THE ENGLISH STATE IN 1857. — THE LAW OF ENGLAND THAT OF AMERICA UNTIL THE REVOLUTION. — RAPID DETERIORATION IN EVERY STATE EXCEPT SOUTH CAROLINA. — THE LAW OF THE ENGLISH, IRISH, SCOTTISH, AND AMERICAN PRAYER BOOKS RECOGNIZES NO DISSOLUTION OF MARRIAGE EXCEPT BY DEATH. — REMARRIAGE OF "THE INNOCENT PARTY" IN THE AMERICAN CHURCH. — THE VERDICT OF EXPERIENCE. — SUM OF THE TEACHING OF THE NEW TESTAMENT.

XXXII. — SOLEMINZATION OF MATRIMONY: THE OFFICE 333

MARRIAGE AMONG CHRISTIANS ALWAYS CELEBRATED WITH RELIGIOUS RITES. — FORBIDDEN BY CUSTOM DURING LENT SINCE THE FOURTH CENTURY — THE PURPOSE OF BANNS AND LICENCE. — "IMPEDIMENTS" AND THE TABLE OF PROHIBITED

CONTENTS

CHAPTER — PAGE

DEGREES. — DIRIMENT AND ECCLESIASTICAL IMPEDIMENTS. — THE MEDIÆVAL SERVICE BEGAN AT THE CHURCH PORCH. — THE ESPOUSAL OR "ENGAGEMENT." — THE NUPTIALS OR BETROTHAL. — "THE MAN ON THE RIGHT HAND." — "OBEY" — THE RING — OMISSIONS IN THE AMERICAN OFFICE. — HOOKER ON THE NUPTIAL COMMUNION. — THE SCOTTISH PROVISION FOR A EUCHARIST.

XXXIII. — VISITATION AND COMMUNION OF THE SICK 341

VISITATION REQUIRED IN HOLY SCRIPTURE, AND PLEDGED IN ORDINATION VOW. — THE SALUTATION OF PEACE — "SPECIAL CONFESSION" AND "ABSOLUTION" VOLUNTARY. — ANOINTING OF THE SICK IN BOOK OF 1549. — AUTHORITY OF OUR LORD AND OF S. JAMES — THE LAMBETH CONFERENCE ON UNCTION OF THE SICK — VARIATIONS IN AMERICAN, SCOTTISH, AND IRISH OFFICES. — COMMUNION OF THE SICK. — RESERVATION OF THE HOLY SACRAMENT. (SEE ALSO CHAPTER XX). — RUBRIC CONCERNING "SPIRITUAL COMMUNION."

XXXIV. — BURIAL OF THE DEAD 349

INTERMENT THE CUSTOM OF BOTH THE JEWISH AND THE CHRISTIAN CHURCH — CREMATION OR INCINERATION. — MEDIÆVAL SERVICES VERY ELABORATE. — BULK OF PRESENT SERVICE FOUND IN THE ANCIENT USE. — "IN THE MIDST OF LIFE, ETC." — ITS USE PECULIAR TO ANGLICAN COMMUNION. — VARIATIONS IN AMERICAN, IRISH, AND SCOTTISH OFFICES. — BENEDICTION OF A GRAVE. — EUCHARIST AT BURIAL IN BOOK OF 1549.

XXXV. — OTHER OCCASIONAL OFFICES: CHURCHING OF WOMEN, ETC. 356

CHURCHING OFFICE VARIES LITTLE FROM THAT OF SARUM. — WHY CALLED "CHURCHING." — VARIATIONS IN AMERICAN AND IRISH BOOKS — VALUE OF THE OFFICE — THE COMMINATION OFFICE PRACTICALLY IDENTICAL WITH THE MEDIAEVAL USE. — WHOLLY OMITTED BY THE AMERICAN CHURCH IN 1789. — THE SUPPLICATIONS WITH SOME ADDITIONS RESTORED IN 1892 AS A "PENITEN-

xxiv CONTENTS

CHAPTER PAGE

TIAL OFFICE." — FORMS OF PRAYER FOR USE AT SEA. — AMERICAN AND IRISH OFFICE FOR VISITATION OF PRISONERS. — FAMILY PRAYERS IN AMERICAN BOOK. — THREE SERVICES OMITTED FROM ENGLISH BOOK IN 1859.

XXXVI. — THE ORDINAL: THE WITNESS OF HOLY SCRIPTURE 363
PREFACE. — OUR LORD EVER LOYAL TO PRIESTHOOD OF JEWISH CHURCH. — HIS METHOD OF PREPARING FOR HIS OWN CHURCH. — CHOOSES TWELVE AS HIS MASTER BUILDERS. — TRAINS AND EMPOWERS THEM. — GIVES THEM "COMMANDMENTS" WHICH ARE ONLY KNOWN BY THEIR ACTS — "APOSTOLIC SUCCESSION" SEEN FROM THE BEGINNING. — THE SECOND ORDER, ELDERS, PRESBYTERS, OR PRIESTS — BISHOP, MEANING OVERSEER, APPLIED AT FIRST TO BOTH APOSTLES AND PRESBYTERS. — CONFINRD LATER TO APOSTLES. — THE THIRD ORDER, DEACONS.

XXXVII. — THE ORDINAL: THE WITNESS OF ANCIENT AUTHORS 372
ALL CHURCH WRITERS IN THE FIRST THREE CENTURIES AGREE IN REGARDING THE THREE ORDERS AS OF DIVINE AUTHORITY. — CLEMENT, IGNATIUS, POLYCARP, HEGESIPPUS, IRENAEUS. — THE HOSTILE JUDGMENT OF GIBBON — HOOKER'S CHALLENGE TO THE PURITANS. — DIOCESAN EPISCOPACY AND APOSTOLIC SUCCESSION TWO DISTINCT THINGS — EVEN IN THE SIXTH CENTURY DIVISION INTO DIOCESES WAS NOT FOUND IN IRELAND AND NORTHERN SCOTLAND — S. JEROME'S STATEMENT. — A SUCCESSION THROUGH PRESBYTERS NOT RECOGNIZED ANYWHERE — ONLY TWO THEORIES EXIST AS TO THE MINISTRY. — THE UNSOUNDNESS OF THE NON-CATHOLIC THEORY SEEN IN "THE DISSIDENCE OF DISSENT."

XXXVIII. — THE ORDINAL: IMAGINED DIFFICULTIES IN THE SUCCESSION 385
SUCCESSION NOT A CHAIN, BUT A NET-WORK. — ANALOGOUS TO ALL CIVIL GOVERNMENT — CONSECRATION BY THREE BISHOPS WITH KNOWLEDGE OF ALL BISHOPS IN THE PROVINCE. — RULE

CONTENTS

CHAPTER

OF COUNCIL OF NICE. — SUCCESSION OF BISHOPS BETTER ATTESTED THAN THE SUCCESSION OF HOLY SCRIPTURE. — "UNWORTHINESS OF MINISTERS" NO BAR. — ARTICLE XXVI, AND BISHOP GORE — PREFACE ONLY STATES UNASSAILABLE HISTORICAL FACTS. — THE STRANGE INTERPRETATION OF "IN THE CHURCH OF ENGLAND," OR "IN THIS CHURCH." — THE GAIN WON BY SELF-CONSTITUTED MINISTRIES NO COMPENSATION FOR THE TERRIBLE LOSS THAT COMES FROM DISUNION — THE VAST MAJORITY OF CHRISTIANS STILL RETAIN THE APOSTOLIC MINISTRY. — THE DECLARATION OF THE LAMBETH CONFERENCE OF 1888.

XXXIX. — ORDINALS PRIMITIVE, MEDIÆVAL, AND MODERN 393

THE ORDINAL ALWAYS EMBEDDED IN THE OFFICE FOR HOLY COMMUNION — THE WITNESS OF THE EARLY CHURCH ORDERS. — PRAYER WITH LAYING ON OF HANDS THE ESSENTIAL ACT OF ORDINATION. — DIFFERENCES OF USAGE AT ORDINATION OF BISHOPS — THE NORMAL FORM OF PRAYER FOR BISHOPS AND PRIESTS. — PRIESTS UNITE IN ORDINATION OF PRIESTS. — DEACONS ORDAINED BY BISHOP ALONE. — MEDIÆVAL ORDINALS OVERLAID BY CUSTOMS WHICH OBSCURED THE TRUE NATURE OF ORDINATION. — "BESTOWAL OF THE INSTRUMENTS." — BORROWED FROM FEUDAL CUSTOMS — OTHER CEREMONIES WHICH TENDED TO CONFUSION. — COMPARISON OF THE PRESENT ROMAN ORDINAL WITH THE PRESENT ENGLISH. — THE REVISED ORDINAL ISSUED IN 1550. — FEW CHANGES IN 1552. — FORM FOR CONSECRATION OF A CHURCH OR CHAPEL ADDED TO THE AMERICAN BOOK IN 1799, AND TO THE IRISH IN 1877. — THE OFFICE OF INSTITUTION OF MINISTERS ADDED TO THE AMERICAN BOOK IN 1804. — THE ARTICLES OF RELIGION, — APPENDIX GIVING OUTLINE OF SARUM ORDINAL.

XL. — CONCLUSION 405

THE APOSTOLIC LITURGY. — TRACED TO ALL ENGLISH SPEAKING LANDS — ITS MANY TRANSLATIONS, AND MANY HUMAN STRAINS. — CRANMER'S WORK AND HIS DIFFICULTIES — HIS GREATNESS AND HIS INFIRMITIES — CANON MASON'S ESTIMATE

CHAPTER OF THE MAN. — SUMMARY OF ABUSES REMEDIED AND BENEFITS GAINED. — THE LARGE PLACE GIVEN TO HOLY SCRIPTURE. — DR. DÖLLINGER'S COMMENT ON THIS. — CREDIT DUE TO THE PURITANS. — THE SUPERB LITERARY STYLE OF THE BOOK THOUGH LARGELY A TRANSLATION. — THE JUDGMENT OF LIDDON, MACAULAY, AND A ROMAN CATHOLIC WRITER. — YET STILL CAPABLE OF IMPROVEMENT AND ADAPTATION TO NEW CONDITIONS.

INDEX 413

PRIMITIVE WORSHIP
& THE PRAYER BOOK

PRIMITIVE WORSHIP & THE PRAYER BOOK

PART I. RATIONALE AND HISTORY

CHAPTER I
PRACTICAL REASONS FOR A LITURGY

"*Form and ceremony are the manners of religion   The waterpots at Cana in Galilee were empty forms, until the servants filled them at the word of Christ, and then they ran with wine. And even so, a liturgy is an empty form, but the man who worships in spirit and in truth may fill it with his heart.*" — W R HUNTINGTON.

THERE is something very suggestive in the popular name, "*The* Prayer Book," which is commonly given to the manual of devotion of the English-speaking Church. It plainly implies that it has no rivals. In Mr. Gladstone's carefully selected library at Hawarden he had a collection of thirty "improvements" on the book, and when he showed them to visitors he used to remark with a smile that not one of them had ever reached a second edition. It would seem to be true of a people's Prayer Book as it is said to be of a poet, *Nascitur, non fit;* it is born, and not made.[1]

---

[1] In marked contrast with this is the attempt of the eminent Puritan, Baxter, author of *The Saints' Rest*, to construct a complete liturgy in two weeks. He was a member of the Savoy Conference in 1661, and he tells us how he laid everything aside and carried the work to completion. "Hereupon," he says, "I departed from them and came no more among them till I had finished my task, which was a fortnight's time" (Luckock, *Studies in the Pr. Bk.* p. 177).

4 PRIMITIVE WORSHIP & THE PRAYER BOOK

The actual title of the volume is "The Book of *Common* Prayer," and the word "Common" calls our attention to a great fundamental principle of Divine worship which had been for many centuries largely ignored in the Church, and is still ignored by almost all modern denominations of Christians who have separated from the ancient national Catholic Churches of Europe. The use of "a tongue not understanded of the people" during the Middle Ages made it practically impossible for the services of the Church to be *common*, that is, so that the people, as at the first, might "lift up their voice with one accord" in common.[1] There is, indeed, a place and a real use for extemporaneous prayer, as there was in the early days of the Church before liturgies assumed their definite form, and also for that silent prayer which pours itself out to God without articulate words. But in public worship the non-use of a book has had exactly the same effect in modern days as that of an unknown tongue in mediæval days, leaving the service almost entirely to the minister, just as once it left it to the priest.[2]

The full title of the book, moreover, is worthy of note. It is "The Book of Common Prayer, and Administration of the Sacraments, and Other Rites and Ceremonies" — not of the Church of England, or the Church in the United States of America, but "of *the Church*," that is, "the Holy Catholic and Apostolic Church" of the Creed, or, as the Te Deum has it, "the holy Church throughout all the world." But this particular book containing these Offices of "the Church Catholic" is "according to the Use of the Church of Eng-

---

[1] Acts iv, 24.

[2] Milton objected to a liturgy as "a supercilious tyranny" imposed on ministers, but it has been remarked that he did not often attend the services of these Puritan ministers, or else he might have made the discovery that every minister is not a Milton.

REASONS FOR A LITURGY 5

land," or of some other national branch of the Church, as that of Ireland, or the United States of America.[1]

And so the title "Common Prayer" challenges our attention, and bids us ask, Is such a book a necessity? And if so, What authority has it in reason, in Scripture, and in history? Here at the outset it is pleasant to remember what a change has come over the minds of many earnest Christian people, in English-speaking lands especially, during the last half century, concerning this question of the value of forms of prayer. The Puritan Westminster Assembly of Divines in 1643 condemned in no measured terms the use of this very Book of Common Prayer. It was ungodly and superstitious, they said. "It has produced an idle and unedifying ministry, which contented itself with set forms." And mere verbal condemnation was not all which the book received. The power of the Puritan civil government was brought to bear upon those who dared to follow the dictates of their conscience and worship God as their forefathers had done for more than a thousand years. In August, 1643, the Puritan Parliament issued an order prescribing that any one using the Book of Common Prayer should be fined five pounds (the equivalent today of five times that sum) for the first offence, ten pounds for the second, for the third a year's imprisonment. Nor was this to apply only to the public use of the book. The law was aimed even at its private use. It was meant to pursue men and women into the secrecy of

---

[1] It is to be remembered that the word "Use" in this place signifies the customary form of Divine Service (*divinum officium*) and Liturgy in a particular country or diocese. It is so employed in the Preface "Concerning the Service of the Church" in the English Book. "Whereas heretofore there hath been great diversity in saying and singing in Churches within this realm, some following Salisbury use, some Hereford use, and some the use of Bangor, some of York, some of Lincoln, now from henceforth the whole realm shall have but one use."

their own houses, and he who could be convicted of using the book even with no eye but God's upon him was subject to the same pains and penalties as the minister who presumed to read it for a congregation of Christian people.[1]

Nor was this state of things confined to England. The same stern course was adopted by the Puritan settlers of New England even at an earlier date. It seems hard to credit it now, that in 1629 the authorities of Massachusetts Bay forbade English Churchmen to enjoy the services of their Prayer Book even in a private dwelling, and that on their refusal to comply, two at least of their number were shipped off to England as "factious and evil-conditioned" persons.[2] In Scotland the same state of things continued even to the close of the eighteenth century, though there political reasons had much to do with the question. Seabury, the first American Bishop, was consecrated in 1784 by the Bishops of the ancient "Catholic remainder" of that country, called the Scottish Episcopal Church, but the service in the city of Aberdeen had to be performed in secrecy, as it was a crime punishable with fine and imprisonment for more than five persons, in addition to the family, to read the Church service even in their own house.[3]

These facts are noted here, not for the purpose of stirring up the embers of old feuds, for Churchmen were also guilty of intolerance of Dissenters, but to serve as a background to that marvellous and welcome contrast which we behold today. The old Church still holds fast to the same Prayer Book which was then despised and reviled as a meaningless mummery. She has not changed, but those who formerly opposed her have changed. Whole Christian bodies whose

---

[1] See Canon Perry's *History of the Church of England*, chap. xxix.
[2] *Ibid.* p. 609.
[3] See Lloyd, *Sketches of Church History in Scotland*, p 106.

REASONS FOR A LITURGY

traditions for three centuries were radically against forms of prayer are found today seeking the old paths of the Church's worship. Prejudice is breaking up, and here and there where fifty years ago liturgic worship was looked upon as formal and heartless, forms of prayer are being freely used. An American Presbyterian divine (Professor Hopkins) wrote concerning this fifty years ago: "The number of Presbyterian ministers who openly advocate the use of some form of prayer is large, and the number of those who hope and anxiously wait for it, much larger. That the Churches themselves are ready to welcome some such improvement is plain enough. That the ministry themselves also feel the want of a liturgy is constantly showing itself." Then he adds that "to make the preaching of the Gospel consist exclusively in the delivery of sermons is a fatal mistake. All appropriate worship of God through Jesus Christ is a preaching of the Gospel. . . . The Apostles' and Nicene creeds are full of the Gospel. . . . There is more of Christ in the Te Deum and the Litany alone than is commonly found in two entire Presbyterian services."[1]

Nor is this reaching out after the reverent ways of the immemorial liturgic worship of the Church the only sign of a better mind on the part of our separated fellow Christians. There is also a growing tendency everywhere for the observance of the Christian Year as well. This is all the more striking because in this later movement it is its fasts rather than its festivals that have been sought. Christmas and

---

[1] It was in response to this growing feeling that the General Assembly of the Presbyterian Church in the United States of America appointed a committee to compile a book of prayers which, under the title of "The Book of Common Worship," was "published by authority, for voluntary use in the Churches," in 1906. It is a useful collection of prayers largely drawn from the Book of Common Prayer and other ancient sources, but not arranged in accordance with liturgical principles.

8 PRIMITIVE WORSHIP & THE PRAYER BOOK

Easter have long been more or less observed among them, but now there is a very general effort being made by earnest ministers and laymen of many denominations to secure the observance of Lent in part or in whole.

But all this is only by way of preface to the many practical and historical reasons which form the ground on which Churchmen have used forms of prayer, not merely for three hundred years, but for eighteen hundred years and more. No great custom among men can be really understood unless we know its *raison d'être* and its history. We must ask therefore first concerning the worship of the Church of Christ on what grounds it has from the beginning adopted what is called the liturgic method.

With the historic English-speaking Church worship by means of a liturgy is not a discovery, but a heritage. It is no method of her own devising any more than the language she speaks, or the letters she uses in writing. It has been handed down through all the Christian centuries and hallowed by the use of a hundred generations. It comes to us from the Tabernacle and the Temple. It comes to us from the Upper Room where the last Paschal Supper of the Older Church was eaten and the new sacrament of God's infinite love was instituted to take its place. It comes from the very Cross itself, even at the moment when the sacred Blood is dripping from the pierced Hands, and Feet, and Side, and thorn-crowned Head. For if at any time thought and feeling should be untrammelled and extemporaneous in their utterance, it is now. Yet what are the words we hear? "My God, My God, why hast Thou forsaken Me?" and again, "Into Thy hands I commend My spirit,"[1] the old familiar forms of prayer that the Boy and Man of Nazareth had said and sung in the liturgic worship of His synagogue

---
[1] Ps. xxii, 1; xxxi, 6.

REASONS FOR A LITURGY

and of the Temple, petitions from that book of Psalms which formed the core of the ordered worship of Israel, as it has ever since continued to form the core of all Christian offices of devotion.

Our first reason, then, for using a liturgy or form of prayer, instead of extemporaneous devotions, is that the highest and best experience in every age, Jewish as well as Christian, has proved it a necessity for unity of worship. Public prayer differs from private in that it must be common prayer, that is, prayer in which every member of a congregation can intelligently join, by voice sometimes, by heart and mind always. This is clearly impossible where the prayers are composed anew for each separate occasion, and sometimes composed on the spur of the moment. Extemporaneous prayer is of course most necessary for private use, though even there not exclusively so. But when we come to public worship, whatever else such extemporaneous prayer may be, no matter how earnest or heartfelt, it cannot be said to be common or united prayer. It does not even escape being a *form* of prayer. It is necessarily a form made for the people to adopt as their own but, not knowing it beforehand, they cannot be said to make it their own and send it up to the throne of grace as the solemn united intercession of God's Church.

To extemporaneous prayer the people can listen, and give or withhold their approval as their judgment may dictate. But this involves criticism, and criticism and devotion are irreconcilable foes. They cannot live under the same roof. As soon as criticism enters, devotion flies away. Indeed, the thought oftentimes left in the people's mind about such prayers is that they are not so much addressed to God as to the assembled congregation; and these form an audience sitting comfortably in their pews, rather than a body of worshippers bending humbly on their knees. Hence we are accustomed to read in the newspapers about prayers that are more like oblique sermons, others that resemble political speeches, and some that are described as "eloquent."

In order to escape these evils the Church in every age and land has provided forms of prayer for her people. If prayer is to be common, there must of necessity be some form known beforehand. This is acknowledged by all in regard to one part of public worship, namely, the singing of hymns. And hymns for the most part consist of either prayer or praise. That they are in verse does not alter the fact that they are forms of prayer.

In addition to the reasons already given for the necessity of forms in the public worship of the Church, there must be mentioned their use in guarding against irreverence or eccentricity on the part of the minister, and in safeguarding the people from the introduction of error or untruth. A single incident out of many will show what is constantly in danger of taking place, where there are no forms of devotion or recited creed to anchor minister and people to the "faith once for all delivered to the saints." The First Congregational Church in Dorchester, Massachusetts, now Unitarian, celebrated its 250th anniversary in 1880. On that occasion the pastor made this statement in explanation of the fact that the original belief of the congregation had been so quietly revolutionized. "The change," he said, "was made gradually; there was no division or strife, no scar of conflict; so gradually that there is nothing whatever in the church records which shows just where the church ceased to be Calvinistic [that is, "Orthodox"] and became Unitarian. Under the leadership of the Rev. Dr. Harris the old church and its company sailed from one latitude to another without straining a timber, without mutiny, and just as comfortably

REASONS FOR A LITURGY

as the 'Mary and John' and her voyagers crossed the billows of the deep" (1629). It is sufficient to say that this voyage from the true faith in our Lord's Godhead could never have occurred if the ship's course had been guided by the chart and compass of its common worship. A creed, no matter how orthodox, that is carefully stored away on the bookshelves of scholars is a dead thing. A creed that is recited by millions of voices, and is sung and prayed by millions of lips and hearts, can alone be a living power.[1]

There are of course other weighty reasons for the use of forms of prayer, derived from the authority of our Lord and the universal practice of His Church. These will be considered in the next chapter. Here we have only treated of the practical use and benefit of a liturgy, first, as a necessary vehicle of "common" or united worship; second, as the guardian of reverence in the presence of God; and in the third place, as a safeguard of the people from error in the minister, and as a conservator of the true faith of the Church from age to age. On this practical side of the question the following words of an able and most thoughtful writer are worth remembering:

"Form and ceremony have their place — a secondary place, no doubt, but still a place. They are the manners of

---

[1] What is true of the Congregational society in Dorchester is true of perhaps the majority of the older Congregational societies of New England. It is true also of the English Puritans of the seventeenth century. The Rev. H N. Oxenham in his translation of Dr. Dollinger's *Reunion of the Churches*, p. 127, has this note: "The English Presbyterians have not disappeared altogether, though their numbers are diminished through the lapse of a large proportion into Socinianism It was stated in the *Eclectic Review* for February, 1832, that out of 258 Presbyterian congregations in England 232 had become Unitarian." The Latin proverb, *Lex orandi, lex credendi*, or as it is in its old English form, Man's rede, man's crede, has many other illustrations.

religion, and though we be as yet, while this earthly life lasts, only in the outer courts of the palace of the Great King, it cannot be amiss for us to bear ourselves as those might do who hoped one day to stand before the throne. Meanwhile this charge of emptiness [of forms and ceremonies] need trouble us not at all, for it is of the very nature of a form, whether devotional or ceremonial, that it be empty until some one fills it. An outline sketch is an empty form; the artist, so the phrase runs, 'fills it in.' A basket is an empty form of wicker-work; the gardener fills it with roses. The waterpots at Cana in Galilee were empty forms, until the servants filled them at the word of Christ, and then they ran with wine. And even so, a liturgy is an empty form, but the man who worships in spirit and in truth may fill it with his heart."[1]

---

[1] *Popular Misconceptions of the Episcopal Church* by the Rev. W. R. Huntington, D.D., p. 13.

CHAPTER II

The Authority of our Lord and of the Scriptures for a Liturgy

"*They found Him in the Temple.*" — S. Luke ii, 46.
"*As His custom was, He went into the synagogue on the Sabbath day.*"
— S. Luke iv, 16.

BESIDES the reasons for the use of liturgic forms of prayer to be found in common sense and experience, as stated in the previous chapter, we have others based on the direct warrant of Holy Scripture and the universal practice of the Church. Our first appeal is to the Old Testament with its history of God's ancient Church of Israel.

It is to be remembered at the outset that every liturgy, whether Jewish or Christian, must of necessity be a growth, though always a growth from a definite principle or seed. It is admitted also that among Christians and Israelites alike in their private devotions, and under exceptional circumstances, even in their public service, "free" or extemporaneous prayer must always be possible. We are considering now, however, the common worship of the Church as a congregation. Here we have the most unquestioned evidence, even in the earliest Old Testament days, of the adoption of the principle that unity and order and dignity could only be obtained by a prearranged form which all should fill with their hearts' desires, and all could intelligently follow. In the days of the journeying in the Wilderness the very words are given to the priests for pronouncing God's blessing upon the congregation.[1] A form of prayer is provided to be used

---
[1] Numb. vi, 22–27.

whenever the sacred ark moves onwards before the people, and whenever it rests.[1] A Thanksgiving service is provided for the offering of the first fruits of the harvest,[2] and another liturgic form is given in the same chapter when the third year's tithes are solemnly presented in God's house.[3] These instances are taken from the very earliest days when the Church was yet in its infancy and incomplete. What that worship became in later days under the inspired direction of Samuel, David, and Solomon, we may gather in part from that marvellous collection of prayers, confessions, praise, and thanksgiving which, in the Psalter, as we call it, became, under the guidance of God, the most wonderful book of devotions the world has ever known. Great Hebrew scholars tell us, moreover, that the Jews had not only fixed forms, but also a fixed order, both in the Temple and in their synagogues. The Temple worship consisted of prayers, psalms, lessons from Holy Scripture, sacrifices, and incense; the synagogue worship, of prayers, lessons, and exhortations only.[4]

Was there any change of principle required by the new dispensation which our Lord brought in? Was human nature so altered as to make such a change either necessary or desirable? In other words, was liturgic worship, which had divine sanction for fifteen hundred years, one of those "beggarly elements" that was to pass away when the fulness of Christ was come? Let us consider the facts of the case. Our Lord had not only been accustomed to the ordered ritual of Temple and synagogue as a Child and Youth. Even as a grown Man He was constantly to be found in His place as a worshipper. S. Luke speaks of His going into the synagogue of His childhood at Nazareth *"as His custom was."*[5]

---

[1] Numb x, 35-36
[2] Deut. xxvi, 1-11.
[3] *Ibid.* verses 12-16.
[4] See S Luke iv, 16, Acts xiii, 15.
[5] S. Luke iv, 16.

AUTHORITY OF OUR LORD

Thither from days of infancy He had been led by the hand of His devout mother Mary and His foster-father Joseph, and when manhood came He had not outgrown either the temper or the habit of the little Child. The synagogue, much more the Temple, was still His spiritual home. With eager enemies all about Him, ready to take advantage of every slight or seeming breach of churchly usage, it is not once charged against Him in all His life that He was a despiser or impugner of that solemn worship which for fifteen centuries had been the prescribed rule and custom of God's holy Church.[1]

Here, therefore, it is important to know something of the character of the worship in Temple and synagogue to which our Lord and the first Christians had all their lives been accustomed. The synagogue was only a kind of parish house in town and village, wherever ten families of Jews were found in Palestine or in heathen lands. Unlike the Christian parish church, it had neither priesthood, altar, nor sacrifice, which were only to be found in what might be called the great cathedral church of the nation in Jerusalem, where God had "set His Name," and promised His especial Presence.[2] In the Temple every Israelite was only bound to worship three times in the year at the great feasts. In both synagogue and Temple, however, the worship was according to a set form, or, as we call it, liturgical. Apart from the sacrifices, the worship of the Temple, while much more elaborate, with its trained and vested choirs of priests and Levites, differed only in degree from that of the synagogue.

The following account of the synagogue service in His own village of Nazareth, as He found it on that Sabbath Day

---

[1] Of His remarkable zeal for the ancient ritual year of Israel see *The Christian Year: Its Purpose and its History*, by the Author, chapters 4 and 5.

[2] Deut. xiv, 23–25, 2 Chron. vi, 20.

in the first year of His public ministry, when, "as His custom was," He entered to take part in the familiar worship there, is taken from the description of a learned Jewish Christian, a priest of the Church of England, Dr. Edersheim:

On His entrance, or perhaps before that, the chief ruler, a layman, would request Him to act as the leader or minister for that occasion. The Lord Jesus would ascend the platform or bema, and, "standing at the lectern, would begin the service by two prayers, which in their most ancient form, as they probably existed in His time, were as follows: —

"'I. Blessed be Thou, O Lord, King of the world, who formest the light and createst the darkness, who makest peace and createst everything; who in mercy givest light to the earth, and to those who dwell upon it, and in Thy goodness, day by day, and every day, renewest the works of creation. Blessed be the Lord our God for the glory of His handiworks, and for the light-giving lights which He has made for His praise. Selah.[1] Blessed be the Lord our God who has formed the lights.

"'II. With great love hast Thou loved us, O Lord our God, and with much overflowing pity hast Thou pitied us, our Father and our King. For the sake of our fathers who trusted in Thee, and Thou taughtest them the statutes of life, have mercy upon us, and teach us. Enlighten our eyes in Thy Law; cause our hearts to cleave to Thy commandments; unite our hearts to fear and love Thy Name, and we shall not be put to shame, world without end. For Thou art

---

[1] *Selah.* "This word occurs 71 times in the Psalter . . It is universally agreed that *Selah* is a liturgical or musical sign of some kind. Its reference to the Temple music is evinced by the fact that 31 of the 39 Psalms containing it are inscribed in their titles *Lamenatseach* [To the chief musician]. . . . The meaning may be 'Lift up! Loud!' a direction to the orchestra . . . Or it may mean [as in this prayer] 'Lift up your benediction'" (Hastings' *Dictionary of the Bible, s. v.*).

a God who preparest salvation, and us hast Thou chosen from among all nations and tongues, and hast in truth brought us near to Thy great Name — Selah — that we may lovingly praise Thee and Thy Unity. Blessed be the Lord, who in love chose His people Israel.'"

After this followed what may be designated as the Jewish Creed, called the *Shema*, from the word 'shema,' or 'hear,' with which it begins. It consisted of three passages from the Pentateuch.[1] The "recitation of the *Shema* was followed by this prayer:

"'True it is that Thou art Jehovah, our God, and the God of our fathers, our King, and the King of our fathers, our Saviour, and the Saviour of our fathers, our Creator, the Rock of our Salvation, our Help, and our Deliverer. Thy Name is from everlasting, and there is no God beside Thee. A new song did they who were delivered sing to Thy Name by the sea-shore; together did all praise and own Thee King, and say, Jehovah shall reign, world without end! Blessed be the Lord who saveth Israel.'"

"This prayer finished, he who officiated took his place before the Ark [the Holy Chest containing the sacred rolls of the Law and the Prophets], and there repeated what formed the prayer in the strictest sense, or certain 'Eulogies' or Benedictions. . . . After this the priests, if any were in the Synagogue, spoke the blessing, elevating their hands up to the shoulders (in the Temple, above the head). This was called the lifting up of hands. In the Synagogue the priestly blessing was spoken in three sections, the people each time responding by an Amen. . . . If no descendant of Aaron were present, the leader of the devotions repeated the usual priestly benediction.[2] After the benediction followed

---

[1] Deut. vi, 4–9, xi, 13–21, Numb. xv, 37–41.
[2] Numb vi, 23–26

the last Eulogy, which, in its abbreviated form (as presently used in the Evening Service), is as follows:

"'O bestow on Thy people Israel great peace for ever. For Thou art King, and Lord of all peace. And it is good in Thine eyes to bless Thy people Israel at all times and at every hour with Thy peace. Blessed art Thou, Jehovah, who blesseth His people with peace!'

"The liturgical part being thus completed, one of the most important, indeed, what had been the primary object of the Synagogue service, began. The *Chazzan*, or minister, approached the Ark, and brought out a roll of the Law. . . . On the Sabbath, at least seven persons were called upon successively to read portions from the Law [according to a prescribed lectionary], none of them consisting of less than three verses. . . . Upon the Law followed a section from the Prophets, the so-called *Haphtarah*. . . . This was immediately followed by an address, discourse, or sermon, that is, where a Rabbi capable of giving such instruction, or a distinguished stranger, was present. . . . The service closed with a short prayer, or what we would call an 'ascription.'"[1]

In the Temple, where sacrifices were offered, and where only the priests and Levites officiated, the services were of course on a grander scale. "These included the daily offering of a lamb on the altar of burnt offering, in the morning and at even, accompanied with a meat offering (flour and oil), and a drink offering (wine). On the Sabbath two lambs were offered instead of one. There was a daily offering of incense on the altar of incense in the morning before, and in the evening after the daily sacrifice. In connection with the offering of the burnt sacrifice, there was vocal and instrumental music; the priests blew silver trumpets, and the

---

[1] *Life and Times of Jesus the Messiah*, Book III, chap. x.

AUTHORITY OF OUR LORD

Levites played on various instruments. A special psalm was appointed for use on each day of the week, viz., on Sunday, Ps. xxiv; on Monday, Ps. xlviii; on Tuesday, Ps. lxxxii; on Wednesday, Ps. xciv; on Thursday, Ps. lxxxi; on Friday, Ps. xciii; on the Sabbath, Ps. xcii."[1]

Following is the substance of Dr. Edersheim's account of the service described by S. Luke,[2] when it was the lot of the priest Zacharias, the father of John the Baptist, to burn incense in the Temple. This privilege came to a priest only once in a lifetime, and it was on this occasion that the angel Gabriel announced to Zacharias the coming miraculous birth of his son. The officiating priest ascended the steps leading to the Holy Place where stood the golden altar. Here he was preceded by two assistant priests, one of whom spread coals on the altar, while the other arranged the incense for convenient use. The two assistants then retired, and Zacharias was left alone in the Holy Place to await the signal of the presiding priest for making the offering. Meanwhile "the whole multitude of the people were praying without at the time of incense" (verse 10).

One of the prayers offered by the priests and people conjointly at this part of the service, as preserved by tradition, is as follows:

"Be graciously pleased, Jehovah our God, with Thy people Israel and with their prayer. Restore the service to the oracle of Thy house; and the burnt offerings of Israel, and their prayers, accept graciously in love; and let the service of Thy people Israel be ever well pleasing unto Thee. . . . Appoint peace, goodness, and blessing; grace, mercy, and compassion for us, and for all Israel Thy people. Bless us, O our Father, all of us as one, with the light of Thy Countenance. For in the light of Thy Countenance hast Thou,

---
[1] Warren, *Liturgy of the Ante-Nicene Church*, p 189   [2] 1, 5-26.

Jehovah our God, given us the law of life, and peace. . . . Blessed be Thou, Jehovah, who blessest Thy people with peace."[1]

It was then to such services as these that our Lord and His disciples alike had been accustomed all their life long. In the early days of His ministry, before the rulers had succeeded in making the mass of the people His enemies, the worship of the village synagogues naturally gave our Lord His best opportunities for teaching and preaching. Hence we read that after His Baptism and Temptation He returned to the country of His childhood, and, it is added, "He taught in their synagogues, being glorified of all. And He came to Nazareth, where He had been brought up; and, *as His custom was*, He went into the synagogue on the Sabbath day."[2]

But we are not dependent only on our Lord's example in this regard. We have His distinct precept also, and His clear directions, concerning the worship of that new Church — "My Church" He calls it — which He is about to build on the foundation of His twelve Apostles.[3] When His disciples came to Him one day asking Him to teach them how to pray as the Baptist had taught his disciples,[4] "He does not tell them to trust to the passing feelings of the moment, and shun as coldness everything which is not extemporaneous."[5] On the contrary He gives them the very words of that most perfect and complete of all prayers that were ever uttered, which we call especially "The Lord's." It may even be said of this prayer that its brevity, its conciseness, its differentiation from every other prayer composed by man, compel the confession that Some One far above humanity must have

---

[1] *The Temple, its Ministry and Services*, pp. 139, 140.
[2] S. Luke iv, 15, 16.   [3] S Matt. xvi, 18
[4] S. Luke xi, 1.   [5] Bishop W. I. Kip.

been its author. In other words, it is a miracle in words.¹ And our Lord bids His disciples use this prayer, not merely as a model or guide, but in its very language. "When ye pray," He commands, "*say*, Our Father," and all that follows.

Moreover, it is surely a very striking fact that, amid many vicissitudes and many shortcomings, Christians in every age have never failed to keep this precept of their Lord to the letter. Year after year, hour after hour, that prayer has been the very key to Heaven for countless multitudes. "Though men should speak with the tongues of angels," writes Hooker, "yet words so pleasing to the ears of God as those which the Son of God Himself hath composed were not possible for men to frame." He quotes also the language of S. Cyprian, the great martyr Bishop of Carthage in the third century: "Seeing that we have an Advocate with the Father for our sins . . . sith His promise is our plain warrant, that in His Name what we ask we shall receive, must we not needs much the rather obtain that for which we sue, if not only His Name do countenance, but also His speech present our requests?"²

What greater proof, then, could our Lord give concerning what He meant the worship of His Church to be? Not only did He show His approval of the liturgic method by His

---

¹ Compare the Ten Commandments in these respects.

² *Ecc Pol* V, xxxv, 3. The doxology, "For Thine is the kingdom," etc , is not used liturgically in the Latin Church. It appears in the Scottish Book of 1637. In the English Book it was added only in 1662. The critics reject it from S. Matthew vi, where it seems to have been first introduced from some such liturgy as those of S. Mark and Armenia. Thus used, it is an act of praise, and it is because of the penitential character of the prayer at the beginning of the office for Holy Communion and elsewhere, that the doxology is omitted there. See Freeman, I, 108, and P. and F., p. 374.

own constant presence in synagogue and Temple, as Child and Man; not only does He *not* condemn the use of forms, while severely denouncing formalism, but He Himself uses forms, and teaches His disciples, and through them His whole Church, to use forms in their approaches to His Father's throne. It was in response to their request that He should "*teach* them to pray, as John also taught *his* disciples," that He said, "When ye pray, say, Our Father," etc. It is as if He said, "Use these very words that I give you. They will sum up all the things for which you need to pray. They will save you also from wandering thoughts, and from those 'vain repetitions' and 'much speaking' by which 'the heathen' think to make God hearken." And though the voice that gave us the prayer is no longer heard by the outer ear, its very words are being uttered today all over the earth, and in every tongue, as no prayer was ever uttered before.[1]

---

[1] In S. Luke xi, 2, our Lord gives *the very words* of the prayer, as His disciples had asked ("When ye pray, *say*"), in the words "our," "we," "us," He implies that it is intended primarily at least for "common" worship. In S. Matt. vi, 9, He gives His prayer to the multitude as a *pattern* for their other prayers ("*After this manner* pray ye").

CHAPTER III

"They Continued Stedfastly in the Prayers"

> " . . . The parson — I knew not his name,
> And the brethren — each face was unknown;
> But the Church and the prayers were the same,
> And my heart claimed them all for its own."
> — BISHOP COXE.

WE come now to a third reason for the use of forms of prayer. Our final appeal is to the practice of the first Apostles, the men who knew best "the mind of Christ."[1] We have already seen to what kind of worship the Apostles and first Christians had been trained as children, and had been familiar with as men. They were all devout Jews, brought up, as their Master had been, in village synagogue and city Temple. It would then be passing strange if they should adopt some new and unheard-of method of worship when they proceeded to set up the Church as Christ commanded them. But nothing of this revolutionary character do we find, for revolutionary indeed it would have been.

It is noteworthy in this connection that, even after the coming of the Holy Ghost and the establishment of the Church, we find the Apostles attending diligently the services of the Temple. It is especially recorded that they, together with the multitudes baptized on Pentecost, "continued daily with one accord in the Temple," while they celebrated their own peculiar Christian service, the "Breaking of Bread," or Holy Communion, "at home."[2] About this time also we are told, S. Peter and S. John "went up into

---
[1] 1 Cor. ii, 16. [2] Acts ii, 46, Rev. Ver.

the Temple at the hour of prayer, being the ninth hour" (3 P.M.),[1] the hour of the evening sacrifice. About twenty-five years after his conversion we find S. Paul also in the Temple, and actually uniting with other Jewish Christians in offering sacrifices there according to the Law.[2] Again and again also, we find S. Paul, and S. Barnabas, and Apollos, with their companions entering the synagogues of the various cities which they visited on their journeys in Asia Minor, and in Greece, not, we may be sure, merely to preach, much less to criticize, but to join also devoutly in the ancient worship of their fathers.[3]

In the Acts of the Apostles, which, let us remember, is the first, and also the inspired, volume of the history of "the Holy Catholic and Apostolic Church" of the Creed, we have, moreover, the record of what constituted distinctive Christian worship in these earliest days when the Apostles, whom our Lord Himself had trained and taught, were still alive. There is first "THE BREAKING OF THE BREAD," or Holy Eucharist, or Holy Communion, which we shall consider later on; and second, there are "THE PRAYERS," in both of which, we are told, the Apostles and all the Christian flock "continued stedfastly."[4]

Let us note this latter phrase especially in this connection. It is not "prayer," as would be the case if the service were what is called "extemporaneous" or "free." Nor is it merely "prayers" but, as in the original Greek and the Revised Version, "*the* prayers," that is, the accustomed prayers which, even in that year when S. Luke was writing his history (A.D. 66, or earlier), formed the ordinary worship of the Christian flock. "They continued stedfastly in *the*

---
[1] Acts iii, 1   [2] Acts xxi, 26
[3] See Acts ix, 20, xiii, 5; xiv, 1; xvi, 13; xvii, 2, 17; xviii, 4, 26.
[4] Acts ii, 42

prayers," those familiar prayers, he seems to say, which we Christians for thirty years past have known and loved.

How it came to pass that the first Christians in Jerusalem had such a body of prayers, or ordered service, ready at once to their hand, may easily be guessed by those who bear in mind what a glorious prayer book and liturgy these men had been accustomed to ever since their childhood. They knew it far better than we know ours today, for they knew it almost universally by heart. In the absence of printed books, such as we possess in abundance, faithful Jews committed these devotional treasures to memory. Their language was "familiar as household words," and in adapting them to their worship as Christians it would be only necessary to add to their prayers such words as "through Jesus Christ our Lord," or "all this we ask in the Name of Thy Son Jesus, our only Mediator and Advocate," in obedience to His repeated command and promise concerning asking "in His Name."[1] They had, moreover, the very words of the prayer which He Himself had given them. Their familiar Hebrew Psalms, also, with other hymns from the Old Testament, and the four great Gospel Hymns as yet unwritten,[2] only needed the addition of such words as those suggested by the baptismal formula, "Glory be to the Father, and to the Son, and to the Holy Ghost," to make them distinctly Christian. Here therefore the Church, at the very beginning, had a rich treasure of devotional forms ready to her hand, with which to conduct her service of "Common Prayer." As time went on, of course new occasions would add to her treasures, especially round the central act of her worship in the Break-

---

[1] S. John xiv, 13, 14; xv, 16, xvi, 23, 24, 26. For examples in the early Greek offices see Freeman, I, pp 64–67.

[2] Ex xv, 1–19; Deut xxxii, 1–44; 1 Sam. ii, 1–11; Is. xxxviii, 10–21; S. Luke i, 46, sq , ii 14; 29, sq.

ing of the Bread, or Holy Eucharist. But here was enough for a nucleus and a beginning. What follows must be the slow growth of Christian experience.

A single recorded example of early Christian worship, within a few weeks of our Lord's ascension, bears definite witness to this inherited tendency and liturgic training of the first disciples. In the fourth chapter of the Acts we are given a picture of a Christian service which was occasioned by a sudden emergency, one therefore where we would naturally suppose all rules of liturgic worship would be forgotten or set at naught. The Apostles Peter and John had been arrested and imprisoned, and after their release they return at once to their fellow disciples. It is at this moment of fear and joy that this band of Christians with their clergy hold a service of thanksgiving and prayer. But though the occasion was most exceptional, nevertheless, so far as Holy Scripture informs us, there is nothing exceptional or extemporaneous in their devotions. The prayer which they offer has all the dignity and soberness of an accustomed service. It has also the unmistakable *upward* look of the Psalter, as contrasted with the *inward* look of many modern prayers and hymns. Its very words, we are told, were joined in audibly by every Christian present. "They" — and not merely their leader — "lifted up their voice to God with one accord, and said," — and then the very language of this "common" prayer is given us, plainly showing that it was not a new prayer coined for this special occasion, but an accustomed form suited to any occasion of public worship in troublous times.

In various passages of the epistles we find what seem to be allusions to the liturgic worship of the Apostles' days. Writing to Timothy, whom he had left as the Bishop over the Church in Ephesus, S. Paul exhorts him to "hold fast

STEDFAST IN THE PRAYERS 27

the form of sound words" which he had delivered to him,[1] where the reference is evidently either to a creed, or to a form of prayer. Writing to the Roman Church we find a similar expression, "that form of doctrine, which was delivered you."[2] There are also many passages throughout the epistles, some of a metrical or rhythmical character, introduced with the words, "as it is written," or "it is a faithful saying," of which the language is nowhere found in the Old Testament or in the New, and it has seemed probable to scholars that these are all quotations either from familiar Christian hymns, or from prayers already used in the worship of the Church.[3]

The first of these passages, which occurs in one of the earliest books of the New Testament, is given in the Revised Version as follows: "As it is written,

> Things which eye saw not, and ear heard not,
> And which entered not into the heart of man,
> Whatsoever things God prepared for them that love Him."

The quotation has a certain resemblance to Is. lxiv, 4: "Since the beginning of the world men have not heard, nor perceived by the ear, neither hath the eye seen, O God, beside Thee, what he hath prepared for him who waiteth for him." But Dr. John Mason Neale has pointed out that, when compared with the original Greek of the Septuagint (that is, the version of the Old Testament usually quoted by the writers of the New Testament and by our Lord), "literally not one word is the same in Isaiah as in S. Paul."[4] It will be observed

---

[1] 2 Tim. i, 13.   [2] Rom. vi, 17.
[3] 1 Cor. ii, 9; xv, 45, Eph. v, 14, 1 Tim. i, 15; iii, 1; iv, 8, 9; 2 Tim. ii, 11, 12, 13, 19, Titus iii, 8.
[4] *Essays on Liturgiology*, p. 416.

also that the passage as literally translated in the Revised Version is ungrammatical, being only the *fragment* of a sentence. But "the exact words of the quotation, with the ungrammaticalness supplied," are found in the liturgy which had its home in Jerusalem, that named after S. James. Even S. Paul's words in the verse following, "For the Spirit searcheth all things, yea, the deep things of God," are also found word for word in the Post-Sanctus of the same liturgy.[1] Though most frequently the liturgies in their later form quote from the New Testament, it would seem that here we have the New Testament quoting from the liturgy.

For this and other reasons it seems evident that a Christian liturgy, after the model to which our Lord and His Apostles had been accustomed in the Temple and synagogue, was formed and used before the Christian Scriptures were written or completed. Thus liturgic worship is one of those "customs" and "traditions" which bear fully the test that S. John applies to them as claiming our obedience, namely, that they have existed in the Church "from the beginning."[2] What the present writer has said elsewhere concerning the ritual year of the Church is equally applicable to its method of worship. "It is remarkable, though too often overlooked, how frequently the words 'tradition,' 'custom,' and 'way,' or their equivalents, occur in the New Testament. . . . S. Paul in writing to correct certain evils in Corinth gives as a sufficient reason for some things his own 'ways in Christ.' As a sufficient argument against another practice in the same Church he writes, 'We have no such custom, neither the Churches of God'; and he says in the same chapter, 'Hold fast the traditions even as I delivered them unto you.' To the Thessalonian Church he says, 'Stand fast, and hold the

---
[1] *Essays on Liturgiology*, p, 417.   [2] 1 John ii, 24; iii, 11; 2 John 6.

traditions which ye have been taught, whether by word or our epistle.'"[1]

Of course we cannot expect to find such customs and traditions embodied, or even described, in the New Testament. It is enough to learn that among the first converts to Christ, in the days of the original Apostles, the principle of liturgic worship was already a life-long inheritance, that it was instinctive, and, above all, that it had the definite example and precept of our Lord Himself. Christian worship possessed undoubtedly all its essential elements in what the writer of the Acts calls "the Breaking of the Bread and the Prayers."[2] It had behind it also the traditions and customs of more than a thousand years, and in its distinctly Christian character it required only time for its development. This had to come slowly. For the first three centuries the Church was under the ban of the Roman Empire. It had to worship for the most part in secrecy, and where and as it could. It had few, if any, church buildings. It had to be content to hold its services in "upper rooms," and hidden retreats such as the underground cemeteries or catacombs at Rome afforded its members.

It is plain, then, to one who accepts the authority of Christ and His Scriptures that the way of an ordered form of devotion in the public worship of God is the way which Christ desired, as it was the way which He Himself trod while He was on earth, and the way in which His Apostles followed after He was gone. And so, these ancient liturgic treasures—enriched as the years went on, adapted to the varying ways and genius of nations and races, penetrated and suffused

---

[1] *The Christian Year: Its Purpose and its History*, p 35. See 1 Cor. iv, 17; xi 2, 16, Rev. Ver ; 2 Thess. ii, 15, iii, 6, Acts xix, 9, 23; xxiv, 14, Rev. Ver.

[2] ii. 42.

with the spirit of saints and martyrs, breathing their hopes and bearing the marks of their conflicts — have been hallowed by the use of more than fifty generations of Christians, and claim our grateful reverence and use today.

It is true that, in spite of these strong sanctions for liturgic worship, we must be careful to estimate accurately the real use and purpose of forms of prayer. Like every other thing in this world, even the Holy Scriptures themselves, they can be perverted and abused. We must distinctly remember that forms of prayer, no matter how beautiful or rich in thought, are not in themselves prayers. They are at best only so many golden censers, such as those which S. John gazed on in his great vision of the opened Heaven, and the divine worship and liturgy which he witnessed there. To be of value in God's sight they must be like these, not mere burnished vessels, fair to the eye, but heaped with living fires, and laden with precious spices of penitence and love. For that "incense," adds S. John, "is the prayers of the saints."[1] The most beautiful of forms, not excepting even that which we call our Lord's own prayer, are but empty vessels until we fill them with our hearts' desires. Only then can it be said of them, as it is said in S. John's great vision concerning "the prayers of all the saints" — "the smoke of the incense ascended up before God."[2]

---

[1] Rev. v, 8.   [2] Rev. viii, 3, 4.

CHAPTER IV

"They Continued Stedfastly in the Breaking of the Bread"

"The bread which we break, is it not the communion of the Body of Christ?"
— 1 Cor. x, 16

WE have hitherto considered only the question of "the Prayers," that is, liturgic worship in general, or rather the principle which underlies all use of forms of prayer in the public worship of God. We have seen that without forms there can be no such thing as "*common* prayer"; that forms are necessary also for reverence, for protection from distraction of thought and from the vagaries or peculiarities of individual ministers, and especially for the preservation of the faith from generation to generation. We have seen also how forms have the positive sanction, not only of the Old Testament and the Church of Israel, but also of the example and the precept of our Lord, and the practice of His Apostles. We have now to consider one other of those four bonds and marks of unity in the Church as it came fresh from the hands of Christ, and in which every Christian "continued stedfastly," namely, "THE BREAKING OF THE BREAD."[1]

THE BREAKING OF THE BREAD is the one great act of united worship which we know our Lord, with dying lips, enjoined upon His Church. It is around this act, therefore, that the whole liturgic worship of the Church has grown up. This is its heart and centre. The word liturgy, in fact,

---
[1] Acts ii, 42.

in its strict sense signifies only that office which is provided to celebrate in due form this divine rite.[1]

There are five words by which the Sacrament is called or referred to in the New Testament.

1. THE BREAKING OF THE BREAD or its equivalent occurs only in the following passages of the New Testament: Acts ii, 42, 46; xx, 7, 11; 1 Cor. x, 16.[2] The reason for the name is of course obvious. The thought involved in it, however, is evidently not so much that of eating or partaking of the divine food, as of the act by which that food, in the person of Christ, became ours by being broken and offered on the cross. This our Lord foretold by His action in the Upper Room when He took the bread and "brake it,"[3] symbolizing that dreadful event which must take place before His Body can become for all the world the very "Bread of Heaven" and "of Life."[4]

2. The second name for this holy Sacrament in the New Testament, THE LORD'S SUPPER, occurs only in 1 Cor. xi, 20, where S. Paul is correcting some grievous evils which had crept into its celebration in the Church in Corinth. Some have been inclined to interpret the Apostle as speaking here only of the *Agape*, or Love Feast,[5] which in those early days

---

[1] Liturgy, in Greek, *leitourgia*, is derived from *leitos*, public, or belonging to the people, and *ergon*, work It occurs in the following passages of the New Testament, where it is variously translated, "ministration," "ministry," and "service " S. Luke i, 23, 2 Cor. ix, 12; Phil ii, 17, 30; Heb. viii, 6, ix, 21. In its application therefore to the Holy Communion it early acquired the meaning of *the* service or ministration, that is, the special work or service of the people in worship

[2] Some, with doubtful reason, have seen also in the action of our Lord on the evening of His resurrection, in the home of the two disciples of Emmaus, a reference to the Sacrament S. Luke xxiv, 35.

[3] S Luke xxii, 19

[4] S John vi, 48, etc.   [5] Compare Jude 12, and 2 Peter ii, 13.

"THE BREAKING OF BREAD"   33

preceded the celebration of the Sacrament, in evident imitation of the "supper" which preceded the Institution in the Upper Room,[1] but which became such a source of abuse here in Corinth among half-trained converts from heathenism, that it was soon abandoned everywhere in the Church.[2] This view, however, is untenable in the light of history. A canon of the third council of Carthage in the fourth century (A.D. 397) calls the sacrament "the Lord's Supper" (*Coena Domini*).[3] S. Augustine in the same century speaks of S. Paul in his letter to the Corinthians as "giving to the receiving of the Eucharist the name of the Lord's Supper," and of his reproving them "for not distinguishing between the Lord's Supper and an ordinary meal", and that "we neither compel, nor do we dare to forbid, any one to break his fast before the Lord's Supper on that day on which the Lord instituted the Supper."[4] Again in his "Correction of the Donatists"[5] he says, "The Supper of the Lord is the unity of the body of Christ."[6]

---

[1] S. Luke xxii, 20

[2] As a partial remedy for the time being, S. Paul directed that all should "tarry one for another," and that "if any hungered he should eat at home," and he promised to "set the rest in order when he came" (verses 33, 34). The result seems to show that, when he came to Corinth, he put the love feast *after* the Celebration instead of before. "It is a fair inference from the language of Pliny's letter to Trajan that, in Bithynia, in A.D. 112 (when he wrote) the severance had already taken place, and that the Eucharist was then celebrated by itself at an early hour in the morning" (Warren, *Lit of Ante-Nicene Church*, p 122).

[3] See Bingham, *Antiq.* XXI, c. 1, 30.

[4] Ep. LIV, v, 7; vi, 8; vii, 9, *to Januarius*.

[5] vi, 24.

[6] The name was in use in the twelfth century, as witnessed by a tract on "the Lord's Supper," *De Coena Domini*, attributed to Cyprian, but really the work of Arnold, a friend of S. Bernard. See note by Keble in his edition of Hooker, Book V, lvi, 9. "In the Middle Ages it was a very

3. The third word is EUCHARIST. It is more than probable that when S. Paul is rebuking the Corinthian Church for another breach of order, namely, for using a language in divine service which is not understood by the people, he is referring to the celebration of the same sacrament of which he had just been speaking. He asks, "If thou bless with the spirit [that is, the bread and wine as in 1 Cor. x, 16], how shall he that filleth the place of the unlearned say the Amen at thy giving of thanks?" or, as it is in the original, "thy Eucharist" (*eucharistia*).¹ Whether this be so or not, it is certain that this name, which has its origin in that significant action of thanksgiving (*eucharistesas*)¹ by which our Lord made of common bread and wine the sacrament of His Body and Blood, is the name in most common use in primitive days and is still the most common name in the Oriental Churches.²

---

common name for the Eucharist" (P. and F p 432). It is used also in the *Catechism of the Council of Trent* in the sixteenth century, chap iv, qu. 5. Some ancient writers speak of it as "The Mystical Supper", among them S Hippolytus, A D 220, Cyril of Alexandria, A D. 412; S. Nilus, A D 440 (Scudamore, *Not Euch* p. 5).

¹ 1 Cor xiv, 16.

² Four independent accounts of the institution of the Holy Sacrament are given us in the New Testament; one by S Matthew, who was present (xxvi, 26, etc), one each by S. Mark and S. Luke, who were not present, but obtained their account from others who were (S. Mark xiv, 22, etc ; S Luke xxii, 19, etc.); and one by S. Paul, who tells us he received his knowledge of the institution directly from the Lord Jesus (1 Cor. xi, 23; Eph. iii, 3, Gal. i, 12), probably on that occasion which he describes in 2 Cor. xii, when he "was caught up into Paradise, and heard unspeakable words." In all these accounts the same word, *eucharistesas*, is used to describe the act of consecration. It is noteworthy, moreover, that in S John (who gives no account of the institution, but, as in the case also of Holy Baptism, only gives our Lord's preparatory teaching on the Sacrament) the same word, *eucharistesas*, is used in that symbolic act of multiplying the

"THE BREAKING OF BREAD"

4. The fourth title is the HOLY COMMUNION. As employed by S. Paul, however, this is not so much a name as a description of one aspect of the Sacrament, namely, its purpose in making each recipient a "partaker of the divine nature,"[1] "through the veil, that is to say, the flesh" of God's Incarnate Son.[2] S. Paul says, "The cup of blessing which we bless, is it not a communion of the blood of Christ? The bread which we break, is it not a communion of the body of Christ?"[3] The Apostle, it will be observed, does not employ it here as a *name* for the Sacrament, but we see here the origin of the name. It is not until the fourth century that we find it used as an equivalent for the Breaking of the Bread, or the Eucharist, or the Lord's Supper,[4] that is, for the Sacrament itself and not for *participation* of the Sacrament, as in S. Paul's use of the word. It was doubtless the thought of joint communion or fellowship with one another as well as, and as a result of, communion with Christ that caused this one feature to be adopted later as a *name* of the Sacrament.

5. Still another name which has a scriptural basis or origin

---

bread in the feeding of the five thousand, which served as the text for His sermon in the synagogue of Capernaum the day following, when He gave His wonderful discourse concerning His Flesh and Blood. See S John vi, 11, etc Though "Eucharist" is not found in the English Book, it is used in the Scottish Liturgy and also in the Office of Institution in the American Book.

[1] 2 Peter i, 4.
[2] Heb. x, 20.
[3] 1 Cor x, 16, Rev Ver
[4] "S. Hilary (Tract on Ps lxviii), A.D 354, calls it 'the Sacrament of the Divine Communion', and S. Basil (Ep. xciii, tome iii) A D. 370, speaks of those who 'have Communion at their own house.' S Chrysostom (Hom. xxvii in 1 Cor), A D. 398: 'Hast thou not heard how the three thousand who were partakers of the Communion persevered continually in the prayer and the doctrine?'" (Scudamore, *Not Euch.* p. 7).

is "THE BLESSING," or "EULOGIA." S. Paul has in mind the action of our Lord when He "took bread and *blessed* it,"[1] in that passage where he writes, "The cup of blessing which we bless."[2] The name is frequently used by S. Cyril of Alexandria in the fifth century, as when he says, "They remain altogether without share or taste of the life in sanctification and bliss, who do not receive the Son through the Mystical Blessing."[3]

This sacred rite, called by these various names, had been instituted by our Lord for the perpetual use of His Church on the night before He suffered. It was a new rite, but it was also the successor and fulfilment of an older one, the greatest of all in the Church of Israel, the Passover. It was in fact the *Christian* Passover. It had nothing corresponding to it in the worship of the synagogues. There the service consisted only of prayers, scripture lessons, and exhortations. There was neither altar, nor priesthood, nor sacrifice. The ordinary ministrants were laymen, though occasionally a priest was present to give the benediction in the words prescribed by the Law.[4] The synagogue had only a platform, and a lectern or pulpit, from which the ruler led the people in their devotions and from which they heard the words of lawgiver, and prophet, and priest from the Scriptures of the Old Testament, or were addressed in sermon or exhortation. On the other hand, the Breaking of the Bread had its only counterpart and origin in the services of the Temple, the chief of which was the Passover, with its lamb slain, and its blood offered in sacrifice, after which the body was roasted whole and eaten with bitter herbs,

---

[1] S. Matt. xxvi, 26
[2] 1 Cor. x, 16.
[3] *Comm in S. Joh. Evang.* vi, 54. For the use of "*Mass*" see chap. xiii.
[4] Numb. vi, 22, etc.

"THE BREAKING OF BREAD" 37

unleavened bread, and a mixed cup of wine and water, in the home.[1]

It was then at this greatest of all the feasts, typifying and foreshadowing, as it had done for fifteen hundred years, the one "full, perfect, and sufficient sacrifice" of the true Lamb of God who was to come, that Christ ordained the sacrament and feast of the Breaking of the Bread. So closely did He associate the new act, which was to be the core and centre of His future worship, with that of His older Church that He used some of the material elements of His last Passover, namely, unleavened bread, and the mixed cup of wine and water, as the material elements of His first Eucharist. Of old they had been but bare and empty symbols pleading before God the true Sacrifice that was to come, and tokens to His people of that future Deliverer who would say, "I am the living Bread which came down from heaven; if any man eat of this Bread he shall live for ever: and the Bread that I will give is My Flesh, which I will give for the life of the world."[2] Henceforth they are no longer empty symbols and "shadows," but sacramental memorials before the Father of "His precious death and sacrifice,"[3] and also instruments whereby His people are to be kept united with His Incarnate Person and made to receive the benefits of His atoning death and resurrection. For the day of mere

---

[1] See Ex xii, 1-29 The cup of wine is not mentioned here, though it is commanded in the continual burnt offering in Numb. xxviii, 7, and is evidently referred to in the words of the Psalmist, "I will receive the cup of salvation," in Ps. cxvi, which formed part of the great paschal "hymn" sung by our Lord and the Twelve at the last Passover in the Upper Room. This was called the *Hallel*, and consisted of Pss cxiii to cxviii, the first portion of which was sung during the offering of the lambs in the Temple, and the latter portion in the home.

[2] S. John vi, 51.

[3] Prayer of Consecration.

"shadows" and "beggarly elements"[1] is past. The day of realities has come. The Eternal Word has been "made flesh," and He is "full of grace and truth."[2]

It was for this holy rite that the Lord Jesus had prepared His disciples a year before in His great discourse in the synagogue of "His own city,"[3] Capernaum. His teaching there about "eating His flesh, and drinking His blood" was very mysterious and startling, so much so that "many of His disciples went back, and walked no more with Him," and He turned sadly to the Twelve and asked, "Will ye also go away?" It is then Peter answers for the rest, "Lord, to whom shall we go? Thou hast the words of eternal life. And we believe and are sure that Thou art that Christ, the Son of the living God."[4] The mystery was just as insoluble to them as to others, but though they could not understand, they trusted. Then one year later they found the clue to all their difficulties when, in the Upper Room,[5] He instituted the sacramental rite which gave them the very things which He had promised.

After the descent of the Holy Ghost on Pentecost, we see in their minds no trace of doubt or difficulty. There is no more questioning as to "*How* this man can give us His flesh to eat."[6] In fact, nothing is more remarkable than the quiet unhesitating way in which, hereafter, the Apostles

---

[1] Col. ii, 17, Gal iv, 9.   [3] S Matt. ix, 1.
[2] S. John i, 14   [4] S John vi, 66-70.

[5] Jewish houses were usually provided with an "upper room," "the most honorable and the most retired place, where from the outside stairs entrance and departure might be had without passing through the house." See Edersheim, *Life and Times of Jesus*, II, 484. It was doubtless here, "at home," especially in view of our Lord's choice of the room, that the Christians were accustomed to have their distinctive act of worship, which of course was out of the question in the Temple.

[6] S. John vi, 52.

"THE BREAKING OF BREAD"

proceed to act. This new mysterious rite, just as mysterious as ever, becomes at once, and in the most casual way, the chief act and the centre of all their worship as Christians. "They continued stedfastly . . . in the Breaking of the Bread, and in the Prayers." Their old familiar service in the Temple, with its grand liturgic setting, was indeed not neglected, but their new rite, with its infinitely richer promise, was now their distinctive, and even *daily*, act of Christian worship. And this was necessarily in their homes; "day by day, continuing stedfastly with one accord in the Temple, and breaking bread at home." Even long after the Day of Pentecost, in every recorded instance where the character of Christian public worship is referred to in the New Testament, the Breaking of the Bread appears as the central act.[1]

---

[1] Acts 11, 46, Rev. Ver.; xx, 7; Cor xi, 20; xiv, 16.

CHAPTER V

Christian Worship in the First Three Centuries

"The roots of the present lie deep in the past, and nothing in the past is dead to the man who would learn how the present came to be what it is"
— Bishop Stubbs.

LET us now in thought take a journey backwards to the age immediately succeeding that of the Apostles. What we find there everywhere is the united or "common" worship of the Church, in liturgical prayers, gathering around the Breaking of the Bread, or Holy Eucharist. All the earliest buildings for Christian worship of which we have any record, all allusions of historians or early writers and preachers, as well as all the most ancient liturgies, testify to the fact that in the first days all such worship had as its centre an altar or holy table [1] on which were celebrated the sacred mysteries which our Lord had instituted to take the place of the Paschal memorial sacrifice and feast. Whether such places for Christian meetings are found in some subterranean chamber of the Catacombs, or some upper room in a private house, or some transformed Roman basilica or court of justice after the Empire became nominally Christian, we find the same

---

[1] In the Old as well as in the New Testament the words "altar" and "table" are used interchangeably In Ezek xli, 22, we read, "The altar of wood was three cubits high, . . . and he said unto me, This is the table that is before the Lord" Compare Ezek xl, 39–44; xliv, 16, Mal. i, 7, 12 See also S Paul's comparison of "the table of the Lord" with the heathen "altar" or "table of devils" in 1 Cor x, 21 Bingham gives evidence beginning with Ignatius and Irenaeus, that the common, if not exclusive, use in the first two centuries was "altar." See Book VIII, vi, sec. 11, sq

pattern everywhere. It is that of the ancient Temple in Jerusalem with its altar and its divinely appointed priesthood, and not that of the synagogue with its platform or *bema*, and its lay services of prayer, and instruction, and exhortation alone. Or rather this earliest Christian worship combined both methods in one; the prayers, the reading of the Scriptures, and the instruction of the synagogue, with the memorial pleading of the one sacrifice for sin, and the intercessions and benedictions of the priests, which were peculiar to the Temple.

During the ages of persecution, nearly down to 313, but little attempt was made to build churches. Christians had to meet where they could in private houses or temporary oratories, sometimes "in dens and caves of the earth." As early, in fact, as A.D. 259 the edict of the Emperor Gallienus gave to the Church for the first time the legal rights of a *religio licita*, that is, of a college or corporation in law. Henceforth it could build and hold churches, and freely worship in them, and within a short time, writes the German historian Neander, "many splendid structures had already arisen in the large cities." What is very important to note, however, is that as soon as persecution was past and large churches were built, only one type is found, and that, modelled not on the synagogue as a place chiefly of instruction, but on the Temple as a place of worship.[1] Descriptions of these first

---

[1] It is surely very noteworthy that again and again S Paul speaks of the Church spiritually, or the individual member thereof, as " The *Temple* of God," but never as a *synagogue* See 1 Cor in 16, 17; vi, 19; 2 Cor. vi, 16, 2 Thess ii, 4, also S John in Rev iii, 12; vii, 15; xv, 8 The Apostles had no reason for pleasant recollections of the synagogue, where they were often imprisoned and beaten Hence S. John speaks of "the synagogue of Satan," Rev. ii, 9; iii, 9 Only once in fact do we find the word applied to a Christian "assembly," where the Greek word is "synagogue," namely, in S James ii, 2.

city churches are given us by Eusebius, the Father of Church History (A.D. 266–340), and other writers, and in the "Church Orders" of the fourth century. (For the general plan see the frontispiece facing title page of this book.) From these we learn that, while details differ, the general plan of all was the same, testifying, as do the Liturgies, to one fundamental principle of construction and worship which was already, even in the days of persecution, the established rule. Most city churches of the fourth century were of the type of the cathedral church of Tyre as described by Eusebius, namely, an oblong nave or central portion, with semi-circular apse (sometimes three) at the east, a narthex or porch at the west, and single or double aisles on the north and south. Some of these churches were round, some square, some octagonal, some were in the shape of a cross with transepts. But one fundamental feature was common to all, namely, that a special place, generally at the east end and elevated above the floor of the body of the building, was reserved for the holy table or altar, and marked off or closed in by rails (*cancelli*), or gates and veils, from the nave. In addition to these main features there was frequently a large court or churchyard at the west, with fountain or basin for cleansing the hands and face before entering the church. The baptistery, an oblong building with a circular font in the centre, was also usually placed in this courtyard.[1]

Concerning the synagogue Canon Warren writes: "It should be borne in mind that synagogues in the first century A.D. were a comparatively modern institution, and had no

---

[1] For the names and uses of the different parts of the church see Bingham, Books VIII and XVIII, Maclean, *Ancient Church Orders*, chap. iv; *Early Christian Worship*, Lec. III; Duchesne, *Christian Worship*, chap. xxi.

IN THE FIRST THREE CENTURIES 43

hereditary claim on the reverence or affection of either Jews or Christians. . . . There is no reference to synagogues in the Old Testament. . . . Synagogues were village institutes and police courts as well as halls of worship. Within their precincts cases were tried, prisoners were sentenced, and the sentences were carried out. Our Lord said, 'They shall lay their hands on you, and persecute you, delivering you up to the synagogues, and into prisons.' 'Beware of men, for they will deliver you up to the councils, and they will scourge you in their synagogues.'[1] S. Paul tells how 'I imprisoned and beat in every synagogue them that believed . . . I punished them oft in every synagogue, and compelled them to blaspheme.'[2] . . . Surely, with such painful and degrading associations and recollections, the synagogue would not have been the quarter to which the first Christians would have turned to find a model, either for their proceedings or their services. Their thought would more naturally centre round the Temple, which our Saviour, and His Apostles after Him, regularly frequented, and which was, *par excellence*, the house of God."[3]

Another element lacking in the synagogue besides altar, sacrifice, and priesthood, was the recitation or chanting of the Psalter, which has always been a central feature of Christian worship, as it had been of the worship of the Temple. In regard to this an eminent French Protestant, Mons. E. de Pressensé, says: "Its cradle was not the synagogue, where the frigid service consisted only of reading and prayer, without any intermingling songs of praise. Christian song comes directly from the Temple, the offspring of that grand Hebrew poetry uttered by lips touched by

---

[1] S. Luke xxi, 12, S. Matt. x, 17, S. Luke xii, 11.
[2] Acts xxii, 19, xxvi, 11.
[3] *Liturgy of the Ante-Nicene Church*, pp. 191, 192.

the live coal from off the altar, the sublimest lyric expressions ever given to the griefs and yearnings of the human heart." [1]

At the cleansing of the Temple it is evident that our Lord had that holy place in mind, and not the synagogue, as the model for the future worship of His Church, when He adopted the prophecy of Isaiah (lvi, 7, Rev. Ver.) as His own and said, "Is it not written, My house shall be called the house of prayer *for all the nations*?" In His Sermon on the Mount also, which contains the laws for the Church of "all the nations," and not merely for that generation of the Jewish Church, our Lord implies that it will have a worship similar to that of the Temple, with an "altar" to which Christians will bring their "offerings," as devout Israelites had always done to the altar in Jerusalem.[2]

In a similar manner S. Paul speaks of Christians having a sacrificial worship (real though unbloody) corresponding to that of the Jews. Referring to the worship of the Temple, which still existed when he wrote his epistle to the Hebrews (assuming that he is the author), he comforts these Jewish Christians, who were taunted by their fellow countrymen with having abandoned the true worship of God, by telling them, "We [Christians] have an altar, whereof they have

---

[1] *Christian Life and Practice in the Early Church*, p. 277, qu. by Warren, *Lit.* etc p. 191. Oesterley, in *The Psalms in the Jewish Church*, chap viii, while admitting that "the *original* object" of the synagogue was "the study of the Law, rather than worship," gives proofs of the *later* use of the Psalms. There is no reference to them, however, in the New Testament. Prof. Cheyne says, "There is no evidence that psalmody formed part of the public worship in the early synagogues," but he adds, "I can with difficulty believe that prayer did not include praise " *Bampton Lec.* p. 14. See also Bingham, XIII, v, 4.

[2] S. Matt. v, 23, 24.

IN THE FIRST THREE CENTURIES 45

no right to eat which serve the [Jewish] tabernacle,"[1] that is, who have not accepted the faith that has turned these shadows into realities. In his first letter to the Corinthians, written earlier, he makes this same comparison between the Christian service and that of the Temple with its altar and its sacrifices. "Behold Israel after the flesh: are not they which eat of the sacrifices partakers of the [Jewish] altar?" But Christians have another and a better altar, whereby they are "partakers" (literally communicants) "of the Body and Blood of Christ."[2] All which goes to show that the Church in its earliest days found in the Temple, and not in the synagogue, the model of its Liturgy.[3]

Sacrificial language concerning the Holy Eucharist (offering, oblation, sacrifice) is so common in the writers of the first three centuries, that it is only necessary to quote some words of one of the earliest of these, namely, Justin Martyr, about A.D. 139. Arguing with Trypho, a Jew, he says: "We are the true high priestly race, as even God Himself bears witness, saying that in every place amongst the Gentiles sacrifices are to be offered well pleasing to Him and pure. So then God referring beforehand to the sacrifices which we offer through this Name — even those which Jesus the Christ instituted, that is to say, through the Eucharist of the Bread and the Cup — and which are presented by

---

[1] Heb xiii, 10   Even the Puritan Richard Baxter says, "'We have an altar whereof they have no right to eat' seems plainly to mean the Sacramental Communion." *Christian Institutes*, 1, p 304; qu by Bp. C Wordsworth on Heb. xiii, 10   "Instances of the use of the word 'table' or 'holy table' are comparatively rare in Ante-Nicene literature." Warren, *Lit. of Ante-Nicene Church*, pp 70, 71.

[2] 1 Cor. x, 16, 17, 18.

[3] It is plain that Duchesne is mistaken when he writes that "the worship of the Temple did not influence the Christian Liturgy," p. 46.

Christians in all places throughout the world, bears witness that they are well pleasing to Him." [1]

At the first, of course, the Christian Liturgy, like all God's gifts to man, was only in embryo. All the essential elements of future growth were there indeed from the beginning, as they are in the acorn or the egg. The development must come later according to the genius of the nation in which the Church was planted. For the Apostles to have made a complete liturgy would have defeated this purpose. They had, however, the words and actions of our Lord distinctly in remembrance. They knew His great prayer of intercession, His solemn blessing and thanksgiving, and His whole tone and manner in instituting the great Mystery.[2] Moreover they had the very words of the prayer which He had given them at their own request,[3] and which they could not fail to use in such an act of united worship. But besides all this they had, as we have already seen, that liturgic training and instinct which could not fail to make them adopt the same reverent methods in their worship as those to which both they and their Master had been accustomed all their life long.

When therefore we come to inquire what was the actual custom of the Church concerning this central act of Christian worship, in the days immediately succeeding that of the Apostles, it is not surprising to find everywhere one rule, and one only, namely, that of a liturgical form, though doubtless with some freedom as to extemporaneous prayer.[4]

---

[1] Dial. cum Trypho, c cxvi, cxvii.

[2] S. John xvii; S Matt. xxvi, 26, sq.; S. Mark xiv, 22, sq.; S. Luke xxii, 19, sq.; 1 Cor. xi, 23, sq.

[3] S. Luke xi, 1, sq

[4] While "the structural skeleton" was the same everywhere, and forms were no doubt in use from the beginning, Dr. Frere says, "the officiant was not at first bound to them. As time went on, the liberty of using

IN THE FIRST THREE CENTURIES 47

In the two earliest notices of Christian worship after the death of S. John (A.D. 100 or 104), — the letter of Pliny the Younger, propraetor of Bithynia from A.D. 103 to 105, to his friend the Emperor Trajan concerning the Christians in his province, and the Apology of Justin Martyr, born about A.D. 114 — the Holy Communion, or Eucharist, as Justin calls it, is described as the chief act of Christian worship, though few details are given.

Pliny's letter was written only four years at the utmost after the death of S. John, and already the Christians had become numerous in his province. Describing their worship he says they "were accustomed to meet on a set day, before it was light, and to sing a hymn together alternately [*secum vicissim*, that is, antiphonally, like our modern choirs, as well as those of the Temple] to Christ as a God, and to bind themselves by a sacrament [in Latin, *sacramentum*, an oath or mystery for it acquired the double meaning] . . . not to commit thefts, robberies, or adulteries," etc., and he adds, "after this was done, their custom was to depart, and meet together again to take food."[1]

---

extempore forms was curtailed, till it was restricted to special orders of the ministry, such as the 'prophets' or the episcopate, and finally to all intents and purposes it disappeared" Procter and Frere, *A New Hist. of the B C P*, pp 433-4

[1] Ep x, 96 The food here is evidently the Agapé, or feast of charity or love (Jude 12), for the abuse of which we saw S Paul rebuking severely the Church in Corinth, and which, as a result of his promised visit shortly afterwards to that city for the purpose of "setting in order" such irregularities, was made to follow, instead of preceding, the celebration of the Lord's Supper. See 1 Cor xi, 20 to end. In the next century Tertullian says, "The Sacrament of the Eucharist we receive in assemblies held even before dawn" (*De Cor Mil.* c. iii, tom iv, p. 293), while the love-feast was postponed till the evening. The love-feast "survived, especially on the occasion of a funeral, down to at least the fifth century" (Tertullian, *Apol.* 39 See Duchesne, p. 49, note).

The "hymn" (*carmen*) spoken of by Pliny may have been one of the Psalms, especially those of the *Hallel*, cxiii to cxviii, sung by our Lord and His Apostles at the institution of the Sacrament in the Upper Room.[1] But besides the whole Psalter, the *Magnificat*, the *Benedictus*, the *Gloria in Excelsis*, and the *Nunc Dimittis*,[2] there were doubtless already many Christian hymns current in the Church, of which we are given fragments quoted by S. Paul and S. John.[3]

Justin, surnamed Martyr, was a heathen philosopher, born in Palestine at what is now called Nablous about A.D. 110, and suffered martyrdom in 165. He became a Christian before 140, and addressed an Apology or Defence of the Christians to the Emperor Antoninus Pius (136–161), and the Roman Senate, in which he gives the following description of the worship of Christians:

"On the day called Sunday, all who live in cities or in the country gather together to one place, and the memoirs of the apostles or the writings of the prophets are read, as long as time permits; then, when the reader has ceased, the president verbally instructs, and exhorts to the imitation of these good things. Then we all rise together and pray, and, as we before said, when our prayer is ended, bread and wine and water are brought, and the president in like manner offers prayers and thanksgivings to the utmost of his power [and, *at considerable length*, as in chap. lxv], and the people assent, saying Amen; and there is a distribution to each, and a participation of that over which thanks have been given, and to those who are absent a portion is sent by the deacons. And they who are well-to-do, and willing, give

---

[1] S Matt xxvi, 30.   [2] S Luke i, 46–56, 68–80, ii, 14, 29–33.
[3] See the following passages. Eph v, 14, 1 Tim iii, 16, Rev. iv, 11, v. 9, 10, 12, 13, vii, 12, xi, 17, xii, 10, 11, 12, xv, 3, 4, xix, 1, 6, 7. See also Eph. v, 19, Col. iii, 16, and Acts xvi, 25.

what each thinks fit; and what is collected is deposited with the president, who succors the orphans and widows, and those who, through sickness or any other cause, are in want, and those who are in bonds, and the strangers sojourning among us; and in a word takes care of all who are in need. Sunday is the day on which we all hold our common assembly, because it is the first day on which God, having wrought a change in the darkness and matter, made the world; and Jesus Christ our Saviour on the same day rose from the dead." [1]

"And this food is called among us *Eucharistia* [Eucharist], of which no one is allowed to partake but the man who believes that the things which we teach are true, and who has been washed with the washing that is for the remission of sins, and unto regeneration, and who is so living as Christ has enjoined. For not as common bread and common drink do we receive these; but in like manner as Jesus Christ our Saviour, having been made flesh by the Word of God, had both flesh and blood for our salvation, so likewise have we been taught that the food which is blessed by the prayer of His Word, and from which our blood and flesh by transmutation are nourished, is the flesh and blood of that Jesus who was made flesh." [2]

It is evident that, in this defence addressed to a heathen Emperor and Senate within forty years after the death of S. John, Justin is confining himself to the bare order of the service followed in the Christian congregations. It could not be expected that, in such a document, he would give much detail, or any formularies of prayer that were employed. His omissions, however, can be made good by the help of Christian documents belonging to the same period. One of the earliest of these is found in the epistle of Clement, Bishop

---

[1] *First Apology*, chap lxvii. [2] Chap. lxvi.

of Rome, to the Corinthians, written before the year 100.[1] This affords us at least an illustration of the *kind* of prayer which the rulers of the Church were accustomed to employ at their gatherings for worship.[1]

Following is a portion of the prayer recorded by Clement:

Thou hast opened the eyes of our hearts that they may know Thee, Thou the sole Highest among the highest, the Holy One who rests in the midst of the holy ones. Thou who abasest the insolence of the proud, who scatterest the machinations of the people, who exaltest the humble and puttest down the mighty; Thou who givest riches and poverty, death and life, sole Benefactor of spirits, God of all flesh; Thou whose regard penetrates the abyss, and scans the works of men; Thou who art our help in danger; Thou who savest us from despair, Creator and Overseer of all spirits; Thou who hast multiplied the nations upon earth, and chosen from among them those who love Thee through Jesus Christ, Thy well-beloved Servant, by whom Thou hast instructed, sanctified, and honored us. We beseech Thee, O Master, be our help and succor. Be the salvation of those of us who are in tribulation; take pity on the lowly, raise up them that fall, reveal Thyself to those who are in need, heal the ungodly, and restore those who have gone out of the way. Appease the hunger of the needy, deliver those among us who suffer in prison, heal the sick, comfort the faint-hearted; that all people may know that Thou art the only God, that Jesus Christ is Thy Servant, and that we are Thy people and the sheep of Thy pasture. . . . We confess Thee through the High Priest and Ruler of our souls, Jesus Christ, through whom glory and majesty be to Thee now, and throughout all generations, for ever and ever. Amen.[2]

---

[1] Clement is probably the same person mentioned by S. Paul as one of his "fellow labourers" in Philippi, which was a Roman "colony" (Phil. iv, 3; Acts xvi, 12). He is thus identified by Eusebius, the historian of the Church, writing in the fourth century (*Hist. Eccl* , iii, 16)   S. Paul says his "name is in the Book of Life"

[2] 1 Ep. 59–61, qu. by Duchesne, *Christian Worship*, pp. 51, 52.

IN THE FIRST THREE CENTURIES 51

The *Didache*, or *Doctrine of the Apostles*, a document discovered in Constantinople in 1873 by Bryennios Philotheos, at that time head-master of the higher Greek School in that city, but later the Metropolitan of Nicomedia, is recognized by scholars as "a very ancient writing, contemporary, at the latest, with S. Justin" (A.D. 110–165). In this we find the following:

"As to the Eucharist, we give thanks in this wise. First for the chalice: 'We thank Thee, our Father, for the Holy Vine of David, Thy Servant, which Thou hast made known to us by Jesus Thy Servant. Glory to Thee for evermore!'

"For the bread: 'We thank Thee, our Father, for the life and the knowledge which Thou hast made known to us by Jesus, Thy Servant. Glory to Thee for evermore! As the elements of this bread, scattered on the mountains, were brought together into a single whole, may Thy Church in like manner be gathered together from the ends of the earth into Thy kingdom; for Thine is the glory and the power, through Jesus Christ, for evermore!'

"After you are satisfied return thanks thus: 'We thank Thee, Holy Father, for Thy holy Name, which Thou hast made to dwell in our hearts, for the knowledge, faith, and immortality which Thou hast revealed to us through Jesus, Thy Servant. Glory to Thee for evermore! It is Thou, mighty Lord, who hast created the universe for the glory of Thy Name, who hast given to men meat and drink that they may enjoy them in giving Thee thanks. But to us Thou hast given spiritual meat and drink, and life eternal through Thy Servant. We give Thee thanks for everything, because Thou art mighty. Glory to Thee for evermore!'"[1]

During the first three Christian centuries, however, we find no record of a complete liturgy. "There may be several reasons assigned for this," Bingham says. "One is that the Bishops at first made every one their own liturgy for the

---

[1] Duchesne, pp. 52, 53.

private use, as we may call it, of their own particular churches. And therefore the use of them not extending further than the precincts of their own dioceses, there was little knowledge of them beyond the bounds of those churches, and not much care to preserve them but only for the use of such churches, for which they were particularly designed. That every Bishop had at first this power and privilege to compose and order the form of Divine Service for his own church, I have showed in another place." [1]

A second reason is seen in the fact that, down to the year 313, when Constantine, the first Christian Emperor, proclaimed religious toleration, the Church was again subject to persecution as an illegal society (*religio illicita*) by the pagan government of Rome. During this period, Bingham says, "It is not improbable but that, as a late learned French writer [Renaudot] has observed, the ancient liturgies were for some ages only certain forms of worship committed to memory, and known by practice, rather than committed to writing. . . . This seems very probable, because in the persecutions under Diocletian [A.D. 303], though a strict inquiry was made after the books of Scripture, and other things belonging to the Church, which were often delivered up by the *traditores* [Christian *traitors*] to be burnt, yet we never read of any ritual books, or books of Divine Service, delivered up among them. . . . We are not thence to conclude (as some weak men might be inclined to do) that therefore they had no liturgies or set form of Divine Worship in these persecuting ages of the Church; because there are undeniable evidences to the contrary; but we are only to conclude that they did not so generally compile them in books as in after ages, but used them by memory, and made them familiar to the people by known and constant prac-

---

[1] *Antiq* Book XIII, chap v, sect i.

IN THE FIRST THREE CENTURIES 53

tice, as many now use forms of prayer at this day without committing them to writing." [1]

This absence of written liturgies was doubtless due also to that *disciplina arcani*, or rule of secrecy, which grew up in the early days out of a mistaken or exaggerated view of our Lord's command "not to cast pearls before swine," [2] which forbade heathen or unbelievers to be present at the administration of Baptism or the Holy Communion, and which withheld from them the highest teaching of the Church in regard to the doctrine of the Holy Trinity, and the sacraments. This rule evidently did not exist in the days of S. Paul, for he speaks of the possibility of unbelievers coming into Christian assemblies,[3] nor in the second century, when Justin Martyr wrote freely about Christian belief and practice, though with proper reserve. Bingham considers that it did not originate before the beginning of the third century.[4] Though proceeding from good motives, the *disciplina arcani* only provoked persecution. It caused suspicion and false inferences in the minds of the heathen and their rulers, as all secrecy is apt to do. In later days, even in heathen countries, a reverent prudence has been found a better fulfilment of Christ's command about "casting pearls" than this doctrine of reserve. It is for this and similar reasons that, during the first three centuries, "we find only isolated references, passing allusions [to the liturgy and worship of the Church], scattered among authors of the most diverse character." [5] When we reach the fourth century, however, all is different. There, like some underground river, it emerges into the light of day.

---

[1] *Antiq.* Book XIII, chap. v, sect. 3.   [3] 1 Cor. xiv, 23–26.
[2] S. Matt. vii. 6   [4] *Antiq.* Book X, chap. v, 3.
[5] Duchesne, p. 54   For these allusions, etc. see Bingham, *Antiq.* Book XIII, c v, 4, 5, 6.

What is true, moreover, of liturgies is true also of churches.

We could not expect to find references to the character of church buildings in the pages of the New Testament inasmuch as Christians had at first to worship just as they best could, in private rooms or in the open. While under the ban of the Roman Empire until 313, as already stated, their services had to be conducted for the most part in secret, as in the Catacombs or subterranean cemeteries of the city of Rome. The only reference we find in the New Testament to the accessories of Christian worship are noteworthy, however, as showing what was its real centre. These are the Eucharistic Altar or Holy Table, and the Eucharistic Cup or Chalice.[1] Though we find a few references to church buildings in the third century by Cyprian, Tertullian, and Origen,[2] it is not until the fourth century, when the ban was removed under Constantine, that we begin to find detailed descriptions of buildings and services.

The earliest account of church buildings is given in the *Didascalia*, a document which is dated by scholars as of the year 250, and was later incorporated into the so-called Apostolic Constitutions (A.D. 375). This is a treatise on Church life, and incidentally mentions "holy churches," with presbyters' seats "in the part of the house which is turned to the east," the Bishop's throne in the midst of them; the laymen also sitting "in another part turned to the east," behind the presbyters; the women behind them, while all pray toward the east.[3] From other Church orders of the fourth century we learn that the eastern end of the building, the

---

[1] 1 Cor x, 16, 21; xi. 25-28; Heb. xiii, 10.
[2] See Warren, *Liturgy of Ante-Nicene Ch.*, pp. 67-73.
[3] See Maclean, *Ancient Church Orders*, p. 35; Warren, *Lit. of A.-N. Ch.*, pp. 43, 44.

IN THE FIRST THREE CENTURIES 55

bema or sanctuary, was raised three steps above the nave, and upon this was placed the altar with the Bishop's throne behind it, and the seats of the presbyters in a semicircle on either side of him. The deacons arrange the congregation, attend the door, and keep order. There are chambers toward the east, to the north and south of the sanctuary, which are used as sacristies by the clergy. The church is like a ship (Latin, *navis*, hence nave); the Bishop is the helmsman, the priests are his officers, the deacons in trim garments are sailors and head rowers, the laymen are passengers.

A plan of the round Church of the Resurrection (*Anastasis*), built by Constantine early in the fourth century over the Holy Sepulchre, and of the Basilica of the Holy Cross, built close by to the west, with a porch or court connecting the two, will be found in the *Lectures of S. Cyril*, Archbishop of Jerusalem, translated by R. W. (afterwards Dean) Church (Oxford, 1838), with the description given by Eusebius the Church historian, on which the plan is based.[1] It was in this basilica that the lectures to his candidates for Baptism were delivered by S. Cyril in the Lent of 347 or 349. In the recently discovered *Peregrinatio* of a lady from Gaul named Etheria (or Silvia) we have a very interesting account of the churches which she visited in that city about the year 385.[2]

These descriptions and allusions give unmistakable corroboration to the testimony of all the liturgies that the earliest worship of the Christian Church was based, not on that of the synagogue with its platform, and reading desk, and lay officials only, but on that of the Temple with its altar, its priesthood, and its sacrificial service.

---

[1] Pp. xxiv–xxix.
[2] See Duchesne. *Christian Worship*, pp. 490–523.

CHAPTER VI

The Parent Liturgies

"The same kind of synthetic criticism which traces back all known languages to three original forms of speech, can also trace back the multitude of differing Liturgies which are used by the various Churches of East and West to a few, — that is to say, four or five, — normal types, all of which have certain strong features of agreement with each other, pointing to the same liturgical fountain." — J H Blunt.

DURING the years that the Church was under the ban of the Roman Empire as an illegal or unlicensed religion (*religio illicita*), suspected as hostile to the imperial government, with which the worship of the heathen gods was inextricably entwined, it was natural that little progress would be made in rendering the services of the Church with much external beauty. There were few permanent church buildings. There were lulls, indeed, when the rulers ceased to persecute, but no one knew when the order might go out to crush the new religion. The Christians had to gather as best they could. Necessity knew no law. A table or a shelf would serve as an altar. Ordinary dress would suffice for a vestment. Instrumental music was impossible. Yet in spite of all these disadvantages it is abundantly evident that the worship of the Church everywhere was marked by extreme solemnity and dignity. In all the glimpses we obtain during this period we find no trace of eccentricity or familiarity in the presence of God. The Breaking of the Bread or Eucharist is the centre round which all worship gathers, and the tone of the prayers is one of profound reverence and elevation of thought.

THE PARENT LITURGIES 57

Though the liturgies in the earliest days were not generally committed to writing for the reason that I have already given, it is unquestioned that the use of them, though in a somewhat fluid state, in the first three centuries was universal. The absence of original documentary evidence of this fact need not surprise us. When it is remembered that out of all the manuscript copies of the New Testament, which must have existed in these three centuries, not one has come down to our own day, and only two from the fourth and two from the fifth century, we need not wonder that we have no manuscript of the liturgies of this period. This fact is all the more striking when it is recalled that the New Testament was an unchangeable record, possessing the highest possible authority as containing God's final revelation to men, whereas the liturgies, while clearly defined in their general character, were variable according to the people or race among whom they were used, and subject to revision and enrichment at the hands of the Bishops of every diocese. It is not, then, to be expected that manuscript copies of the many forms of the Liturgy would be so carefully preserved and handed on to future ages as were the sacred Scriptures.

Modern liturgical scholars are generally agreed in reckoning all the ancient liturgies in existence today, of which there are more than a hundred, as traceable to six principal types known by the names of the Apostles with whom they were traditionally connected, or by the names of the places in which they have been in use. These are (1) the Syrian, of S. James; (2) the Egyptian or Alexandrian, of S. Mark; (3) the Persian, of SS. Adeus and Maris, including that of the Christians of S. Thomas on the Malabar coast of India; (4) the Byzantine, of S. Chrysostom, represented by the present Greek and Armenian rites; (5) the Ephesine, of S. John or

S. Paul; (6) the Roman, of S. Peter, originally Greek for three centuries, and not Latin.

The Syrian Liturgy was that which was used throughout the patriarchates of Jerusalem and Antioch, which included the countries of Judea, Syria, Mesopotamia, and some provinces of Asia Minor. This liturgy, Palmer says, "merits our particular attention for several reasons. First, because the Church of Jerusalem was the mother Church of Christendom, and the faithful first received the title of Christians at Antioch;[1] secondly, because the Liturgy used there appears likewise to have prevailed to a great extent in the adjoining regions; and thirdly, because we have more ancient and numerous notices of this Liturgy in the writings of the Fathers than of any other in existence."[2]

This does not imply that the liturgies now in use in these Churches have remained absolutely unchanged through all these centuries. That is not true of any liturgy. Many revisions and enrichments take place from time to time in all liturgies in adaptation to changed conditions or new needs. Among men specially gifted for this purpose Basil, commonly called "the Great," Bishop of Caesarea in Cappadocia about A.D. 370, whose patriarchate extended from the Hellespont to the Euphrates, has a most prominent place. It is this improved form of S. Basil which has been used from time immemorial throughout the whole of Asia Minor.[3]

The Byzantine seems to be only another form of this Liturgy of S. James. It still bears the name of S. Chrysostom, "the golden-mouthed" Bishop of Constantinople, as

---

[1] Acts xi, 26.

[2] *Origines Lit*, I, pp. 15, 19. A list of sixty-four liturgies belonging to this family is given by Brightman in *Lit Eastern and Western*, pp. lviii–lxi. See also Neale and Littledale, *Prim. Lit.* pp. xi, xii.

[3] Palmer, I, 45, 48.

THE PARENT LITURGIES 59

enriched by him while he was still a priest of the Church in Antioch (386–397). This is today "the normal Liturgy of the Eastern Church."[1]

It is concerning the many forms of this great oriental liturgy used throughout the East that Palmer writes: "Whoever compares these venerable monuments will not fail to perceive a great and striking resemblance throughout. He will readily acknowledge their derivation from one common source; and will admit that they furnish sufficient means for ascertaining all the substance, and many of the expressions, which were used in the solemn *Anaphora* of the partriarchates of Antioch and Jerusalem, before the Council of Chalcedon, A.D. 451."[2]

Concerning the earliest form of the parent liturgy we obtain our knowledge chiefly from four sources, (1) THE CATECHETICAL LECTURES OF S. CYRIL, Bishop of Jerusalem in A.D. 349; (2) THE PRAYER BOOK OF BISHOP SARAPION, the contemporary and friend of Athanasius (c. A.D. 350); (3) the collection of early documents of the Church called THE APOSTOLICAL CONSTITUTIONS; and (4) THE SERMONS OF S. JOHN CHRYSOSTOM, Bishop of Constantinople, A.D. 397.

(1) Cyril delivered his CATECHETICAL LECTURES about the year 347 when he was still a priest of the Church in Jerusalem. They were instructions addressed to candidates preparing for Baptism, Confirmation, and Holy Communion.

---

[1] Neale and Littledale, p. xx Duchesne says, "It has ended by supplanting the older liturgies in all the Greek patriarchates of the East. It is in use in the national Church of Greece, and in those of Servia, Bulgaria, Roumania, etc. . In these latter countries, where the liturgical language is not Greek, translations are employed which are made from the Greek text used in the Patriarchate of Constantinople . . . In Greece the liturgical language is Greek; in Georgia, Georgian, in Roumania, Roumanian; in the other countries Slavonic" *Christian Worship*, pp 71, 72, and note.

[2] *Orig. Lit*, pp 28, 29. For what is meant by *Anaphora*, see p. 67.

The twenty-third and last of these lectures, as "the finish to their spiritual edification," gives an account of the holy Sacrament as it was celebrated in that city. He describes briefly one after another the different parts of the service. Assuming that the bread and wine have already been brought to the altar, he begins by speaking of the washing of the hands of the priest "as a symbol," he says, "that ye ought to be pure from all sinful deeds"; of the kiss of charity[1] as "the sign that our souls have banished all remembrance of wrongs"; the *Sursum Corda*, "Lift up your hearts," followed by "Let us give thanks to the Lord"; the *Sanctus*, or *Trisagion*, "Holy, Holy, Holy"; the prayer for the Holy Spirit upon the elements, "that He may make the bread the Body of Christ, and the wine the Blood of Christ"; the prayer for the common peace of the Church, for kings, soldiers, sick, afflicted, etc.; the commemoration of those who have fallen asleep before us, Patriarchs, Prophets, Apostles, Martyrs, etc.; the Lord's Prayer; the Invitation, "O taste and see," etc. And finally he adds this practical direction:

"Approaching therefore, come not with thy wrists extended or thy fingers open; but make thy left hand as if a throne for thy right, which is on the eve of receiving the King. And having hallowed thy palm, receive the Body of Christ, saying after it, Amen. Then after thou hast with carefulness hallowed thine eyes by the touch of the holy Body, partake thereof, giving heed lest thou lose any of it; for what thou losest is a loss to thee as it were from one of thine own members. For tell me, if any one gave thee gold dust, wouldest thou not with all precaution keep it fast? How much more cautiously then wilt thou observe that not a crumb falls from thee, of what is more precious than gold and precious stones?

"Then after having partaken of the Body of Christ, approach also to the Cup of His Blood; not stretching forth

---

[1] 1 Cor. xvi, 20, 1 Peter v, 14.

THE PARENT LITURGIES 61

thy hands, but bending, and saying in the way of worship and reverence, Amen, be thou hallowed by partaking also of the Blood of Christ. . . . Sever not yourselves from the Communion; deprive not yourselves, by the pollution of sins, of these Holy and Spiritual Mysteries."[1]

(2) THE PRAYER BOOK OF SARAPION, a Bishop in the Nile Delta, is "the first collection to which the name of Service-book can properly be given." It was discovered in the Monastery of Mount Athos, and was first published in 1899. It contains only the portions of the service said by a Bishop at ordination, in the Holy Communion, and other services, but nothing so complete is met with again until the seventh century. No information is given about what is said by the assistant clergy or the congregation.[2]

(3) The third chief source of the original form of the Apostolic Liturgy is the book called THE APOSTOLIC CONSTITUTIONS, which is generally admitted to be not later than the fourth century. The book is "a description by some private author of the rites used in the Church of his day; a service book incorporated in a treatise."[3] The early character of many of the documents contained in the book is evident from the fact that "they describe the Church of primitive times in its antagonism with heathen life, and in its over-depressed and, humanly speaking, mean condition, when as yet 'not many wise men after the flesh, not many mighty, not many noble, were called.'"[4]

---

[1] *Lectures of S. Cyril*, translated by R. W. Church, Oxford, 1838, pp. 273, sq.

[2] This is one of many recent discoveries made in the last years of the nineteenth century, and described by Bishop Maclean in *Recent Discoveries* etc , S. P C K , 1904 See also P and F *New History, etc* , p 5.

[3] Dr Frere, *Principles of Religious Ceremonial*, and P. and F. *New His.* etc. p 4.

[4] *Dic of Doctr and His Theology*, ed by J H Blunt, p. 149. See also Canon Warren, *Lit Ante-Nicene Church*, p 255.

The books of this collection treat of many subjects, moral and religious duties, clerical functions, consecration of Bishops, clerical marriage, fasts and festivals, Holy Baptism, the Holy Eucharist, the Lord's Day, etc. The eighth and last book, among other things such as the election and ordination of Bishops, contains a liturgy which is commonly called the Clementine as attributed to Clement, one of the earliest Bishops of Rome, and supposed to be the companion of S. Paul mentioned by him in Phil. iv, 3. Of this document Palmer says, "The liturgy which bears the name of Clement, Bishop of Rome, is certainly a monument of venerable antiquity. I cannot think, however, that it is an accurate transcript of the liturgy of any Church. In the first place there is no evidence that it was used anywhere. Secondly, although from its title we should say that it was the liturgy of the Roman Church, it is nevertheless totally unlike the primitive liturgy of that Church, while it agrees in substance and order with the liturgies of the East. . . . In its order, its substance, and many of its expressions, the Liturgy of Clement is identical with that of S. James." [1]

(4) The fourth chief source of our knowledge of the original Liturgy of S. James is found in THE HOMILIES OR SERMONS OF S. CHRYSOSTOM while he was still a priest of the Church of Antioch (386–397). As his description corresponds generally to that given by Cyril in his Lectures, it will not be necessary to reproduce it here. The service in Antioch in the latter part of the fourth century was evidently the same in substance as that in Jerusalem in 347.[2]

The following portion of the *Anaphora* of the Liturgy of

---

[1] *Orig Lit*, I, pp. 37, 38

[2] Duchesne says, p 56, "Bingham was the first to form the project of collecting and putting into order these scattered data " *Antiq* XIII, chap vi.

THE PARENT LITURGIES

S. James, as revised by S. Chrysostom, which, as already stated, is "the normal liturgy of the Eastern Church" today, is of much interest as showing the close correspondence with the English, but more especially with the Scottish and American forms.

The Priest taking the Air[1] *from the Holy Gifts, lays it on one side, saying,*
The grace of our Lord Jesus Christ, and the love of God the Father, and the fellowship of the Holy Ghost, be with you all.
Choir. And with thy spirit.
Priest. Lift we up our hearts.
Choir. We lift them up unto the Lord.
Priest. Let us give thanks unto the Lord.
Choir. It is meet and right to worship the Father, the Son, and the Holy Ghost, the consubstantial and undivided Trinity.
Priest. It is meet and right to hymn Thee, to bless Thee, to praise Thee, to give thanks to Thee, to worship Thee, in every part of Thy dominion. For Thou art God, ineffable, inconceivable, invisible, incomprehensible, the same from everlasting to everlasting; Thou and Thine Only-Begotten Son, and the Holy Ghost. For Thou broughtest us forth to being from nothing, and when we had fallen didst raise us up again, and gavest not over till Thou hadst done every thing that Thou mightest bring us to heaven, and bestow on us Thy kingdom to come. For all these things we give thanks to Thee, and to Thine Only-Begotten Son, and Thy Holy Ghost, for Thy benefits which we know, and which we know not, manifest and concealed, which Thou hast bestowed upon us. We give Thee thanks also for this ministry which Thou hast vouchsafed to receive at our hands:· although there stand by Thee thousands of Archangels, and ten thousands of Angels, the Cherubim, and the Seraphim that have six wings, and are full of eyes, and soar aloft on

---
[1] The "air" is the name in the Eastern Church for the veil for covering the sacred vessels.

their wings, singing, vociferating, shouting, and saying the triumphal hymn:

Choir. Holy, Holy, Holy, Lord of Sabaoth; heaven and earth are full of Thy glory. Hosanna in the highest: blessed is He that cometh in the Name of the Lord: Hosanna in the highest.

Then the Deacon, taking the asterisk from the holy disk,[1] *signs it with the sign of the cross, and having saluted it, replaces it.*

Priest. We also with these blessed powers, Lord and Lover of men, cry and say, Holy art Thou and All-Holy, Thou and Thy Only-Begotten Son, and Thine Holy Ghost. Holy art Thou and All-Holy, and great is the majesty of Thy glory:

Who didst so love Thy world as to give Thine Only-Begotten Son, that whoso believeth in Him might not perish, but might have everlasting life: Who having come, and having fulfilled for us all the dispensation, in the night wherein He was betrayed, or rather surrendered Himself for the life of the world, took bread in His holy and pure and spotless hands, and gave thanks, and blessed, and hallowed, and brake, and gave to His holy Disciples and Apostles, saying, (*aloud,*) Take, eat: this is My Body which is broken for you for the remission of sins.

Choir. Amen.

Priest, (*in a low voice,*) Likewise after supper He took the cup, saying, (*aloud,*) Drink ye all of this: This is My Blood of the New Testament, which is shed for you and for many for the remission of sins.

Choir. Amen.

Priest, (*in a low voice,*) We therefore remembering this salutary precept, and all that happened on our behalf, the Cross, the Tomb, the Resurrection on the third day, the Ascension into heaven, the Session on the right hand, the second and glorious Coming again, (*aloud,*) in behalf of all, and for all, we offer Thee Thine own of Thine own.

---

[1] The "asterisk," or star, is a device formed of two crossed arches of metal, intended to support the "air" or veil, when it is placed over the paten, or "disk."

THE PARENT LITURGIES 65

Choir. Thee we hymn, Thee we praise: to Thee we give thanks, Lord, and pray to Thee, our God.

Priest, (*in a low voice,*) Moreover we offer unto Thee this reasonable and unbloody sacrifice: and beseech Thee and pray and supplicate; send down Thy Holy Ghost upon us and upon these proposed gifts.

[*Here follow brief prayers by the Deacon and Priest kneeling.*]

The Priest standeth up, and thrice maketh the sign of the Cross on the Holy Gifts, saying,

And make this bread the precious Body of Thy Christ.

Deacon. Amen. Sir, bless the holy cup.

Priest. And that which is in this cup, the precious Blood of Thy Christ.

Deacon. Amen. *And pointing with his orarion*[1] *to both the Holy Things,* Sir, bless.

Priest. Changing them by Thy Holy Ghost.

Deacon. Amen, Amen, Amen.

Then the Deacon bows his head to the Priest, and saith,

Holy Sir, remember me a sinner.

Then he stands in his former place, and taking the fan,[2] *fans the oblation as before.*

Priest. So that they may be to those that participate, for purification of soul, forgiveness of sins, communion of the Holy Ghost, fulfilment of the kingdom of heaven, boldness towards Thee, and not to judgment or to condemnation.[3]

The following beautiful prayer for the departed is taken from the same liturgy:

And remember them who with purity of heart, and sanctity of soul and body, have departed from this world, and have come to Thee, O God. Them who from the first Adam, the first made of our creation, in all generations have pleased Thee, and confessed Thee, and have hoped for and expected

---
[1] The "orarion" is a stole

[2] The "fan," now "generally made of silver and in the shape of the heads and wings of cherubim" (Neale, *Prim. Lit,* p xxix, note), was originally intended to prevent flies from settling on the elements.

[3] Neale, *Primitive Liturgies,* pp. 112–115.

the manifestation of Thine Only-Begotten Son, and have desired to see His great and glorious day. Them who in the spiritual bosom of Baptism, have put Thee on splendidly, and have believed in Thy Name. Give them rest in Thy celestial habitations, in the Paradise of delights, in the tabernacles of light, in quiet dwelling-places. Enter not into judgment with them, O Lord, for in Thy sight shall no man living be justified; for there is only One who hath appeared upon earth, pure and without blemish.[1]

Dr. Neale gives many other examples of prayers for the faithful departed as found in the primitive liturgies, and makes this observation upon them: "The more they are examined, the more clearly two points will appear. (1) That prayers for the dead, and more especially the oblation of the blessed Eucharist for them, have been from the beginning the practice of the Universal Church. (2) And this without any idea of a purgatory of pain, or of any state from which the departed soul has to be delivered as from one of misery." [2]

The Syrian, or S. James family of liturgies has probably more than fifty branches, throughout the East from Palestine to Russia. The Alexandrian or S. Mark family has about twenty branches tracing their source to Egypt. The Persian has five, one of these being that used from time immemorial by the Christians of S. Thomas, as they call themselves, of Malabar. The Petrine family has only one liturgy, the Roman. That of S. John, or Ephesus, has two chief branches, the Gallican and the so-called Mozarabic, though it is claimed by some modern liturgists that these derived their oriental character, not directly from Ephesus, but from Milan where the Liturgy of S. Ambrose had certain Roman features mingled with its distinctly oriental original.

---

[1] Neale, *Primitive Liturgies*, p 253
[2] *Ibid.* p. 248. See also Mason, *The State of the Faithful Departed*, p. 110.

THE PARENT LITURGIES 67

Akin also to that of Milan was the Use of Aquileia in the civil province of Triest, and known as the Patriarchine.[1]

The general order of the great parent liturgies, as given by Dr. Neale, is substantially as follows: Every liturgy contains two parts, the PRO-ANAPHORA, or preparation, and the ANAPHORA, or celebration proper. The PRO-ANAPHORA begins with a prefatory prayer, a hymn, or antiphon, or introit (literally, "he enters"), accompanying the solemn bringing in of the Gospels from the sacristy or prothesis. This is called "the Little Entrance," and is followed by the *Trisagion*, or *Ter-Sanctus* ("Thrice Holy"), the Lections (Epistle and Gospel for the day, and in some rites a selection from the Old Testament, called the Prophecy), and prayers after the Gospel, when those not yet admitted to the Holy Communion are required to leave. This portion of the Pro-Anaphora was called the *Missa Catechumenorum*, or Mass of the Catechumens. The second part of the Pro-Anaphora consisted of prayers accompanying the solemn bringing in of the elements of Bread and Wine. This is called "the Great Entrance," and is followed by the Offertory, the Kiss of Peace (*Pax*), and the Creed.

The ANAPHORA (literally, the Oblation, or Offering) begins with the *Sursum Corda* ("Lift up your hearts"), the Proper Preface (if there be one), and the Triumphal Hymn ("Therefore with angels and archangels," etc.), *Benedictus qui venit* ("Blessed is He"), the Consecration, the great Intercession for the living and the departed, the Prayer of Intense Adoration, the Confession or Prayer of Humble Access, the Communion, Thanksgiving, and Dismissal.[2]

A comparative table is given below showing the component parts of the four parent liturgies which represent the

---
[1] For a further consideration of this see chap. vii, pp. 77, 78.
[2] *Prim. Lit*, pp xv–xviii, and 48, 113, 131, 163.

COMPARATIVE TABLE, SHOWING THE LEADING FEATURES OF FOUR PARENT LITURGIES, AND OF THE ENGLISH, SCOTTISH, AND AMERICAN LITURGIES

S JAMES	S MARK	S JOHN	S PETER	ENGLISH [1]
1 Prefatory Prayer and Introit.	1 Prefatory Prayer and Introit	1 Prefatory Prayer and Introit	1 Prefatory Prayer and Introit	1 Prefatory Prayer with Introit (hymn) preceding
2 Trisagion ("Holy God, holy and mighty, holy and immortal")	2 Trisagion	2 Gloria in Excelsis ("Glory be to God on high")	2 Gloria in Excelsis	
3 Lessons from the Old and New Testaments	3 Epistle and Gospel	3 Epistle and Gospel	3 Epistle and Gospel	3 Decalogue (Old Testament lesson), with Kyries (Lord, have mercy), and Epistle and Gospel
4 Oblation of Elements	4 Oblation of Elements	4 Oblation of Elements	4 Oblation of Elements	4 Oblation of Elements
5 Creed	5 Creed	5 Creed	5 Creed	5 Creed
6 Kiss of Peace	6 Kiss of Peace			
7 Prayer for the whole Church	7 Prayer for the whole Church	7 Prayer for the whole Church		7 Prayer for Church Militant with commemoration of faithful departed
8 Sursum Corda ("Lift up your hearts")	8 Sursum Corda	8 Sursum Corda.		6 Kiss of Peace, represented by "Ye who do truly, etc"
9 Ter Sanctus ("Holy, holy, holy")	9 Ter Sanctus	9 Ter Sanctus	8 Sursum Corda	8 Sursum Corda
10 Words of Institution	10 Words of Institution		9 Ter Sanctus	9 Ter Sanctus
11 Oblation	11 Oblation	11 Oblation	10 Words of Institution	10 Words of Institution
12 Invocation of the Holy Ghost	12 Invocation of the Holy Ghost	12 Invocation of the Holy Ghost	11 Oblation	11 Oblation
13 Prayer for the living	13 Prayer for living	13 Prayer for living	13 Prayer for living	
14 Prayer for the faithful departed	14 Prayer for the faithful departed	14 Prayer for faithful departed	14 Prayer for faithful departed	
15 Lord's Prayer	15 Lord's Prayer	15 Lord's Prayer	15 Lord's Prayer	15 Lord's Prayer.
16 Communion	16 Communion	16 Communion	16 Communion	16 Communion
17 Thanksgiving	17 Thanksgiving	17 Thanksgiving	17 Thanksgiving	13 } Prayer for "all Thy whole Church."
18 Dismissal with blessing	18 Dismissal with blessing	18 Dismissal by the deacons, saying "The mysteries are complete."	18 Dismissal with blessing (This liturgy is wanting in the Invocation of the Holy Ghost (12) The Kiss of Peace and the Prayer for the whole Church (6 and 7) have substitutes).	14 } 17 Thanksgiving 2 Gloria in Excelsis. 18 Dismissal with blessing.

[1] The Scottish and American differ from the English in possessing the Invocation (12) and in having the Oblation (11) restored to its ancient place between the words of Institution (10) and the Invocation (12) The Scottish Liturgy places the prayer for "the Whole Church" (7) ending with the Lord's Prayer (15), immediately after the prayer of Consecration (10, 11 and 12)

THE PARENT LITURGIES

worship of the Christian Church in the days of persecution, that is, before the year 313. These same general features are found also in all other liturgies, national or local, heretical or orthodox, which are derived from these originals. The essential oneness of all, in spite of the utmost difference in language, and wording, and order, and detail, must force on any unprejudiced student the conclusion that all have had one common origin. This is the more remarkable because of the vast distance of national or racial Churches one from another (as Abyssinia, Ethiopia, Malabar, the British Isles), the difficulties of ancient travel, together with the recognized authority of each Bishop to modify or adapt the worship to the requirements of his own diocese. It follows that there is only one place and one time where and when such an original could have been framed, namely, Jerusalem, and the years immediately following the Ascension, while the Apostles were still gathered together in that city. It has been said with much reason, "Probably before the Apostles separated for their several spheres of missionary work, they met and agreed, under the guidance of the Holy Ghost, upon the essentials of Eucharistic worship." These would form the foundation and framework which Bishops, and doctors, and missionaries of the Church, having special gifts for the work, would build upon and enrich with treasures of devout thought and supplication. On no other theory can we explain the remarkable unity in essentials, together with endless variety of detail, in all extant liturgies.

CHAPTER VII

THE BRITISH AND IRISH LITURGIES

"When one wishes to explain a science little known, the simplest method is to give an account of its history. In this way the knowledge insinuates itself into the mind of the reader, just as it was formed in that of successive generations, people follow, so to speak, the science step by step; and with this knowledge they proceed, from its simplest elements to its most complex theories" — PAUL DE RÉMUSAT, *Sur une Revolution dans la Chimie, 1855.*

WE are now in a position to trace the sources from which the liturgy of the British and English Churches was derived. But before approaching this question it is necessary to understand something of the history of the early Church in the British Isles. At what date Christianity found its first footing in Britain it is impossible to say. The claim that S. Paul preached in Britain after his promised visit to Spain [1] rests on no certain authority. In his day, and for 350 years afterwards, the island, as far north as the Clyde, was a province of the Roman Empire (from 54 B.C. to A.D. 418). The northern portion and Ireland were, to their own loss, never conquered by Roman arms. Southern Britain was ruled by Roman officials and subjected to Roman laws, just as India is ruled today by the British, and the Philippine Islands by the United States. About the year 120 Ptolemy, the astronomer and geographer, enumerates fifty-six British cities with Latin names, and there is every evidence from the ruins of theatres, villas, baths, coins, vases, etc., that these cities once contained a flourishing population.

---

[1] Rom. xv, 24, 28.

BRITISH AND IRISH LITURGIES

The first converts would therefore most naturally be among these Latin-speaking colonists, soldiers of the Roman army, officials of the government, merchants, and such natives as were brought into immediate contact with them. One fact is clear, whatever the source of the founding of the Church in Britain, before the withdrawal of the Roman armies and governors in A.D. 418 the Church was fully organized. Its many dioceses, each under its own Bishop, were united into three provinces. Each province had its Archbishop. The Bishop of London was the Archbishop of the southern province; the Bishop of York of the northern; and the Bishop of Caer-Leon on Usk of the Welsh or western province.

In the persecution by the Emperor Diocletian, A.D. 303, the British Church had many martyrs, such as Alban, Julius, and Aaron. Three Bishops of the Church attended the Council of Arles in France, A.D. 314, and at the great General Council of Nice, A.D. 325, two priests were present representing the British Bishops.

Another fact is of importance here, one which has its analogy and counterpart in India under British rule, and in the Philippines under that of Americans. The historian Bede, in the eighth century, tells us that Latin had become "a common language for the Angles, Britons, Picts, and Irish."[1]

"In quite early days," writes Canon Warren, "Latin and not any form of Gaelic, may have been, if not the vernacular language, at least a language understood by all the members of the Christian Church in Britain. Tacitus informs us that the Roman language was adopted by the leading inhabitants of Britain under the 'policy' of Agricola. Most of the writings of the British, Scottish, and Irish authors of the first six centuries, all the extant Psalters and

[1] *His. Eccles.* I, i.

72 PRIMITIVE WORSHIP & THE PRAYER BOOK

Books of the Gospels, and the few liturgical fragments which have been preserved, are written in the Latin language by scribes who not only understood what they wrote, but were so far masters of the language in which they were writing as to have compiled a special British and Irish version of the old Latin text of the Bible for use in their own Church. The ecclesiastical use of the ancient Celtic tongue, if this theory is correct, commenced when the Church began to include among its members and to receive into its priesthood persons who were ignorant of Latin; but even then it was confined to the rubrics, and to sermons and addresses." [1]

Though the introduction of the Latin language was doubtless justifiable in the early days of the Church in England, its continuance by the stupid conservatism and unscriptural policy of the later Papacy when the language of the people became fixed, was worse than a blunder. To this day Rome by canon forbids the translation of the liturgy into the vernacular of every country where it has sway, though the very Latin service which it insists on as sacrosanct is itself a translation from the Greek, when Latin had become the language of the people.[2] Yet as late as A.D. 1215 a canon

---

[1] *Lit. and Rit.* etc., pp. 156, 157. The sources of information in regard to the ancient British Liturgy and Ritual are (1) Scattered notices in the works of contemporary Irish and British writers of the 5th, 6th, and 7th centuries (2) Scattered notices in Celtic manuscripts such as the Catalogue of the Saints of Ireland, Leabhar Breac, etc. (3) Fragments of the ancient Liturgy in the following Irish Missals, the Stowe (ninth century), Drummond (eleventh century), and Corpus (twelfth century): in the Books of Mulling, and Dimma (seventh century), Deer, and Armagh (ninth century), etc. (4) Illuminations in Celtic manuscripts. (5) Architectural remains of churches, inscriptions, sculptured crosses, book-covers, pastoral staves, bells, chalices, etc See *Lit and Ritual*, etc., pp. viii and ix.

[2] See Littledale, *Reasons against Joining the Church of Rome*, pp. 87–89.

BRITISH AND IRISH LITURGIES 73

of the Lateran Council under Pope Innocent enforced "the celebration of Divine Service according to the diversity of ceremonies and languages."[1]

But side by side with this partially Roman and bilingual character of the ancient British Church, we find her making the most thorough-going assertion of her "independence of the Roman Church, in her origin, mission, and jurisdiction."[2] It is true that Bede, the historian of the English Church in the eighth century, attributes the conversion of England to the agency of the Roman Bishop, Eleutherus (A.D. 171–190), in the time of the British prince Lucius.[3] "This story," Canon Warren says, "is now known to have originated in Rome in the fifth or sixth century, 300 years or more after the date assigned to that event. In the eighth century Bede introduced it into England, where by the ninth century it

---

[1] Luckock, *Studies in the Prayer Book*, p. 30 It is noteworthy, moreover, that more than five hundred years before England regained the use of the vulgar tongue, the Bohemians in 977 wrested from the court of Rome the use of the vernacular in their Liturgy, and they still retain the Slavonic tongue in spite of various efforts on the part of Rome to take it away The Liturgy of the old kingdom of Georgia is in Georgian, that of Rumania in Rumanian (that is, *Roman*, akin to Italian), that of Russia in Slavonic, which owes its translation to S Cyril, a native of Thessalonica, who was a missionary to the Bulgarians in the ninth century. "He adopted Greek characters so far as they went; but its twenty-two literal forms went but a little way in supplying the forty-three which he found to be necessary for a language of inexhaustible richness and beauty, . . the rival of Greek in flexibility, its superior in copiousness " . . Slavonic is still used in Russia, but "children are taught both languages (Russ and Slavonic), which form the commencement of their education " The Greek Liturgy is still allowed in Sicily, Calabria, and Apulia (See Neale, *Essays on Liturgiology*, pp. 200, 206, 212; also Duchesne, *Christian Worship*, p. 72, note)

[2] Warren, *Lit and Rit*, p 29

[3] *His. Ecc.* i, 4.

had grown into the conversion of the whole of Britain, while the full-fledged fiction, connecting it specially with Wales and Glastonbury, and entering into further details, grew up between the ninth and twelfth centuries." [1]

It is to be remembered, moreover, that during the first three centuries, while the Empire was still powerful and still pagan, the Church in the city of Rome was only a struggling and persecuted body whose membership was chiefly among a Greek-speaking population, and with its liturgy in the Greek language, which was also the language of commerce. No such claims of universal supremacy, as were afterwards made by the Roman Bishops, were at this time thought of. It is moreover a significant fact that in the year 596, when Gregory sent Augustine and his missionary priests to convert the heathen Angles and Saxons in Britain, he seems strangely ignorant of the existence of any Church planted there by Roman influence, or owing allegiance to the Roman see, which it would have done if Rome had been its founder. In fact, we know that when Augustine endeavored to exercise authority over the British Bishops, with one consent they refused to recognize such a claim as a thing before unheard of. "We will have none of these things which you require," they said at the conference in 602, "nor will we have you as our Archbishop." [2]

And this independent character of the British Church continued long after the days of Augustine, even down to the end of the eighth century. As early as 432, that is, 164 years before Gregory sent Augustine to the Anglo-Saxons, the work of christianizing the Irish, or as they were then called, the Scots, was begun by a British Christian, edu-

---

[1] *Lit. and Rit*, p. 30, and compare Haddan and Stubbs, *Councils and Ecc Doc*, i, pp. 25, 26.
[2] Bede, *His. Ecc.* ii, 2.

BRITISH AND IRISH LITURGIES 75

cated and ordained in France, Patrick, or Succat, as his British name was called.[1]

Columba, a member of this Irish, or as it was then called, Scottish, Church of S. Patrick, became in 563 the Apostle of the heathen Picts of Albania (not called Scotland till the tenth century), where he christianized the whole of the North and North-West, and the adjacent islands. S. Columba's successors at Iona converted in a similar way the whole of the Anglo-Saxon population north of the Humber, some of them carrying their labors as far south as Suffolk and Cornwall. "Irish missionary zeal sought a vent even beyond the confines of Britain. Early in the sixth century (A.D. 511) the Irish S. Fridolin appeared at Poitiers, Strasbourg, and Seckingen near Basle, as the pioneer of future missionary hosts. Late in the sixth and early in the seventh centuries S. Columbanus and S. Gall, with their companions, traversed Gaul, Italy, and Switzerland, founding their chief monasteries at Luxeuil, Bobbio, and S. Gall. . . . Less

---

[1] "He was thus double-named, like the Apostle Paul, who bore a Roman as well as a Jewish name from his youth up." (Prof. Bury, *Life of S. Patrick*, p. 23) In this scholarly volume by the Regius Professor of Modern History in the University of Cambridge (England), the author makes a strong argument against the common view that Patrick's birthplace (Bannaventa, as given in his autobiography, or "Confession") is identical with Dumbarton on the Clyde. His grandfather, Potitus, was a priest of the British Church, and his father, Calpurnius, was a deacon, and also a decurion, or member of the municipal council of a Roman town "We have no evidence," writes Prof. Bury, "that there were Roman towns with municipal constitutions in Strathclyde. . . . The Rock of Clyde, at the extreme end of the Northern Wall, is the last place we should expect to find the *uillula* (farmhouse) of a Roman decurion; and the opinion that the home of Calpurnius was in that remote spot cannot be accepted without better evidence than an anonymous statement which we cannot trace to any trustworthy source" (*Ibid* pp , 323, 324) He is inclined to look for the birthplace "in the regions of the lower Severn" (*Ibid.*, p. 17).

76 PRIMITIVE WORSHIP & THE PRAYER BOOK

known Irish missions also carried Christianity to the Faroe Isles c. A.D. 725, and to Iceland A.D. 795. . . . All the great leaders in this Celtic wave of missionary enterprise were of Irish origin." [1]

These facts are very important as bearing directly on the original source of the Liturgy of the British and English Churches. They show us "a vast Celtic communion existing in Great Britain and Ireland, and sending its missions among the Teutonic tribes on the Continent, and to distant islands like Iceland; Catholic in doctrine and practice, and yet with its claims to Catholicity ignored or impugned by the Church of Rome; with a long roll of saints, every name of note on which is either that of one like S. Columbanus taking a line wholly independent of Rome, or, like Bishop Colman at the Synod of Whitby [664], directly in collision with her; having its own liturgy, its own translation of the Bible, its own mode of chanting, its own monastic rule, its own cycle for the calculation of Easter; and presenting both internal and external evidence of a complete autonomy." [2]

It has been already pointed out that during the first two centuries the Church in the city of Rome was a mere struggling and persecuted body, chiefly composed of Greek-

---

[1] Warren, *Lit. and Ritual of the Celtic Church*, pp. 25, 26. See also *Ireland and the Celtic Church*, by Prof. Stokes.

[2] *Ibid*, pp. 45, 46. It is very noteworthy also that in S. Patrick's "Confession," or autobiography, and his "Letter" to the Christian subjects of Coroticus on the Clyde, as well as in his Life dictated by Aedh, Bishop of Sletty (died A.D. 698), and preserved in the Book of Armagh, there is complete silence as to any commission from a Bishop of Rome. S. Patrick describes himself only as a Bishop in Ireland, deriving his commission directly from God (*Ibid*, pp 36, 37) In fact the Church of Ireland was the last in Europe to submit to Rome It was not until the synod of Kells in 1152 that the Irish Church accepted the Roman Missal, and palls for her four Archbishops.

BRITISH AND IRISH LITURGIES 77

speaking people and using a liturgy in Greek. It was not then in a position to send out missionaries to such a distant point as "the other world" (*alter orbis*), as Britain was then regarded, though, as we have already seen, Christian soldiers in the imperial army, and Christian traders and merchants may have carried the beginnings of a Christian community to the coast towns and the camps in that country. All the facts seem to point to a source closer by, namely Gaul, separated from Britain by a channel which, at its narrowest point, had only eighteen miles of sea.

In the year 208 the famous Church writer, Tertullian, a priest of the Church in Carthage, is the first to speak definitely of a Church in regions of the Britons "not yet visited by the Romans."[1] Irenaeus, the Bishop of Lyons, a disciple of Polycarp, who was a disciple of S. John, while naming, in A.D. 176, the branches of the Church then in existence, makes no allusion to any Church in Britain.[2] But the following year a terrible persecution broke out in Celtic Gaul, the district around Lyons and Vienne, and it is probable that the Christian refugees became the means of establishing the Church beyond the narrow sea of the Channel sometime between 176 and 208. However this may be, there are certain oriental features in the remains of the Celtic liturgy and ritual which make it most probable that they are to be traced to this source and time.[3] "It is well known," writes Duchesne, "that the Gallican Liturgy, in the features dis-

---

[1] *Britannorum inaccessa Romanis loca, Adv Jud* vii

[2] *Haer*, i. 10.

[3] Canon Warren while treating of the Celtic Liturgy calls our attention to the employment of the fan, which is still an accessory of liturgic worship in the Eastern Church, and also to the use of the Greek word "disc" for the paten. *Lit of Celtic Church*, pp 143, 144

tinguishing it from the Roman use, betrays all the characteristics of the Eastern liturgies." Instead, however, of adopting the view of most English liturgiologists that the Gallican Liturgy, which is the acknowledged source of the Celtic of the British Isles, is the Liturgy of Ephesus imported into Gaul by the founders of the Church of Lyons, he is inclined to trace these oriental characteristics through the use of Milan, which was the imperial and ecclesiastical rival of old Rome in the fourth century. "From the moment when Rome became no longer the centre of attraction [by the removal of the seat of empire to Milan and Constantinople] . . . Milan could not fail to have the preference over all other Churches." . . . "Many of the most important Milanese peculiarities in discipline and worship," he adds, "have a distinctly Oriental character." [1]

But through whatever channel, Ephesine or Milanese,

---

[1] Pp. 92–94. According to Neale also, this Milanese or Ambrosian Liturgy (so-called after S. Ambrose, the great Bishop of Milan, its reviser in the fourth century) is "the Ephesine moulded by contact with the Petrine" or Roman. (*Essays*, p 171) Canon Warren, in his article on *Liturgy* in the Ency Brit. 11th ed , writes concerning the assumed Ephesine origin of the Hispano-Gallican, that it "lacks proof and may now be regarded as a discredited hypothesis." His own discussion of the subject in the same article, however, seems rather to support the opposite contention. The presumption appears to point clearly to Ephesus as the source of the liturgies of both Spain and Gaul; by S. Paul directly for the former (Rom. xv, 24), and by S. John indirectly through Irenaeus, Bishop of Lyons (circa 130–200), for the latter. The internal evidence seems to point strongly in the same direction. See Warren's article, p. 797, and Freeman, II, p. 404. That they were modified by the Milanese in the fourth century, as Duchesne argues, just as the Celtic and British were modified by the Roman in the seventh century, is reasonable enough. It is difficult, however, to see how this can affect the fact of its original source being Ephesus or some other Eastern region.

BRITISH AND IRISH LITURGIES 79

the Liturgy was first introduced into Gaul, the close early connection between the Gallican and the British people and Churches tends strongly to confirm the view that the British and Celtic Churches derived their liturgic customs from the East through Gaul. During the fourth and fifth centuries there was constant commercial intercourse between the two countries, while many British Christians emigrated from Wales and Cornwall to Armorica and Brittany. Many Gallican Bishops such as S. Martin of Tours, Hilary of Poictiers, Victricius of Rouen, Germanus of Auxerre, and Lupus of Troyes, visited, or made their influence felt on the British Church between A.D. 350 and 450, a full century and a half before the Roman mission of S. Augustine. Many ancient British churches are dedicated to Gallican saints, as at Canterbury and Whithern to S. Martin, and in Cornwall and Wales to Germanus and Lupus. Many Gallican saints are still commemorated in the modern English calendar, as they had been in its earlier British form.[1] The British Church employed the same Paschal cycle as that of Gaul, and used S. Jerome's second revision of the Latin translation of the Psalter as used in Gaul, while the Roman Church continued to use his first revision down to the year 1566.

In the Celtic and British liturgies there are also close resemblances to Gallican usage in the Scripture lessons, the proper prefaces, the position of the benediction, prayers for the faithful departed, the *Benedicite*, the ritual use of only two colors, white and purple, the use of "bidding" prayers ("Let us pray for," etc.). Another marked feature of the Gallican and British, as of the modern English, use is the employment in the rubrics of the imperative, "shall say," or "let him say," instead of the indicative, "he saith," as

---

[1] See Gwynne, *The Christian Year*, chap. xvii.

80 PRIMITIVE WORSHIP & THE PRAYER BOOK

in the Roman.[1] It was on these grounds in addition to many others such as single instead of trine immersion, and the omission of unction, in Baptism, the allowance of consecration of a Bishop by a single Bishop instead of by three as required by the Council of Nice, etc., that Gildas, the British chronicler, made the exaggerated assertion about the year 570, "The Britons are at variance with the whole world, and are opposed to Roman customs."[2] It is evidently then to Gaul, and to a branch of the parent Liturgy of S. John and Ephesus, and not to Rome, that we must look for the origin of the British Liturgy. It has been tersely said, "Rome may have been a stepmother of the Church of England, but assuredly the orthodox East has been her Mother."[3]

As resemblances are often pointed out between the British and English Liturgies and the so-called Mozarabic, it is well to note that this ancient use of the Church of Spain is only a modified form of the Gallican. The word is derived from the Arabic, *Arab most Arabe*, which means an Arab by adoption. The term, however, is a misnomer as the liturgy was used long before the Arabic invasion. This national Spanish use was replaced in the eleventh century by the Roman Liturgy by the continuous efforts of the Roman see, "with that intolerance of other rites which has so incalculably injured ecclesiastical antiquity." It was used in six churches in Toledo and many others throughout the country until 1842

---

[1] "The rubrics of all other Churches, Jewish or Christian, Eastern or Western, Orthodox or otherwise, from Rome to Malabar, are in the indicative 'The Priest doth' so and so In the Gallican, Spanish, English, and in them alone, the imperative is used throughout: 'Let the Priest do so and so'" (*Prin. Div. Ser.* II, 401) "Even as regards the contents of the rubrics, it may be safely affirmed that there is not one in the whole office exactly agreeing with the Roman" (*Ibid*, p. 418).

[2] See Warren, *Lit. and Ritual*, etc., pp. 59, 61–76, 167.

[3] Lowndes, II, 545.

when most of them were suppressed by the government. It is now confined to one chapel in Toledo and to three other parishes where it is authorized. A peculiarity of the Mozarabic, like that of the English, is that it contains many little addresses to the people.[1]

---

[1] See Neale, *Essays on Liturgiology*, pp. 132, 134, 149, 171, and Pullan, *His. Bk. C. P.*, pp. 18, 19.

CHAPTER VIII
GROWTH OF THE ENGLISH LITURGY

"If all the liturgies of all the ancient Churches throughout the world be compared amongst themselves, it may be easily perceived that they had all one original mould." — HOOKER.

SHORTLY after Gregory, "that greatest and most lovable of Roman Bishops,"[1] sent Augustine on his mission to convert the Angles and Saxons, who had driven the British Christians of the older Church into the mountains and wilds of Wales and Cornwall, he gave him directions concerning the liturgy and customs which he was to provide for the new Church among his converts from heathenism. The Pope's letter was in reply to questions which Augustine had put to him two years before and was dated in the summer of 601. Canon Bright says, "Gregory, who was deeply interested in liturgical questions, and revised and re-edited the 'Sacramentary' of his predecessor Gelasius, and brought the Eucharistic ceremonial to what he considered an elaborate perfection, was at the same time far from being a pedant or a bigot on such points: he advised, on the contrary, a wise eclecticism. Let Augustine 'collect into a sort of a bundle' the best usages of Rome, of Gaul, or of other Churches, whatever he had found to be most pious, religious, righteous and most likely to be pleasing to God, and so form a ritual of the English Christians, who were as yet young in faith and could become accustomed to whatever was given to them. There was no need to stick blindly to the Roman observances

---

[1] W. Bright, *Early English Church History*, p. 34.

THE ENGLISH LITURGY 83

as such."[1] And he adds, "For things are not to be loved for the sake of places, but places for the sake of good things."[2] In passing, it is well to observe the marked contrast between this broad-minded policy of the great Bishop of the seventh century and the course now and for long pursued by his successors in that see, by which the national Liturgies of France, Spain, and every other country where the Papacy has control, are suppressed and supplanted by that of Rome.

It is not possible to say to what extent Augustine made use of Gregory's suggestion as to preparing a composite Liturgy for the young Anglo-Saxon Church. He probably did not possess the necessary faculty which was so conspicuous in his master Gregory, and besides was too busy with his rough missionary work to give much time to liturgical affairs. He seems to have contented himself therefore with establishing the Roman use in part, just as a modern English or American Bishop would establish the Anglican service in a heathen land, but with certain modifications. These, in Augustine's case, would naturally be derived from his knowledge of the Gallican liturgy acquired during his stay in Gaul, and in this he would doubtless have the sympathy of Queen Bertha of Kent (whose Saxon husband, Ethelbert, was his first convert), and the help of the Gallican Bishop who was her chaplain, and who conducted the Church services according to the Gallican use, in the little Church of S. Martin in Canterbury.[3]

More than a century passed away before the ancient British Churches and those founded by Augustine drew to-

---
[1] *Early English Church*, p. 57.
[2] Bede, *His. Ecc.*, 1, 27.
[3] "The Anglo-Saxon books abound in Gallican details." Duchesne, p. 99, and compare Freeman, *Prin. Div. Ser.* III, 418.

84 PRIMITIVE WORSHIP & THE PRAYER BOOK

gether. Augustine's untactful and imperious treatment of the British Bishops and their natural hostility to the race that drove them from their land, as well as their different traditional usages, were the chief occasion of this delay. Though the Celtic Churches of Britain and Ireland, as we have seen, did such splendid work abroad, and though the Scottish-Irish Church was the chief agent in winning the greater part of England (Northumbria, Norfolk, Suffolk, Essex, and Mercia, or the country bordering on North Wales) to the faith of Christ, it took much time and mutual forbearance to bring the two races and the two branches of the Church into formal and genuine unity.[1] It is noteworthy, however, that this union was effected 150 years before the seven petty Saxon kingdoms were united, as they were in 827, under King Egbert. Even at the end of the eighth century this modified Roman use of Augustine had not entirely supplanted the modified Gallican of the earlier period. The older Church of the Britons still clung tenaciously to its usages. We find that as late as 747, when the Council of Clovesho passed a canon requiring the use of the Roman Liturgy, the Celtic Liturgy still retained its hold in the land. Fifty years later the Scottish Liturgy introduced by the missionaries from Iona, was still in daily use in the Church of York, and a letter of Alcuin, the famous Yorkshire headmaster of the great school of Charlemagne,[2] written from France to Eanbald, Archbishop of York, tells us that there were then in use some service books "that did not entirely agree with the Roman." In Scotland the Celtic Liturgy

---

[1] Theodore, a Greek of Tarsus in Cilicia, who became Archbishop of Canterbury in 668, and "was as able and energetic as he was conscientious," did much to secure this unity. "He doubtless made concessions," Duchesne says, p 99.

[2] See Lingard, *Anglo-Saxon Church*, I, 229.

THE ENGLISH LITURGY 85

remained in use until the eleventh century when the saintly Queen Margaret, cousin of Edward the Confessor, and wife of King Malcolm Canmore, took steps to get it abolished.[1] It was not until 1200 that the Church of Wales was fully united with the Church of England.

After the Norman Conquest in 1066 the Liturgy of the united Celtic and Anglo-Saxon Churches, now called the Church of England,[2] received a new impress at the hands of Osmund, a Norman Count, who was consecrated in 1085 as Bishop of Salisbury, and was Chancellor also of England under the Conqueror. The efforts to bring the ancient British rite and that introduced by Augustine into complete accord, or rather, to supplant the older rite with the new, had not been completely successful. Nothing is more tenacious in its hold on mind and heart than traditional customs of devotion, and the ways of the older Church were not, and could not be, completely eradicated. The result was that many variations of the Liturgy existed throughout the land at the time of the Conquest. It was to correct as far as possible this lack of national uniformity that Osmund is said to have revised the books which he found in his own diocese of Sarum or Salisbury. In 1087 he remodelled, after the pattern of the use of Rouen, the daily services of the Church, in the volume then known as the Portiforium; the Liturgy proper, or Communion Service, in the Missal; and probably also the Baptismal and other "occasional" offices in what was called the Manual. It was these and some other books that constituted the "Sarum Use," that is, the Prayer Book

---

[1] See Warren, *Lit and Ritual*, etc. pp 76, 77, 155, and Bright, *Early English Church*, p. 90

[2] "It was not until Eadgar's day [King from 958 to 975] that the name of Britain passed into the name of Engla-land, the land of Englishmen, England" (Green, *His English People*, I, p. 9).

of the Diocese of Salisbury.[1] This revision was so acceptable that it was introduced into other dioceses of the land, and became the principal devotional rule of the Church of England for more than four centuries. Its use was soon adopted also in the Churches of Wales and of Ireland.[2]

Even down to the year 1549 when the first revised Prayer Book was appointed for the whole Church, "great diversity within this Realm" continued, "some following Salisbury Use, some Hereford Use, and some the Use of Bangor [Wales], some of York, some of Lincoln."[3] "At S. Paul's Cathedral, and perhaps throughout the Diocese of London, there was an independent Use until A.D. 1414; and probably there were several others in Cathedral Churches, while the Roman system was adopted by most monasteries."[4]

As the copies of the Sarum use which we possess belong to a much later period than the eleventh century, we have no means of knowing just what changes Osmund or his successor, Bishop Poore, introduced into the service books.

---

[1] Dr. Frere takes the view that Osmund was only the author of the endowment of the Cathedral, and of its constitution, which soon became the model for other cathedral bodies He says, "There is no evidence that S. Osmund's work dealt with the liturgical arrangements· it was left to Richard Poore, first as Dean and then as Bishop, at the beginning of the thirteenth century, when the see was transferred from Old Sarum to New Sarum, and from the old Norman cathedral which has perished to the existing Early English building, both to develop more fully in his Consuetudinary the constitutional legislation of S Osmund, and to add to this a full code of liturgical rules " *New His of the B. C P.*, p 15. Palmer says, "When the Archbishop of Canterbury celebrated the liturgy in the presence of his province, the Bishop of Salisbury acted as precentor of the college of Bishops, a title which he still retains." *Orig Lit.* I, xi. 187.

[2] See Blunt, *Ann Pr Bk* p xviii, Palmer, *Origines*, I, xi, 187.

[3] *Concerning the Service of the Church*, in the Preface to the English Book of Common Prayer.

[4] Blunt, *Ann. Pr. Bk.*, pp. xviii, xix.

THE ENGLISH LITURGY

We do know, however, that at the beginning of the sixteenth century all the services, not only for the Holy Communion but for the Daily Prayers, Holy Baptism, Confirmation, Ordination, etc., had become very complicated and difficult even for the clergy, and many superstitious accretions had gathered around the ancient devotions of the Church. "As early as the year 1516," writes Archdeacon Freeman, that is, fifteen years before Henry VIII's break with Rome on account of his marriage with his brother's widow, "we discern the first indication of a steady design and endeavour, never afterwards abandoned, of amending the existing condition of the ancient English Service-books. In that year appeared an edition of the Sarum Breviary [Portiforium, or Book of Daily Prayers], differing so widely, at least in point of arrangement and method, if not in its actual contents, from all previous editions, that a peculiarly informed antiquarian has not hesitated to designate it by the title *Reformatum.*" In these changes, he adds, "we discern two, at least, of the leading principles which governed the Revision of 1549: first, the simplification of the use of the Office; and secondly, the increased provision of Holy Scripture." [1]

"In 1531," writes Mr. Blunt, "this Reformed Edition of the Salisbury Portiforium or Breviary was reprinted; and two years later the Missal [Office for Holy Communion] was published, reformed on the same principles; in the latter special care being taken to provide an apparatus for enabling the people to find out the places of the Epistles and Gospels. A fresh impulse seems thus to have been given to the use of the old English Prymers, in which a large portion of the Services (including the Litany) was translated into the vulgar tongue, and also a third of the Psalms, and to which in later times the Epistles and Gospels were added. In 1530 also had been published an admirable commentary on some

---

[1] *Prin. Div. Service*, Vol. II, Intro., p. 102.

88 PRIMITIVE WORSHIP & THE PRAYER BOOK

of the daily services (in which the greater part of them is translated into English), under the title of 'The Mirroure of our Ladye,' which furnishes a strong indication of the endeavours that were being made to render Divine Service intelligible to those who could not read Latin.

"In 1541 another amended, and still further reformed, edition of the Salisbury Breviary was published, in the title-page of which it is said to be purged from many errors. By order of Convocation (March 3, 1541–2) this was adopted throughout the whole province of Canterbury, and an uniformity secured which had not existed since the days of Augustine. With this edition an order was also put forth that Lessons should be read in English after the Te Deum and Magnificat."

We have now, before her complete break with the Bishop of Rome, reached the end of the third great period in the history of the worship of the Church of England. Each of these stages consists of a term of about five hundred years. The first is the period during which the Apostolic Liturgy found its way from Jerusalem, through Ephesus and Lyons, modified possibly by that of Rome through Milan, to the Celtic Church in the British Isles. It is bounded by the time when the Angles and Saxons from Germany drove the Christians of South Britain from their homes. The second period is that beginning with the year 601 when the Anglo-Saxon converts under Augustine received from him a liturgy partly Roman, partly Gallican, which, after the blending of the ancient British Church with that of the Anglo-Saxons, had now elements and characteristics of both communions, thus combining to make what, from the middle of the tenth century, was known henceforth as the Use of the Church of England. The third period is that which we have been just considering, beginning with the Norman Conquest, the

---

[1] *Ann. Pr. Bk.*, p. xix.

THE ENGLISH LITURGY

introduction of the higher education and culture of the Continent through the Bishops and clergy of Norman birth, especially by the work of Osmund, and Poore, and with it all, in the course of time, much of the superstition and the erroneous teaching and practice of the Churches of the Continent in communion with Rome.

But against this deterioration in worship as in life there was constant protest, especially throughout the fourteenth and fifteenth centuries. It was during this time that there were established such collegiate schools as that of S. Mary Winton, by William of Wykeham, Bishop of Winchester, in 1382; that of Eton by Henry VI in 1440; of Higham Ferrers by Chichely, Archbishop of Canterbury, about the same time; of S. Paul's Cathedral, by Dean Colet, sixty years later; and colleges at Oxford and Cambridge, of which these schools were meant to be feeders. From these and similar schools of learning and religion proceeded the influences that were ever tending to challenge and curb the usurped and tyrannical claims of the Papacy as it had developed since the pure days of the first Gregory, surnamed the Great, to whom England and her Church owed so much, religiously and intellectually. These were largely the sources of the ferment in Church and Nation which at last brought about that reformation in doctrine, and worship, which found its best illustration in 1549 in the "First Prayer Book of Edward the Sixth," that is, "The Booke of the Common Prayer and Administration of the Sacramentes, and Other Rites and Ceremonies of the Churche: after the Use of the Churche of England." How this revision of the ancient offices of the Church was accomplished must be the subject for our next consideration.

CHAPTER IX

THE BEGINNINGS OF REFORM

"There was never anything by the wit of man so well devised, or so surely established, which in continuance of time hath not been corrupted As, among other things, it may plainly appear by the Common Prayers in the Church, commonly called Divine Service." — Preface to the English Prayer Book.

BEFORE proceeding to consider the method by which the ancient offices of worship of the Church were brought to their present condition, it will be necessary for us to understand something of what is called the English Reformation. This was far from being a sudden catastrophe which broke out and was completed in the later days of Henry VIII. On the contrary, it may be truly said that it covered a period of two hundred years or more, namely, from the middle of the fifteenth century (c. 1450) to the middle of the seventeenth (1662). Even in the eleventh, twelfth, and thirteenth centuries we find protests of Englishmen against the interference of the Bishops of Rome in the affairs of the English Church. When Gregory VII, the famous Hildebrand, the most extreme exponent of papal assumptions, took upon him to grant the crown of England to William of Normandy, the Conqueror met his later claims by the declaration that he would not do fealty for his kingdom, or permit any papal legate to set foot on English soil without royal permission.[1] In 1076, when Gregory commanded all married clergy of the English Church to put away their wives, a council of the English Church refused to allow the

---

[1] Stubbs, *Constitutional History*, I, p. 310.

BEGINNINGS OF REFORM   91

new regulation, and up to 1102 the parochial clergy were generally married. In 1164 the council of Clarendon forbade all appeals to Rome without the King's consent. When King John (1199–1216) agreed to make the whole kingdom subservient to the Bishop of Rome, the clergy, barons, and people, calling themselves "The Army of God and the Church," under the leadership of Stephen Langton, Archbishop of Canterbury, rose up against John, and on the 15th of June, 1215, compelled the King to sign the Great Charter (*Magna Charta*), the first article of which reads: "The Church of England shall be free, and shall have her rights entire, and her liberties uninjured."[1] "It was," writes Hore, "the army, not only of the barons against the King, but of the Church against the Pope."

The "Statute of Provisors," beginning, "Whereas the Holy Church of England was founded, etc.," passed by Parliament in 1350, and the statutes of "Praemunire," passed in 1353, 1365, and 1393, left scarcely a vestige of papal authority in England. They forbade the appointment by the Bishop of Rome to any bishopric or other Church dignity in England, and prohibited the carrying of suits to the Roman

---

[1] "*In primis . . . quod Anglicana Ecclesia libera sit, et habeat jura sua integra, et libertates suas illaesas.*" Attention is called to the fact that the name of the Church recorded here is that which she had from the beginning in the sixth century, the Church of the English, and not the Church of Rome in England Roman canon law was never recognised in England, and there was no Church of Rome in England until 1570 when the Roman Bishop, finding that the Church would no longer submit to his unlawful claims, sent foreign priests into the country, by whom certain members of the ancient Church of the land were induced to forsake their parish churches, and form a new schismatical body. The first Roman bishops only appeared in England in 1623, and it was not until 1850 that they ventured to call themselves bishops of English dioceses. Up to that time they only assumed the disused titles of certain bishoprics *in partibus infidelium*, that is, in heathen countries.

court, or the obtaining of any appointments, bulls, or excommunications from Rome, under penalty of confiscation and perpetual imprisonment.[1]

This traditional attitude of the English Church is well summed up in the words of Archdeacon Manning before his forsaking his mother Church for the Roman obedience: "If any man will look down the line of early English history, he will see a standing contest between the rulers of this land and the Bishops of Rome. The Crown and Church of England, with a steady opposition, resisted the entrance and encroachment of the secularized ecclesiastical power of the Pope in England. The last rejection of it [in 1534] was no more than a successful effort after many a failure in struggles of the like kind." We need not wonder that when Dr. Manning became a prelate of the Roman communion he declared that "the appeal to history is treason."

But the beginnings of reform of abuses in the Church are perhaps best seen in the work of Wicliffe, Rector of Lutterworth, and "a celebrated teacher in the university of Oxford . . . enthusiastic and fearless in temper, solid in attainment, brilliant in argument, fierce and unsparing even for the Middle Ages in denunciation. . . . Worldly position, political power, temporal wealth, seemed to Wicliffe to be absolutely incompatible with the clerical office. Like S. Francis of Assisi, he believed that in the life of poverty was to be found the true following of Christ. But unlike S. Francis he vindicated his position by attacking those who held a different theory instead of simply living out his

---

[1] See Gibson, *Codex*, pp. 74, 80–87, 1222. Even long before the Norman Conquest the aggressions of the Roman Bishop were invariably resisted, as in the notable case of Wilfrid, Archbishop of York in the seventh century, upheld by Rome, but condemned by an English synod; and the similar case of Stigand, Archbishop of Canterbury, in the eleventh century.

own life on his own theory. In fact he was a polemic, not a saint."[1]

Wicliffe obtained a ready following among the poor. "The dumb mass who had suffered in silence so long had found a voice and a leader." With all his ability, however, and his enthusiasm, he was not well-balanced. His speculations in theology were condemned by the Church, and his teaching caused many of his clerical students to become communists, and advocates of the seizure of all property. For this he was also formally condemned in 1382, but he was allowed to pass the rest of his days in peace at his country rectory of Lutterworth, without ever being called upon to retract his heresy. "There he busied himself with the most important work of his life, the translation of the Bible into English. In its Latin translation — the Vulgate — the Bible had always been in the hands of the scholar; parts of it, such as the Gospels and Epistles, had been frequently translated into English since the days of Bede [673–735] and Ælfred [849–901]. Every person who could read was able in the Middle Ages to procure without difficulty those parts of the Bible which were used in the Church services. But to Wicliffe England owes the translation of the whole Bible, and the original of our present version, written in prose which by its nerve and strength has done much to fix for ever the genius of the English language."[2]

These were some of the steps which heralded and led the way to the work of thorough reform of the Church in Eng-

---

[1] Wakeman, *History of the Church of England*, p. 150. Bishop Stubbs of Oxford, the eminent historian, describes this book as "the most precious history of the Church of England that has ever been written, a book scholarlike, lucid, full of matter, full of interest, just and true, and inspired with faith, hope, and charity, as few Church histories, or any other histories, have ever been written."

[2] *Ibid*, pp. 151, 152.

land. Much was done in the sixteenth century, not by the Church but by the State, which is not to be defended. Chief among these things was the destruction of the monasteries, and the appropriation of their property to the enrichment of royal favorites. The monasteries were undoubtedly the strongholds of Roman influence as being removed from the control of their own Bishops, and subject only to the Pope. They had also outgrown the usefulness of their early days when they were centres of missionary operations, schools of learning, of book-making, and of art; their inmates the drainers of swamps, the intelligent farmers of the land, the architects of churches, and the overseers and almoners of the poor. Their very usefulness and their prosperity had become the occasion of their corruption, and this proved too strong a temptation to unscrupulous statesmen to despoil them, instead of applying their wealth, to the foundation of more modern schools of learning such as that great Churchman, Cardinal Wolsey, did when he partly carried out his plans for Christ Church College at Oxford, and his Grammar School at Ipswich. The Church's work of reformation was properly concerned for the most part with her teaching, and her offices of worship, and this was done, though often under great difficulties, through the orderly and legal instrumentalities of her houses of Convocation, the clerical representative bodies of the provinces of Canterbury and York; while the two houses of Parliament, all its lay members, at this time necessarily communicants of the Church, represented the laity.

We have already seen (in 1516, 1530, 1531, and 1533) a beginning of this work of reform, while the Church and State alike still permitted a certain measure of authority to the Roman see, or at least before they formally rejected that authority. In 1534, however, the bold and final step was

BEGINNINGS OF REFORM 95

taken which opened up the way to independent action by the Church. On March 31 of that year the Convocation of Canterbury voted, "That the Roman Bishop has no greater jurisdiction given to him by God in this kingdom than any other foreign bishop." On June 1st, York voted, "That the Roman Bishop has not *in the Holy Scriptures* any greater jurisdiction in the kingdom of England than any foreign Bishop."[1] Individual Bishops such as Shaxton of Salisbury, Robert of Chichester, Longland of Lincoln, Lee of York, Tonstal of Durham, and the chief abbots with their monks, all preached or signed instruments renouncing the Pope's authority and supremacy. "This universal renunciation, though no doubt influenced by authority and pressure, is one of the most remarkable facts in the history of the Reformation."[2]

This was the final event which prepared the way for the thorough revision of the Church's books of devotion. Other and kindred work in the publication of the whole Bible in English (1539), and declarations in regard to points of doctrine and morals, was of course also undertaken by the Church in her corporate capacity, but in view of the purpose of this volume we must confine ourselves solely to the consideration of what deals directly with the offices of public worship.

The first definite step in this direction, beyond those already mentioned, was taken in 1542, when Cranmer, Archbishop of Canterbury, laid before Convocation a proposal to amend the service books. In the session of Feb. 21, 1543, the Archbishop "signified to the House that it was his Majesty's will that 'all mass-books, antiphoners, portuisses

---

[1] Wilkins, III, 782.
[2] See Perry, *History of the Ch. of England from the Accession of Henry VIII*, chap. vi, pp. 102, 103.

96 PRIMITIVE WORSHIP & THE PRAYER BOOK

[*portiforia*, or breviaries] in the Church of England, should be newly examined, corrected, reformed, and castigated from all manner of mention of the Bishop of Rome's name, from all apocryphas, feigned legends, superstitious orations, collects, versicles and responses,'" etc. A committee of eight persons consisting of Bishops Shaxton of Salisbury and Goodrich of Ely, with three of the Lower House of clerical representatives joined to each of them, was appointed to undertake the work. At a later date the committee was much enlarged. Shaxton died, and Cranmer, Archbishop of Canterbury, became chairman, with six other Bishops including Goodrich associated with him. The number of the members from the Lower House remained unchanged.[1]

It is noteworthy that the first work accomplished and put forth by this committee was the translation and revision of the Litany, which the King urged on account of the miserable state of Christendom, distracted by wars and other troubles. It was the hand of Cranmer that wrought this exquisite piece of devotion, using the old Latin "processions," but altering and adding as seemed in his judgment to answer best the purpose of such a supplication. This was sung for the first time in S. Paul's Cathedral on the 18th day of October, being S. Luke's Day and a Sunday, 1544, and ordered to be *sung* in every parish church in England. This service, together with a chapter in English from the Old Testament, and one also from the New, was the whole amount of English service which was *authorized*, though it is probable that more was used irregularly, during the reign of Henry.

Nothing more was accomplished in the reformation of worship in Henry's lifetime, his death occurring on Jan. 28, 1547. The King's part in the reformation was not in matters of doctrine and worship, except so far as we have seen above.

---
[1] Blunt, *Ann. Pr. Bk.*, p. xxii.

BEGINNINGS OF REFORM

In these respects he lived and died, for the most part, in the beliefs and practices of what was called "the old learning," the ways of mediæval England. And this was well for the Church as it "had the effect of hindering fanatical and hasty proceedings, and allowing the Church slowly and carefully to mature her services and her teaching."[1] All that Henry really accomplished by his dominating character and absolute authority as King, was the support which he gave to setting the Church completely free from all control of Rome, something which, though representing thoroughly the mind of the English people, could not then have been done without his powerful help.

---
[1] Perry, chap. x, p. 176.

CHAPTER X

THE FIRST REFORMED PRAYER BOOK

"*They had a profound disbelief in theory, and knew better than to commit the folly of breaking with the past. They were not seduced by the French fallacy that a new system of government could be ordered like a new suit of clothes. They would as soon have thought of ordering a suit of flesh and skin It is only on the roaring loom of time that the stuff is woven for such a vesture of their thought and experience as they were meditating.*"
— J. R. LOWELL.[1]

WE must now consider the character of the work which the committee of Convocation had to do. The Prayer Book as we have it today is sometimes spoken of as a "compilation," and the men who formed it its "compilers." Nothing could be farther from the fact. The duty laid on them was to "examine, correct, reform, and castigate," etc., the service books that had been used from time immemorial in the Church, but which, in the course of the years, had become cumbered with useless ceremonies, difficult rules, and many erroneous notions. They were to be revisers and not compilers. There had been many revisions of the Liturgy of the Church Catholic in many lands and in many ages of the past. S. Basil of Cæsarea and S. Chrysostom of Constantinople had done much in the fourth century for the Liturgy of Jerusalem and Antioch. Leo (440–461), Gelasius (492–496), and Gregory the Great (590–604), all Bishops of Rome, had done similar things for the Roman Liturgy. The name of S. Ambrose attaches to another revision used in his archdiocese of Milan. We do not know however to what

---

[1] *Address on Democracy and the Adoption of the American Constitution.*

THE FIRST REFORMED BOOK 99

extent these various revisers were responsible for the points of difference between their versions and the originals.[1] We have already learnt what Augustine was directed to do for the new Church of the English, and what doubtless many other Bishops and Priests in England did afterwards to bring about that merging of the old Celtic use with that of Augustine. We have learnt also of the notable work attributed to Osmund in 1087, or to his successor Bishop Poore a century later, which drew from a writer in 1256 the declaration that the Church of Salisbury was "conspicuous above all other Churches, like the sun in the heavens, diffusing its light everywhere, and supplying their defects."[2] About the time of Osmund's work Gregory VII, or Hildebrande (1073-1085), revised and *abbreviated* the Daily Offices, which after that were called the *Breviary*, though the favorite title for the book in England was Portuary or Portuisse.[3]

Nor was the felt need of revision confined to the Church of England in the sixteenth century. Hermann, Archbishop of Cologne, attempted such a revision, and Cardinal Quignonez, a Spanish Bishop, revised the Breviary and published it under the sanction of Pope Clement VII in 1536, but this was suppressed in 1576.[4] Similar then to the work which these had done, or were attempting, was that of the learned committee appointed by the lawful authority of the Church of England in her Convocations in 1543. It was most appropriate that the successor of Osmund in the see of Salisbury should be made its chairman.

The service books which the committee was required to "examine, correct, reform, and castigate" were both many

---

[1] See Freeman I, 38.   [2] Blunt, *Ann. Pr Bk*, p. xviii.
[3] Luckock, *Studies*, etc., p xxviii, and Maskell, *Mon. Rit*, I, lxxxvi.
[4] As late as the year 1911 another thorough revision of the Breviary and Psalms was made by the Church of Rome.

and cumbersome.[1] The following list represents the chief books in use at the time immediately preceding the Reformation: —

1. The Portiforium, or Portuary, or Portuisse, containing the daily offices for the Seven Canonical Hours.

2. The Legenda, a book of readings from Holy Scripture, the acts of saints, the sufferings of martyrs, discourses of Fathers and Popes, etc.

3. The Antiphonarium, containing the antiphons, or anthems, for the Canonical Hours.

4. The Graduale, containing the antiphons for High Mass, so called from short phrases after the Epistle sung "*in gradibus.*"

5. The Psalterium, or Psalter, divided into certain portions for the service of the Hours.

6. The Troperium, containing certain verses sung before or after the Introit.

7. The Ordinale, Pica, or Pie, a book of rubrics, which regulated the whole manner and ritual of the services, and which had become so complicated that the revisers said that "many times there was more business to find out what should be read, than to read it when it was found out." [2]

8. The Sacramentary contained the prayers relating to the Sacraments, including in that term Holy Orders, Mar-

---

[1] Maskell in his *Monumenta Ritualia*, Vol I, pp cxciv-vi, gives a list of more than one hundred different books used more or less in the service of the Church.

[2] Preface, *Concerning the Service of the Church*, in the present English Prayer Book. The letters of the Pica being smaller than the usual text, the early printers gave the name to a medium size of type The initial letters were in red, hence the word rubric, from the Latin *ruber*, red From the confused appearance of a page of pica it is thought that the custom originated among printers of calling any portion of type which is in utter disorder by the name of "pie."

THE FIRST REFORMED BOOK

riage, etc., in addition to Holy Baptism and the Holy Eucharist.

9. The Missal, which contained only the service for the Holy Eucharist, without the Introits, Epistles, or Gospels, though sometimes these were also included.

10. The Manual was a book of occasional offices, such as Visitation of the Sick, Churching of Women, Burial of the Dead, etc.

11. The Pontifical was a book of offices for the use of Bishops, containing services for Confirmation, Ordination, etc.[1]

Few copies of these books remain, inasmuch as the statute of 1549 ordered their destruction. Many were of course written by hand, as Gutenberg's invention of movable types (of wood) did not take place before 1438, and it was not until 1471 that Caxton set up his press in London. But whether written or printed, most of these service books were destroyed, or had the name of the Bishop of Rome erased from them during the reign of Henry or Edward.

The following books may be taken as fairly representing the books which the committee of Convocation had before them as the materials for their work of revision: — (1) The Salisbury Portiforium, Missal, Manual, Pontifical; (2) The Diocesan Uses of York, Hereford, Bangor, Lincoln, etc.; (3) The reformed Breviary of Cardinal Quignonez (1535–1536); (4) The Consultation of Hermann, Archbishop of Cologne (1545); (5) The Prymer, a book of private devotions, generally in English, containing (about A.D. 1400) Matins, Evensong, and Compline (the last of the Seven Canonical Hours), the seven Penitential Psalms, the Gradual Psalms (cxx–cxxxiv), the Litany, the Lord's Prayer, the

---

[1] For an interesting account of the contents of these books see P. and F. *New His.* etc , pp 15–20.

Creed, the Commandments, etc.; (6) The "Great Bible," the translation of Bishop Coverdale, which had been revised in 1539 under the direction of Archbishop Cranmer, and became the foundation of the "Authorized Version" in present use; the Prayer Book Psalter being that of the "Great Bible" practically unchanged.

The committee continued their deliberations for six years. In the meantime Henry had died (Jan. 28, 1547), and young Edward, his son, a mere boy, was on the throne, with his uncle, the Duke of Somerset, as "Protector." Next year a service in English for the reception (not consecration) of the Holy Communion by the people was adopted, but this did not set aside the first part of the service, which remained still in Latin. In 1549 the committee reported to Convocation the result of their labors in the all-English volume which is known as "the First Prayer Book of Edward VI," and it was adopted by them. Parliament, which was then, and had been from earliest days, the House of Laymen, or Lay Deputies, every member being of necessity in communion with the Church, gave its approval also, and the book was published under the title "The Book of Common Prayer and Administration of the Sacramentes, and other Rites and Ceremonies of the Churche; after the use of the Churche of England."

The book came into use on Whitsunday, June 9th, 1549. It possessed the full authority of the Church as declared by the Bishops and representative Clergy in Convocation, and her representative Laymen in Parliament.[1] No other Prayer

[1] That the First Book of Edward had the sanction of both Convocations is proved beyond a doubt by two letters of the king See P and F , 50, 51. Even the parliamentary Act which substituted the Book of 1552 declared that the First Book contained nothing "but what was agreeable to the Word of God and the Primitive Church," and that such objections as had been made to it proceeded "rather from the curiosity of the ministers and mistakers than of any worthy cause."

THE FIRST REFORMED BOOK 103

Book had that joint sanction until one hundred and twelve years later (1662), when the book in present use in the Church of England was approved in a similar manner. The book was adopted also by the Convocation of the Church of Ireland in 1551, but most unfortunately no attempt was made at the time to translate the service into either Welsh or Irish. Thus the native Irish fell under the influence of Roman priests whom the Pope sent into the country, and the Welsh fell away into dissent of various kinds.[1]

The contents of this first revised book were as follows: —

1. The Preface, with a few verbal changes, the same as "Concerning the Services of the Church" in the present English Book. 2. The Order for the Psalter. 3. The Order for the Rest of Holy Scripture. 4. The Calendar. 5. Matins and Evensong, substantially as in the present Book, but beginning with the Lord's Prayer, and ending with the Third Collect, with the provision that on the six greatest festivals, of which Epiphany is one, the Creed of S. Athanasius be substituted for that of the Apostles at Matins. 6. The Introits (selected Psalms), and the same Collects, Epistles, and Gospels, as in the present Book, but taken from the "Great Bible." 7. The Office for the Holy Communion. 8. The Litany. 9. Baptism, Public and Private. 10. Confirmation. 11. Matrimony. 12. Visitation, Anointing, and Communion of the Sick. 13. Burial. 14. The Churching or Purification of Women. 15. A Commination, or Prayers to be used on Ash-Wednesday. 16. A Declaration concerning excessive Ceremonies (now placed at the beginning of the English Book). 17. Directions in regard to the use of surplice, albe, vestment (chasuble), rochette, cope, hood, etc. 18. The Ordinal.

---

[1] There was no Welsh translation until 1657, and no Irish until 1608 when one was made by O'Donnell, Archbishop of Tuam. As there was no Irish printing press, and few could read the Irish letters, the Irish Parliament of 1560 adopted the expedient of authorizing the use of a Latin translation of the Book of 1559. See P. and F., pp. 107, 108, 143.

In the previous year (1548) it had been ordered that the Laity should receive the Communion in both kinds, in accordance with Christ's ordinance, and with the universal custom of the Church up to the year 1415, when it was first forbidden to give the cup to the people by the Council of Florence. Concerning this restoration of the cup Palmer writes: —

"In all the Eastern Churches the sacrament has been given to the laity in both kinds, even to the present day. It is true that they are not given it separately, but at the same moment, by means of a particle of bread dipped in the cup; but this is merely a variety of discipline, which does not in the slightest degree affect the verity of the Communion in both kinds. The same custom formerly prevailed all through the Western Churches, but in later times the laity were in most places entirely deprived of the sacrament of Christ's Blood; in order to obviate inconveniences which some persons thought might follow from an obedience to Christ's commands, and the practice of the Catholic Church.

"It was not remembered that God could prevent His sacraments from real profanation; and that proper instruction might suffice, as it had done in primitive times, to teach the people their duty."[1]

Another most notable feature of the First Book was the restoration of the Invocation, or *Epiclesis*, that is, the prayer for the Holy Ghost upon the elements, which was, and still is, lacking in the Roman office, but is part of every other known liturgy in the world. This was happily restored to the Scottish Book in 1637, and to that of America in 1789.

The complete order for the Holy Communion in the First Book was as follows: —

1. The Lord's Prayer, and the Collect as at present. 2. A Psalm as Introit, followed by the threefold Kyrie (Lord,

---

[1] *Orig. Lit*, II, iv, 20. See also Bingham, *Ant.* XV, v, 1, 2, 6. Our Lord seems to have had this very error in view when He said "Drink ye *all*," though He did *not* say "Eat ye all."

THE FIRST REFORMED BOOK 105

have mercy. Christ, have mercy. Lord have mercy, etc.). 3. The Gloria in Excelsis. 4. Collect for the day, and another for the King. 5. Epistle and Gospel. 6. The Nicene Creed. 7. Sermon. 8. The Exhortation to Communion, unless an exhortation has already been given in the Sermon. 9. The Offertory, with the oblation of Bread, and Wine, "putting thereto a little pure and clean water." 10. *Sursum Corda* ("Lift up, etc."), with Proper Preface. 11. *Sanctus.* 12. Prayer for the Whole State of Christ's Church, substantially as in present Prayer Book, but with commemoration of all the saints, "and chiefly the glorious and most blessed Virgin Mary," and commendation of "all other Thy servants, which are departed hence from us with the sign of faith, and now do rest in the sleep of peace." 13. The Prayer of Consecration, as follows: — O God, heavenly Father, which of Thy tender mercy diddest give Thine Only Son Jesu Christ to suffer death, etc. . . . until His coming again" [as in the present Book]: "Hear us, O merciful Father, we beseech Thee; and with Thy Holy Spirit and Word vouchsafe to bless and sanctify these Thy creatures of Bread and Wine, that they may be unto us the Body and Blood of Thy most dearly beloved Son Jesus Christ: Who, in the same night that He was betrayed, etc. . . . drink it in remembrance of Me" [as in present Book].

"Wherefore, O Lord and heavenly Father, according to the institution of Thy dearly beloved Son our Saviour Jesu Christ, we Thy humble servants do celebrate and make here before Thy divine Majesty, with these Thy holy gifts, the memorial which Thy Son hath willed us to make: having in remembrance His blessed Passion, mighty Resurrection, and glorious Ascension: rendering unto Thee most hearty thanks for the innumerable benefits procured unto us by the same; entirely desiring Thy fatherly goodness mercifully to accept this our Sacrifice of praise and thanksgiving; most humbly beseeching Thee to grant, that by the Merits and Death of Thy Son Jesus Christ, and through faith in His Blood, we and all Thy whole Church may obtain remission of our sins, and all other benefits of His Passion. And here we offer and present unto Thee, O Lord, ourselves, our souls and bodies, to be a reasonable, holy, and lively sacrifice unto Thee; humbly beseeching Thee, that whosoever shall be partakers of this Holy Communion may worthily receive the most precious Body and Blood of Thy Son Jesus Christ; and be fulfilled with Thy grace and heavenly benediction, and made one body with Thy Son Jesu Christ, that He may dwell in them, and they in Him. And though we be unworthy (through our manifold sins) to offer unto Thee any Sacrifice, yet we beseech Thee to accept this our bounden duty and service, and command these our prayers and supplications, by the ministry of Thy holy Angels, to be brought up into Thy holy Tabernacle before the sight of Thy divine Majesty; not weighing our merits, but pardoning our offences, through Christ our Lord; by whom and with whom, in the unity of the Holy Ghost, all honour and glory be unto Thee, O Father Almighty, world without end.   Amen.

Let us pray.

As our Saviour Christ hath commanded and taught us, we are bold to say: Our Father, etc.

Then shall the Priest say,
The peace of the Lord be alway with you.

The Clerks. And with thy spirit.

The Priest. Christ our Paschal Lamb is offered up for us once for all, when He bare our sins on His Body on the Cross; for He is the very Lamb of God that taketh away the sins of the world: wherefore let us keep a joyful and holy feast with the Lord."

14. "You that do truly, etc.," followed by Confession, Absolution, and Comfortable Words, as in the present Book. 15. Prayer of Humble Access. 16. Communion, with the words of administration as in the first half of the present form, while the Clerks sing "O Lamb of God, etc." (as in the Gloria in Excelsis), and one of a selection of verses from Holy Scripture. 17. The prayer of Thanksgiving (the same as the second post-Communion prayer in the English office). 18. The Blessing, as in the present Book.[1]

---

[1] For the vestments of the Celebrant see chap xxvii.

THE FIRST REFORMED BOOK

It is of this Book of 1549 it has been said that it is "the noblest monument of piety, of prudence, and of learning which the sixteenth century constructed" (Hardwick). It was the ancient service to which people had been accustomed, purified, simplified, and "clothed in English, the beauty of which has been rarely equalled, and never surpassed, even in the best age of literary excellence." So clear were the Revisers on this point that Archbishop Cranmer, with some exaggeration, offered to prove that "the order of the Church of England, set out by authority of Edward VI, was the same that had been used in the Church for fifteen hundred years past." "Their aim," it has been said, "was restoration, not a complete revolution in Church worship; and in the process of attaining it they exercised the most careful discrimination between the old and the new, and while cutting away without hesitation the later overgrowths, preserved with scrupulous care the ancient landmarks."

Thus four objects in addition to the removal of erroneous teaching, were distinctly kept in view throughout: First. That the whole of the services should be in the vernacular, "the tongue understanded of the people," in accordance alike with common sense and the teaching of Holy Scripture. Second. To bring order out of the utter confusion of many rubrics and many books, so that one book only, together with the Bible, should be sufficient for clergy as well as for worshippers. Third. That the reading of Holy Scripture should have much larger place. Fourth. That, "where heretofore there hath been great diversity in saying and singing in churches within this Realm: some following Salisbury use, some Hereford use, some the use of Bangor, some of York, and some of Lincoln: now from henceforth, all the whole Realm shall have but one use."

Thus gradually, by action of the Church herself, through

her lawful clerical and lay deputies, in Convocation and Parliament (and not by any foreign or secular power), in continual revisions through more than a century, the ancient offices of Christian worship were adapted to new conditions of race, and land, and times. In this the Church was only fulfilling our Lord's precept: "Every scribe which is instructed unto the kingdom of heaven is like unto a man that is an householder, which bringeth forth out of his treasures things new and old." [1] Thus step by step came the Book of Common Prayer which, during the next hundred years, after various reactions and restorations, assumed practically the form in which we have it today.

---

[1] S. Matt. XIII, 52.

CHAPTER XI
REACTION AND RESTORATION, 1552-1662

"Poor wanderers, ye are sore distrest
To find that path which Christ has blest,
Tracked by His saintly throng;
Each claims to trust his own weak will,
Blind idol! — so ye languish still,
All wranglers, and all wrong.

"Wanderers! come home! when erring most
Christ's Church aye kept the faith, nor lost
One grain of Holy Truth
She ne'er has erred as those ye trust,
And now shall lift her from the dust,
And reign as in her youth." — LYRA APOSTOLICA.

IN spite of the confessed beauty, conservatism, and true Catholicity of the first Prayer Book, and the great learning and patient labor bestowed upon its production through six years, there was a small but vigorous party growing up in England which favored more radical changes. This movement was fostered by the "Protector" Somerset, uncle of the boy king, and the other men in power in the State. It was by their means chiefly that the First Book was displaced within three years, and another produced and forced on the unwilling Church in 1552. It is important to remember that this Second Book was never submitted to the Convocation of Bishops and representative Clergy. It was drawn up by a few Bishops and clergy appointed by the Council of State, and only possessed the authority of a Parliament which had been carefully packed for the purpose. "The Church," writes Canon Dixon, "was held dumb throughout this period, by the positive orders of the Council." [1]

The Church therefore was in no way responsible for this Second Book. The changes from the First Book were due almost wholly to the meddling interference of foreigners such as Calvin (by letters), Peter Martyr, who had been made Regius Professor of Divinity in Oxford, Martin Bucer, who occupied the similar chair in Cambridge, and others who sought asylum in England, and were infected with the extreme Protestantism of Germany and France. Admitted only as "lodgers," it has been said, "they attempted to turn the landlord out of his house." [2] Somerset and the members of the Council were in thorough sympathy with these views, but the value of the Protector's opinions may be gathered from the fact that he "desired to pull down Westminster Abbey and use the materials for building a palace for himself, and was only bought off by the Dean and Chapter by the surrender of twenty manors. Then, for the construction of Somerset House he destroyed the church of S. Mary-le-Strand, and the cloister of S. Paul's Cathedral." [3] He also "destroyed the palaces of three Bishops (Llandaff, Chester, and Worcester), in the Strand; attempted to demolish S. Margaret's, but his workmen were beaten off by the parishioners," all to provide building materials for his new palace.[4] It was at this same time, namely, "in the autumn and winter of 1552–3," writes Mr. Froude, "that no less than four commissions were appointed with this one object; to go over the oft-trodden ground, and share the last spoils which could be gathered from the churches. . . . The halls

---

[1] *History of the English Church*, III 5; iv, 73.
[2] Archdeacon Denison.
[3] S Baring-Gould, *The Church Revival*, p 5
[4] W. Sinclair, *Memorials of S Paul's Cathedral*, p 141.

REACTION AND RESTORATION

of country houses were hung with altar-cloths; tables and beds were quilted with copes; knights and squires drank their claret out of chalices, and watered their horses in marble coffins."[1] Some of the treasures of S. Paul's Cathedral are still to be seen in Spain.[2]

It was then under these circumstances, and under these adverse influences that the Second Prayer Book was produced in 1552. "This Second Book, which was the First Book revised, defaced, and generally maltreated," wrote Dr. Morgan Dix, "was put forth in the vain hope of conciliating certain radicals and ultra-reformers in England, whom nothing would have satisfied but the extirpation of the whole Catholic system; and certain foreigners, who, having rejected the Episcopate and the Catholic traditions, were founding new churches on an independent basis, and inaugurating presbyteral and congregational disciplines, with inordinate boasts of their value and purity."[3] Even Bullinger could say of the Second Book, writing to some exiles in Frankfort, that "Cranmer, Bishop of Canterbury, had drawn up a Book of Prayer [the First] a hundred times more perfect than this that we now have."[4]

The worst alterations were those made in the service for Holy Communion. Besides verbal changes in various places the chief alterations are as follows: —

1. The Invocation of the Holy Spirit upon the elements (the *Epiclesis*), which was in every known liturgy in the world, *except* the Roman, and mediæval and present English, was omitted from the Prayer of Consecration.[5]

---
[1] Froude, *History*, V, 458   [2] Ford's *Handbook of Spain*, I, 440, II, 959
[3] *Intro to Reprint of the First Pr Bk* , New York, 1881
[4] Gasquet and Bishop, *Edward VI and the Book of Common Prayer*, p 287
[5] The substitute in the Roman liturgy makes no reference to the Holy Spirit, but prays that "Almighty God may command that these [oblations] may be borne by the hands of Thy holy angel to Thy highest altar

2. The Consecration Prayer was reduced almost to the bare recital of the words of Institution, here again, strange to say, virtually adopting the Roman theory that a valid consecration consists chiefly, if not wholly, in the words "This is My Body . . . This is My Blood." The first portion of the prayer in the First Book, the intercession for the whole state of Christ Church, was put in an earlier place, and the last portion containing the solemn oblation, mangled by the omission of the beautiful opening words, "Wherefore O Lord and Heavenly Father," was made a separate prayer to be used after the Communion.

3. The Prayer of Humble Access, "We do not presume," which was fitly placed, as in all ancient liturgies, immediately before the reception, was now put before the Consecration,[1] as were also, with better reason, the Confession and Absolution.

4. The first words of administration of the Sacrament, as in the present book, were omitted entirely, and the latter words, "Take and eat," etc., "Drink this," etc., were put in their place, without any mention whatever of the sacred Body and Blood of our Lord.

5. The word "altar" was entirely expunged, and "table" substituted.[2]

---

in sight of Thy Divine Majesty" Concerning this Duchesne writes: "This prayer is far from exhibiting the precision of the Greek formularies, in which there is a specific mention of the grace prayed for, that is, the intervention of the Holy Spirit to effect the transformation of the bread and wine into the Body and Blood of Jesus Christ," p. 181.

[1] The restoration of this prayer to its original place was adopted by both houses of the General Convention of the American Church in 1889, and by the House of Bishops in 1892, but failed to get final approval in that year, by the lack of only one vote of the House of Clerical and Lay Deputies in Committee of the Whole.

[2] For the Scripture and primitive use of the word "altar" see chap v, pp. 40, 45.

REACTION AND RESTORATION 113

6. The Introit Psalm before the Collect for the day, the *Agnus Dei* ("O Lamb of God, etc."), and other appropriate sentences of Holy Scripture to be sung while the people were communicating, were omitted.

7. The *Gloria in Excelsis* was moved from its ancient place at the beginning of the office to its present possibly more appropriate place at the end.

8. The words of Holy Scripture, "Hosanna in the Highest, Blessed is He that cometh in the Name of the Lord," were expunged from their ancient place in the *Sanctus*.[1]

This Second Book had happily a brief existence. Edward died July 6th, 1553, and all England, which was still at heart Catholic, though not Roman, welcomed Mary the elder daughter of Henry. In 1554 the old Latin service was restored, but in spite of early promises of tolerance, bitter persecution of those holding to the need of reformation in the Church followed, and this alone did more than anything else to make Englishmen for ever opposed to everything Roman. Happily Mary also died after a brief reign on November 17, 1558, and her sister, Elizabeth, was crowned according to the old unreformed service. A commission, however, was at once named to examine both the Books of Edward VI.

Their work was a very difficult one. "The Marian Bishops were uncompromising in their desire to maintain things as they were, and the Protestant divines were for the most part

---

[1] While it is true that the general character of the changes in the Second Book were bad, some things were added which were far from being of the Puritan order. Such are the Absolution that speaks of "power and commandment" given to the Priests "to declare and *pronounce* Absolution and Remission of Sins" introduced into Matins and Evensong, the declaration as to the regeneration of infants in the Baptismal Service, the retention of the sign of the cross in Baptism, and of kneeling at Holy Communion. But these things could not counterbalance the evil wrought by the maltreatment of the Eucharistic Office.

hot Zwinglians. They had passed beyond Luther, and even Calvin . . . . The Queen herself was opposed to both extremes — and she certainly would have preferred her brother's first Prayer Book to the second. The result was a compromise."[1] Many of the objectionable features of the Second Book were removed. The first words of administration in the Holy Communion were restored and both parts of the formula remain to this day. But by far the most important change was that of the famous "Ornaments Rubric." "The accustomed place of the Church, Chapel, or Chancel" is substituted for "the place where the people may best hear," and the prohibited vestments, "alb, vestment and cope" are restored.[2]

The Book was used at S. Paul's Cathedral on May 15, 1559, and was gradually accepted by the nation. It is noteworthy in this connection that out of 9,400 clergy compelled to submit to the Roman obedience under Queen Mary, "not more than one hundred and eighty-nine preferred to resign their benefices rather than use it."[3] From this time forward, however, by the freedom accorded to the Puritan exiles returning from their quarrels in Frankfort and Geneva, their attack upon the Church and the Prayer Book was bitter and unrelenting for one hundred years to come. On the other hand, while "there is good reason for believing that in the early days of the reign, Pope Pius IV was prepared to recognize the Prayer Book in return for a recognition of his own supremacy, the conflict with the Roman dissenters became bitter also, especially after Pius V published his bull of excommunication in 1570."[4]

---

[1] Canon Bright, *His Intr to Pr. Bk. of Queen Elizabeth*, p. viii.
[2] See chap xxvii.
[3] Maclear, *Pr. Bk. Comm* , p 9.
[4] P. and F., p. 111

REACTION AND RESTORATION 115

At the Hampton Court Conference in 1604 under James I a few trifling changes were made in the Prayer Book, chiefly by way of "explanation." During the Commonwealth under Cromwell and the Puritan Parliament (1645–1660), the use of the Book, in private as well as in public, was strictly prohibited under severe penalties of fine and imprisonment, and a Presbyterian "Directory for the Public Worship of God in the Three Kingdoms" was established. And so, writes Bishop Jeremy Taylor, "The worship of God was left to chance, indeliberation, and a petulant fancy."[1]

On the restoration of Charles II in 1660 another conference was held at the palace of the Savoy in London in the hope of appeasing the opposition of the Puritan party. This consisted of twenty-one Churchmen and twenty-one Presbyterians, twelve of the former being Bishops, and nine Priests. At the outset Sheldon, Bishop of London, requested the Presbyterians to present a formal list in writing of all their grievances. The challenge was accepted, and they set to work. At the same time they appointed Baxter, the most famous of their number, to prepare for them what they deemed a better manual than the Prayer Book, and this he produced within two weeks, though it had taken sixteen hun-

[1] *Works*, v, 235 To use the Book of Common Prayer in public or in private was punishable by a fine of five pounds for the first offence, ten pounds for the second, and for the third by "one whole year's imprisonment without bail or mainprize" To say or do anything in opposition to the Directory might be punished by a fine of five pounds, or fifty pounds, at the discretion of the magistrate The Westminster Assembly (so-called from its meeting in S Margaret's Church, Westminster) consisted of ministers and laymen appointed by the Parliament in 1643 as a substitute for the ancient Convocation, and for the definite purpose of carrying out the provisions of the Scottish oath, called "The Solemn League and Covenant," a deliberate pledge to overturn the Church and "extirpate episcopacy." It was this body, which continued in session for six years, and adopted the Directory.

dred years to produce the Book which they wanted to displace!¹

The list of objections was soon ready, and contained among other things the following: — All responses in the service to be omitted, the Litany changed to "one solemn prayer," extemporaneous prayer to be allowed, the word "Minister" to be substituted for "Priest," and "Lord's Day" for "Sunday," one long prayer to be substituted for Collects, no surplice to be worn, no Lent or Saint's day to be observed, no kneeling at the reading of the Commandments, no lessons to be read from the Apocrypha, the General Confession to be said by the Minister alone, no kneeling at the reception of the Holy Communion, no sign of the cross to be used in Baptism, "the example of the Apostles" not to be alleged for Confirmation (as in the last Collect but one in that service), no ring to be used in marriage, no reverence at the Name of Jesus, etc.

It is of the authors of this list and their sympathizers that the revisers say in the Preface to the English Book: — "Such men are given to change, and have always discovered a greater regard to their own private fancies and interests, than to that duty they owe to the public." "Of the sundry alterations proposed to us," they say, "we have rejected all such as were either of dangerous consequence (as secretly striking at some established doctrine, or laudable practice of the Church of England, or indeed of the whole Catholick Church of Christ), or else of no consequence at all, but utterly frivolous and vain. But such alterations as were tendered to us, as seemed to us as in any degree requisite or expedient, we have willingly, and of our own accord, assented unto."

---

[1] For a most interesting description of the members and their work see Luckock, *Studies in the Prayer Book*, 162 sq

REACTION AND RESTORATION 117

At the meeting of Convocation in November, 1661, the committee was appointed which prepared the new revision of the Prayer Book, and to this body was presented the report of the Savoy Conference. Much of the work had in fact been accomplished already, and on the 20th of December the Book "was adopted and subscribed by the Clergy of both Houses of Convocation, and of both provinces."[1] In April, 1662, it received the approval of Parliament, as representing the laity, being the only Book which had this constitutional approval of both orders in the Church, clerical and lay, since the adoption of the First Prayer Book of 1549.

The changes were not many. The Epistles and Gospels were taken from the Authorized Version of 1611. The Psalter of the "Great Bible" of 1539, which had endeared itself to the people, was allowed to remain. Some occasional prayers were added. Two new offices were composed, one for the baptism of adults which, the revisers said, "by the growth of Anabaptism, through the licentiousness of the late times crept in amongst us, is now become necessary, and may be always useful for the baptizing of natives in our plantations, and others converted to the faith." The other addition, namely, Prayers for those at Sea, testifies also to the colonial enterprise and growing power of the nation. Since this time the English Prayer Book, except as regards some occasional offices, has remained unaltered.

The Irish Convocation (August-November, 1662) examined and unanimously approved the Prayer Book, and its use for the Church of Ireland was enjoined by the Irish Parliament in 1666, thus giving it the sanction of the representative Irish laity, all members being necessarily communicants of the Church, as in England.

---
[1] Procter and Frere, p. 194.

"The Prayer Book of 1662," writes Mr. Wakeman, "marks the close of the long liturgical struggle, just as the Savoy Conference marks the close of the long political struggle, in which ecclesiastical parties in England had been engaged since the Reformation. By it, in worship, just as in doctrine and discipline, the Church definitely refused to break with historical Christianity, definitely refused to rank herself with the Protestant churches of Europe, reiterated and to the best of her power enforced her claim to be the Catholic Church of Christ in England.

"The assertion of these principles necessarily involved the ejectment of unordained ministers from all benefices of which they held possession. It was manifestly impossible that a Church which taught that the power of the priesthood could be transmitted only by the hands of a Bishop, could allow those who had never received Episcopal ordination still to receive emoluments of Church benefices, and affect to administer the sacraments. . . . On that day (S. Bartholomew's Day, 1662) two thousand Independent, Baptist, and Presbyterian ministers, who were either unable in conscience to use the Prayer Book or were unwilling to submit to Episcopal ordination, were obliged to leave their benefices and go forth, as the Clergy of the Church had done twenty years before to certain poverty and possible persecution." [1]

It is of this Book, which comes to us from the Upper Room bearing the marks of many conflicts, and breathing the spirit of martyrs and of saints through wellnigh nineteen centuries, it has been thoughtfully said: — "The Book of Common Prayer has been used by some twelve generations of men and women and children in England; it has been carried into all the colonies of English people everywhere; it

---

[1] *The Church and the Puritans*, pp. 198, 199.

was used on this continent [America] as soon as the English Churchmen set foot on it, and it has been constantly used in our land since the settlement of Jamestown in 1607, when the Book (as revised in 1559) was not sixty years old. Its words are on the lips of Christian people all the world over, and its thoughts are in their hearts, and we feel sure that it will be used, and that its influence will extend as long as there shall be English-speaking Christians on the earth." [1]

---
[1] Dr S. Hart, *Book of C. Pr*, p 5. Since 1662 no change has been made in the English Prayer Book An attempt at revision in 1689, which would have toned down the Church's teaching, happily failed The corporate action of the Church was stifled by Crown and Parliament until 1852 when the Convocations were permitted to meet again for business. But even thus the State has so hampered the Church that no effort to enrich her services, and adapt them to modern conditions, has proved successful, with the exception of that for a revised Lectionary, and more freedom in the use of the Book, which was approved by Act of Parliament in 1872.

CHAPTER XII
THE SCOTTISH, AMERICAN, AND IRISH REVISIONS

"And thou, true Church of Scotland,
Cast down, shalt not despair;
When dowered wives are barren,
The desolate shall bear. . . .

"When o'er the western waters
They seek for crook and key,
The Lord shall make like Hannah's
Thy poor and low degree!
Thou o'er new worlds the sceptre
Of Shiloh shalt extend,
And a long line of children
From thy sad breast descend."
— BISHOP COXE, *Christian Ballads.*

THIS seems a fitting place to give some account of the later fortunes of the Church and Prayer Book in Scotland, the United States, and Ireland. The ecclesiastical changes in North Britain formed a marked contrast to those in England. There it was a revolution rather than a reformation. The leaders were not learned Bishops and Priests acting with duly constituted authority in their convocations or synods, but Priests of radical views acquired from Germany and Switzerland, who were determined to cut themselves off, "root and branch," from the ancient Scottish Church with its thousand years of history, and therefore also from other five hundred years which connected it with the Apostolic age. It was in 563 that S. Columba with his band of missionaries from the north of Ireland landed on the little western island of Iona, called in later ages I-Columbkill, that is, the Island of Columba's Church. It was in 1560 that the lay Parliament at Edinburgh rejected the ancient

Divine government of the Church, and its liturgical and reverent worship.

For political reasons the outer form of episcopacy was retained for a time in order to secure the property and income of the Church. Laymen were given the title and some of the authority of Bishops, so that they might draw the revenues of the sees. "It was a device of Highland farming, when a cow had lost her calf, to place the skin, stuffed with straw, before her eyes, to make her yield her milk more freely."[1] The name given to the make-believe calf was "tulchan," and so these titular "bishops," who were used as decoys, and only received a mere fraction of the revenues, while the Regent and the nobles were enriched, came to be called in contempt "Tulchans."

During the next hundred years, in the reigns of James I and the two Charleses, various attempts were made to restore the Apostolic Ministry, and with it the ancient liturgic worship. In 1633 a committee of Scottish Bishops, with Archbishop Laud, and Bishops Juxon and Wren as advisers, was appointed to adapt the English Prayer Book for use in Scotland, and in 1637 this Book, in which much of the Communion Office of the Book of 1549 had been incorporated, was approved. The method of its introduction into the parishes, however, was unwise and unfortunate. The people, either in Assembly or in Parliament, had not been consulted, and the Book was thrust upon them by royal edict, without opportunity for clergy or laity to examine it beforehand. It was not then to be wondered at that it was not welcomed. A new bishopric had been established at Edinburgh, and the Book was first used in the Cathedral of S. Giles in that city on the Seventh Sunday after Trinity, July 23, 1637. When the Dean was beginning to read the collect for the day, "Lord of all

---

[1] Lloyd, *Sketches of Church His in Scotland*, p. 72

power and might," Jennie Geddis, an old herb-woman, sprang up and flung her stool at his head. The Bishop tried to restore peace, but the scene ended in a riot, and the riot ended eventually in a revolution which once more abolished Episcopacy in Scotland.

Under Charles II the ancient Ministry and worship were partially restored, but in 1689, under William of Orange, the Church was again disestablished and deprived of her property, and Presbyterianism established in her stead. Henceforth the "Catholic Remainder," as those were called who clung to the ancient Church of Scotland, were subjected to a series of penal laws, and their numbers greatly diminished. This condition, however, was largely owing to the mistaken notion, shared in with the Nonjurors in England, that Church and King must stand together, and that their allegiance was due, not to the new line of the Georges from Hanover, but to the Stuarts.

In 1764 the Scottish Bishops made a slight revision of the Eucharistic Office of 1637, and it was this Liturgy which Dr. Samuel Seabury, the first American Bishop, consecrated by three Scottish Bishops in the upper room of a house in Aberdeen on Nov. 14, 1784, introduced into his Diocese of Connecticut, and which was adopted in substance by the whole American Church in 1789.[1]

Bishop Seabury, after his consecration in 1784, always used

---

[1] The reason for this secret service was the fact that all persons more than four in number, besides the family, attending a meeting conducted by an Episcopal Clergyman who had not taken the oath of allegiance to King George, were subject to a fine of five pounds for the first offence, and imprisonment for two years for the second. The death in 1788 of Prince Charles Edward, the last of the Stuart claimants to the throne, paved the way for relief. In 1792 the repressive law was repealed, and the Scottish Church had at last restored to her the full freedom of her worship. In 1797 the Book was translated into Gælic.

SCOTTISH, AMERICAN, IRISH

the Scottish Prayer of Consecration in his own Diocese. In a letter to Bishop White, dated June 29, 1789, in view of the General Convention of that year, referring to the meagre Prayer in the English Office, he wrote: — "The Consecration is made to consist merely in the Priest's laying his hands on the elements and pronouncing 'This is My body,' etc., which words are not consecration at all, nor were they addressed by Christ to the Father, but were declarative to the Apostles. This is so exactly symbolizing with the Church of Rome in an error, an error, too, on which the absurdity of Transubstantiation is built, that nothing but having fallen into the same error themselves could have prevented the enemies of the Church from casting it in her teeth. The efficacy of Baptism, of Confirmation, of Orders, is ascribed to the Holy Ghost, and His energy is implored for that purpose; and why He should not be invoked in the consecration of the Eucharist, especially as all the old Liturgies are full to the point, I cannot conceive." [1]

The independent organization of the American Church originated in a meeting of "The Corporation for the Relief of Widows and Orphans of Clergymen of the Church of England" in the three Provinces of Pennsylvania, New York, and New Jersey, held in New Brunswick, N. J., May 11, 1784. At this meeting it was agreed to form a "Continental representation of the Episcopal Church," which took place in the city of New York on October 6 and 7 that same year. It was at the next meeting, September 27 and 28 in Philadelphia, consisting of sixteen Clergymen and twenty-six Laymen, that certain radical changes in the English Book,

---

[1] *Journals of General Convention*, edited by Bishop W. S. Perry, III, pp. 387, 388. The Scottish Prayer, with slight verbal alterations, was adopted by the Convention the following September, and the revised Book came into use on October 1, 1790.

after hasty consideration, were *proposed*, in addition to some required for political reasons which were the only ones *adopted*. This was the origin of the so-called "Proposed Book" published in April, 1786, but generally disapproved from the beginning.[1]

This is the account given by Horace Wemyss Smith, great-grandson of the Rev. Dr. William Smith, the President of the House of Clerical and Lay Deputies in 1789, as to the way in which the Scottish Prayer of Consecration was adopted by the American Church. Bishop Seabury of Connecticut and Bishop White of Pennsylvania constituted the whole House of Bishops at the time. They were in favor of the Scottish Office, but the Lower House was doubtful. In their anxiety they sent for Dr. Smith, who himself was a Scotchman, for a private conference. "He agreed to introduce the new Office to the House of Deputies, and recommend it for adoption. The next day he informed the House of the document entrusted to him, and of its variations from the Office of the Church of England. A storm began to brew, and hoarse whispers of popery reached his ears. He rose in his place, and, exclaiming 'Hear — (pronouncing it *Heyre*) before ye judge,' began to read. Dr. Smith was a superb reader, and withal had just enough of a Scotch brogue to make his tones more musical and his emphasis more thrilling. He soon caught attention, and read his paper through without a single interruption, his hearers becoming more and more absorbed and charmed. When he had finished, the new Office was accepted with acclamations."[2]

---

[1] These proposed alterations will be found in Bishop White's *Memoirs*, pp. 435-447, ed. 1880, and in Bishop Perry *Reprint of the Journals of Early Conventions*, and his *Handbook of the General Conventions*, pp 25-40.

[2] Life and Correspondence of the Rev. William Smith, D.D., Philadelphia, 1880, Vol. II, pp. 290, 291. Concerning these two remarkable

SCOTTISH, AMERICAN, IRISH 125

In the Appendix to this chapter will be found a comparison of the three forms of the Prayer of Consecration of the Holy Eucharist, English, Scottish, and American; also a table showing the genealogy of the four parent Liturgies and of those of the Anglican Communion. For a comparison of the Eucharistic Office as a whole with that of the parent Liturgies see chap. vi, p. 68.

After the disestablishment of the Irish Church a revision of the Prayer Book, which hitherto had been the same as that of the English Church since 1662, was accomplished in 1877. Only a few changes were made, none of which affected any fundamental doctrine. Some canons, however, were enacted, among other things requiring that the "Communion Table" should be movable and of wood, forbidding the use of Eucharistic lights, crosses on the altar or its covering, incense, wafer bread, the mixture of water with the wine in Holy Communion, and the carrying of crosses or banners in processions.

Among the changes made in the American Prayer Book in 1789 was one of a serious and unfortunate character which was allowed to creep into the title page, as it would seem, without formal or positive action on the part of the Convention. The Church had indeed the wisdom to retain the first part of the title of the Book, namely, "The Book of Common Prayer and Administration of the Sacraments, etc. of the Church," that is, of the Holy Catholic Church of all ages and all lands. But she was not so wise in yielding

---

men, White, the friend of Washington, and Seabury, whom God raised up to be the first Bishops of the American Church, John Williams, the successor of Seabury, has said in reference to the results to the Church of the Convention of 1789 "We are mainly indebted, under the overruling wisdom of the Holy Spirit, to the stedfast gentleness of Bishop White, and the gentle stedfastness of Bishop Seabury."

to the popular prejudice of Puritans and Dissenters against the Church, when, without formal adoption, she allowed the words "According to the Use of the Protestant Episcopal Church in the United States of America" to be placed there.[1]

Nearly a century later, after the disestablishment and disendowment of the Church of Ireland, an extreme section of that Church urged a similar abandonment of her true and ancient title ever since the days of her founder, S. Patrick, and to her honor she rejected it. So far, in fact, from acceding to the demand to call herself the "Protestant Episcopal Church," while reaffirming her character as "reformed and Protestant," she declared herself to be "the Ancient Catholic and Apostolic Church of Ireland."[2] More recently the Archbishops and Bishops of the Irish Church refused to receive a communication of State that was sent to them because it was addressed to the "Protestant Episcopal" Bishops, and in 1902 issued a declaration against "the increasing misuse of the term Catholic to describe without any qualifying designation that body of Christians only who acknowledge the supremacy of the Bishop of Rome." The Church of England has persistently pursued the same course through all her history, never having adopted the title Protestant either in her Prayer Book, or by canon. When the Convocation in 1689 was asked to adopt an address to King William III, thanking him for his zeal for the Protestant religion, it refused "lest," as it said, "the Church of England should suffer diminution in being joined with foreign

---

[1] The title seems to have been first used by a meeting of Clergy of the Diocese of Maryland at Annapolis in August, 1783, but its adoption even then was a distinct usurpation of the legal name of the Moravians of Pennsylvania and North Carolina, who were designated as a "Protestant Episcopal Church" by an Act of the English Parliament passed on May 12, 1747.

[2] Prayer Book, *Preamble and Declaration*.

SCOTTISH, AMERICAN, IRISH 127

Protestant churches." In all this these two Churches have been wiser than their American sister.

Among the many objections urged against this title are the following: — (1) Protestant stands for controversy, contest, uncharity, division. It is a silent but eloquent testimony to this discredited signification of the word that not one of the principal sects of England or America has thought it desirable to incorporate it in its official name. (2) Whatever *positive* meaning may be claimed for the word as a "witness *for*" (*testis pro*), it is now, and for a long time has been, used only in a *negative* sense as a "witness *against*." Edmund Burke, himself an Irish Churchman, said in 1792, "A man is certainly the most perfect Protestant who protests against the whole Christian religion." In fact long before Burke's day the word had fallen into such disrepute that an Irish Churchman, writing in 1714, speaks of "Atheists, Deists, Socinians, Sectarians, going under the name of Protestants." [1] And since Burke's day the word has taken on such new meaning in Germany that his definition of "the most perfect Protestant" has found its literal fulfilment in the last words of Strauss, the rationalistic author of a "Life of Jesus," when he declared, "We are no longer Christians, but still continue to be Protestants." It is evident then that the words of Hamlet's mother, "The lady doth protest too much, methinks," [2] may have other and wider applications.

(3) Neither Protestant nor Episcopal (unless the latter word be regarded as synonymous with Apostolic, which it is not)[3] is a real definition of the Church, inasmuch as it proclaims only an incidental relation to other religious bodies of recent date, and is therefore itself denominational and sectarian. In other words it classes the national Ameri-

---
[1] Froude, *The English in Ireland*, I, 331.   [2] Act III, sc. 2.
[3] See chap xxxvi.

128 PRIMITVE WORSHIP & THE PRAYER BOOK

can branch of the Holy Catholic Church, in the eyes of "the man in the street," as merely one of two hundred "other churches" which have, or may have, an equal claim on his attachment. The real question is not, Is the Church Protestant against Roman claims and Romish doctrine? That she is Protestant in this sense, as in many others, there is no doubt whatever. The term was justly applied to her by some of her greatest and most Catholic divines, from Laud and Andrewes to Cosin and Jeremy Taylor. But this is altogether aside from the propriety of making the word an essential part of her official title, where no incidental and temporary characteristic has any rightful place.

(4) Again, the title is unhistorical and unscriptural. For the first one hundred and eighty-two years of the Church in America it was known only by its local title "of England," as the branches of the Church were known in Apostolic days — the Church "in Corinth," "in Philippi," "in Rome," "of Galatia," because the land was then politically part of England. One cannot imagine the Apostle S. John speaking of "the Protestant Episcopal Church in Ephesus," or S. John Chrysostom being described as a Bishop of "the Protestant Episcopal Church in Constantinople," though there were more evils to protest against in their day than in ours.

(5) Finally, the name is novel as well as unhistorical. It is only since 1789 that the words "Protestant Episcopal" have been on the title page. Bishop Cleveland Coxe, whose loyalty to what are called "Protestant principles" cannot be questioned, speaking of the condition of the American Church in 1789, has said, "A much more humiliating token of our position at that day was the consent of even the Catholic Seabury to permit our truly Apostolic Church to be known, even in its external conditions, as 'the Protestant Episcopal Church in the United States of America.' I hold this," he

SCOTTISH, AMERICAN, IRISH

adds, "to be a jumble of words which nothing but familiarity can render tolerable to an enlightened mind. . . . Nor can any tribute be paid to the Papacy more entirely acceptable, than the surrender to its followers of the Catholic name, its prestige, and its logical force."[1]

APPENDIX

The English Prayer of Consecration[2]

Almighty God, our heavenly Father, who of Thy tender mercy didst give Thine only Son Jesus Christ to suffer death upon the Cross for our redemption; who made there (by His one oblation of Himself once offered) a full, perfect, and sufficient sacrifice, oblation, and satisfaction, for the sins of the whole world; and did institute, and in His holy Gospel command us to continue, a perpetual memory of that His precious death, until His coming again; Hear us, O merciful Father, we most humbly beseech Thee; and grant that we receiving these Thy creatures of bread and wine, according to Thy Son our Saviour Jesus Christ's holy institution, in

---

[1] The remarkable growth of conviction in the American Church in regard to this question is shown by the following facts. The first definite effort in behalf of restoring a Scriptural and traditional title to the Church was made in the House of Clerical and Lay Deputies of the General Convention which met in Boston in 1877, when a memorial and resolution from the Diocese of Wisconsin was presented by the Rev Dr. James De Koven, Warden of Racine College This proposal received only the vote of two clerical Deputies of that Diocese, namely, Dr De Koven, and Dr Cole, and the vote of one other Deputy from the Diocese of Alabama. Not a single vote was cast for it by any Lay Deputy In 1910 in Cincinnati a resolution was offered to alter the title page of the Prayer Book so as to read, "The Book of Common Prayer and Administration of the Sacraments and other Rites and Ceremonies of the Holy Catholic Church according to the Use of that portion thereof known as The Episcopal Church in the United States of America" This resolution was adopted by a majority of the Dioceses in the Clerical Order, but failed of passage by the lack of one vote in the Lay Order.

[2] The Prayer in the revised Irish Book is the same as the English.

remembrance of His death and passion, may be partakers of His most blessed Body and Blood; who, in the same night that He was betrayed, took Bread; and, when He had given thanks, He brake it, and gave it to His disciples, saying, Take, eat, this is My Body which is given for you: Do this in remembrance of Me. Likewise after supper He took the Cup; and, when He had given thanks, He gave it to them, saying, Drink ye all of this; for this is My Blood of the New Testament, which is shed for you and for many for the remission of sins: Do this, as oft as ye shall drink it, in remembrance of Me. *Amen.*

(It will be observed that in the English Invocation there is no mention of the Holy Spirit.)

The American Prayer of Consecration

(In the American Prayer — which is almost the same as the Scottish — italic type marks additions to, or alterations from the English. The portion beginning, "And we earnestly desire," is in substance the first Post-Communion Prayer of the English Book.)

ALL *glory be to thee*, Almighty God, our heavenly Father, *for that thou*, of thy tender mercy, didst give thine only Son Jesus Christ to suffer death upon the Cross for our redemption; who made there (by his one oblation of himself once offered) a full, perfect, and sufficient sacrifice, oblation, and satisfaction, for the sins of the whole world; and did institute, and in his holy Gospel command us to continue, a perpetual memory of that his precious death and sacrifice, until his coming again: For in *the night in which* he was betrayed, he took Bread; and when he had given thanks, he brake it, and gave it to his disciples, saying, Take, eat, this is my Body, which is given for you; Do this in remembrance of me. Likewise, after supper, he took the Cup; and when he had given thanks, he gave it to them, saying, Drink ye all of this; for this is my Blood of the New Testament, which is shed for you, and for many, for the remission of sins; Do this, as oft as ye shall drink it, in remembrance of me.

WHEREFORE, O Lord and heavenly Father, according to the institution of thy dearly beloved Son our Saviour Jesus Christ, we, thy humble servants, do celebrate and make here before thy Divine Majesty, with these thy holy gifts, which we now offer unto thee, the memorial thy Son hath commanded us to make; having in remembrance his blessed passion and precious death, his mighty resurrection and glorious ascension; rendering unto thee most hearty thanks for the innumerable benefits procured unto us by the same. *The Oblation*

AND we most humbly beseech thee, O merciful Father, to hear us; and, of thy almighty goodness, vouchsafe to bless and sanctify, with thy Word and Holy Spirit, these thy *gifts and* creatures of bread and wine; that we, receiving them according to thy Son our Saviour Jesus Christ's holy institution, in remembrance of his death and passion, may be partakers of his most blessed Body and Blood. *The Invocation*

AND we earnestly desire thy fatherly goodness, mercifully to accept this our sacrifice of praise and thanksgiving; most humbly beseeching thee to grant that, by the merits and death of thy Son Jesus Christ, and through faith in his blood, we, and all thy whole Church, may obtain remission of our sins, and all other benefits of his passion. And here we offer and present unto thee, O Lord, our selves, our souls and bodies, to be a reasonable, holy, and *living* sacrifice unto thee; humbly beseeching thee, that we, and all others who *shall be* partakers of this Holy Communion, may worthily receive the most precious Body and Blood of thy Son Jesus Christ, be *filled* with thy grace and heavenly benediction, and made one body with him, that he may dwell in us, and we in him. And although we *are* unworthy, through our manifold sins, to offer unto thee any sacrifice; yet we beseech thee to accept this our bounden duty and service; not weighing our merits, but pardoning our offences, through Jesus Christ our Lord; by whom, and with whom, in the unity of the Holy Ghost, all honour and glory be unto thee, O Father Almighty, world without end. *Amen.*

132 PRIMITIVE WORSHIP & THE PRAYER BOOK

The Scottish Prayer of Consecration

In the Scottish Liturgy the Oblation has these additional words at the end: — "and looking for His coming again with power and great glory." The Invocation is as follows:— "And humbly praying that it may be unto us according to His word, we Thine unworthy servants beseech Thee, most merciful Father, to hear us, and to send Thy Holy Spirit upon us and upon these Thy gifts and creatures of bread and wine, that being blessed and hallowed by His life-giving power, they may become the Body and Blood of Thy most dearly beloved Son, to the end that all who shall receive the same may be sanctified both in body and soul, and preserved unto everlasting life." The Consecration is followed (not preceded as in the English and American Books) by the Prayer "for the Whole State of Christ's Church," the words "militant" and "militant here in earth" being omitted.

Committees for revision of the Prayer Book, in addition to that in the American Church, have been at work in the Church in England and in Canada for several years. The Canadian Church alone, however, has authorized the publication and tentative use of a revised Book (Cambridge University Press, 1915), subject to ratification at a later Synod. The chief features of this revision are:— Greater freedom in use of the Psalter, a new Lectionary, additional Sentences for the Church Seasons, permission to shorten Matins, Evensong, and Litany on week days, and in combination with Holy Communion on Sundays, permission to confine the response, "Praise Him, etc." in the *Benedicite* to the end of groups of verses, many additions to the Occasional Prayers, the Athanasian Creed to be said alternately by Priest and People, with permission to omit the minatory verses, 2, 28 and the last, and an explanatory rubric, enlargement of the Confirmation Office, and modification of the Commination Service. The feast of the Transfiguration is elevated to be a red letter day, with Collect, Epistle, and Gospel. Special services are provided for the Accession Day, for Missions, Harvest Thanksgiving, Institution and Induction of Ministers, and Consecration of Churches and

GENEALOGY OF THE CHIEF LITURGIES

The Mozarabic is still used in a few churches in Spain. For the connection of the Milanese with the Transalpine or Gallican, see Duchesne, pp. 88, 89.

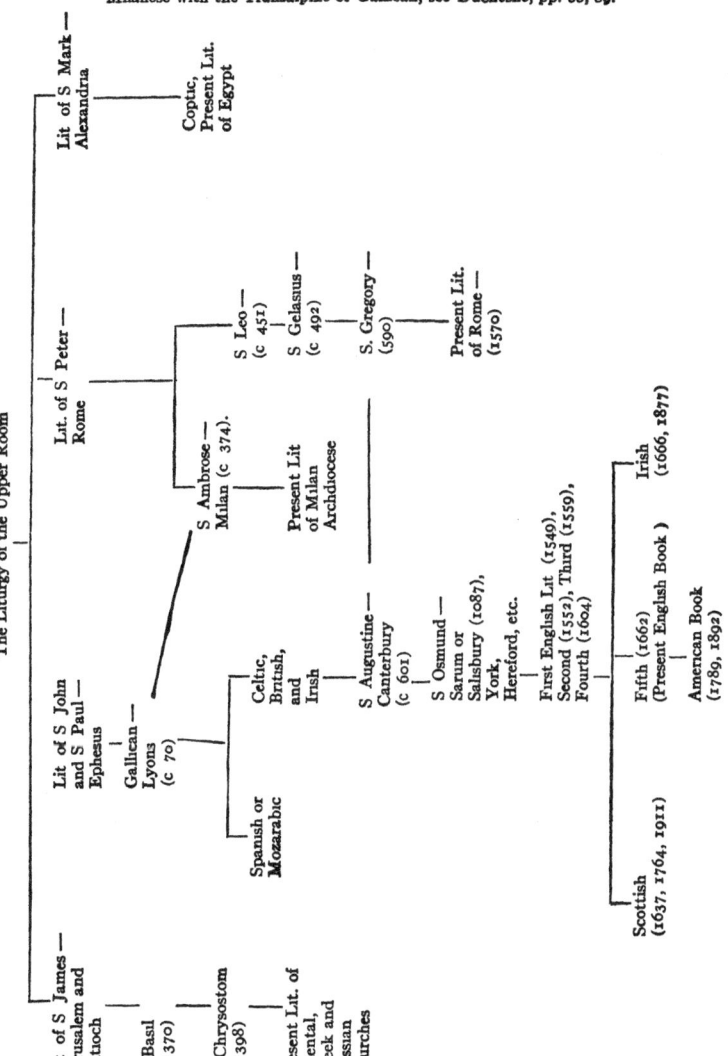

Chapels, for all of which Collects, Epistles, and Gospels are provided. There are also forms for Laying Foundations, and for Consecration of a Church-Yard or Cemetery, and of a Grave. The only material change in the Communion Service is the addition of the Summary of the Law to the Decalogue. It is much to be regretted that the opportunity was not taken to adopt a richer and a more primitive form for the Prayer of Consecration, such as that possessed by the Scottish and American Churches. The American Church in the General Convention of 1913 appointed a Revision Committee which recommended certain changes and enrichments in 1916, and was continued in office to report again in 1919. The Convocations of Canterbury and York have not yet issued any complete report of their work (1917).

PART II. THE PRAYER BOOK AND WHAT IT TEACHES

CHAPTER XIII

THE HOLY COMMUNION — THE PREPARATION OR PRO-ANAPHORA

"*Jesus came to them and spake unto them, saying, All authority hath been given unto Me in heaven and on earth. Go ye therefore, and make disciples of all nations, baptizing them into the Name of the Father and of the Son and of the Holy Ghost; teaching them to observe all things whatsoever I have commanded you and lo, I am with you alway, even unto the end of the world.*" — S. MATT. xxviii, 20, R. Ver.

THE services of the Prayer Book may be divided into three distinct classes; (1) those intended for public worship (the Holy Communion, the Daily Offices of Matins and Evensong, and the Litany); (2) the Occasional Offices for Priests (Holy Baptism, the Solemnization of Matrimony, Churching of Women, Visitation and Communion of the Sick, Burial of the Dead, etc.,); (3) Occasional Offices for Bishops (Confirmation, Ordination, etc.).

"THE ORDER FOR THE ADMINISTRATION OF THE LORD'S SUPPER, OR HOLY COMMUNION,"[1] though placed after the daily Offices of Prayer, which are in a measure its preparation, is the core and centre of all Divine Worship as being the only service ordained by our Lord for the united worship of all of His people. For this reason, in the first glow of enthusiastic love for their crucified Lord, the first Christians

---

[1] For the various names given to the Holy Sacrament in Scripture and the Primitive Church see chap. IV.

are found celebrating it "daily," and when this became impracticable anywhere, on every Lord's Day at the least.[1] This has been the rule of the whole Catholic Church in all ages. And the reason for this is evident. The Holy Communion, according to our Lord's command, is the ordinary and not extraordinary service for all Christian people. Hence the office with which it is celebrated is called specifically "THE LITURGY," literally, "The People's Service" from the Greek *laos*, the people, and *ergon*, work.[2]

The full title given to the Office in the First Book of Edward in 1549 was "THE SUPPER OF THE LORD, AND THE HOLY COMMUNION, COMMONLY CALLED THE MASS." This last title was omitted in 1552, and has never been restored. The word had come to represent only one essential aspect of the service, namely its "continual remembrance [before God] of the sacrifice of the death of Christ," and that in a manner wholly unwarranted by Scripture or the Primitive Church, to the neglect of the other equally essential aspect which required the faithful to "eat and drink" in fulfilment of Christ's command, in order to obtain the full blessing of the Sacrament. This purpose of the Sacrament as a Holy Communion had been sadly ignored, partly owing to the perverted teaching in regard to its sacrificial character, partly to the novel enforcement of private confession to a Priest as a condition of Communion, and partly to rigid rules in regard to fasting.

It is a curious fact that this word Mass has absolutely no theological significance in itself, though it is held in utter disrepute by the great body of the English-speaking world on account of its association with the false views and super-

---

[1] Acts ii, 46; xx, 7; 1 Cor xi, 20; xiv, 6.
[2] For a full account of the reasons for this see chaps. xviii and xix.

HOLY COMMUNION, PREPARATION 137

stitious practices connected with its use in mediæval days. The word in early days was innocent enough. It is the English form of the Latin word *missa*, which means nothing more than "sent," in allusion to the *dismission* or sending away of the congregation by the Deacon at the close of the service, when he said, *Ite missa est*, which may be freely rendered, as in the oriental service, "Let us depart in peace." It was used in this general way "for every part of Divine Service,"[1] since the fourth century, and it is this lack of any real significance as applied to the Holy Communion, in addition to the ineradicable prejudice regarding it among English-speaking people, that forms the strongest argument against recent attempts to restore it to popular use.[2] Though removed from the title of the Office, we retain a reminder of it in the popular names for the feasts of the Nativity, the Purification, and S. Michael and All Angels (Christ*mas*, Candle*mas*, and Michæl*mas*).[3]

---

[1] Bingham, XIII, i, 4.
[2] Dr. Pusey asks, "Why should people say 'Mass' instead of the Holy Eucharist? . . . They might have gone far to Catholicize England if they would have taught as dear John Keble did. . . . Now they only strengthen a party" (*Spiritual Letters*, p. 251).
[3] S. Ambrose of Milan in the fourth century uses the word in a letter to his sister (*Op* ii, 853). Etheria, or Silvia, the author of the newly discovered *Peregrinatio*, describing a journey which she made to Jerusalem about the year 375, "uses the word for all meetings, for the [daily] offices as well as for the Liturgy" (Duchesne, p. 491). Kellner says that the word came only to be applied, though not exclusively, to the Holy Eucharist in the sixth and seventh centuries (*Heortology*, p. 432). In *Romeo and Juliet* Shakespeare puts it into the mouth of Juliet addressing Friar Lawrence, where the reference is to an afternoon service: "Are you at leisure, holy father, now; or shall I come to you at evening Mass?" (IV, i, 38) Freeman thinks that "*perhaps* it is connected with the Hebrew *Missah*, a free-will offering" as in Deut. xvi, 10. (*Prin. Div Ser.* II, ii, p. 440, note.) It

Before speaking of the Office itself it will be necessary to say something about the rubrics which precede it. The American Church has omitted the first of these requiring notice by intending communicants the day before, but this rule had already in 1789 become a dead letter in England, as it is today. In regard to the rubric concerning the "repulsion" of an unworthy communicant, it is to be remembered that this is not an act of excommunication, which is the exclusive prerogative of the Bishop, but only a temporary exclusion. No person who has been confirmed can be regarded otherwise than as a possible communicant.

The last rubric in regard to the place where the Holy Table shall stand has been a source of remarkable and prolonged controversy in England from the sixteenth century to the present day. The Puritan party insisted on having the "Table," as they called it, placed where the Priest could be distinctly heard. This was a natural result of violent reaction against the utter perversion of the old service when the Priest mumbled the Office in a voice inaudible, and in "a tongue not understood of the people." The alleged object of the Puritans seemed worthy enough, but their method was certainly very objectionable and revolutionary. The Book of 1549 made no change in the place for the Altar, but the Book of 1552 adopted the present rubric directing that the "Table, at the Communion-time, shall stand in the Body of the Church [that is, the Nave], or in the Chancel, where Morning and Evening Prayer are appointed to be said." [1]

seems strange, however, to find that the popular prejudice against the word does not exist in Germany, or the Scandinavian countries It is still in use in the Lutheran Prayer Books of Germany, Sweden and Denmark.

[1] So far as the actual Communion was concerned, this had some show of precedent in the custom of the Eastern Church in always communicating the people at the gate of the choir or sanctuary The object of the Puritans, however, was not that of the Eastern Church, namely, to guard the sanc-

HOLY COMMUNION, PREPARATION 139

This aim of the Puritan party became for a time completely successful when, on September 1, 1641, a tyrannical and illegal order of the House of Commons, then in rebellion against the King, was issued commanding all church-wardens to "forthwith remove the Communion Table from the east end of the church or chancel into some other convenient place." In 1662, after the Restoration, vigorous efforts were made to correct these abuses; nevertheless, for a long time, the evil custom continued in many country churches, and it was not until the following century that the restoration of the Altar to its ancient place against the eastern wall was accomplished generally throughout the Church.[1]

All this has an important bearing on the further direction of this rubric concerning the position of the Priest at the *beginning* of the service where he is bidden to stand "at the north side of the Table." The Puritan party insisted, as we have seen, on its standing with its sides turned north and south, "table-wise," instead of east and west as formerly. But when the altars were put in their ancient place, this direction remained, and as a result the whole question of the position of the Priest at the beginning of the office was

---

tuary from irreverence, but to degrade the character of the Sacrament to that of a mere social religious feast, the people actually receiving in their seats where it "cannot be discovered whether they kneel or no, while they receive, and the Minister cannot possibly come with any convenience at them which are placed farthest in their seats" (Letter of Archbishop Laud to the Bishop of Lincoln). It was a frequent and bitter charge against Laud that "he placed the Holy Table altar-wise at the upper end of the chancel, and placed a rail before it" (Scudamore, pp. 159, 163).

[1] A few examples of the former evil custom were still said to exist in England in 1876, but outside of England probably not a single case can be found where the removal to "the body of the church" exists today. It is surely time therefore for removing from our Prayer Book this reminder of days of confusion and irreverence long since past (See Scudamore, *Not. Euch.*, pp 161, 162.)

left, and is still left, in complete confusion.[1] In the American Book "north side" is changed to "right side." In the Scottish Liturgy the rubric says, "standing *at* the Holy Table."

The Order for the Holy Communion in every Liturgy, ancient and modern, has two very distinct divisions, the PREPARATION and the CELEBRATION. These are called in the Eastern Church the PRO-ANAPHORA, down to the *Sursum corda* ("Lift up your hearts"), and the ANAPHORA, or OFFERING (which may be said to include the actual Communion); and in the Latin Church, the ORDINARY OF THE MASS, and the CANON. The word Ante-Communion, though it does not correspond exactly to the Pro-Anaphora, is the only word in common use among us today. "Communion," however, has come to signify with us, though inaccurately, "the *Celebration* of the Communion," and not merely the act of communicating, so that Ante-Communion in the sense of Ante-Celebration is as nearly the equivalent of Pro-Anaphora as any word we can employ. The title of the Scottish Liturgy expresses the distinction with great accuracy. It is "For the *Celebration* of the Holy Eucharist, and *Administration* of Holy Communion."

It will be observed that the Lord's Prayer, with which the service begins, is to be said by the Priest *alone*, as is evident by the way in which the Amen is printed, not in italic but in roman type. This is a remnant of the old English rule for the Priest to make his own preparation privately in the sacristy before entering.[2]

The introduction of the Ten Commandments, with the

---

[1] See the "Lambeth Judgment" of Archbishop Benson *in re Read and Others versus the Lord Bishop of Lincoln*, 1890, pp 18-45.

[2] The liturgic rule throughout the Prayer Book is that when Amen is in italics, it is a response by the people When it is in roman or ordinary type, it is not a response, but is part of the prayer and, as in this case, is

HOLY COMMUNION, PREPARATION 141

ten-fold *Kyrie* ("Lord have mercy, etc.") has been thought by some to be a liturgical novelty, as having no place in the older service books. It finds its analogy, however, in the primitive custom in the early liturgies of reading here a portion of the Old Testament, in addition to the Epistle and Gospel from the New. These Old Testament Lections disappeared from both the Eastern and Western liturgies at an early date, though traces of them are found as late as the ninth century. The Armenian Liturgy is the only one that retains the three Eucharistic Lections.[1]

It is to be remembered, moreover, that for three hundred years the Commandments had been recited and explained in the English Church publicly once a quarter,[2] and that, together with the Creed and the Lord's Prayer, they were

to be said by the Minister alone, or, as in the General Confession, by Minister and People together. Another important rule of printing worth remembering is in regard to the use of capitals. Capitals are frequently used in other places than the beginning of sentences, or proper names. The purpose here is to guide the eye of the reader, and in the case of prayers to be said by Priest and People together, as in the Confessions, they have the additional purpose of making the clauses so distinct that the congregation may be able to say them in unison without lagging or confusion. Bearing this rule in mind it will be seen that the "General Thanksgiving" is *not* meant to be said in unison as it has only the usual capitalization at the beginning of each sentence, and the Amen is in italics. Here the word "General" has reference to things, and not to persons, as in the "General Confession."

[1] See Duchesne, pp. 168, 577B. It is worthy of note also that the Commandments were recited daily in the Temple as part of the Shema. (See Warren, *Lit. A. Nic. Church*, 195) The Summary of the Commandments given by our Lord in S. Matt. xxii, 37-41 was introduced into the Non-juror's Office of 1718, to the exclusion of the Commandments It was added to the Scottish Office later as an alternative, and in 1789 was adopted by the American Church to be used in the same way on any day, provided the Decalogue was read once each Sunday. P. and F., p. 478, note

[2] See Johnson, *English Canons*, II, 283, 520.

contained in the popular private Prayer Books in use in mediæval days called Prymers. They have here the further very useful purpose (especially as they are explained in the "Duty to God and our Neighbor") of providing communicants with a most wholesome method of self-examination before they "presume to receive that Holy Sacrament." In this connection the ten-fold *Kyrie* may be regarded as a substitute for the penitential Litany with which the earliest liturgies began the Office, and which is still the use of the Eastern Church. It has been well said that the Kyrie is the natural cry of the human heart in the presence of God's eternal law.[1]

---

[1] Dr. Pusey "held that the introduction of the Commandments into the Communion Service, and the injunction that they should be set up at the East end of every church, was a protest of the Reformers against the antinomian tendency of the Lutheran doctrine of Justification" (Baring-Gould, *The Church Revival*, p. 272). Does not this same reason still hold good as against certain similar tendencies of today, when it is claimed that "the Ten Commandments have no place in practical politics," international as well as national?

In view of a common objection to the fourth Commandment in particular, it should be noted that this is the primal law "for man" (S Mark ii, 27), and not for Hebrews only. In fact there is not in it the faintest trace of Judaism. On the contrary it directs us back to creation's dawn, and not to Abraham or the Red Sea, for the reason or illustration of its observance. Nor is there anything of a ceremonial character required for its observance but only rest from the burden of labor, and the keeping of it "holy." Moreover "the seventh day" only denotes the *proportion* of time and not any particular day of the week, which, for the Hebrews before the Exodus, is supposed to have been Friday, the day being changed to Saturday, after the Exodus, that being the actual day of the week when the first Passover was celebrated, the day of their "resurrection" from the bondage of Egypt. See Ex. xii, 14, 17, Deut v, 14, 15 One of the earliest of the Church Orders, the Ethiopic *Didascalia* (about A D 335), calls Saturday "the Jewish Sabbath," and the Lord's Day "the Christian Sabbath" (Maclean, *Ancient Ch. Orders*, p. 57).

HOLY COMMUNION, PREPARATION 143

The rubric prescribing that the Priest shall "turn to the People, and rehearse distinctly" the Commandments is noteworthy as an example of the manifest intention of the Church throughout all services, namely, that they shall be read in such a manner that all may hear to their edification. This is a very marked feature of the English Book, where the following directions (omitted from the American Book for some strange reason) occur, and which experience proves are by no means unnecessary: — The Sentences in the Daily Prayers are to be "read with a loud voice"; the Lord's Prayer "with an audible voice"; and the Lessons are to be read "distinctly" and "with an audible voice; he that readeth so standing and turning himself, as he may best be heard of all such as are present." This rule as being that of common sense is plainly meant to apply to the Eucharistic Lessons, and to all other parts of the service. It surely implies also that they shall be read at such a pace that the Minister as well as the people can let their thought follow the words, instead of conveying the impression that the chief object is to get through as speedily as possible. In regard to reading the service in general, the saying attributed to Garrick concerning some of the Clergy in his day may be found applicable to some in ours also: — "While we actors speak unreal words as if they were real, these Clergy speak real words as if they were unreal."[1]

---

[1] It is strange that any intelligent clergyman should think or do otherwise, though as early as the sixth century "a severe law" of the Emperor Justinian was found necessary, Bingham tells us, "commanding all Bishops and Presbyters to make the Divine Oblation, and the prayers used in Baptism, not in secret, or with a low mumbling voice, but so as all the faithful might hear them" (*Antiq*, XV, iii, 33) Concerning the custom of intoning the Lessons, while admitting that "the practice may be very ancient", Duchesne says, "It was necessarily introduced as soon as the Christian assemblies became very large," and with the object of enabling

"the officiating minister to make himself heard." He attributes the use of the *Secreta* (so-called) in the Mass, that is, "the custom of pronouncing in a low voice certain formularies which were evidently intended in the first instance to be heard by every body," to "the same reason — namely, the difficulty of maintaining a high intonation in a large building" (p 118). There is of course a place for genuine *Secreta*, that is, silent prayers by the Priest, as at the preparation or presentation of the oblations, and elsewhere, especially at the close of the Eucharistic Office, where it has been the good custom of the Western Church for the Priest to recite silently the Gospel for Christmas Day (S. John 1, 1-15).

CHAPTER XIV
THE COLLECTS

"*For twelve hundred years the Collects have been as manna in the wilderness to devout spirits, and are, next to Scripture itself, the clearest standard whereby genuine piety may be discerned, the surest guide by which its progress may be directed, the highest mark to which its wishes would aspire.*" — ALEXANDER KNOX.

AS the Collects, Epistles, and Gospels are part of the Eucharistic Office, their appointment for every Sunday and Holy Day, and even for week-days (where a celebration is desired or practicable), shows clearly the mind of the Church in regard to the frequency of the Sacrament as being the same as that which, in the last chapter, we found to be the rule of the New Testament, and of the whole Church in all ages.[1] It has been the plain intention of the Church also in every revision of the Prayer Book that no exception should be made of Good Friday. "The appointment of an Epistle and Gospel," writes Mr. Blunt, "is a *prima facie* evidence that Consecration on Good Friday was intended to supersede the Mass of the Pre-sanctified [the reserved Sacrament from Maundy Thursday] which had been hitherto used, and Communion was of course intended to follow. The practice of the Church of England since the Reformation certainly seems to have been to celebrate the Holy Communion on this day."[2]

---

[1] See the first rubric for Advent Sunday, and those for Holy Innocents, the Circumcision, Epiphany, and Ash-Wednesday after the Gospel, also the proper Prefaces.

[2] *Ann Pr Bk*, pp. 101-2. This was the practice of Bishop King of Lincoln, and of S. Paul's, London, under Dean Church, Canon (afterwards Dean) Gregory, and Canon Liddon. See Liddon's *Life*, by Johnston, pp. 331-2. For an account of how the omission of Consecration grew up in the Church, see Scudamore, *Notitia Euch.*, xvii, sec. 3.

The COLLECT is peculiar to the offices of the Western Church. It has no existence in the East. A Collect may be called the sonnet of devotion. Like the sonnet of poetry it is condensed in form, comparatively short, and aims at a single point, or at two points closely connected with each other. In contrast "with such wordy effusions as exist in Knox's 'Book of Common Order,'" writes Canon Bright, the Collects "say so much in saying so little; address the Most High with such adoring awe, and utter man's needs with such profound pathos, yet with such a calm intensity — assailing 'Heaven's door,' as our great poet says, with the 'forceful knocking' of determined faith;[1] are never weak, never diluted, never drawling, never ill-arranged, never a provocation to listlessness; exhibit an exquisite skill of antithesis, and a rhythmical harmony which the ear is loth to lose."[2]

Moreover, beautiful as were most of the English collects in their Latin dress, they were fortunate also in their sixteenth century translators, chief of whom was Cranmer. The gift indeed seems to have been almost peculiar to that age, and it has been well said, "It is with a Latin collect as with a Greek ode or an Italian sonnet: no matter how wonderful the diction, the charm of it is as a locked secret until the thing has been Englished by genius akin to his who first made it out of his own heart."[3] At the last revision of the Prayer Book (1662) a number of prayers like that for "All Conditions of Men" are called collects, but they have not the true character of the class.[4]

---

[1] *Lyra Innocentium.*   [2] *Ancient Collects*, pp. 199, 200.
[3] Dr. W R. Huntington.
[4] The characteristic feature of the prayers also in the Book which Baxter had the temerity to produce in two weeks (see p. 115) is lengthiness. The sentence with which the Book begins contains eighty-three words by actual count!

THE COLLECTS

There are three necessary parts in every true Collect. (1) The Invocation, usually addressed to God the Father, and containing a reference to some attributes of His character. (Only three in our Prayer Book are addressed to our Lord, and only one to the Blessed Trinity.) (2) The Petition, consisting of one or more clauses. (3) The Conclusion, expressing the grounds of our petition, "through Jesus Christ," or a recognition of His union with the Father and the Holy Ghost; or, as in the Collect for S. Stephen's Day, a reference to His present power and will to help.[1]

Fifty-eight of the Eucharistic Collects in the Prayer Book are translations from those of the ancient English Use, and are found also in the Roman Sacramentary as revised by Gregory the Great (Bishop from A.D. 590 to 604). (A list of these and other Collects in the Prayer Book is given in the Appendix to this chapter.) The following Collects were newly composed for the First Book of Edward, Cranmer being the probable author: — First and Second in Advent, Christmas, Circumcision, Quinquagesima, Ash-Wednesday, I in Lent, the Third for Good Friday, I and II after Easter,

[1] There need be no doubt as to the meaning of the word Collect. An explanation common today, namely that the prayer received its name from the assumption — rarely true — that it *collects* the thought of the Epistle and Gospel, is without any foundation whatever. The *history* of the word tells unmistakably its real origin. The Collect in its original use was the first prayer in the Eucharistic service, that is, after the people are *collected* "After saluting the congregation ['the Lord be with you'] the celebrant calls on them to pray for him in the introductory prayer, which is called the *collecta*, because it was said as soon as the people were assembled . *Colligere plebem* is the ordinary expression for calling the people together for worship. The meaning of the word *collecta* is made perfectly clear in the rubrics of the Gregorian Sacramentary relating to the Litany days. The prayer prescribed for use at the church whence the procession sets out is called '*ad collectam.*'" (Duchesne, pp. 166, 167, and note.)

S. Thomas, SS. Philip and James, S. Matthew, S. Luke, SS. Simon and Jude, All Saints, and parts of those for the Conversion of S. Paul and S. Bartholomew. III Advent and VI Epiphany were added in 1662.

It will be observed that few of the Collects for Saints' Days are translations from the ancient English Use. The reason for this is that most of these were addressed to the individual Saints by name, asking their prayers ("pray for us," *ora pro nobis*). For the first seven centuries there was nothing to support this custom but certain rhetorical apostrophes resting on an "if," the possibility that in some way the departed may hear or be informed of our prayers. But none of these is an invocation except in the sense in which Tennyson invokes the spirit of his friend Arthur Hallam: —

"Be near me when my light is low,
   When the blood creeps, and the nerves prick
   And tingle; and the heart is sick,
And all the wheels of being slow."

It was not until the eighth century that the invocations were introduced into the Litany in the West, and "the opinion of praying to Saints had not the full growth for an article of faith till after 1335." [1] That the Saints, and all the faithful departed, pray for those who are still in the thick of life's conflict cannot be doubted, without assuming that they have lost the love of their neighbor, which is an evident impossibility. Even the once selfish Dives is represented by our Lord as remembering his brethren on earth. How much more then the faithful Christians in Paradise.[2] But that the

---

[1] Twysden, *His. Vindication*, ix, 21, pp. 214 sq. See Procter, *His. B C P*, pp 249, 298, and Mason, *Purgatory*, etc , pp 112 sq.

[2] S Luke xvi, 23, etc , compare Rev. vi, 9, 10. Concerning this Charles Kingsley speaks of "the help" we ought to receive "from our blessed dead,

THE COLLECTS

faithful departed can hear *our* petitions to themselves is quite a different as well as a doubtful matter. It is true that invocation does not necessarily imply worship of the Saints, but only asking their intercession with God, as one might ask the intercession of a friend still on earth. Nevertheless the custom has proved dangerous to ignorant Christians in the past, and tends undoubtedly to put the direct mediation of our Lord into the background. Moreover, it has no sanction in Holy Scripture, nor in the primitive liturgies.

The remarkable skill and added beauty of Cranmer's work in the revision may be seen by comparing the following Collects with the Latin originals: —

"O Almighty God, who alone canst order the unruly wills and affections of sinful men; Grant unto Thy people, that they may love the thing which Thou commandest, and desire that which Thou dost promise; that so, among the sundry and manifold changes of the world, our hearts may surely there be fixed where true joys are to be found; through Jesus Christ our Lord." The original reads: — *Deus, qui fidelium mentes unius efficis voluntatis, da populis tuis id amare quod præcipis, id desiderare quod promittis, ut inter mundanas varietates ibi nostra fixa sint corda ubi vera sunt gaudia. Per, etc.* [1]

"O Lord, who never failest to help and govern them whom Thou dost bring up in Thy stedfast fear and love; Keep us, we beseech Thee, under the protection of Thy good providence, and make us to have a perpetual fear and love of Thy holy Name; through, etc." The original reads:)—

Sancti nominis tui, Domine, timorem pariter et amorem fac

---

who surely will not use their power — the augmented spiritual power of their present state — for themselves, but as Christ uses His, for those they love" (*Daily Thoughts from the Writings of C. Kingsley*, p 95).

[1] IV after Easter.

nos habere perpetuam; quia nunquam tua gubernatione destituis, quos in soliditate tuæ dilectionis instituis. Per Dominum, etc.[1]

These two Collects illustrate the method by which the more severe and epigrammatic wording of the Latin is transformed, rather than translated, into the tender and flowing language of "English undefiled."[2]

"Not a few of the ancient collects which have thus been preserved to us," writes Canon Bright, "are rich in interest, historical or liturgical. The daily collects for Peace, and V Trinity enable us to feel what Roman or Italian Churchmen felt in the latter half of the fifth century, when sieges and barbaric invasions made men's hearts fail for fear, — when Rome but narrowly escaped the Huns, and did not escape the Vandals, and the Western Empire passed away before Odoacer, and Odoacer was overthrown by Theodoric. . . . Lord Macaulay, in a well-known passage, has spoken of the ancient collects in the Prayer-Book as having 'soothed the griefs of forty generations of Christians.' No one indeed would say that the collect-type of prayer could meet all the requirements of Christian devotion. There are deep needs and frequent occasions for which its restraint of expression

---

[1] II after Trinity.

[2] The Scottish Prayer Book has added special Collects, Epistles, and Gospels for the Festivals of S. Kentigern, the earliest missionary to Scotland (Jan. 13), S. Patrick (March 17), S Columba (June 9), S. Ninian (Sept. 16), S. Margaret of Scotland (Nov. 16), and for the Dedication Festival of a Church, Thanksgiving for Harvest, the Solemnization of Matrimony, the Burial of the Dead, and additional sets for Christmas and Easter; also a special Gospel for the Lent Ember Days, and an Epistle, with two alternative Gospels, for the September Ember Days. The American Church added in 1892 Collects, Epistles, and Gospels for the Feast of the Transfiguration (August 6), and for a first Communion on Christmas Day and Easter Day.

THE COLLECTS

would seem too cold, and its measured orderliness too elaborate. . . . Yet, all this allowed for, the best specimens of the class are a goodly heritage of Western Christendom, which, for its purpose, may be set against the glowing poetry and the exuberant adoration with which, in the words of a great liturgical writer, the Eastern Church 'soars up to God.' . . . A thoughtful poet of our Church has put into touching words the desire to carry the Sunday Collect through the varied life of the week,

'That so my steps may turn to practice clear,
And 'scape those ways where feverish fancy burns;'
and he has described it as the constant renewal of
'a tale of better things
Like tune that pleased our childhood's pensive ear,'
which
'Still as we grow old is doubly dear.'" [1]

APPENDIX TO CHAPTER XIV

For the originals of the Collects, as given by Canon Bright (*Ancient Collects*, pp. 208, sq.), we are indebted as follows:—

1. To the Sacramentary of S. Leo, Bishop of Rome (440–461), seven, namely, 3rd after Easter, 5th, 9th, 10th, 12th, 13th, 14th, after Trinity.

2. To S. Gelasius (492–496), twenty-nine, namely, Morning and Evening Collects for Peace, Evening for Aid against Perils, Collect for Clergy and People, 4th in Advent, Innocents' Day, Palm Sunday, Second for Good Friday, Easter Day, 4th, 5th, after Easter, 1st, 2nd, 6th, 7th, 8th, 10th, 11th, 12th, 15th, 16th, 18th, 19th, 20th, 21st, "Assist us mercifully," "Almighty and everliving God," in the Confirmation Service, "O most merciful God," in the Visitation Office, "O Lord, we beseech Thee," in the Commination or Penitential Office for Ash-Wednesday.

---
[1] *Prayer Book Commentary*, pp 92–96 See also Freeman, *Prin. Div. Ser.* I, p. 274; Dean Goulburn, *The Collects of the Day;* and Isaac Williams, *The Cathedral*, p. 15.

3. To Gregory the Great (590–604), thirty-three, namely, S. Stephen, S. John Evangelist, Epiphany, 1st, 2nd, 3rd, 4th, 5th, after Epiphany, Septuagesima, Sexagesima, 2nd, 3rd, 4th, 5th, in Lent, first for Good Friday, Second half of Easter Collect, Ascension, Whitsunday, 3rd, 4th, 17th, 22nd, 23rd, 24th, 25th, after Trinity, Purification, Annunciation, S. Michael and All Angels, "We humbly beseech Thee, O Father" (Litany), "O God, whose nature and property," "Prevent us" ("Direct us"), "Almighty and immortal God" (Baptismal Service), First part of the first Collect in Burial Office.

The following classification of the Collects, as given by Canon Bright,[1] may assist many in their private or family devotions: —

1. *For the Spirit of acceptable Prayer.* 3rd and 10th after Trinity.
2. *For Repentance.* Ash-Wednesday, S. John Baptist.
3. *For Pardon.* "O God, whose nature," Septuagesima, 4th in Lent, 12th, 21st, 24th, after Trinity, First in Commination (Penitential Office for Ash-Wednesday).
4. *For Faith.* Trinity, S. Thomas, S. Mark, Annunciation.
5. *For Hope of Heavenly Blessedness.* 2nd in Advent, S. Stephen, 4th after Easter.
6. *For Love.* Quinquagesima, 2nd, 6th, 7th, after Trinity.
7. *For Faith, Hope, and Love.* 14th after Trinity.
8. *For Purity.* Innocents, Circumcision, 6th after Epiphany, 1st in Lent, Easter Even, 1st after Easter, 18th after Trinity, Purification, "Almighty God, unto whom" (Communion Office).
9. *For Unworldliness.* 4th after Easter, Ascension, S. John Baptist, S. James, S. Matthew.
10. *For Devotion of the Will to God.* Second Evening Collect, 20th and 25th after Trinity, S. Andrew.
11. *For Renewal.* Christmas Day.
12. *For Illumination.* S. John Evangelist.

---

[1] *Ancient Collects*, pp. 231, sq.

THE COLLECTS 153

13. *For Right Intentions.* 5th after Easter, 9th after Trinity.

14. *For the Carrying-out of such Intentions.* Easter Day, "Prevent us" ("Direct us").

15. *For Grace to know God's Will.* First after Epiphany, Whitsunday.

16. *For Grace to do God's Will.* 1st and 4th in Advent, 1st, 11th, 13th, 17th, 20th, 25th after Trinity, SS. Philip and James.

17. *For Grace to Use God's Gifts.* S. Barnabas.

18. *For Grace to love God's Word.* 2nd in Advent, S. Paul, S. Luke, S. Bartholomew.

19. *For Defence against Danger, or Deliverance from Evil.* 2nd and 3rd Morning Collects, 3rd, 4th, 5th, after Epiphany, Sexagesima, 2nd, 3rd, 5th, in Lent, 2nd, 3rd, 8th, 15th, 16th, 20th, 22nd, after Trinity, S. Michael.

20. *For Comfort.* Sunday after Ascension, Whitsunday.

21. *For Guidance.* 4th, 19th after Trinity, "Assist us," and "O Almighty Lord" (in Post-Communion).

22. *For the Benefit of Christ's Example.* Palm Sunday, 2nd after Easter.

23. *For the Benefit of Christ's Sacrifice.* 2nd after Easter, Annunciation.

24. *For Conformity to the Christian Standard.* 3rd after Easter, All Saints.

25. *For Peace.* 2nd Morning and Evening Collects, 2nd after Epiphany, 5th after Trinity.

26. *For the Church and its Work.* Collect for Clergy and People, S. John Evangelist, 5th after Epiphany, Good Friday, 5th, 15th, 16th, 22nd, after Trinity, S. Matthias, S. Peter, S. Bartholomew, SS. Simon and Jude.

27. *For Final Blessedness.* Epiphany, 6th and 13th after Trinity, [Transfiguration, in American Book].

28. *At the Close of Prayers.* 12th, 23rd, after Trinity, "Assist us," "Almighty God, the fountain of all wisdom," "Almighty God, Who hast promised to hear."

CHAPTER XV

EPISTLES, GOSPELS, CREED, AND SERMON

"*O make Thy Church, dear Saviour,
A lamp of purest gold,
To bear before the nations
Thy true light as of old;
O teach Thy wandering pilgrims
By this their path to trace,
Till, clouds and darkness ended,
They see Thee face to face.*" — BISHOP W. W. How.

THE EPISTLES AND GOSPELS are the same, with few exceptions, as in the old English Use. Out of ninety Epistles only twenty-one (and of these only four for Sundays) differ from that of Salisbury; out of ninety Gospels only five (and only one for Sunday) differ from it.[1] The guiding principle of these lections from Holy Scripture is of course the teaching of the Christian Year. From Advent on to Trinity Sunday we have the unfolding of the life of our Lord in His Incarnation, Birth, Circumcision, Manifestation, Baptism, Fasting, Temptation, Crucifixion, Resurrection, Ascension, and the sending of the Holy Ghost. From Trinity to Advent Sunday the practical side of the Christian

---

[1] The liturgical independence of the English Church has here a further witness in the fact that no less than thirty-three Epistles and the same number of Gospels are different from those of the Roman Use, as follows: Both the Epistles and the Gospels for all the Sundays in the Trinity season (26), the Epistles for the Third and Fourth in Advent, S. Mark, S. James, S. Bartholomew, S. Luke, SS. Simon and Jude (7); and the Gospels for the four Sundays in Advent, Second in Lent, S. Barnabas, and S. Bartholomew (7).

EPISTLES, GOSPELS, SERMON 155

life is illustrated, as in the earlier portion the life of faith and worship receives the chief emphasis.[1]

Readings from the Old Testament must necessarily have been the only lections possible in Divine Service until the New Testament came gradually into being. It is to be remembered that the Holy Communion was celebrated for twenty years before the earliest book of the New Testament was written, namely, the first Epistle of S. Paul to the Thessalonians; and probably a longer period before the first Gospel was written. The passages of the Old Testament would naturally be such as those in which our Lord unfolded "all things written in the Law, and in the Prophets, and in the Psalms" concerning Himself.[2] This "prophetic" lection, as it was called, continued for many centuries. The Armenian Liturgy has preserved the "prophetic" lection, and that of Milan still makes use of it on certain days.[3]

The origin of the EPISTLE, which for several centuries was called the "Apostle,"[4] is evidently to be found in the injunction of S. Paul that his letters should be "read," that is publicly, "in the Church."[5] The immemorial place for reading the Epistle is the south-west corner of the altar, and from a lower step, sometimes from a lectern; and for the Gospel the north-west corner (*cornu sinistrum*, or *cornu Evangelii*), and from an upper step.[6]

Though the Gospels, at least in their written form, did not come until after the Church had spread into Europe, there is no extant liturgy that does not contain a provision for a

---

[1] For a full consideration of this subject, see the Author's *The Christian Year Its Purpose and its History*.
[2] S. Luke xxiv, 44
[3] Duchesne, p. 195.
[4] Scudamore, *Not. Euch.* VI, iii, 24.
[5] Col iv, 16, 1 Thess v, 27.
[6] *Not. Euch.* VI, vi, 258.

156 PRIMIITVE WORSHIP & THE PRAYER BOOK

GOSPEL lection. It was the custom of the Primitive Church, as seen in the *Apostolical Constitutions*, to sit at the reading of the Scriptures (except the Gospel), and at the sermon. "To sit during the Epistle is the ancient custom, and to stand during the Gospel."[1] Kneeling at the Epistle, which has been somewhat practised of late, has no good authority anywhere. In the First Book of Edward (1549) the ancient custom of saying "Glory to Thee, O Lord" (*Gloria Tibi*) was continued, and though omitted from the English Book since 1552, the tradition has been universally preserved. It was restored to the Scottish Prayer Book in 1637, and to the American in 1789. The Scottish Book has at the end of the Gospel the response, "Thanks be to Thee, O Lord, for this Thy glorious Gospel," but there was no response in the old English liturgies.[2] There is no direction to say "Here endeth the Gospel," after the example of the ending of the Epistle, because the Creed which immediately follows is the continuation and the full declaration of the Gospel, of which the portion read is but a fragment.[3]

The proper CREED for the Holy Eucharist is that which is called the Nicene from having been drawn up, so far as the clear declaration of our Lord's perfect Godhead is concerned, at the First General Council held in Nice in Asia Minor in 325. From the beginning there had been a brief "form of sound words," or "form of doctrine,"[4] summing up in simple language the great fundamental facts of the Gospel, and framed around the three-fold formula given by our Lord for the admission of disciples into His sacred school.[5] The Nicene Creed did not add to this belief in Father,

---

[1] Dearmer, *Parson's Handbook*, p. 199, Maskell, *Anct. Lit*, p. 50; *Not. Euch*, 248.
[2] *Not. Euch.* 264.
[3] Rev. xiv, 9.
[4] 2 Tim. i, 13; Rom. vi, 17.
[5] S. Matt. xxviii, 19.

EPISTLES, GOSPELS, SERMON 157

Son, and Holy Ghost, but brought out more clearly its meaning in opposition to the heresy of Arius, a priest of Alexandria, who denied the true Godhead of the Lord Jesus. Though taught to all the baptized from the earliest days, the Creed was not formally introduced into the Liturgy until the year 471 in Antioch, and until 511 in Constantinople. In Rome it was not so used until the first half of the eleventh century.[1]

The custom of bowing at the Name of Jesus is said to have originated at the Council of Nice, to emphasize the reverence due to the Son of Man whose true Deity had been despised by Arius. The rule of bowing the head at every mention of this holy Name is required by Canon 18 of the Church of England, "As it hath been accustomed; testifying by these outward ceremonies and gestures . . . their due acknow-

---

[1] Duchesne, pp. 84, 172. For a history of the three forms of the Creed see chap. xxv.

The original Creed of Nice, or Nicaea, ended with the words, "We believe in the Holy Ghost." (In the acts of the councils "we" is always employed, but in the Greek liturgies it is the singular, "I," as with us.) The rest of the Creed was added at the Second General Council in Constantinople in 381, chiefly for the purpose of condemning the heresy of Macedonius, who denied the Divinity of the Holy Ghost.

The addition of the words, "and from the Son," commonly known as "the Filioque" from the words in Latin, is said to have been made in the Spanish Church in the fifth or sixth century in order to guard some new attempt to deny the true Divinity of our Lord. It was finally inserted in the Roman Creed about the year 850, chiefly, it is said, through the influence of Charlemagne, to whom is ascribed the authorship of the great hymn to the Holy Ghost, "Veni Creator Spiritus" "It has never been accepted by the whole Church, and however true the doctrine which it sets forth, its introduction into the Creed, without sufficient authority, has been the cause of the schism of the Church of Christ into Eastern and Western Christendom, the most extensive division, and the most lamentable occurence in ecclesiastical history" (F. E. Warren, *Pr Bk. Comm*, p. 20).

ledgment that the Lord Jesus Christ, the true eternal Son of God, is the only Saviour of the world."[1]

This is the only place where a SERMON is provided for. In the Middle Ages sermons were only occasional. Though there is no provision in the Book for a prayer before the Sermon, some form of invocation or prayer is appropriate, and is customary. The fifty-fifth Canon of the Church of England, and the Scottish Book provide forms of a *Bidding Prayer* to be used by preachers. The English form begins, "Ye shall pray for Christ's Holy Catholic Church, . . . and especially for the Churches of England, Scotland, and Ireland." It then specifies rulers and magistrates, clergy and people, and concludes with the Lord's Prayer. It is still used in cathedrals, college chapels, and some parish churches.[2]

---

[1] See also S Paul's remarkable reverence for this Name, as pointed out in the author's, "*The Christian Year*, etc., pp. 59, 60.

[2] "These addresses to the people, or 'biddings,' called 'Prefaces' in the Gallican Liturgies, are a distinct mark of Ephesine origin" Warren, *Lit of Celtic Church*, p 167, note.

CHAPTER XVI

THE OFFERTORY, PRAYER FOR THE CHURCH, EXHORTATION, AND INVITATION

"Thy prayers and thine alms are come up for a memorial before God." — ACTS X, 4.

IN the Primitive Church there was no such thing as a pewed church building. All the support of the Clergy, the care of the poor, and of buildings, came from the voluntary offerings of the people, and "the altar," according to our Lord's command in the Sermon on the Mount,[1] was naturally considered the most fitting place for such gifts. In the earliest days the opportunity to make an offering at the altar was a privilege, and only those who were in the full communion of the Church were allowed to do so. It is important to remember in this connection that the endowments, glebe lands, tithes, and invested funds, as well as the Church buildings, in all old Christian lands, are very rarely the gift of the State. They are the voluntary gifts, for the most part, of the Church's own members, high and low, rich and poor alike, through many centuries. Exactly the same process is going on in new countries today, where endowments for parish, and school, and college, and hospital are being created by the voluntary offerings of Christian people.[2]

An essential part of the OFFERTORY (which is correctly applied also to the sentences said or sung at this part of the service) consists of the bread and wine for the Holy Com-

---

[1] S. Matt., v, 23, 24.
[2] See the author's *Gospel in the Church*, Senior Grade, p. 221, for the character of endowments in the Church of England.

munion. To the latter of these a little water is usually added, according to primitive custom, though no direction is given in the Prayer Book.[1] Concerning the wine it ought to be unnecessary to say that unfermented juice of the grape, or "must," has never been regarded as wine. It is an assured fact that what is called wine among the Jews was a *fermented* product.[2] The learned Jewish Christian, Dr. Edersheim, writing to Canon Bright in 1882, quotes from the Talmud in proof of his assertion that "the wine used at the Paschal Supper was undoubtedly fermented and intoxicating. . . . In fact, to *avoid* intoxication, the Paschal wine was almost always 'mixed' (as was the common custom in drinking wine), the ordinary proportion being two parts of water to one of wine, . . . *strong* wine in that of three parts water. . . . Still further, to show that the natural fermentation could not possibly be ranked with *leaven*, the principle is distinctly laid down in the Talmud that 'the juice of the fruit does not produce leavening.'"

This "fruit of the vine,"[3] moreover, has been the universal use of the Church from the beginning. No other product of the grape than one with the necessary amount of alcohol could be available in every climate and for "all nations," as our Lord meant it to be. This fact has also a direct bearing on "all" receiving from one cup, as did the Apostles in the Upper Room. Our Lord was assuredly aware of the antiseptic character of wine, as testified, if need be, by His

---

[1] The mixing of water with the wine, though not as a ceremonial act, was pronounced lawful in the trial of Bishop King of Lincoln in 1890. The Scottish Book has the following rubric, "It is customary to mix a little pure water with the wine in the eucharistic Cup"

[2] The following references out of many show this beyond a question; Gen ix, 24; xlix, 12; 2 Sam xiii, 28; Prov xx, 1; Eph. v, 18, 1 Pet. iv, 3.

[3] S. Mark xiv, 25.

parable of the Good Samaritan,¹ and the thought was doubtless in His mind when He first administered it to all from a *common* cup. This has special significance for the Clergy, who are much more exposed to infection than the laity, inasmuch as they are obliged to consume what remains in the cup after all have drunk. Nevertheless it is a well assured fact, as every insurance actuary can testify, that the Clergy have the highest longevity of any class or profession.

There are doubtless cases, however, as in epidemics of infectious disease, where "intinction," or the dipping of a portion of the consecrated Bread into the wine, might be employed, as is the use of the Oriental Churches. In any case, the novel and utterly irreverent method of "individual cups," in contravention of our Lord's action in the Upper Room, and of the custom of nineteen centuries, and in destruction of the symbolism of the single cup, is wholly unnecessary.²

As to the kind of bread to be used, the First Book explicitly required "unleavened bread." The present English Book, in one of the final rubrics, declares that "bread such as is usual to be eaten shall *suffice*." In other words, this is the minimum, but whatever is used, it is declared, must be "the best and purest wheat bread that conveniently may be gotten." It is unquestioned that thin unleavened bread was the kind in which our Lord instituted the Holy Eucharist. As the Passover was the Feast of Unleavened Bread, when all leaven was commanded to be put away,³ no other bread was possible to a loyal Jew. The use of unleavened, or "wafer" bread⁴ is therefore only following the example of Christ.

---

¹ S. Luke x, 34.
² For ancient methods of administration see Bingham, XV, v.
³ Ex xii, 15, xiii, 7.
⁴ Ex. xxix, 2.

162 PRIMITIVE WORSHIP & THE PRAYER BOOK

Other reasons for its use are the fact that it is less liable to crumble, and that it is always ready, not being subject to decay like ordinary bread.[1]

It is to be observed that the rubric, with good reason, and according to ancient usage, distinctly requires that the elements are not to be placed on the altar until *after* the alms have been placed there. One evident purpose of this is to give opportunity for their preparation at the Credence while the alms are being collected. There is no mention of this table or shelf in the Prayer Book, but some such receptacle is implied of necessity. Its usual place is on the south side of the chancel.[2]

The position of the "PRAYER FOR THE WHOLE STATE OF CHRIST'S CHURCH MILITANT," which is equivalent to the "Great Intercession" found in every known Liturgy, varies in different offices. In the East its usual place is after the Prayer of Consecration. "In the Roman Liturgy it occurs partly before and partly after the Words of Institution. In the ancient Gallican and Mozarabic Liturgies it occurred in the same position which it now occupies in the Anglican Liturgy."[3]

---

[1] Among Lutherans and Moravians the use of common bread would be regarded as the height of irreverence. Among the Scotch-Irish Presbyterians the use lingered even after their transplantation to America. Mrs. Earle notes in her work on "The Sabbath in Puritan New England" (p. 122), that the custom continued in the Londonderry settlement in New Hampshire during the 17th century, where "thin cakes of unleavened bread were specially prepared for this sacred service." In the Oriental Church the bread is leavened, but a special bread is made carefully for the purpose.

[2] In the Oriental Church the elements are prepared in, and brought from, the *Prothesis*, or Sacristy, with a special service, and this is called the Great Entrance, in contradistinction to the bringing in of the sacred books, which is called the Little Entrance.

[3] Warren, *Pr. Bk. Comm.* p. 103.

OFFERTORY, EXHORTATION, &c   163

It is as all-inclusive as the Litany, and possesses intercessions for (1) the Catholic Church and its Unity; (2) Christian Rulers; (3) Bishops and other Clergy; (4) the People; (5) the Afflicted; (6) Commemoration of the Departed.[1]

Though there is no direction here for those who do not intend communicating to withdraw, it has been the unfortunate custom for great numbers not only of non-communicants but of communicants to leave the church after this prayer just when the service is about to rise to its highest point. Even loud organ music, which has been well named by Bishop Cleveland Coxe, the "soul dirge," has been employed to cover (and encourage) their withdrawal. This custom happily

---

[1] In all the Primitive Liturgies there was here a distinct prayer for the Faithful Departed, such as that found on page 65. It was owing to the extreme perversion of this unquestionably Scriptural and Primitive practice in mediæval days, when the greater part of the Intermediate State was turned into an "abbreviated hell" called Purgatory, that direct prayer for the rest, peace, progress and refreshment of the faithful departed was unwisely omitted, and the words "militant here in earth" inserted in 1552. (They are omitted in the Scottish Book) In the first Post-Communion Prayer of the English Book (which is part of the Consecration in the first Book of Edward, the Scottish, and the American Books) prayer for the Faithful Departed is definite and real in the petition that "we *and all Thy whole Church* may obtain remission of our sins, and all other benefits of His Passion." Concerning this clause, Bishop Cosin, one of the most learned members of the committee of revision in 1661, wrote, " By 'all the whole Church' is to be understood as well those that have been heretofore and those that shall be hereafter as well as those that are now the present members of it." For a somewhat full discussion of this question see the author's *Some Purposes of Paradise*, pp 67–75. The Russian Metropolitan being asked by Dr. Ingram, Bishop of London, what struck Russian Churchmen as the chief defect of Anglicans, replied, "We marvel at the way you English people forget your dead — by far the largest part of the Church. Our children are taught to think of their dear parents as living in the next room."

is becoming less frequent. In primitive days when the Church was in the midst of heathen, the catechumens not yet admitted to Holy Baptism were required to depart at an *earlier* part of the service. When this rule ceased to be enforced the custom was for those who did not communicate to remain until the actual Communion of the people began, and then to withdraw during the singing of Communion antiphons by the choir.[1] This surely is a custom well worthy of consideration as the lesser of two evils. It would at least avoid the unseemly confusion of withdrawal at the moment when it jars on every reverent mind, while the effect would be almost entirely neutralized if done when communicants begin to approach the chancel.

This, however, is by no means intended as an encouragement of the notion of some *quasi* sacramental virtue in what is called "non-communicating attendance." It is rather in order that those who remain, "before whose eyes Jesus Christ is openly set forth crucified"[2] may be led on by the attractive power and persuasion of the service to partake of the Divine Food, as well as to plead the atoning Sacrifice. "Was there a Passover heard of," writes Bishop Andrewes, "and the lamb not eaten? Time was when he was thought no good Christian, that thought he might do one without the other, no *celebremus* without *epulemur*."[3]

Two "Warnings" for Communion are placed here in the English Book, but were removed to the end of the Office of the American Book in 1892. The "Exhortation" to Communion which follows has, in several sentences, a remarkable similarity to a form used in the earlier days of the English

---

[1] See Duchesne, p. 187.

[2] Gal. iii, 1, R. V.

[3] *Sermons*, II, 298–9. Concerning the bearing of fasting Communion upon this question see pp 191, sq.

OFFERTORY, EXHORTATION, &c 165

Church, beginning "Good men and women, y charge you by the Auctoryte of holy churche." [1]

THE INVITATION (as it is called in the Scottish service), "Ye that do truly, etc," is really part of the *Exhortation* immediately before the celebration, and may be regarded as a substitute for the ancient "Kiss of Peace," as in the Liturgies, or "Holy Kiss," or "Kiss of Charity," as in the Epistles.[2] The Clementine Liturgy says: "Let the Deacon say to all, 'Salute one another with a holy kiss; and let them of the Clergy salute the Bishop; the laymen, laymen; the women, women.' . . . The ancient custom appears to have been well kept up in the West until the thirteenth century, when we first read of an instrument [*deosculatorium*] which, after being kissed by the Priest, and the Deacon after him, was by the latter handed to the Communicants who thus, in another manner, expressed their mutual love, viz., by all kissing the same thing." [3] The ancient "Kiss of Peace" occupied the same place, before the *Sursum Corda*, as it does at present.[4]

---

[1] Maskell, *Mon. Rit*, 348, 349 It is important to observe that the "warnings" are not "notices." The place for the "notice" is provided for immediately after the Creed. In the English Book the "warning" is to be read "after the sermon." As the Holy Eucharist is the normal service for every Lord's Day at the least, it is not intended that either "notice" or "warning" should be given every Sunday, but only "if occasion be," as is said in the rubric after the Creed See Dearmer, *Parson's Handbook*, pp 317, 318, and Blunt, *Ann Pr Bk.*, p. 176 So full and clear, however, is the teaching of these warnings concerning the Holy Sacrament, and the necessary preparation for it, that one or other might well be read before the three great feasts.

[2] Rom. xvi, 16, 1 Cor xvi, 20; 1 Peter v, 14.

[3] Scudamore, *Not. Euch*, pp 497, 501

[4] The mistaken interpretation of this Invitation which would make it apply to *all* persons in the congregation who are "in love and charity with their neighbors, etc ," and irrespective of their being confirmed, is explicitly

166 PRIMITIVE WORSHIP & THE PRAYER BOOK

contradicted by the rubric at the end of the Confirmation Office, which says, "There shall none be admitted to the Holy Communion, until such time as he be confirmed, or be ready and desirous to be confirmed." The same interpretation would logically include the *unbaptized*, as no mention in the Invitation is made of Baptism any more than of Confirmation. The plea that the rubric in the Confirmation service was adopted in 1281 by Archbishop Peckham of Canterbury only goes to show the sad "neglect of the sacrament of Confirmation . . . in evil days. . . . To cure this damnable neglect," he adds, "we ordain that none be admitted to the sacrament of the Lord's Body and Blood that is not confirmed, except at the point of death, unless he have a reasonable impediment " So far from this showing that Confirmation was "an informal service," and one of many "mediæval ceremonies," it clearly sets it on the high position which Holy Scripture and the whole Catholic Church give it, namely, as the completion of Holy Baptism, the instrument appointed by our Lord for the "receiving of the Holy Ghost" in all His fulness by penitent and believing souls, and one of the six "foundations," or "principles of the doctrine of Christ" (Acts viii, 15, 16, xix, 2, etc ; Heb vi, 1, 2). This does not imply that every devout Christian, unconfirmed through ignorance or prejudice or lack of opportunity, is under all circumstances to be rejected from the Holy Communion. We may well rejoice that "the pure river of water of Life" overflows its banks, and that "the cup of blessing which we bless," "runneth over," to those who are, as an old Father of the Church expressed it, of the soul of the Church, though not externally of its body (Rev. xxii, 1; 1 Cor. x, 16; Ps. xxiii, 5).

It is told of Bishop Samuel Wilberforce that he once asked an Irish maidservant if she thought he, a heretic from the Roman point of view, could possibly enter Heaven, and she replied, "Certainly, your lordship." When he asked her how could that be, she promptly answered, much to the amusement of the Bishop, but with sound theology and common sense, "By your invincible ignorance, my lord"! It is to be remembered that for 177 years (1607-1784) no Churchman in the English colonies, now the United States, was able to receive Confirmation, and yet, if otherwise fitted, he was admitted to the Holy Communion. See also chap. xxx.

CHAPTER XVII

CONFESSION, ABSOLUTION, COMFORTABLE WORDS

> "*Each morn and eve, the Golden Keys,*
> *Are lifted in the sacred hand,*
> *To show the sinner on his knees*
> *Where heaven's bright doors wide open stand.*
>
> *On the dread altar duly laid*
> *The Golden Keys their witness bear,*
> *That not in vain the Church hath prayed,*
> *That He, the Life of Souls, is there*" — KEBLE.

IN the First Book the CONFESSION AND ABSOLUTION were placed immediately before the Communion of the people, but the present place is manifestly better inasmuch as it is a preparation not only for Communion, but also for the Consecration, Oblation, and Intercession. In the old English, as in the Roman Liturgy, there was a confession (the *Confiteor*), "first prescribed, so far as appears, by the Council of Ravenna in 1314." But this is only a mutual confession by the Priest and his assistants to each other, and a *mutual prayer* for pardon. "It may appear singular that there was no Confession to be said by all the people in the mediæval Liturgies; but not to mention the obstacle arising from the use of the Latin language, we must remember that the laity communicated rarely; and that, when they did so, their Communion was generally preceded by an act of private Confession to the Priest." [1]

It is well known that there was no compulsory confession to a Priest anywhere in the Church in early days, as a con-

---
[1] Scudamore, *Not. Euch.*, pp. 510, 511.

dition of Communion. Even heinous offences were required to be confessed in public, and the custom was continued until it was found to be the occasion of needless scandal. Auricular confession to a priest in private (literally, *to the ear*) was only made obligatory in the Western Church by the fourth Lateran (Roman) Council in 1215. It is not the rule today, and never has been, in the Oriental Churches of Greece, Russia, Armenia, etc.

Our present rule is simply a return to the primitive custom of *voluntary* confession to a Priest in a case of necessity.[1] The first "Warning" in the English Book does not forbid such private confession, and private absolution, but says, "And because it is requisite that no man should come to the Holy Communion but with a full trust in God's mercy, and with a quiet conscience; therefore if there be any of you, who by this means [self examination] cannot quiet his own conscience therein but requireth further comfort or counsel, let him come to me, or to some other discreet and learned Minister of God's Word and open his grief; that, by the ministry of God's holy Word, he may receive the benefit of absolution, together with ghostly counsel and advice, to the quieting of his conscience, and avoiding of all scruple and doubtfulness." Concerning this Mr. Blunt writes: "One of the most remarkable of the peculiar features of the Anglican Communion Offices is the anxious carefulness shown by the Church to ensure that communicants shall approach the Lord's Table after due preparation and with right dispositions. The mixture of grave warning and tender encouragement in this Service is indeed truly

---

[1] Speaking of private confession as a habit, Mr. Baring-Gould says, "It enfeebles the moral fibre, and makes weak natures become weaker . I have often enough heard young Romanists talk of being 'whitewashed'" (*The Church Revival*, p. 306).

CONFESSION, ABSOLUTION, &c 169

wonderful. There is nothing like it in the Offices of any other Communion."[1]

The ABSOLUTION, which is the same as that in both the First and Second Books, is taken, with a slight change, from the prayer of the assisting "Ministers" for the absolution of the Celebrant after he has said the *Confiteor* in the old English Use. "Authority thus to remit sin, as to exercise in other ways 'the Ministry of Reconciliation',[2] is derived from the original grant of our Blessed Lord to the first rulers of His Church: — 'Receive ye the Holy Ghost. Whose soever sins ye remit, they are remitted unto them; and whose soever sins ye retain, they are retained.'[3] The Priest is acting on this commission whenever, as the guardian of any spiritual privilege [for instance, the 'one Baptism for the remission of sins,' as in the Nicene Creed, and Acts ii. 38], he imparts it to one whom he deems worthy, and denies it to another whom he deems unworthy."[4]

---

[1] *Ann Pr. Bk*, p. 179. Liddon says of Dr. Pusey, "Neither now [1844], nor at any other time in his life, did he treat the practice of private confession as a matter of absolute obligation on the part of anyone. Besides, he had extreme difficulties in his own case. He was so overwhelmed with the consciousness of his sins that he shrunk from making a confessor of one of those friends with whom he was associated in common work, and outside this circle, there was no one whom he could choose as a spiritual guide" *Life of Pusey*, III, p 96 The American Prayer Book *alone* omits "that by the ministry of God's holy Word he may receive the benefit of absolution," but in view of our Lord's solemn words, which are repeated over the Priest at his ordination, omission in this case does not necessarily mean prohibition. The Scottish and Irish Books retain the words.

[2] 2 Cor. v, 18.

[3] S. John xx, 22, 23.

[4] Scudamore, *Not Euchar.*, p. 515. See also chaps xxxiii and xxxvi.

Archbishop Bramhall (of Armagh, 1660–1663) says the power of "the Keys of the Kingdom of Heaven" (S. Matt. xvi, 19), to loose or bind, is exercised in many ways: "By Baptism, by the Sacrament of the Lord's

"There is somehow an idea," writes Mr. Sadler, "that even a delegated and conditional power of Absolution is too sacred a matter to be exercised by man; but when we attentively consider it, is it one whit more difficult to apprehend that man can absolve than that man can administer the Lord's Supper? . . . Is it one whit more easy to believe that one man can be the instrument, in God's hands, of communicating to another that inward part, to which the Saviour applies such terms as His Body and His Blood, than to believe that the same man can, in the Name of the same Omnipresent Saviour, and by the use of certain words, make his penitent fellow-sinner a partaker of the Atonement purchased by the breaking of that Body of Christ, and the shedding of His Blood? . . . But it has been objected that the Apostles had this power conferred upon them because they had the power of 'discerning spirits,' and that the latter gift is necessary to the right exercise of Absolu-

---

Supper, by Prayer, by preaching the Word of Reconciliation, by special Absolution: 'Whose sins ye remit they are remitted.' . . . God remits sovereignly, imperially, primitively, absolutely, the Priest's power is derivative, delegate, dependent, ministerial, conditional " (*Protestants' Ordination Defended*, V. 213, in Anglo-Catholic Library)

Concerning this "power and commandment to His Ministers to declare and pronounce to His people, being penitent, the Absolution and Remission of their sins" (see the Absolution in Morning and Evening Prayer), Bishop Brownell of Connecticut (1819-1865), in his comments upon the Ordinal in his "Family Prayer Book," quotes Archbishop Secker (1693-1768) as follows: "This power, being bestowed for the edification of the Church, must be restrained, not only by general rules of order, but according to particular exigencies of circumstances. But how little soever exerted, the power is inherent in the office of priesthood. And though we are no more infallible in our proceedings and sentences than temporal judges are in theirs, yet our acts as well as theirs are to be respected as done by competent authority. And if they are done on good grounds also, 'Whatsoever we bind or loose on earth will be bound or loosed in heaven.'"

CONFESSION, ABSOLUTION, &c 171

tion. But they who say this totally mistake the nature and intent of this gift. . . . It appears to me little short of blasphemy to suppose that this 'discerning of spirits' was a 'discerning of the thoughts and intents of the heart'; for this latter is, throughout Scripture, ascribed to God only, as one of His incommunicable attributes; and yet we find that good men scruple not to ascribe this divine power to the Apostles, in order to avoid granting to their successors a power of absolution, on the very face of it delegated, ministerial, subordinate, and conditional. . . . The person who absolved, absolved not infalliby as a judge, but conditionally as a servant or minister . . . *always referring the ratification of his act to the Searcher of hearts.*" [1]

THE COMFORTABLE WORDS with which the Preparation, or Pro-Anaphora, ends are peculiar to the revised English Liturgy, and need no apology. They are a very beautiful enrichment, such as the wisdom and devotion of other revisions throughout the centuries have given to this highest office of the Church's worship. The words of S. John that tell of the scene before the throne in Heaven, and the "Advocate with the Father, Jesus Christ the Righteous," the Eternal "Propitiation for our sins," is surely a wonderfully fitting close to the act of preparation, and an equally fitting prelude to the exclamation which forms the beginning of the Anaphora, Canon, or essential part of every great Liturgy in the world, namely, the *Sursum Corda*, "Lift up your hearts," with its response, "We lift them up unto the Lord." [2]

[1] *Church Doctrine Bible Truth*, pp. 234 sq

[2] The only two exceptions where the *Sursum Corda* is absent are two Liturgies of no special note, namely, the Syro-Jacobite of S Chrysostom and of John of Antioch. For the bearing of this minor but most striking feature on the Apostolic origin of *all* the Liturgies, see *The Christian Year*, p. 37.

CHAPTER XVIII

THE CELEBRATION: ANAPHORA OR CANON

"*Whene'er I seek the Holy Altar's rail,*
    And kneel to take the grace there offered me,
It is no time to task my reason frail,
    To try Christ's words, and search how they may be;
Enough, I eat His Flesh and drink His Blood,
More is not told — to ask it is not good" — NEWMAN.

THE SURSUM CORDA marks the beginning of the actual celebration of the mystery which our Lord ordained as His perpetual memorial, and for the spiritual food of His people. Here therefore is the keynote of the whole service. It is not merely a Communion whereby each separate soul may feed on the spiritual food of Christ's Body and Blood, though that in itself is one of the marvelous and blessed *gifts* of the Sacrament. It is infinitely more than a mere token of communion and fellowship between Christian brethren, one with another; though that also is true. It is, first of all, the great act of the whole body of the Church in thanksgiving (*eucharistia*), adoration, and intercession with the Father, in union with Him of whom we are "branches" and "members",[1] and who is our Eternal Advocate, and "the Propitiation for our sins." For it is to be noted that throughout the whole service no prayer is addressed to the Son, or to the Holy Ghost, but to the Father only. We have here at the outset, if we but heed it, the correction of the too prevalent error of regarding the service merely as a "Communion." It brings us at once,

---

[1] S. John xv, 5; Eph. v, 30.

THE ANAPHORA OR CANON 173

after due preparation of confession and absolution, into the very courts of that Heaven which Christ has "opened to all believers," and in union with "Angels, and Archangels, and all the Company of Heaven."

"Back to Christ" is a good watchword of our day when rightly understood as a call to the study and imitation of Him as revealed in the New Testament story. But better still is that which we find here so deeply imbedded in all the liturgies of the world: "Up to Christ! Lift up your hearts to Him. Behold Him still pleading for us 'in the midst of the throne,'[1] mighty to save to the uttermost all who come to Him in penitence and love." It was the watchword of S. Stephen, and of every true believer after him: "Behold, I see the heavens opened, and the Son of Man standing at the right hand of God."

THE SERAPHIC HYMN, OR TERSANCTUS, usually followed by the *Benedictus qui venit* (*Blessed is He that cometh*, *etc.*) has its place here in all the ancient liturgies. The corresponding Greek word is TRISAGION which, like the Latin TERSANCTUS, means Thrice Holy. We have here one other reminiscence of the Temple service (in addition to one in the Lord's Prayer), where the third of the Eighteen Benedictions recited in the Temple daily, is as follows:— "Hallowed be Thy Name on earth as it is hallowed in heaven above, as it is written by the prophet, And one calls to the other, and says — Holy, Holy, Holy, is the Lord God of Sabaoth; the whole earth is filled with His glory."[2] It is preceded on certain festivals by what are called PROPER PREFACES, which connect it with the course of the Christian Year. It is to be regretted that only five of these Prefaces (for Christmas, Easter, Ascension Day, Whitsunday, and Trinity Sunday), were retained in our various revisions.

---
[1] Rev v, 6.   [2] Warren, *Lit and Rit. Ante-Nicene Church*, p. 195.

The old English use had in addition Proper Prefaces for the Epiphany, Ash-Wednesday, the Annunciation, the feasts of the Apostles and Evangelists, and some minor festival days. Some of these might well be restored in any future revision.[1]

The American Prayer Book has an alternate form for Trinity Sunday, while retaining "Holy Father" in the introduction, as follows: "For the precious death and merits of Thy Son, Jesus Christ, our Lord, and for the sending to us of the Holy Ghost, the Comforter; who are one with Thee in Thy Eternal Godhead." This may have been introduced in 1789 on account of the somewhat ambiguous language of the first Preface, evidently the result of a printer's error, the substitution of "or" for "of," which, like the similar error of "straining *at* a gnat" instead of "straining *out*," in our Authorized Version of S. Matt. xxiii, 24, our ultra conservatism has forbidden us to correct ever since 1549.[2]

---

[1] The Scottish Book has additional Proper Prefaces for the Epiphany, the Purification, the Annunciation, Feasts of Apostles and Evangelists, All Saints' Day, the Consecration of Bishops, the Ordination of Priests and Deacons, the Dedication of a Church, and the Anniversary

[2] The Latin of the Sarum Use, which is the same as that of the Sacramentary of Gelasius (A D 494), is "*Quod enim de Tua gloria revelante Te credimus, hoc de Filio Tuo, hoc de Spiritu Sancto sine differentia discretionis sentimus,*" which is manifestly "without difference *of* inequality," that is, without such difference as would constitute inequality For difference there is unquestionably, as there must necessarily be between the Three Divine Persons. All are equal and "of the same Substance," but, as the Athanasian Creed warns us, we must "neither confound the Persons, nor divide the Substance" Our continued mistranslation of this ancient Preface comes perilously near committing us to this error, which it is hoped a new revision will correct, as the equally egregious printer's mistake above referred to has already been corrected in the Revised New Testament. See Blunt, *Am Pr. Bk*, 184, and *Orig Lit.* IV, xv, p. 125.

THE ANAPHORA OR CANON 175

The beautiful PRAYER OF HUMBLE ACCESS, as it is called in the Scottish Book ("We do not presume, etc."), though composed in 1549, is found in substance in all the ancient liturgies. There, however, as in the First Prayer Book of Edward, and in the present Scottish, it occupied a place immediately before reception. While something may be said for the change as a fitting act of self abasement, recalling the confession of the centurion, "Lord, I am not worthy that Thou shouldest enter under my roof,"[1] and of the Syrophenician woman,[2] its presence here breaks the continuity of that lofty act of worship and adoration beginning with "Lift up your hearts," and continuing through the Prayer of Consecration.[3]

THE PRAYER OF CONSECRATION is to be said by the Priest "standing before the Table," or, as it was in the First Book of Edward, "standing humbly afore the midst of the altar." In the First Book it began, as we have seen, with what is now the Prayer for Christ's Church Militant as far as "any other adversity," followed by a commendation of the living and the faithful departed, and the Invocation of the Holy Spirit upon the elements as in all the ancient Liturgies. The present English Canon of Consecration, following the emasculated one of 1552, begins with the address, "Almighty God, our heavenly Father, who of Thy tender mercy didst give Thine only Son Jesus Christ to suffer death upon the Cross, etc.," followed by a petition, faintly suggestive of the Invocation, that "we receiving these

---

[1] S. Luke vii, 6   [2] S. Mark vii, 28.

[3] The two Houses of the American General Convention in 1889, and the House of Bishops in 1892, adopted the proposal of the Committee of Revision to put this prayer in its ancient place, but it failed, by the lack of a single vote of the Committee of the whole in the House of Clerical and Lay Deputies, to receive the required ratification of the Convention of 1892.

Thy creatures of bread and wine, etc., may be partakers of His most blessed Body and Blood," and ends with the manual acts of breaking the bread, and "laying the hand upon every vessel" etc., while repeating our Lord's words of Institution. This may be confidently asserted to be the weakest part of all the present English Book. While the act of consecration, bald and brief as it is, is undoubtedly valid, no precise words or moment being fixed for consecration in the earliest liturgies, it is certainly very far from the dignity and richness of every ancient Use.

In his *Alliance of Divine Offices*, first published in 1659, the learned Hamon L'Estrange called attention to the singular inconsistency of the English revisers of 1552 in actually adopting the Roman theory of consecration of the Sacrament by the omission of the Invocation of the Holy Spirit on the elements. He says, "The recitation of these words (This is My Body, etc.) pass in the common vogue for a consecration; were I Romishly inclined, I should rather impute unto them the power of transubstantiation, for that a bare narrative can be qualified to consecrate is certainly new divinity, unknown to Scripture, and antiquity interpreting it".[1] For it is a fact that the Roman Liturgy, alone among all the great Liturgies of the world, is curiously lacking in having no Invocation of the Holy Spirit upon the elements. Instead, it asks that they may be carried "by the hands of Thy holy angel to Thy sublime altar," that thereby "we may receive the sacred Body and Blood of Thy Son, etc." Concerning this Duchesne acknowledges that "this prayer is far from exhibiting the precision of the Greek formularies."[2]

---

[1] chap. vii, K.

[2] *Christian Worship*, p. 181 See also above, chap. xii, p. 123 in letter of Bishop Seabury to Bishop White. Compare Ffoulkes, *Prim.*

THE ANAPHORA OR CANON 177

Much is lost to us by regarding this Sacrament merely as a Communion. It is indeed that channel of Christ's pardon and grace which has been aptly termed by Bishop Jeremy Taylor "the extension of the Incarnation," and by Dr. Liddon, "the certified point of contact" with His glorified and life-giving Humanity. Nevertheless, this is far from all that our Lord had in mind for our blessing. The first purpose of the Sacrament is declared to be, as the Catechism clearly puts it almost in His own words, "for the continual remembrance [before God, and before man] of the sacrifice of the death of Christ." That is, here is the sublime occasion when the whole Church ("we," and not merely the officiating Priest, who is but the Church's mouthpiece) pleads on earth, as Christ in His "unchangeable priest-

---

Consecration, 466–9. Concerning different forms of the Invocation Bishop Maclean writes "By an 'explicit Invocation' is meant one which prays that the elements may become or be made the Body and Blood of Christ to the end that the communicants may be blessed, by an 'implicit Invocation' one which omits the express reference to the change in the elements." *Ancient Church Orders*, p 41 Examples of both kinds are found in the Liturgies, but the greatest and most ancient have explicit formulæ. See Neale and Littledale, *Prim Lit*, 1869, pp 24, 51, 85, 114, 134 The Scottish Invocation has *all* the most ancient features, explicit prayer for the Holy Spirit on "these gifts, etc , that they may become the Body and Blood of Thy most dearly beloved Son " The American, while *explicitly* invoking "Thy Word [that is, the Lord Jesus] and Holy Spirit, to bless and sanctify these Thy gifts, that we, receiving them, etc , may be partakers of His most blessed Body and Blood," is *implicit*. In this it follows some early Liturgies, e. g. that of Sarapion. (See Maclean, *Anct. Ch. Orders*, p. 54) The English together with the Roman, though valid, is defective in omitting mention of the Holy Ghost, and in having only an *implicit* Invocation "that we receiving these Thy creatures, etc. may be partakers, etc."

In *A Prayer Book Revised*, prepared by "many liturgical scholars," and with a preface by Bishop Gore of Oxford (1913), the Scottish and American Prayers of Consecration are recommended. The Prayer of Humble Access also is put in its original position immediately before the Communion.

hood,"[1] "a Lamb as it had been slain,"[2] still bearing in His glorified Body the five wounds of His cross, the tokens of His unchangeable love, pleads for us "continually" in Heaven. That "one oblation of Himself once offered" upon the Cross, whereby He "made a full, perfect, and sufficient sacrifice for the sins of the whole world," can never be repeated; but His work of intercession as "a Priest for ever," and also "a sacrifice for ever" (Ps. cx, 4; Heb. x, 12), continues "until His coming again."

For though the mystery of an "atoning" sacrifice remains, and may for ever remain, it is to be remembered that no sacrifice consists in the mere infliction of death. As all sacrifice is necessarily a conscious, a moral, and not a mere physical act, every such act must be "a *living* sacrifice." Such was Abraham's when, in giving his loved and only son, whose unwilling death could in itself have no more moral or spiritual value than that of a lamb or an ox, he gave himself. Such too was our Lord's, though in His case "unto death, even the death of the cross." "I consecrate Myself," He said.[3]

In order to understand what our Lord meant by "Do this in remembrance of Me," we must bear in mind the nature of the solemn service in which He had been then engaged, and out of the very elements of which He ordained the infinitely loftier service which was its fulfilment. The Paschal lamb of which they had partaken had been offered to God "in remembrance" beforehand of the true Lamb of God who should "take away the sins of the world" in reality and not merely in type. It was the mute sign on which the Divine Father was called to look as an *anamnesis* or memorial of the promised Redeemer. For 1500 years the Church of Israel had been pleading this in obedience to

---
[1] Heb. vii, 3, 24. [2] Rev. v, 6. [3] Phil. ii, 8; S John xvii, 19.

THE ANAPHORA OR CANON 179

the Divine command, but ignorant of its true fulfilment. Now the moment has come to make it clear, and His disciples are bidden "Do this" — offer this, as the word is understood by many of the Fathers — "as My *anamnesis*, My memorial before God and man, until I come."

In the Prayer of Consecration in the First Book of Edward, which was adopted almost without change in the Scottish Book of 1637, and the American as revised in 1789, we see this true sacrificial character of the Holy Eucharist as it is found also in all the primitive Liturgies. This is very different from the popular mediæval notion of "sacrifices of Masses, in the which it was commonly said, that the Priest did offer Christ [*anew*, that is] for the quick and the dead," and which are condemned as "blasphemous fables, and dangerous deceits" in the 31st Article of Religion.

And so the Eucharist is the Church's "sacrifice of praise and thanksgiving," a truer sacrifice by far than any that were ever offered on Jewish altars. These were but faint shadows of the one true Sacrifice that was to come. Ours is the "unbloody sacrifice," like that of Melchizedek of old, "priest of the Most High God"[1] who brought forth no slain beast, but only "bread and wine." With us these elements are no more empty signs of a thing absent, but sacraments filled with the grace and power of Christ's Body broken, and His Blood shed for us. And here we ask God to look on them and "remember His everlasting covenant," as He promised concerning that great *natural* Sacrament of His Love, the "bow in the cloud," "That gracious thing made up of tears and light"[2] of which He said, "I will look upon it, *that I may remember*."[3]

The true idea of the sacrificial aspect of the Eucharist, combined with the fulness of its blessing as a Holy Com-

---
[1] Heb. vii 1.   [2] Coleridge, *Two Founts*.   [3] Gen. ix, 16.

munion, is most happily expressed in the following verses by one who combined the devout spirit of a Christian poet with the learning of a theologian, the late Canon Bright: —

> Wherefore, we sinners, mindful of the love
> That bought us, once for all, on Calvary's Tree,
> And having with us Him that pleads above,
> Do here present, do here spread forth to Thee,
> That only offering perfect in Thine eyes,
> The one, true, pure immortal Sacrifice.
>
> Look, Father, look on His anointed face,
> And only look on us, as found in Him;
> Look not on our misusings of Thy grace,
> Our prayer so languid, and our faith so dim;
> For lo, between our sins and their reward,
> We set the Passion of Thy Son, our Lord.
>
> And then for those, our dearest and our best,
> By this prevailing Presence, we appeal;
> O fold them closer to Thy mercy's breast,
> O do Thine utmost, for their souls' true weal!
> From tainting mischief keep them white and clear,
> And crown Thy gifts with strength to persevere.
>
> And so we come,— O draw us to Thy feet,
> Most patient Saviour, who canst love us still:
> And by this Food, so awful and so sweet,
> Deliver us from every touch of ill:
> In Thine own service make us glad and free,
> And grant us never more to part with Thee.

It is this sacrificial aspect of the Holy Communion which makes clear to us the true nature of *all* priesthood in the Christian Church. It will be observed that in the Prayer of Consecration, as in every other Liturgy, the Celebrant never uses the word "I," but always "we" — "we offer,"

THE ANAPHORA OR CANON 181

"*we* present — *we* ask — *we* bless." And the reason of this is evident. The officiating Priest is but the mouthpiece of the priestly People, their official spokesman, both *with* and *for* his flock. Even his "eastward position" at the altar, as a shepherd going before his flock, shows this. It is here therefore that the People exercise their "royal" and very real priesthood. For they themselves are also consecrated to God, not only in "the washing of regeneration" in Baptism, but even in the Laying on of Hands for the gift of the Holy Ghost in Confirmation, just as the ministerial Priest is consecrated by "the Laying on of Hands" for the same gift in Ordination.[1]

The unreasoning objection to priesthood and "sacerdotalism" in the clergy would not be so often heard if this "sacerdotalism" of Christian laymen, and their great privilege as themselves "priests of the Most High God," were rightly understood and realized. For even under the old Dispensation this was true of every Israelite. "Ye shall be to Me a kingdom of priests" was what God said to ancient Israel.[2] In how much higher sense, then, are they priests of whom it is said that they are "members of Christ," the great High Priest, "of His Body, of His Flesh, and of His Bones," having "put on Christ" in Holy Baptism, and been "anointed" with the Holy Ghost in Confirmation.[3] It is to such that S. Peter writes, "Ye are a chosen generation, a royal priesthood" (ἱεράτευμα, *sacerdotium*); and that

---

[1] Tit. iii, 5; Acts xix, 6; xiii, 3. See also chap xxx. This priestly part taken by the people is further emphasized by the rule of one of the earliest Liturgies, *The Testament of our Lord*, where the congregation say with the celebrant the prayer of Oblation in the midst of the Eucharistic service. See Maclean, *Recent Discoveries*, pp. 14, 102.

[2] Ex. xix, 6.

[3] Eph. v, 30, Gal. iii, 27.

S. John says, "Christ hath made us kings and priests (ἱερεῖς, *sacerdotes*) unto God and His Father."[1]

Here in fact is the solid ground of responsibility in every Christian layman. He too is a priest, and can no more unrobe himself of that which he has "put on," than the ministerial priest can unrobe himself, without disgrace and sin and eternal loss.[2] Well may we say in the half ironical language of the saintly Bishop Leighton, speaking of this priesthood or *sacerdotium* of the layman, "It is not so mean a thing as we think to be a Christian" (*Works*, I. 262). It is of this "mysterious state in which all Christians stand" even now, that Newman has beautifully said, "They are ministers round the throne of their reconciled Father; kings and priests unto God; having their robes washed in the Lamb's Blood, and being consecrated as temples of the Holy Ghost."[3]

But real and glorious as is this universal priesthood, it does not exclude the ministerial priesthood. So far from doing so it seems only to make it the more necessary. For if the universal priesthood of the people of Israel did not

---

[1] Rev. i 6. Commenting on this passage S. Augustine says, "This refers not to the Bishops and Presbyters alone, who are now specially called priests (*sacerdotes*) in the Church, but as we call all believers 'Christians,' so we call all 'priests' (*sacerdotes*), because they are members of the one Priest." *Civ Dei*, xx, 10.

[2] "It is worthy of notice how those Nonconforming bodies, which lay stress in this matter on the authority of S Peter and S. John, have robbed the laity of their prerogative, and precluded them almost entirely from all part in the offering of public worship. A comparison of the ordinary service and the parts assigned to the congregation and the ministers as appointed in the Church and in any Dissenting Chapel will exhibit the contrast in a very marked manner." (Luckock, *Studies in the Prayer Book*, p. 7, note)

[3] *Par. and Plain Sermons*, III. 264.

THE ANAPHORA OR CANON 183

exclude a ministerial priesthood, as the rebels under Korah asserted it did, and as God declared it did not,[1] why should the universal priesthood of the Christian Church interfere with or exclude a ministerial priesthood? There is clearly no contradiction, such as men are fond of assuming, between the general and the special priesthood. It is true the priesthood is of the whole body of the Church. But why should not this function of the *whole* body be exercised by a particular limb, or a particular organ, as in the natural body, or by a particular person, as under the old covenant? That is S. Paul's unanswerable argument when headstrong or ignorant Christians in Corinth opposed his own official character as an Apostle. "The body is not one member, but many. . . . If the whole body were an eye, where were the hearing? . . . Are all apostles?" he asks.[2] "All members have not the same office," is what he reminds his fellow Christians in Rome also.[3] This is simply a necessity in *all* government, in the state, the family, and in any voluntary club, as well as in the Church. And it is in the very act of celebrating the Holy Communion, which is so dependent on the special sacerdotal powers of the ministerial priesthood, that we find the best illustration of this twofold *sacerdotium* — that of the lay priest and of the other, each in his own sphere and "office."[4] There is no setting of one above the other, or putting the ministerial priest between any soul and God. *Both* are sacrificers, pleaders, intercessors, mediators with God, through the one Mediator and Sacrifice. But one is neces-

---

[1] Num xvi, and Jude 11
[2] 1 Cor xii, 14, 17, 29
[3] Rom xii, 4,
[4] Compare Bishop Gore, *The Church and the Ministry, A Review of Dr. Hatch's Bamp. Lec* pp 23, sq.

sarily the mouthpiece of the Body of Christ, and all speak to God through him.[1]

---

[1] On the general subject of the Ministerial Priesthood, see chap. xxxvi–xxxix. Liddon speaks of "sacerdotalism" as "a formidable word, harmless in itself, but surrounded with very invidious associations" (*Univ Ser*, 2nd series, 191) "The chief ideas commonly associated with sacerdotalism, which it is important to repudiate," writes Bishop Gore, "is that of a *vicarious* priesthood. . . . It is an abuse of the sacerdotal conception, if it is supposed that the priesthood exists to celebrate sacrifices or acts of worship *in the place of* the body of the people, or as their *substitute*. This conception had, no doubt, attached itself to the 'massing priests' of the Middle Ages What is the truth then? It is that the Church is one body. The free approach to God in the Sonship and Priesthood of Christ belongs to men as members of 'one body,' and this one body has different organs through which the functions of its life find expression, as it was differentiated by the act and appointment of Him who created it" (*The Church and the Ministry*, pp 84–86) "If Christian laymen would only believe with all their hearts that they are really priests," writes Liddon, "we should very soon escape from some of the difficulties which vex the Church of Christ. Spiritual endowments are given to the Christian layman with one purpose, to the Christian minister with another: the object of the first is personal, that of the second is corporate" (*Univ. Ser*, 2nd series, p. 198) Each is a real priest in his own sphere, and so, in all the worship of the Church, it is never "*I* offer, *I* beseech, *I* intercede," but "*We* offer, *we* beseech, *we* intercede," and that not only for ourselves, but for "Thy whole Church, and for all men."

CHAPTER XIX
CHRIST'S PRESENCE IN THE HOLY COMMUNION

"*What these elements are in themselves it skilleth not, it is enough that to me which take them they are the Body and Blood of Christ His promise in witness hereof sufficeth, His word He knoweth which way to accomplish*" — HOOKER.

IT is very important to observe here that the Church of England and the Churches in communion with her have never formulated any theory as to how our Lord is present in the Holy Sacrament of His Body and Blood. Rome has her metaphysical theory of TRANSUBSTANTIATION, or the change of substance (not of "accidents," or visible form), into the sacred Body and Blood. This theory has been described as "bad theology based on worse psychology," and is declared by our 28th Article of Religion to be "repugnant to the plain words of Scripture," and as "overthrowing the nature of a Sacrament," inasmuch as a Sacrament is defined as having *two* parts," the outward visible sign, and the inward spiritual grace," whereas, according to the theory of a change of substance, only *one* part in reality remains, for the "accidents" are a mere cheat to the eye.[1]

Luther's theory of CONSUBSTANTIATION is perhaps equally objectionable. It is that "after consecration of the Eucharist, the substance of the Lord's Body and Blood co-exists in union with the substance of Bread and Wine, just as

---

[1] Gelasius, Bishop of Rome, in 490 wrote, "By the sacraments we are made partakers of the Divine Nature, and yet the substance or nature of bread and wine does not cease to be in them." For the original see Bingham, XV, v, 4, note 71.

iron and fire are united in a bar of heated iron."[1] The THEORY OF ZWINGLI of Zurich, on the other hand, regards "the Sacraments as mere signs of initiation and of a pledge to continue in the outward society. . . . They are not even pledges of grace."[2] This also is distinctly condemned in the 25th Article of Religion, where it is said that "Sacraments ordained of Christ be not only badges or tokens of Christian men's profession, but rather they be certain sure witnesses and effectual signs of grace . . . by which God doth work invisibly in us."

But all theories in regard to the *how* of Christ's presence in the Holy Sacrament are equally objectionable, and equally useless. Christ has not told us how, and the Church does not presume to define what He has *not* defined. "How can these things be?" Nicodemus asked when our Lord declared to him the mystery of the "water and of the Spirit" in Holy Baptism.[3] "How can this man give us His flesh to eat?" the unbelieving Jews asked when He declared the mystery of the other Sacrament.[4] And in each case the question was only met by a restatement and a fuller declaration of the mystery. The Anglican Communion is content to leave the matter just where our Lord left it when He said of the wind, "Thou canst not tell."[5] The mystery of His Presence in "the outward and visible sign" is no greater, no more comprehensible, He would have us know, than the presence of what we call life in a blade of grass, or an electric current in a piece of wire, or a soul in the body of a man. Physical science and Christian faith are at one in accepting the mystery in each case. Neither cares to ask the useless question "How?"[6] There

---

[1] Blunt, *Dic of Doc and His Theology*, s v
[2] *Ibid* p 812. [3] S John III, 1-14. [4] *Ibid* vi, 52. [5] *Ibid*. iii, 8.
[6] Cf. Hooker V, lxxvi, 12, p 460, Keble's ed.

CHRIST'S PRESENCE 187

was sound theology as well as sound philosophy in the answer attributed to Princess (afterwards Queen) Elizabeth when she replied to the question of one who would entrap her concerning the "how ": —

> "His was the Word that spake it;
> He took the bread and brake it,
> And what that Word did make it,
> That I believe, and take it."

Without attempting to define the *manner* of Christ's presence in the Sacrament, the Prayer Book asserts very clearly, as our Lord did, the *fact* of His presence. The Church is but following Him when, in the Prayer of Humble Access, and elsewhere, she speaks of "eating the Flesh [1] of Thy dear Son Jesus Christ, and drinking His Blood"; of "receiving the most precious Body and Blood," and of "the Body of Christ" as being "given" as well as "taken, and eaten in the Supper," though "only after a heavenly and spiritual manner." And all this is but employing the very language which our Lord employed, knowing perfectly as He did how men would, in these latter days, stumble at His marvelous language as "a hard saying," while He refused to alter or withdraw a single word, even when some of His disciples forsook Him on account of this "hardness." [2]

---

[1] The use of the word "Flesh" here instead of "Body" shows that the Church interprets our Lord's words in St John vi, where "Flesh" alone is used, as a definite instruction in preparation for the Holy Sacrament which He instituted a year later Compare Heb. x, 20

[2] S John vi, 60, 66 Coleridge presses home this point as follows: — "That those [who deny the genuineness of S John's Gospel] should object to the use of expressions which they had ranked among the most obvious marks of spuriousness, follows as a matter of course. But that men who with a clear and cloudless assent receive the sixth chapter of this Gospel as a faithful, nay, inspired record of an actual discourse, should take offence at the repetition of words which the Redeemer Himself, in the per-

188 PRIMITIVE WORSHIP & THE PRAYER BOOK

Hooker, with his keen philosophic sense, strikes at the root of the matter when he writes: "Sith we all agree that by the Sacrament Christ doth really and truly in us perform His promise, why do we vainly trouble ourselves with so fierce contentions whether by consubstantiation, or else by transubstantiation the Sacrament itself be first possessed with Christ, or no?" And again: — "Let curious and sharp-witted men beat their heads about what questions themselves will, the very letter of the word of Christ giveth plain security that these mysteries do as nails fasten us to His very Cross, that by them we draw out, as touching efficacy, force, and virtue, even the Blood of His gored side; in the wounds of our Redeemer we there dip our tongues, we are dyed red both within and without; our hunger is satisfied, and our thirst for ever quenched; they are things wonderful which he feeleth, great which he seeth, and unheard of which he uttereth, whose soul is possessed of this Paschal Lamb and made joyful in the strength of

---

fect foreknowledge that they would confirm the disbelieving, alienate the unstedfast, and transcend the present capacity even of His own elect, had chosen as the most appropriate, and which, after the most decisive proofs that they were misinterpreted by the greater number of His hearers, and not understood by any, He nevertheless repeated with stronger emphasis and without comment as the only appropriate symbols of the great truth he was declaring, and to realize which ἐγένετο σαρξ ["He was made flesh"], — that in their own discourses these men should hang back from all express reference to these words, as if they were afraid or ashamed of them, though the earliest recorded ceremonies and liturgical forms of the primitive Church are absolutely inexplicable, except in connection with this discourse, and with the mysterious and spiritual, not allegorical and merely ethical, import of the same, and though this import is solemnly and in the most unequivocable terms asserted and taught by their own Church, even in her Catechism, or compendium of doctrine necessary for all her members; — this I may perhaps understand, but this I am not able to vindicate or excuse" (*Aids to Reflection*, pp. 351, 352).

CHRIST'S PRESENCE 189

this new wine; this bread hath in it more than the substance which our eyes behold; this cup hallowed with solemn benediction availeth to the endless life and welfare both of soul and body, in that it serveth as well for a medicine to heal our infirmities and purge our sins, as for a sacrifice of thanksgiving; with touching, it sanctifieth; it enlighteneth with belief; it truly comformeth us unto the image of Jesus Christ. What these elements are in themselves it skilleth not, it is enough that to me which take them they are the Body and Blood of Christ. His promise in witness hereof sufficeth, His word He knoweth which way to accomplish; why should any cogitation possess the mind of a faithful communicant but this, O my God, Thou art true, O my soul, thou art happy!" [1]

It is surely a good test of one's freedom from intellectual prejudice to ask ourselves, Do I wish that Christ had used some words about this mystery other than those He has

---
[1] *Eccl Pol.*, V, lxvii, 6, 12. — Hooker elsewhere falls into the very error which he is here guarding others against when he formulates a theory of his own, though a negative one, concerning the "how" of Christ's presence, "The real presence of Christ's most blessed Body and Blood," he writes in this same chapter (section 6), " is not to be sought in the Sacrament, but in the worthy receiver of the Sacrament " Archdeacon Freeman points out that Hooker failed to notice that S. Paul does not say, "The bread which we *eat*, is it not the Communion of the Body of Christ?" but "The bread which we *break*," "the cup which we *bless*" (1 Cor. x, 16; *Prin. Div. Ser.* II Intro p. 208). Hence the 28th Article of Religion declares that " the Body of Christ is *given*" as well as "taken and eaten " To deny this would indeed be to adopt Calvin's theory that it is the faith of the receiver that makes Christ present, and not He who wrought the mystery of the Incarnation at the beginning, namely, "the Holy Ghost, the Power of the Highest," (S. Luke i, 35), "the Lord, and Giver of life," acting through His appointed ministers. The office of faith, S Paul tells us, is to "discern" the Lord's Body (1 Cor xi 29) as *already* present by the "breaking," and the "thanksgiving," and the "blessing," and not to *make* It present.

used, words such as He might easily have used? If He had meant, "This is only a visible token to *remind* you of My Body, but it is not My Body and Blood in any real sense," would He not have said so? But this is just what He did *not* say, and what He did say is very different, very wonderful, unspeakably glorious, the language of the King of heaven and earth, concerning whom it is written, "Eye hath not seen, nor ear heard, neither have entered into the heart of man, the things which God hath prepared for them that love Him" (1 Cor. ii. 9).

One thing only remains to be said concerning this great ordinance in its two-fold aspect, as the "continual remembrance [before God and man] of the sacrifice of the death of Christ," and as the means whereby the power of His incarnate life for holy living is conveyed to every worthy partaker. *It is the one and only act of public worship ordained by Him as His parting gift and command to His Church.* Other services have their use. This is essential to her very existence, and must be "continual," "until He come." Concerning this it has been wisely said: — "If only the Church will trust herself, and the Spirit of God that is in her! Let her concentrate all her power upon her central act of worship. Let her, in hours of perplexity, be content to reassert her central verities, avoiding definitions and deductions, leaving the declaration to do its work by its own spiritual weight and momentum. Let her give freedom, elasticity, variety, to her minor offices. Let her show to living people that she can teach them, in perfectly plain and simple speech, by ways that are intelligible to any human heart that cares to learn, how to live as they ought, and to die in Christ. She has but to be loyal to her own claims, and she shall live."[1]

---
[1] Canon Scott Holland, *Our Place in Christendom*, Lecture VII.

CHAPTER XX

COMMUNION AND POST-COMMUNION

"If I may but touch His garment, I shall be whole" — S Matt. ix, 21.

"*Touch Me not! awhile believe Me* [1]
*Touch Me not till Heaven receive Me
Then draw near, and never leave Me;
Then I go no more*" — Keble.

THE Church has nowhere, either by rubric or canon, laid down any rule in regard to preparation for Holy Communion in addition to the general one of SELF EXAMINATION concerning our repentance and faith, as stated in her Catechism, and in the Office itself. Nowhere, for instance, does she require that a communicant must come fasting to receive the Holy Sacrament. It is true that this was the rule of the Church generally for many centuries, not however because it was the rule "from the beginning," or as a question of essential right or wrong, but as a question of discipline, a detail in the matter of reverent preparation, over which each "particular or national Church" has complete jurisdiction.[2]

That FASTING COMMUNION was not the rule from the beginning is unquestioned. It was "after supper," that is, the Paschal Supper, that our Lord instituted the new spiritual feast of His Body and Blood.[3] In the Church of Corinth, founded by S. Paul, we know that as late as the year 57, when he wrote his first letter to that Church, the Sacrament was celebrated after the *Agapé*, or common love-feast, of which all were partakers.[4] Experience showed, how-

[1] S. John, xx 17. [3] S. Luke xxii, 20.
[2] *Art.* xxxiv. [4] 1 Cor. xi.

ever, that this practice led to serious abuses, probably in other Churches as well as in that of Corinth, and S. Paul with his apostolic authority interposed to correct them. Nevertheless, it is most important to observe that the Apostle, so far from commanding the Corinthians to fast as a necessary prerequisite for Communion, on the contrary says, "If any man hunger, let him *eat at home*, that ye come not together to condemnation." Thus he plainly contemplates that some at least would eat ordinary food before communicating, and without any condemnation in so doing. In other words the whole matter was left to the individual conscience, and this is exactly where the English-speaking Church leaves it also.

How then, it may be asked, did the custom of Fasting Communion grow up? The answer cannot be better expressed than in the words of Bishop Christopher Wordsworth of Lincoln: — "In sub-apostolic times — that is, in the days of persecution — it was usual to receive the Holy Communion very early in the morning. . . . Various reasons may be assigned for this. It may have been introduced on account of the irregularities to which the later reception had given rise at Corinth, and also because the hour, as well as the day, of our Lord's resurrection had a significant propriety for the administration of the Sacrament; and also because it was fit that this holy food should be the first received on that day, and probably also because, in times of persecution, the early twilight morning hour, with its quiet seclusion in the Catacombs, and other places of retreat, was the best that could have been chosen for the assemblies of Christians.

"It cannot be doubted that, at the close of the fourth century, it was the practice of the Church to receive the Communion before any other food, except on one day of

COMMUNION AND POST-COMMUNION 193

the year — namely on Maundy Thursday — the anniversary of the day when the Holy Communion was instituted. On that anniversary it was administered after supper, as a record of the time of its original institution by Christ.[1] All this is readily allowed, and it would be irreverent and presumptuous in us to say that the Church of God did not act wisely in this matter. . . . But it would be also irreverent and presumptuous in us to take upon ourselves to be legislators in ritual matters, and to impose customs, whether derived from the first century or from the fourth century, in a spirit of opposition to the laws and usages of the particular Church in which our lot is cast by the providence of God." [2]

While then it may be true that fasting Communion is the "more excellent way" for those who are physically able, it must not be forgotten that non-fasting and later, voluntary fasting, before Communion was the earliest custom of the Church. Such fasting moreover was not meant as an act of self-mortification, a thing forbidden on all feast days, but only of reverence.[3] Provided, therefore, that one comes with the preparation demanded by S. Paul in his letter to the communicants in Corinth, and by the Church in her Prayer Book, he need have no scruples about taking necessary food before Communion. The whole question of fasting Communion may indeed be summed up in the words — To receive fasting is an ancient and good custom; to communicate is a duty. It is plain then that

---
[1] See the author's *The Christian Year, Its Purpose and its History*, pp. 112, 113.

[2] *Charge to his Diocese* in 1882. See also the unanimous report of a committee of the Canterbury Convocation in 1893.

[3] While the custom of the East is to receive fasting, the responsibility of deciding if one can rightly receive with broken fast is left to the individual conscience

it is wrong to refrain from Communion where the *only* hindrance is the accidental lack of fasting, or the inability to fast.[1]

It is important to observe that the rubric in regard to receiving the Communion requires that it shall be given "into their hands," not fingers. This ancient rule and its reason are taught by S. Cyril, the Bishop of Jerusalem in the fourth century, when, as a priest, he was giving his last instruction to persons preparing for Holy Communion.[2]

---

[1] Compulsory fasting as well as compulsory confession to a priest, as a prerequisite to Communion, had much to do with the rare reception of the Sacrament in the mediæval Church, where only a single Communion in the year was obligatory, though attendance at the Office was required every Sunday. Bishop Kingdon of Fredericton, while defending fasting reception of the Holy Communion, as a custom, tells this anecdote concerning the modern Church of France under the mediæval rules — "A few years ago a Jesuit father, English by birth and education, was conducting a retreat for priests in the north of France. One day at the time of recreation, the parish Priest called on his brethren to sympathize with him in his satisfaction at having that day communicated *two men*. The English Priest was astonished. 'What, only two!' And the answer was, 'I have never seen such a sight before, during the twenty years I have been here as Curé.'" Dr Pusey in 1873 wrote to a correspondent: — "If there had been anything irreverent in receiving the Body and Blood of our Lord after food, our Lord would not so have instituted it. The division of the day at midnight is only arbitrary. When the day begins at sunset, it [that is, the following morning] is the same day." Concerning those unable to come fasting he says, — "I should think that such an one would show more reverence and love for our Lord's Body and Blood by receiving it at a definite time (three or four hours) after light food, or sooner after some liquid, than by excommunicating himself from it, it may be for months together, or being very probably incapable of thought at the time of communicating" See the *Guardian* (London), March 24th, 1897.

[2] *Catech. Lec.* XXIII In order to guard against a superstitious practice in mediæval days the Book of 1549 ordered that "the people commonly receive the Sacrament of Christ's Body in their mouths, at the Priest's hand." The primitive rule was restored in 1552.

COMMUNION AND POST-COMMUNION 195

Reverence requires also that no gloves should be worn, and no handkerchief carried nor veil allowed to droop over the cup. It is surely thoughtless, to say the least, for any one to wipe away from the lips so sacred a thing as that which our Lord calls His Blood. It is prudent of the Priest to retain a slight hold of the cup for the purpose of guarding against accident, but a similar reason will make him insist that the cup shall be firmly taken by "the hands," and not merely placed by him to the lips.[1]

Custom varies much in regard to saying all the words of administration, "The Body etc.," "The Blood etc.," to each communicant. When there are many to receive, the rubric seems to be sufficiently fulfilled if only the precatory portion is used to each, though even a more liberal rule would preserve the spirit of the law. It is very noteworthy that this prayer, "preserve thy *body* and soul," again connects this Holy Sacrament directly with our Lord's preparatory teaching in S. John vi where He associates the resurrection of our bodies with the eating of His Flesh and drinking of His Blood (verse 54).[2]

In the Lord's Prayer, which immediately follows, and is to be said by all as the beginning of their thanksgiving, the "daily bread" should have its highest, and really primary, meaning in the thought of every devout communicant. "I am the Living Bread," said our Lord. "The Bread that I will give is My Flesh."[3] This too is the interpretation in the Church Catechism — "all things needful for our souls and bodies" — both kinds, but first of all for every

---

[1] See also chap. xvi, pp. 160, 161

[2] It is well worth noting that the only word employed in the Prayer Book for the act of receiving the Communion is "communicate." "Commune" suggests a much lower conception, and should be avoided.

[3] S. John vi, 51.

true believer, "the meat that endureth unto everlasting life" (verse 27). John Wesley's comment on the petition for "daily bread" is: "not only the meat that perisheth, but the Sacramental Bread, and Thy Grace." [1]

The first POST-COMMUNION prayer that follows in the English Book is scarcely a prayer of thanksgiving. It forms the concluding part of the Prayer of Consecration in the Scottish and American books. The second, and alternative prayer is the thanksgiving in all the books. It was composed in 1549.

The GLORIA IN EXCELSIS, which is an enlargement of the song of the angels at the Nativity, had a most appropriate place at the beginning of the service in the early liturgies, and in the First Book, as heralding the coming of the Incarnate One to sinful men. In the East it is called the "Great Doxology," and from the earliest days has been a hymn in the daily Morning Office. In mediæval days in England its use was confined in the Eucharistic service to certain seasons, being omitted in Advent, and from Septuagesima to Easter Even. "The English Church at her Revision," Archdeacon Freeman writes, "after restoring the great Hymn at first to continual use, was most infelicitous subsequently in placing it *after* consecration and reception. Even as placed there, indeed, it cannot but serve an excellent purpose; as did the *Agnus Dei* — an extract from the Gloria in Excelsis — placed of old in our own and in the Roman Use between consecration and recep-

---

[1] The Greek word translated "daily" — *epiousion* — occurs only in the Lord's Prayer (S Matt vi, 11, S. Luke xi, 3), and its exact meaning is somewhat uncertain. The best translation seems to be that of the early Syriac version which renders it by "necessary," "the bread of our necessity." The Latin Vulgate gives the word "supersubstantial," which is a literal translation of the Greek, but scarcely conveys its meaning.

COMMUNION AND POST-COMMUNION 197

tion. But, ritually speaking, the transposition is as clear a departure from the ancient method of using it, as its restoration to constant use was accordant therewith." [1]

The BLESSING OF PEACE which closes the service is, as Mr. Scudamore says, at "once the grandest and the most calmly solemn extant." The first clause is taken from Phil. iv 7. Its greatness and dignity are recognized by its being reserved for the use of the Bishop, if he be present, even though a Priest has been the Celebrant.

It is provided that WHAT REMAINS OF THE CONSECRATED ELEMENTS shall be reverently consumed, and not carried out of the Church. The universal custom in the Primitive Church was for the Deacons to carry the Sacrament to the sick, and to those absent for similar reasons. Though this is not now the rule, and though the Church has provided a special office for the Communion of the Sick, this rubric has not usually been construed to forbid the reservation of a portion of the consecrated elements for use in certain extreme cases, as of epidemic, or the insufficiency of Clergy, or the lack of decent conditions in the crowded portions of great cities. There is no direction for what is called the ABLUTIONS, but a proper reverence has dictated the custom of pouring a little water, or water and wine, into the vessels in order to enable the Minister to "reverently" consume any remainder that might still adhere to them.

The custom of RESERVING A PORTION OF THE HOLY SACRAMENT, in order to permit reception by the sick, and others hindered from coming to the public administration, was the universal rule of the Primitive Church as described by Justin Martyr about A.D. 150, and is still the rule of the whole Eastern Church [2] In the Western Church in med-

---
[1] *Prin Div Ser.* I, 225, 226; II, pp 320, 321.
[2] *First Apol* Chap 65.

iæval days reservation had come to be employed in a very different way, namely for purposes of devotion and adoration. "This later Western use of the reserved Sacrament," writes Bishop Gore of Oxford, "as a permanent centre of devotion has not behind it either Catholic or ancient authority. The Eastern Church does not know it, and the ancient Church did not know it. It has not the sanction of our own part of the Church, the Church of England." [1]

In the Book of 1549 this practice of constant reservation was abandoned, and the primitive rule was restored. If the need fell upon a day when the Holy Communion was celebrated in church, the Priest was ordered to "reserve (at the open Communion) so much of the Sacrament of the Body and Blood as shall serve the sick person, and so many as shall communicate with him. And so soon as he conveniently may, after the open Communion ended in the Church, shall go and minister the same, etc. . . . And if there be more sick to be visited the same day that the Curate doth celebrate in any sick man's house," when there is no celebration in the Church, the same rule of reservation is to be observed as at the public celebration. In the Book of 1552 this provision was omitted, and has not since been restored in the English, Irish, or American Books. [2]

---

[1] *Oxford Diocesan Magazine*, Oct., 1915.

[2] In view of the needs of large city parishes, crowded tenement houses, and the lack of decent provision for the externals of a reverent service, both Houses of the Convocation of Canterbury adopted in 1915 the following new rubric (which has not yet, however, become the law of the whole Church of England): — "When the Holy Communion cannot be reverently or without grave difficulty celebrated in private, and also when there are several sick persons in the parish desirous to receive the Communion on the same day, it shall be lawful for the Priest (with the consent of the sick person), on any day when there is a celebration of the

THE SCOTTISH CHURCH has the following rubric: —

"According to long existing custom in the Scottish Church, the Presbyter may reserve so much of the Consecrated Gifts as may be required for the Communion of the sick, and others who could not be present at the celebration in church."

THE BLACK RUBRIC, as it is called, defends the custom of kneeling to receive the Holy Communion against those Puritans who objected to it "either out of ignorance and infirmity, or out of malice and obstinacy." It was appended to the office in 1552, and after being omitted in 1559, was restored in 1662, but with an important alteration. The earlier form had declared that "no adoration was done or ought to be done, either unto the Sacramental Bread or Wine there bodily received, or unto any *real and essential Presence* there being of Christ's natural Flesh and Blood." The words "real and essential Presence" were changed to "any Corporal Presence," thus retaining the protest against transubstantiation, while guarding against any denial of our Lord's real and essential Presence in the Sacrament. The rubric was omitted from the American Book of 1789.

Holy Communion in the church, to set apart at the open Communion, etc.," as in the Book of 1549 It also provides that if the elements are not taken immediately to the sick person, "they shall be kept in such place as the Ordinary shall approve, so that they be not used for any other purpose whatever."

CHAPTER XXI
DAILY MORNING AND EVENING PRAYER: MATINS AND EVENSONG

"Thou makest the outgoings of the morning and evening to praise Thee." — PSALM LXV, 8.

AS we have seen in the Eucharistic Service the fulfilment and successor of the Paschal Service of the older Church, so we find in the daily Offices of MATINS AND EVENSONG [1] the successor of the daily prayers of the Temple and synagogue. The early Christians, in addition to their "Breaking of the Bread," that is, celebrating the Holy Communion, "at home," "continued daily with one accord in the Temple," where prayers were offered up at 9 A.M. and 3 P.M.[2]

It is very noteworthy that only in the Anglican Communion are these two primitive offices of Divine Service preserved for the use of the people. In all other branches of the Catholic Church they are confined to the clergy. It is one of the glories of the English-speaking Church that

---

[1] Acts ii, 46, iii, 1.

[2] Matins, or Mattins, and Evensong are the alternative and more convenient words used in the Calendar of the English Prayer Book. Evensong is the later form of the Anglo-Saxon Evensang for Nones (3 p m), as Nightsang was the name for Vespers (Maskell, *Mon. Rit.* II, viii) It was the popular word even in mediæval times, according to the proverb, "Be the day short or ever so long, At length it ringeth to Evensong " "Beautiful names, good English Reformation words," wrote Dr W R Huntington in 1892, "which it is a great pity to have lost from the American Book in 1789." It is to be hoped that they will be restored in the revision now in progress (1913-1919).

MATINS AND EVENSONG

all her children have this great privilege of daily worship, with its moulding influence of psalm and lesson, creed and prayer, fast and feast, either public or in private, though it may be only valued and used by the few. "The English Church in this matter is the heir of the world," writes Freeman. "She may have diminished her inheritance; but all other Western Churches have thrown it away." [1]

It is then surely well worth remembering that every day throughout the year the prayers and praises of this Book are going up unceasingly to the throne of God from the lips and hearts of devout worshippers wherever the English tongue is spoken. This thought should be an inspiration to every Priest and layman whenever only "two or three are gathered together in His Name." "Were there many at the church today?" was the question put to a clergyman as he returned from a weekday service. "The church was full," was the reply, and to the wondering look of his enquirer he added, "full of angels." That surely is also a fact worth remembering.

There were only two "HOURS OF PRAYER" in the Jewish Temple, namely, at the time of the morning and evening sacrifice, between which hours the Lord Jesus was hanging

---

[1] *Prin Div Ser* I, 279. He quotes also from Ward's *Divine Service·* "Roman controversialists not unfrequently compare the poverty of our two Offices with the richness of their seven." But "the priests of that Church keep these seven Offices to themselves, convents and cathedral choirs alone excepted, and yet that exclusive use is a burden to them. Offices moulded for joint or common use are muttered over in private, and even when sung in choir are *never listened to or joined in* by the people. The laity are absolutely ignorant of the Psalms, which always formed the chief manual of devotion in former days, so much so as to have been called 'the Prayer Book of the Saints.' The seven Penitential Psalms are all that are known among them. In France and England the Sunday Vesper Psalms are also known."

on the Cross as the true "Lamb of God which taketh away the sin of the world,"[1] and of whom these sacrifices were but mute signs and foreshadowings. Devout men were accustomed to mark the noon hour also as a time of prayer, as we find Daniel and S. Peter doing;[2] and the Psalmist says, "In the evening, and morning, and at noon-day will I pray."[3] But for the public worship of the congregation in Israel only the evening and morning service was the rule. It would be most natural that this should become the rule also of the first Christian converts among the Jews. It seems to have become the custom throughout the whole Church as early as the third century.[4] When "the Church of Malabar, said to have been founded by the apostle S. Thomas," writes Archdeacon Freeman, "was discovered by the Portuguese in 1501, 'The priests,' it was found, 'performed the Divine Office twice daily, at three in the morning and five in the evening' a striking testimony, as it would seem, to the general correctness of the view which we have been led to, as to the ancient practice in this matter."[5] This daily worship, which as a service in church was "neither of apostolic nor early post-apostolic date, . . . had nevertheless probably existed in a rudimentary form as private or household devotions, from a very early period, and had been received into the number of recognized public formularies previous to the re-organization of the Western ritual after the Eastern model."[6] Its history is therefore not so easily traced as that of the Eucharistic worship of the Liturgy. Early notices show that it consisted largely

---

[1] S. John 1, 29; Acts iii, 1, x, 30.   [2] Dan. vi, 10; Acts x, 9.
[3] Psalm lv, 18.
[4] Bingham, *Antiq* XIII, ix, 7: Maclean, *Ancient Church Orders*, 59 *sq*.
[5] *Prin. Div Ser.* I, p 236.
[6] *Ibid.* I, p. 219.

MATINS AND EVENSONG

of "psalms, and hymns, and spiritual songs,"[1] especially the great Gospel hymns, *Magnificat, Gloria in Excelsis, Benedictus,* and *Nunc Dimittis.* Lessons from Holy Scripture, which were introduced first into the Eucharistic Office, were not added to the ordinary service, it is thought, until about the beginning of the fifth century,[2] the Divine Office, as it was called later, being primarily, if not exclusively, at first one of prayer and praise alone, the Psalter forming its very core.

In the fourth century we find these early morning and evening services increased in number and much elaborated. This development naturally began in the monasteries, especially those of Palestine and Mesopotamia. The sixth hour or noon seems to have been the first addition, and then an earlier morning service. Other "CANONICAL HOURS," as they were called, "came gradually into the Church, and are all of them owing to the rules of the Eastern monasteries for their original."[3] In later days these were developed into seven in number, known in the Western Church by the names of Nocturns, or Matins, Prime, Tierce, Sext, Nones, Vespers, and Completorium, or Compline. As their names imply, these offices were said, Nocturns or Matins at dawn, to which a later appendix was added called Lauds; Prime at the *first* hour according to Oriental reckoning, namely six A.M.; Tierce, or *third,* at nine A.M.; Sext, or *sixth,* at noon; Nones, or *ninth,* at three P.M.; Vespers at six P.M.; and Compline at the *completion* of the day, or bedtime.

The reason for the choice of these hours, which of course could never be observed except in monasteries, or by persons

---

[1] Eph v, 19, Col iii, 16
[2] Freeman, I, 237
[3] Bingham, *Antiq.* XIII, ix, 8.

of great devotion and leisure, has been described in the following verse: —

> At Matins bound, at Prime reviled,
>   Condemned to death at Tierce,
> Nailed to the Cross at Sext,
>   At Nones His blessed side they pierce:
> They take Him down at Vesper-tide,
>   In grave at Compline lay,
> So thenceforth holy zeal observes
>   These sevenfold Hours alway.

Writing concerning the gradual development of this system in the Western Church, Archdeacon Freeman says: — "Not content with enriching — a task which she executed most admirably — her old framework with elements drawn from every region of the East, she multiplied her services at the same time; thus piling together a structure which from its cumbersomeness has fallen into utter decay, leaving but a single fragment erect among its ruins." [1]

It was then out of these services that the revisers of the sixteenth century formed the two offices of our Prayer Book, and thus returned to the use of the earliest days when the people, as well as ecclesiastics and ascetics, took their part in the daily worship of the Church. THE BREVIARY, or, as it was called in England, the PORTUASE, or PORTUARY, was the book which contained these elaborate offices, but as it required four volumes (one for each quarter of the year) to give them with all their fulness of psalm, and hymn, and lesson, and prayer, and antiphon, and rubric, the names which were originally applied to them as signifying *brevity* and *portableness*, became utter misnomers. Matins, Lauds, and Prime were condensed by the revisers into Morning Prayer; while Vespers and Compline were the basis of

[1] *Prin. Div. Ser*, I, p. 232.

MATINS AND EVENSONG 205

Evensong.[1] Nor was this any great departure from what by sheer necessity had become already a well established custom, namely to abbreviate and unite the several offices which, even for ecclesiastics, had become so cumbersome as to be impossible.[2]

It must not be overlooked that Matins and Evensong, as in our present book, are formed upon a definite plan, and follow the lines and order of the earlier services of the Breviary. They have three distinct divisions: — (1) the penitential introduction, consisting of Sentences from Holy Scripture, an Exhortation to repentance, a General Confession, and Absolution, ending with the Lord's Prayer; (2) acts of Praise and Thanksgiving, beginning with the versicles, "O Lord, open Thou our lips" etc., and the Invitatory Psalm, or *Venite*, followed by the Psalter for the day, Lessons from the Old and New Testaments, each followed by other acts of praise, *Te Deum* or *Benedicite, Benedictus,* or Psalm; and (3) Prayers and Intercessions.

The first Revised Book began the service with the Lord's Prayer. THE SENTENCES, EXHORTATION, etc. were added in the second Book (1552), and have been retained ever since.[3] These additions, however, were not without their examples in the earlier daily offices of the English Church. The *Capitula,* or verses from Holy Scripture in the old Lent

---

[1] See Freeman I, 288–9.

[2] Clement VII entrusted the Spanish Cardinal Quignon with the reforming of the Breviary about 1529, and his work was published in 1535. His introduction of so much of Holy Scripture, and omission of doubtful legends, however, caused the Pope to prohibit the book in 1558. An attempted reform of other offices in German was published by Hermann, Prince Bishop of Cologne, in 1542, which was also prohibited and its author excommunicated in 1546.

[3] The American Church in 1892 added other Sentences appropriate to the Church seasons.

services gave the revisers their model here, while "an Exhortation preparatory to Absolution was a regular part of the office for the Visitation of the Sick. Also a *public Exhortation in English* was sometimes used preparatory to Communion, followed by a Confession also in English, and an Absolution in Latin."[1] It was thus evidently intended that this public CONFESSION AND ABSOLUTION, both here and in the Eucharistic Office, should ordinarily take the place of the private or auricular Confession and Absolution that had been the rule of England and the Western Church during the Middle Ages.[2] It did not indeed prohibit such private and particular Confession and Absolution, "if there be any who" by other means "cannot quiet his own conscience."[3] It only provided a service by which all who are not so burdened may receive the benefit of Absolution in accordance with Christ's command.[4]

[1] Procter, 205, 206 In the revision of the American Prayer Book in 1892 the use of the Exhortation was only made obligatory at Matins on Sunday At all other times a substitute was allowed, namely, "Let us humbly confess our sins unto Almighty God." In the earlier services of the English Breviary there was a Confession (*Confiteor*) and Absolution, but it was confined to the Priest and Choir, and was almost wholly precatory. Now the Confession is to be said by "the whole Congregation kneeling," and the Absolution "by the Priest alone standing." The Absolution also is given a more authoritative character. While it still prays for forgiveness and perseverance in repentance, it not only asserts God's readiness to "pardon and absolve," but, through the "power and commandment given to His ministers," it "declares and pronounces to His people, being penitent, the Absolution and Remission of their sins."

[2] See S. John xx, 22, 23; S. Matt. xvi, 19, xix, 18, and see the words spoken to the Priest in Ordination. The American Prayer Book allows here as an alternative the Absolution in the Communion Office.

[3] First Exhortation "when the Minister giveth warning, etc." in the Communion Office

[4] Writing concerning *The Testament of Our Lord*, one of the most *Recent Discoveries Illustrating Early Christian Life and Worship*, p. 84, Bishop

MATINS AND EVENSONG

This penitential and preparatory portion of the service is fitly closed with the Lord's Prayer, which sums up all the needs of God's penitent children, and without which no service can be complete.[1]

Maclean says, "Late comers had to wait till they were brought in by the Deacon, who offered a special petition on their behalf in the Litany 'For this brother who is late, let us beseech that the Lord give him earnestness and labor, and turn away from him every bond of the world,' and so forth. 'In this way,' the Testament naively remarks, 'earnestness is strengthened . . . and the despiser and the slothful is disciplined' This curious feature remains to the present day in the Abyssinian Litany. Perhaps if we adopted this habit of praying for late comers the present unseemly rush during the General Confession and Absolution at Matins might be obviated, and people would be more punctual "

[1] It may be noted here that there is one striking feature of the ancient Choir Offices absent from the revised Prayer Book, namely, the Office Hymns, of which there were 130 in the Portuary alone. Only one, the *Veni Creator Spiritus*, "Come, Holy Ghost," was taken from the other parts of the Service Judging by the two translations of this mediæval Hymn, it may be considered fortunate that no attempt was made on any considerable scale until the 19th century to translate these Hymns for the use of the Church. Though Cranmer was a master of prose, neither he nor his associates seem to have had the gift of poetry.

CHAPTER XXII

THE PSALTER

Jesus said, " All things must be fulfilled which were written . . . in the Psalms concerning Me"

"What the heart is in man, that the Psalter is in the Bible." — JOH. ARND.

"Oh in what accents spake I unto Thee, my God, when I read the Psalms of David, those faithful songs, and sounds of devotion, which allow of no swelling spirit." — S. AUGUSTINE.

THOUGH many of THE PSALMS are of a penitential character, and express the heart's thought of the "afflicted," yet the great majority are either acts of praise and worship, or else of trust, joy, hope, and final victory. It is this dominant note of the Psalter that has made it so dear to the heart of Christians of every age. It is the note struck in the *Venite*, or 95th Psalm, which has been the Invitatory Psalm for Matins in the Western Church from the very earliest days. "It is possible, indeed," writes Archdeacon Freeman, "that this Psalm prefaced the entire Temple service. . . . In the East, the Psalm itself is not used, but only a threefold invitation to praise, or 'invitatory,' based upon the first, third, and sixth verses of it." [1]

One other note of the Psalter is that, unlike all mere poetry of the imagination, it is always the voice of real life

---

[1] *Prin Div. Ser*, I, 75, 402 In the American Prayer Book the *Venite* consists of the first seven verses of the 95th Psalm, and the 9th and 13th of the 96th. The same Book has a similar combination of parts of Psalms in the service for Thanksgiving Day These composite Psalms are found also in English State Services, and there are several in the Mozarabic Offices See Neale and Littledale, *Commentary on the Psalms*. Vol. I, Dissertation I, 69.

THE PSALTER

and real men. For though inspired by God there is nothing in the entire Bible more thoroughly human than the book of Psalms. It is not God speaking to man, as in the Law and the Prophets, the Gospels and the Epistles, but man speaking to God — man in despair, man in doubt, man in sorrow, man in penitence, crying "out of the deep," and from the midst of "the great waterfloods." Or again, it is man in praise and thankfulness, rejoicing in God's glory in earth and sky, in star and flower, or adoring His manifestations of mercy in His Church by the forgiveness of sins and the blotting out of iniquities. The fingers of the inspired musicians have touched all the keys of the human heart. All that men *may* feel finds in the Psalter a responsive chord in all that man *has* felt.

This is why, with an instinct that is unerring, the Church from the first found in the Hymnal of the earlier dispensation the full expression of her soul's deepest longings, and loftiest desires — "the whole music of the human heart swept by the hand of its Maker."[1] The ancient Psalmists had sounded all the depths, and soared to all the heights of the soul's experience, and the Christian Church found here a vehicle of worship prepared by the wisdom of God, ready for her use. Even our Lord upon the Cross found in its very words the full expression of His utmost needs; and not He alone, but myriads of others also have found there "prayers which, like some mysterious vestment fit every human soul in the attitude of supplication; — prayers for every time, place, circumstance; for the bridal and the grave, the storm and the battle, the king and the peasant, the harlot sobbing on her knees on the penitentiary floor, and the saint looking through the lifted portals into the city of God . . . prayers for the

---
[1] Gladstone.

seasons when the Church looks upon the Crucified, and for those when He bursts the bars of the tomb, and ascends to His Father's Throne. Such prayers the world has never seen but once." [1]

But besides its answer to these universal needs, the Psalter possessed another distinct note which made it doubly dear to the Christian mind and heart. The Lord Jesus after His resurrection had told His Apostles that, not only "the Law and the Prophets" had spoken of Him beforehand, but "the Psalms" also,[2] and He had "opened their understanding that they might understand" the things written there "concerning Him." Of this the 22nd Psalm is perhaps the most typical example. It is of this that Archbishop Alexander writes: —

"Loaded with the sins of the world, Jesus began the Psalm upon the Cross to show that it was His. Four out of the last Seven Words certainly are taken from, or refer to, this portion of the Psalter. From the first verse on, there is scarcely a line that might not have come from the pen of an Evangelist; instead of a colourless scene, there is color and detail. . . Burning thirst; violent tension of suspended members, making the frame like that of a living skeleton; rude spectators gambling over the raiment; some wrong, probably piercing, done to the hands and feet; the ἀδημονεῖν, the feeling strange and out of place in God's universe; — all these are represented so vividly, so powerfully, so accurately, that Christian consciousness upon Good Friday turns to this Psalm as naturally and spontaneously as to the nineteenth chapter of S. John. . . . But there is more than this. The Sufferer passes to glory by the edge of the sword (or a violent death), from the lion's mouth, from the claws of the dog, from the horns of the unicorn. . . . The wonder of the Psalm is brought to

---

[1] Archbp. Alexander, *Witness of the Psalms to Christ*, Lect. iv, 127, 128.
[2] S. Luke xxiv, 44.

THE PSALTER

a climax by the ordered development in which all is given. First, He who suffers is laid into the very dust of death. Then, risen from that dust, He proclaims His Name to His brethren, beginning from the Jews, and ending with the Gentiles from the very furthest parts of the earth. To understand all this fully, we must, indeed, remember those deep words, 'He hath made Him to be sin for us . . . who His own self bare our sins in His own body on the tree.' . . . 'Psalmorum clavis Christi fides.' The golden key of the Psalter lies in a Pierced Hand."[1]

This Psalm does not stand alone, the Archbishop adds:—

"It belongs to a class of which there is but one consistent solution. Our Lord's "Humanity found in them a collection of appropriate devotions — Prayer-book, liturgy, hymn-book, fitted and pre-harmonised for a Divine Sufferer and Pilgrim. . . . They are lyrics primarily of the Humanity of our Lord, secondarily of ours."[2] "The references which they contain to the beauty and grandeur of nature may color many pages of geography and natural history. . . . Above all, and without this everything else will be in vain, our people must be taught habitually to see Christ in the Psalter. . . . They must be able to say almost instinctively:— In this Psalm is the voice of the Sorrow and of the Love of Jesus. This Psalm speaks of His Passion. His are the Pierced Hands and Feet. He is the Divine Shepherd. Here I find Him reigning in glory. This is He who comes to Judgment. This Sion and Jerusalem which is spoken of is the Church. This feast is the Eucharist, this Table the Table of the Lord, this Cup the Chalice, this Bread the Body of Christ. The peace of which the Psalmist speaks is the peace that passeth all understanding, the peace to

---

[1] *The Witness of the Psalms*, Lect. I, iii.

[2] *Ibid* Lect. II. The Archbishop, in App. A to Lect. I, gives a carefully prepared list of nearly three hundred quotations from, or references to, the Greek Psalter which occur in the New Testament. One hundred of these are in the Gospels, and most of them have direct reference to our Lord.

the weary when the long day's work is over, the peace of Heaven."[1]

Side by side with the eloquent words of the learned Irish Primate in the nineteenth century it is fitting to set the words of another great preacher of northern Africa in the fourth century. In a well-known passage of his *Confessions*, or spiritual autobiography, his *Apologia pro Vita Sua*, S. Augustine writes: — "In what accents I addressed Thee, my God, when I read the Psalms of David,[2] those faithful songs, the language of devotion which banishes the spirit of pride, while I was still a novice in true love of Thee, and as a catechumen rested in that country house along with Alypius, who was also a catechumen, with my mother at our side, in the dress of a woman but with the faith of a man, with the calmness of age, the affection of a mother, the piety of a Christian. How I addressed Thee in those Psalms! how my love for Thee was kindled by them! How I burned to recite them, were it possible, throughout the world, as an antidote to the pride of humanity."

A thoughtful writer thus sums up the wealth of blessing which the constant use of the Psalter has brought to men through three thousand years: — "There has gathered round every Psalm, nay, round every verse of a Psalm, a vast treasure of spiritual truth brought together by the tears and labors of believers for many generations; the Psalms have been life and light for thousands; they have been turned into the prayers and thanksgivings of innumerable souls from the Lord of Glory Himself in the days of His Humiliation down to the humblest and meanest of His servants; almost every word in them has brought guidance, relief, refreshment to some men."[3]

---

[1] *The Witness of the Psalms*, Lect. VIII.

[2] Though the Prayer Book, in common with S. Augustine, uses this title, *Psalms of David*, it is only because David is the author of most of the Psalms, and he to whom the spirit of ancient psalmody owes its greatest debt. As may be seen by reference to the Bible version, many of the Psalms are by Asaph, some by Moses, Solomon, and others of much later date.

[3] *Practical Reflections on the Psalms*, viii.

THE PSALTER 213

The question of the use of the "IMPRECATORY PSALMS" in the Christian Church is too large and too difficult a subject to be dealt with fully here. Whatever may have been in the mind of the Hebrew Psalmists with their lower ideas and lesser knowledge, two things are to be remembered about these particular Psalms; first, that God's hatred and punishment of sin is expressed by the merciful lips of our Lord and Judge Himself, in language stronger and more terrible than any Psalmist ever used;[1] and second, that the "enemies" against whom the Psalmists bid us pray are foes that "war against the soul." "The broad gates are flung wide open of the city that lies foursquare towards all the winds of heaven; for its ruler is divinely tolerant. But there shall in no wise enter it anything that defileth, neither worketh abomination; for He is divinely intolerant too. And thus when, in public or private, we read these Psalms of imprecation, there is a lesson that comes home to us.... Reading them we must depart from sin, or pronounce judgment upon ourselves. Every known sin of flesh and spirit — these, and not mistaken men, are the worst enemies of God and of His Christ. Against these we pray in our Collects for Peace at Morning and Evening Prayer — 'Defend us in all assaults of our enemies.' — These were the dark hosts that swept through the Psalmist's vision when he cried, 'Let all mine enemies be ashamed and sore vexed.'"[2]

Bishop Butler's characterization of Resentment may also be of some service in this connection. "The indignation raised by cruelty and injustice and the desire of having it punished, which persons *un*concerned — and in a higher de-

[1] See S. Matt. xviii, 6, xxiii, 13 sq.; xxv, 41; xxvi, 24; and cf. Rev. vi, 16.
[2] *Witness of the Psalms to Christ.* Lect. II.

gree those who *were* concerned — would feel, is by no means malice. It is one of the common bonds by which society is held together — a weapon put into our hands by nature . . . which may be innocently employed . . . one of the *instruments of death* which the Author of our nature hath provided . . . not only an innocent but a generous movement of the mind . . . a settled and deliberate passion implanted in man for the prevention and remedy of wrong." [1]

To this may be added the opinions of two representatives of very diverse schools of thought. Dean Stanley writes: — "The duty of keeping alive in the heart the sense of burning indignation against moral evil, against selfishness, against injustice, against untruth, in ourselves as well as in others, — that is as much a part of the Christian as of the Jewish dispensation." These "imprecations," writes Bishop Gore, "are not the utterances of selfish spite: they are the claim which righteous Israel makes upon God that He would vindicate Himself, and let

---

[1] *Sermon VIII*. At least a partial solution of the problem may be found in the theory advocated by the learned Jew, Moses Mendelssohn (1729–1786), who held that the imprecations are not those of the Psalmist himself, but are those uttered by his enemies and persecutors. It is to be remembered that the Hebrew had nothing corresponding to our inverted commas to mark a quotation. The second Psalm is a typical instance of this change from the words of one speaker to another without sign or warning, and of which there are many other examples in the Psalms and Prophets In Psalm cix, verse 27 seems plainly to imply that verses 5–19 are the words of "the ungodly" in verse 1. All difficulties may not be removed by this theory, but those that remain are trifling in comparison, and seem capable of solution. See Luckock, *Spiritual Diff in the Bible and Pr. Bk* , pp. 52–75. "None of the imprecatory Psalms are to be found in the Jewish Prayer Book" of today (Sir Edwd. Clarke, *Pr. Bk. Version Corrected*, xxi).

THE PSALTER 215

their eyes see how 'rightousness turns again unto judgment.'"[1]

One other noteworthy feature of the Psalms as the divinely ordained vehicle of Catholic Christian worship for every race and language is their fitness for translation into other tongues without loss of strength or beauty. "The Church is *Catholic,* languages are *particular,*" Dr. Alexander writes. "And this *difficulty* arises. *Poetry* is somewhat impatient of translation. It is a wine that is too delicate to cross the sea. Few poetical translations have ever been popular, and those few have scarcely been correct representations of their originals. . . . It is certain almost to demonstration, that the Hebrews never possessed the notion of metrical art, as it was practised among the Greeks and Romans. . . . There is little or no discoverable symmetry of *measure* or concurrence of *sound,* addressed to the *ear.* There *is* a symmetry of *sense,* addressed to the intellect [called *parallelism*]. . . . The most frequent form of parallelism is the simple sequence of two following verses which reproduce the same idea in other words. But the parallelism sometimes extends to three, or even four verses; occasionally the two first and the two last rhyme by the idea or thought, occasionally the third corresponds with the fourth, or the fourth with the second." It is this parallelism more than anything else which enabled the Psalms to occupy their place in the worship of the Church among all nations. "Other poetry translated *verbatim* loses the very essence of its poetical character, because it loses the measure and cadence of its words. But Hebrew poetry can only be given in exact translation. It is destroyed by being turned into

---

[1] *Lux Mundi.* Compare also W. T. Davison in Hastings' *Dic. of the Bible,* IV, 159.

verse as much as other poetry is destroyed by being turned into prose." [1]

Of the peculiarities and excellences of our *Prayer Book* version in this respect there is much to be said. It is the translation which formed part of the "Great Bible," based on that of Coverdale, published under the editorship of Archbishop Cranmer in 1539, and ordered to be set up in all churches the following year. It is not so accurate a translation as that of the so-called Authorized Version of 1611, but it bears the mark of Cranmer's admirable felicity of rhythmical English. It has been said of it that it is "the translation of a poet, and not of a dictionary."[2] It is so adapted for musical rendering, and it so endeared itself to the people, that later translations have never been allowed to supplant it.

It is in connection with this version that Liddon writes: — "Every language appears to reach its bloom at a certain period in the history of the nation which speaks and writes it; and thenceforward to decline. And for the English language the sixteenth century was the period of consummate excellence; the decline had begun even at the beginning of the seventeenth. The English writers of the sixteenth century — and Archbishop Cranmer in particular — had an ear for English which has not been given even to the most gifted of their successors; and their work is unapproached in its simple and forcible vocabulary, and still more in the order and beauty of its rhythm. This appears partly in the Collects of the Prayer Book, but

---
[1] *Witness of the Psalms, etc* Lect VI Thus "Hebrew poetry carries its lyric rhythm into the very thought itself." (Moulton, *Modern Reader's Bible*, p. 1431) The musical colon in our Prayer Book version of the Psalter usually marks the division between the two parallel thoughts. Psalm xvii, 3 is an example of a triple parallelism, xviii, 1 of a quadruple.

[2] Sir Edward Clarke.

THE PSALTER 217

especially in the version of the Psalms, which is perhaps the most beautiful thing, without exception, that is peculiar to the modern Church of England. It deserves all that has been said by masters of our language about the Authorized Version, and a great deal more; and we may hope that the danger, if it ever seriously existed, of replacing it in our Daily Services by some substitute of later origin, has passed away for ever."[1]

One other though minor feature which has helped to commend the Prayer Book version to many is that, unlike all modern translations of the Psalms made directly from the Hebrew original, this one was made conjointly from the three versions represented by the inscription on the Cross, "Hebrew, Greek, and Latin." These were (1) the Hebrew text as it had come down in the care of the rabbinical schools; (2) the Septuagint or Greek translation, made by seventy-two learned Jews at Alexandria about B.C. 270, and always quoted by the New Testament authors, and (3) the Latin translation, or *Vulgate* (the revised version of the older imperfect *Italic*), made by S. Jerome about A.D. 390, which since his day, after the eighth century at least, had become the common use of all the Western Church. It is to the Vulgate we owe the Latin headings of our Prayer Book version. These are simply the first words of each Psalm, which in mediæval days had become their familiar titles, as the first Latin words of the *Venite*, the *Te Deum, Benedicite, Magnificat*, etc. have become to us.

It is much to be desired that brief descriptive titles in English might also be given to the Psalms. This would be of great help in their devotional use. Imagine a book of English poetry without titles, or only titles in Latin, and these mere translations of the first words of each poem

---

[1] Preface to *Practical Reflections on the Psalms*, pp ix, x.

in English![1] The abandonment by the revisers of one universal feature in the use of the Psalms in the Western Church makes this adoption of titles in English all the more desirable. I refer to the employment of what were called ANTIPHONS, brief sentences or versicles said or sung before or after a Psalm, illustrating or emphasising some special feature of its character. "There can be no doubt," writes Archbishop Alexander, "that, in many cases, this has been the noblest of all commentaries upon the Psalms for the purpose of public worship, and the best means of drawing out their manifold significance. We may take the First Psalm as a very favourable specimen. On any ordinary day, the Psalm was applied to the Christian's common duty in life by the Antiphon 'Serve the Lord in fear.' If it were the commemoration of a Saint or Martyr, the true root of the saintly character was signified by means of an Antiphon taken from this very Psalm, 'His delight is in the law of the Lord.' On Passion Sunday it was declared that it is Christ who, when hanging on the Cross, made it 'like a tree which brings forth fruit in due season, and whose leaf will not wither.' At Easter the Antiphon is, 'I am that I am, and My counsel is not with the wicked, but in the law of the Lord is My delight. Alleluia.'"[2] "Were any of the methods of service, which were laid aside at our Revision, to be selected for restoration," writes Archdeacon Freeman, "I conceive that the antiphons, with this restricted application to special seasons and to Festivals, would possess a weighty claim upon the Church's consideration. A

---

[1] An imperfect attempt has been made at the end of this chapter to provide such titles in English. If written into one's Prayer Book version they might be found by many an aid to the intelligent use of this great book of the Church's devotion.

[2] Lecture VI.

THE PSALTER

single antiphon, fixed for the season, and said before and after the entire psalmody of each day, would involve comparatively little complexity, and would greatly help to sustain the character of such seasons as Christmas, Lent, and Easter: during the last of which, indeed, such a single antiphon was used." [1]

Writing concerning this method of giving the tone and emphasis to the Psalms proper to the season, Dr. Neale says: — "The same sun-ray from the Holy Ghost rested indeed at all times on the same words, but the prism of the Church separated that colorless light into its component rays; into the violet of penitence, the crimson of martyrdom, the gold of the highest seasons of Christian gladness. Hence arose the wonderful system of antiphons." [2]

There were four methods of singing the Psalms from the earliest times. (1) The *Cantus Directus*, as it was called, the singing of every verse by the full choir, without response. (2) The Antiphonal, each verse, half verse, or parallelism (as marked by colon), being sung alternately by opposite sides of the choir. (3) The Precentor and choir taking alternate verses, or half verses. (4) A solo, sung by a single voice.[3]

In the mediæval Church the Psalter was arranged to be read or sung through once each week. But this was only possible in the monastic bodies, and even there the rule

[1] *Prin. Div. Ser*, I, 122, 123. The Antiphon was undoubtedly overdone, and the Farce seems to be its degenerate offspring "A Farce," writes Dr. Neale, "is the insertion in a Gospel, Epistle, or Canticle, of intercalated sentences, intended to have the same effect as an Antiphon" (*Comm on Psalms*. Diss I, 40, 42). This was carried so far that it became absurd Hence the word came to be used for a ludicrous play as at present. The Farce was given up after the 10th century, and the Antiphon was only said before and after each Psalm — later, before and after several Psalms — and varied according to the day or season, thus giving to the portion its proper tone.

[2] *Comm on the Psalms*, Dissertation I, section 34.   [3] *Ibid.* p 58.

had so many exceptions that it was said by the revisers, "Now of late time a few [of the psalms] have been daily said, and the rest utterly omitted." [1] The present rule by which the whole Psalter is divided arbitrarily into sixty portions may not be ideal, but it has at least the merit of having made the Psalms "familiar as household words" to the vast body of English-speaking lay people as well as clergy, though it is only realized by the few how much they are indebted to this constant repetition for the mould and form of their own spiritual life. It was the remark of M. Taine, who knew England and the English better than any other Frenchman ever did, that the English character, the strong sense of duty and righteousness, had been fostered and consolidated by the constant recitation of the Psalms of David. And in this the Psalter is different from every other religious poetry in the world. It has nothing like it, or even second to it. It has been said of the Vedas or sacred hymns of India, that "they are or have been for ages *dead relics*. . . . known in their real spirit and meaning to a few students. The Psalms are as living as when they were written; and they have never ceased to be, what we may be very certain they have been today, this very day which is just ending, to hundreds and thousands of the most earnest souls now alive." [2]

---

[1] *Concerning the Service of the Church* in the English Book. See also Neale and Littledale, *Comm on the Psalms*, I, Dissertation I, 27.

[2] Dean Church, *The Gifts of Civilization*, pp. 385, 388, 391. The Scottish Church by her Bishops (June, 1915) adopted an ingenious method of using the Psalter, which might well be copied by other branches of the Anglican Communion. The present principle of continuous recitation in sixty consecutive portions is preserved, but these are to be used only on weekdays, not according to the civil Calendar, but to that of the Christian Year, every Sunday having its proper Psalms, and usually fewer in number than at present. Thus the whole Psalter is recited in five weeks

THE PSALTER

It should be needless to point out that the Psalms by their very nature were written to be sung, and were sung antiphonally, that is, by alternate verses, or rather, parallelisms or half verses, by opposite sides of the choirs of Levites in the Temple, and they continued to be sung thus in the Primitive Church. The Church historian Socrates, at the end of the fourth century, attributes the introduction of this method into the Church to S. Ignatius, the martyr Bishop of Antioch, at the beginning of the second century.[1] Duchesne says that "up to the fourth century the Psalms were always sung as a solo," that is, by a precentor, "the congregation repeating the last words of the chant" as a response, which corresponds to our present method when the Psalms are read.[2] S. Ambrose adopted the antiphonal method of singing by two sides of the choir in the Diocese of Milan about 387, as we learn from S. Augustine.[3] Later it was introduced into the Roman Church. "All the verses were chanted to the same melody, but the melody varied with each Psalm."[4] Concerning the use of the *Gloria* Bingham says: — "In all the Western Churches, except the

---

of six days each, or more that ten times in the year on weekdays. Besides this, "nearly all the whole Psalter is recited once in the year on Sundays, the majority of Psalms twice, and some three times." Proper Psalms are provided for Sundays, also for Christmas, Holy Week, Easter Week, Ascension Day, and Whitsun Week. The American Book has twenty Selections of Psalms, in addition to the Proper Psalms for festivals and fasts, which may be substituted for the daily portion at the discretion of the Minister

[1] *His. Ecc*, vi, 8.

[2] It is on account of this *response* by the congregation that the Psalm introduced in the old English use between the Epistle and the Gospel received the name *Respond* This was also called the *Gradual*, either because it was sung (as a solo) at the *gradus*, or ambo, or else while the Deacon was ascending the step (*gradus*) of the altar to read the Gospel.

[3] *Confessions*, iv, 7.   [4] Duchesne, pp. 113-115.

Roman, it was customary also, at the end of every Psalm, for the congregation to stand, and say, 'Glory be to the Father, and to the Son, and to the Holy Ghost": but in the Eastern Churches — only at the end of the last Psalm." [1]

Concerning this musical rendering of the Psalms Hooker, in his defence of the custom as against the objections of the Puritans that this method of singing was the work of the Devil, says: — "As for the Devil, which way it should greatly benefit him to have this manner of singing Psalms accounted an invention of Ignatius [pupil of S. John, and Bishop of Antioch about A.D. 69], or an imitation of the angels of heaven,[2] we do not well understand." Then, after referring to other objections of the Puritans, he asks: — "And shall this enforce us to banish a thing which all Christian Churches in the world have received; a thing which so many ages have held. . . . a thing whereunto God's people of old did resort, with hope and thirst that thereby especially their souls might be edified; a thing which filleth the mind with comfort and heavenly delight. . . . and so fitly accordeth with the Apostle's own exhortation, 'Speak to yourselves in psalms and hymns and spiritual songs, making melody, and singing to the Lord in your hearts,' that surely there is more cause to fear lest the want thereof be a maim, than the use a blemish to the service of God." [3]

---

[1] *Antiq* XIV, 1, 8.   [2] Is xxxvi, 1-3.

[3] *Ecc. Pol*, V, xxxix, 1, 4. The Bampton Lectures of Archbishop Alexander (1876), for their grasp of the true character of the Psalms in their Witness to Christ, in their literary beauty, and the depth and richness of their devotion, stand without a rival. Three other books will be found of much value in this connection. — *Christ, the Key to the Psalter*, by an Oxford Graduate (1888), *Practical Reflections on every Verse of the Psalms*, with Preface by H P. Liddon, (1890), and *The Psalms in Human Life*, by R. E. Prothero (1903), also two Lectures by Dean Church on *Early Sacred Poetry* in *The Gifts of Civilization*.

APPENDIX I TO CHAPTER XXII
SUGGESTED ENGLISH TITLES FOR THE PSALMS

"*As a door bringeth one into the house, so doth the title of the Psalm into the understanding.*" — S. AUGUSTINE.

Book I
PSALM
1. The Way to Blessedness.
2. "Thou art the King of Glory, O Christ" — *An Easter Hymn.*
3. A Morning Hymn of Thankfulness.
4. An Evening Hymn of Trust.
5. A Prayer of Preparation for God's House.
6. Prayer of a Penitent — *A Lenten Litany.*
7. Song of the Slandered Saint.
8. Song of the Devout Astronomer — *An Ascension Hymn.*
9. A Song of the Great Judgment.
10. A Prayer for the Persecuted and the Poor.
11. Childlike Trust in Face of Unbelief.
12. The Tongues of Men and the Words of God.
13. The Cry of an Anxious Heart — "How Long?"
14. God's Judgment on the Unbelieving Fool.
15. God's Picture of a Righteous Man — *An Ascension Hymn.*
16. "In Thy Presence is the Fulness of Joy."
17. The Appeal of the Oppressed.
18. The Resolve of a Grateful Heart.
19. God's Law in the Heavens and in the Heart — *An Epiphany Hymn.*
20. Prayer for a Friend in Trouble.
21. "Thou shalt give him Everlasting Felicity" — *An Ascension Hymn.*
22. The Crucified's Cry of Sorrow and of Victory.
23. The Good Shepherd Song.
24. "Who is the King of Glory?" — *A Song of the Ascension.*

25. A Litany of Penitence and Supplication.
26. A Hymn before the Altar.
27. Three Glorious Titles of God — *A Song of Cheer and Hope.*
28. Strength for the Trusting Heart — *A Song in the Night.*
29. Psalm of the Seven Thunders.
30. "Joy cometh in the Morning" — *A Hymn for Easter Even.*
31. "Into Thy Hands I commend my Spirit" — *The Cry of the Dying Lord.*
32. Blessedness of the Pardoned Soul.
33. The Greatness and the Goodness of God.
34. "O Taste and See how Gracious the Lord is."
35. Prayer of the Persecuted.
36. "In Thee is the Well of Life."
37. "Fret not Thyself because of the Ungodly."
38. Litany of the Penitent.
39. The Shortness and Uncertainty of Life.
40. "I Waited Patiently for the Lord." — *A Plea from the Cross.*
41. Prayer of a Deserted Soul—*A Cry from Gethsemane.*

Book II

42. The Exile's Cry for God's Courts.
43. "That I may go unto the Altar of God" — *A Communion Hymn.*
44. "Our Fathers have told us" — *An Appeal to History.*
45. The King and His Bride — "*Concerning Christ and the Church.*"
46. "Jesus, Emmanuel, God with us."
47. God is the King of all the Earth — *An Ascension Triumph Song.*
48. "The Gates of Hell shall not Prevail against it"— *A Whitsun Hymn.*
49. "Some put their Trust in their Goods."
50. God's Call to Repentance.
51. A Penitent's Prayer for himself and for The Church — *The Great Miserere.*

THE PSALTER

52. "The Man that took not God for his Strength."
53. The Fool and his Folly.
54. "God is my Helper" — *Another Cry from Gethsemane.*
55. Litany of the Oppressed.
56. "In God have I put my Trust."
57. "Under the Shadow of Thy Wings" — *An Easter Song.*
58. "There is a God that Judgeth the Earth."
59. "Deliver me from mine Enemies, O God."
60. The Church's Cry in Days of Anxiety.
61. "When my Heart is in Heaviness."
62. "Rock of Ages."
63. "Early will I seek Thee" — *A Morning Hymn.*
64. Wicked Doers and their Bitter Words.
65. "Thou Crownest the Year with Thy Goodness" — *A Harvest Thanksgiving.*
66. "How Wonderful art Thou in Thy Works."
67. "That Thy Saving Health may be Known among All Nations" — *A Missionary Hymn.*
68. The Church's Trumpet-Call — *A Processional Whitsun Hymn.*
69. "I am come into Deep Waters" — *A Psalm of the Passion.*
70. Prayer of the Poor and Needy.
71. "When my Strength faileth me" — *A Prayer for the Aged.*
72. "All Nations shall do Him Service" — *A Missionary Hymn.*

Book III

73. The End of Prosperous Wickedness.
74. Elegy on the Ruined Temple.
75. God the Righteous Judge.
76. The Church's Song of Victory.
77. Strength in Remembering our Past.
78. The Story of God's Marvels for His Church.
79. Lament over the Ruined City of God.
80. Prayer for the Ruined Vineyard.
81. Glad Hymn for a Great Feast.

82. God's Judgment on the Judges.
83. Judgment on the Church's Enemies.
84. A Longing for God's Courts and Altar.
85. "God so Loved the World" — *The Mystery of the Lowly Incarnation — A Christmas Hymn.*
86. Prayer of a Persecuted Believer.
87. "Jerusalem which is above, the Mother of us all."
88. "My Soul is full of Trouble" — *A Prayer from the Cross.*
89. "I will make Him My Firstborn" — *A Christmas Hymn.*

Book IV

90. "Teach us to number our Days."
91. "Underneath are the Everlasting Arms."
92. "It is a Good Thing to give Thanks" — *A Morning and Evening Hymn.*
93. "The Lord God Omnipotent Reigneth."
94. "How Long, O Lord?" — *The Cry of a Distracted Believer.*
95. The Church's Call to Worship — *Venite.*
96. A Call to the Church and the Nations — *A Missionary Hymn.*
97. Christ is King, let the Earth Rejoice.
98. A New Song of Christ's Marvelous Works.
99. The Name that is above Every Name.
100. A Call to all the Nations.
101. The City of God for the Godly.
102. Medicine for an Aching Heart — *A Prayer for the Sorrowful.*
103. Praise for God's Gifts to the Soul.
104. Praise for God's Greatness in Nature.
105. God's Marvelous Works for His People — *A National Anthem.*
106. God's Mercy and Pardon for His People — *A National Warning.*

Book V

107. "The Wonders that He doeth for the Children of Men."

THE PSALTER

108. "Through God we shall do Great Acts" — *A Song for Ascension Day.*
109. "Though they curse yet bless Thou."
110. The Priest-King, the Sufferer, and the Victor — *A Christmas Song.*
111. "The Works of the Lord are Great."
112. The Blessedness of the Godly.
    (*The Hallel Psalms*, 113–118. "*The Hymn*" of S. Matt. xxvi, 30).
113. "Who is Like unto the Lord?"
114. Triumph Song of the Exodus — *An Easter Hymn.*
115. "Not unto us, O Lord, but unto Thy Name give the Praise" — *Non nobis, Domine.*
116. "Thou hast Delivered my Soul from Death" — *A Communion Hymn.*
117. "Praise Him all ye Nations."
118. "I shall not Die but Live" — *An Easter Song from the Cross.*
119. The Glories and Beauties of God's Law — *A Meditation.*
    (*The Pilgrims' Songs of Ascent*, or *Gradual Psalms*, 120–134)
120. "When I was in Trouble — *The Cry of a Returning Exile.*
121. "He that Keepeth thee will not Sleep."
122. "For the Peace of Jerusalem."
123. Prayer of the Despised Exile.
124. "If the Lord Himself had not been on our Side" — *A National Thanksgiving.*
125. "As the Hills stand about Jerusalem" — *The Exiles' Confidence.*
126. They that Sow in Tears shall Reap in Joy" — *Song of the Freedmen.*
127. "Except the Lord Build the House" — *The Builder's Psalm.*
128. A Song of Wife and Home.
129. A Litany for the Afflicted Church.
130. A Cry out of the Deep — *De Profundis.*
131. "As a Little Child."

132. "An Habitation for the Mighty God of Jacob" — *A Christmas and Consecration Hymn.*
133. The Joy of Brotherly Love.
134. The People's Prayer for their Priests.
135. A Festal Hymn of Praise.
136. "His Mercy Endureth for Ever" — *The Great Hallel of Thanksgiving.*
137. "By the Waters of Babylon" — *Sad Memories of an Exile.*
138. "Though I walk in the Midst of Trouble" — *A Song of Thanksgiving.*
139. "Thou hast Searched me out and Known me" — *A Hymn of God's Omniscience.*
140. The Cry of a Tempted Soul.
141. An Evening Prayer for Protection.
142. "When my Spirit was in Heaviness."
143. "I Flee unto Thee to Hide me."
144. "My Defender in Whom I Trust."
145. "There is no End of His Greatness."
146. "Put not your Trust in Princes."
147. "A Joyful and Pleasant Thing it is to be Thankful." — *A Benedicite.*
148. "All ye Works of the Lord, Bless ye the Lord" — — *A Benedicite.*
149. "Let Israel Rejoice in Him that Made Him."
150. "Let Every Thing that hath Breath Praise the Lord."

The Jews divided the Psalms into five Books; concerning which it has been said: — "God presented Israel with the Law, a Pentateuch, and grateful Israel responded with a Psalter, a Pentateuch of Praise." The author is fully conscious of the imperfect character of this effort to give titles to the Psalms. Though he has found very little in the work of others to assist him in his attempt, he would express his indebtedness particularly for a number of suggestions to *Practical Reflections on the Psalms*, by "an old and honoured,"

THE PSALTER

but unnamed, friend of Canon Liddon, and to Mr. Spurgeon's *Treasury of David*.

It has of course been impossible to point out in the preceding list the many "things written in the Psalms concerning" Christ, as He Himself taught His disciples (S. Luke xxiv, 44, 45). It is to be remembered that *after* this teaching we find nearly two hundred references to the Psalms by apostolic writers in the New Testament. To minds thus "opened to understand the Scriptures," the Psalter was overflowing with Christ and His Gospel, His love, His life, His death and resurrection, His sacraments, His promises. An early tradition says that as He hung on the Cross He not only uttered the first words of the 22nd Psalm, "My God, My God, etc.," but He went on through that great "programme of the crucifixion" to the 23rd, with its cry, "Though I walk through the valley of the shadow of death;" to the 24th, with its glorious promise of heaven; and so through all that follow until He reached the 31st, with the prayer, "Into Thy hands I commend My Spirit," and so ended. Thus, as has been well said, "The golden key of the Psalter lies in a pierced hand."[1] Thus also, we see the wisdom of the Church from the beginning in her constant use of the Psalms, weaving them into her Christian Year, that they may become "familiar in our mouths as household words," and help us to feel and think aright, in penitence, and praise, and thanksgiving, and joyful hope, in presence of the glorious mystery of Incarnate Love.

---
[1] Archbp. Alexander, p. 22.

APPENDIX II TO CHAPTER XXII
MUSIC IN THE CHURCH

It is needless to remark the great place given by Holy Scripture to music, both instrumental and vocal, in the worship of God. Dupanloup, Bishop of Orleans, writes: — "Singing is one of the noblest and strongest ways of expressing the feelings of the soul. As S. Augustine again has said, '*Cantat amor.*' Singing is love; thus everything sings in nature, everything sings in heaven. It is the enthusiasm of the heart. It moves souls. Whence comes it? What is the secret of this mysterious relation between musical things, cadence, rhythm, harmony, melody, and the deepest powers of our being? I know not. *But it is a fact;* this is why everything in the soul sings; why all that is noble, ardent, generous, passionate, breaks out into song."[1] Concerning the faculty and the enjoyment of music in the economy of human life, even such a man as the late Mr. Darwin lets fall the word which theologians are so often blamed for employing. "They are," he says, "among the most *mysterious* faculties with which man is endowed. They awaken dormant sentiments. They tell us of things which we have not seen and [he adds perhaps mistakenly] shall not see."[2]

Socrates, the Church Historian, says that Ignatius, the martyr Bishop of Antioch (circa A.D. 50–115), introduced the custom of antiphonal singing of the Psalms, that is, by opposite sides of the choir or congregation in turn (*vicissim*), and the younger Pliny, governor of Bythinia, in his letter to the Emperor Trajan (A.D. 112) makes a similar statement.

[1] *The Ministry of Catechizing*, English Trans. pp. 180, 181.
[2] *Descent of Man*, II, p 335.

THE PSALTER

They do not speak, however, of the character of the music. The earliest form of music in the Church of which we have record is that called Plain Song, in Latin, *Cantus Planus*, that is, a chant unmeasured by bars as in modern music. It is marked by great simplicity and dignity, and was always sung in unison. Its most distinctive feature is its attempt to give musical expression to the reading of a prose poem, in the most natural manner, and with the utmost freedom. Harmony or homophony (as distinguished from polyphony in fugue and canon, with their *many voices* each singing its own melody) was a much later development. It is profoundly suggestive that, though unadapted to Plain Song, this perfection of musical art, as the symbol of that "peace on earth" proclaimed by the angelic choir over the fields of Bethlehem, was the peculiar work of the Church of Christ.[1]

The origin of Plain Song is probably traceable in a measure to the Jewish Christians, who would naturally sing the simple tones or chants which were endeared to them by the constant use of the great Temple choirs. But doubtless it owes its development in a great degree, when the Church spread among the Gentiles, to the traditional music of the Greeks and Romans. S. Ambrose, Bishop of Milan (A.D. 340–397), introduced the custom into the Church in Italy, and did much to improve the character of these ancient melodies.[2] During the next two centuries, however, Church music degenerated greatly by attempting too much elaboration, and it was given to that Gregory who showed his missionary fervor in sending the monk Augustine to England in 596,

---

[1] It is claimed by musical writers that "England possesses the oldest specimen of polyphonic writing, the famous canon, 'Sumer is icomen in,' now assigned to the year 1226." See *New Inter. Ency.* XVI, p. 482.

[2] For the different methods of reciting or singing the Psalms see p. 219.

232 PRIMITIVE WORSHIP & THE PRAYER BOOK

to bring about, by his love and skill in music, a reform in the direction of greater simplicity and reverence. As formerly the chants were called Ambrosian, from the friend of Monica and her son S. Augustine of Hippo, so henceforth it is from Gregory the Great that we derive the name Gregorian now usually given to the tones of Plain Song.

In the sixteenth century Church music had again become so elaborated and secularized that one of the first acts of the Roman Council of Trent (1545–1563) was an effort for its reformation. In fact Pope Pius IV in 1564 went so far as to appoint a commission to enquire whether music in parts, as distinguished from the unison of Plain Song, should be tolerated in the Church at all. It was chiefly owing to the work of the great Church musician, Giovanni Palestrina, by his skilful adaptation of harmony to the ancient Church tones, that this radical measure was rejected. It is said that such was the Pope's enthusiasm on hearing one of his masses that he exclaimed, "These are the harmonies of the New Song which the Apostle John heard coming out of the new Jerusalem, and which an earthly John [Giovanni] makes us hear in the earthly Jerusalem."

It was not until the sixteenth century that the peculiarly Anglican form of the Church chant arose. By this time the major and minor keys had taken the place of the many ancient "modes," and this change greatly advanced the growth of harmonized music.[1] Though in its later forms,

[1] It seems strange to modern musical ears that the major and minor keys, as we have them now on the organ and piano, were practically unknown to the ancient world, though the key of C natural was long known under the name of Hypolydian. The four keys or "Authentic Modes," as they were called, Dorian, Phrygian, Lydian, and Mixo-Lydian, but named by S. Ambrose, 1st, 2nd, 3rd, and 4th, consisted of the white notes only, as we have them on the piano or organ today, beginning D, E, F, and G To these were added by Gregory four "Plagal Modes," beginning

THE PSALTER 233

varying widely in lightness, melody, and variety from the earlier music, the Anglican chant is historically and musically a development from the ancient modes. The famous *Book of Common Prayer Noted* of John Marbeck (or Merbecke, 1523-1585), chorister and organist of S. George's Chapel, Windsor, "contains the first adaptation of the ancient music of the Latin ritual, according to its then well known rules, *mutatis mutandis*, to the new English translations of the Missal and Breviary." Tallis, organist of Waltham Abbey, the contemporary of Marbeck, pursued the same method, and has been called "the Father of English Cathedral music." In fact the Gregorian chants for the Psalms and Canticles were in use, not only immediately after the Reformation, but far into the seventeenth century. And although the Great Rebellion (1545-1660) silenced the ancient service with its traditional chant, yet the well known work of Clifford, Minor Canon of S. Paul's, gives as the "common tunes" for chanting the English Psalter, etc., correct versions of each of the eight Gregorian tones.

In this connection some notice must be taken of metrical hymns. In the absence of good English translations of the old Latin Office hymns, metrical versions of the Psalms came into use, especially among the Puritan party. In 1549 Sternhold published a version of the first fifty-one Psalms, and in 1562 the whole book was versified by T. Sternhold, J. Hopkins, and others. These were afterwards supplanted by a new version made by N. Brady, D.D., and N. Tate.

---

on the fourth note below the first or "tonic" of the Authentic Scale, and distinguished by prefixing the word "*Hypo*" (under) to the corresponding names of the Authentic, as Hypodorian, etc See an excellent article by Dr Dykes in *Blunt, Ann Pr. Bk.*, pp li-lxv; Oxford *His. of Music;* Helmore, *Plain Song;* and Grove, *Dic. of Music and Musicians*, under Chant, Marbeck, Tallis, etc.

They were sometimes bound up with the Prayer Book, but were not obligatory in England. Strange to say, however, the American Church up to 1872 required that when one of the small collection of hymns bound with the Prayer Book was used, a Psalm or portion in metre should also be sung. These metrical Psalms with few exceptions were entirely lacking in literary quality.

Christian metrical hymns, as distinct from the Hebrew Psalms, came into use from the very beginning, as is evident from such passages as Eph. v, 19 and Col. iii, 16. S. Paul in fact seems to be quoting from an early Easter hymn in the former of these passages (verse 14) as the metrical character of the quotation is evident in the Greek. Compare also 1 Tim. iii, 16; 2 Tim. ii, 11; Rev. iv, 11; v, 9–14; xi, 15–19; xv, 3, 4. Hilary of Poictiers (300–366), Gregory Nazianzen (329–389), and Ambrose of Milan (340–397) are among the earliest of those whose hymns are found in our present collections. The Middle Ages both east and west were rich in such hymns, of which nearly one hundred and fifty in Latin formed the Office hymns of the Church of England. Bishop Ken, Dr. Watts, the two Wesleys, Bishop Heber, Montgomery, and others, from the seventeenth century to the beginning of the nineteenth, wrote many original hymns in English which have stood the test of time, but it was not until after the Oxford Revival, which began in 1833, that the ancient Office hymns were made available to any extent by translation for English Christians. This was also the time when original hymns of the deepest spiritual character and most scholarly finish were produced in large numbers, and composers of the highest musical ability matched them with noble melodies.

CHAPTER XXIII
THE LESSONS AND CANTICLES

"Truth through the Sacred Volume hidden lies,
And spreads from end to end her secret wing,
Through ritual, type, and storied mysteries" — I WILLIAMS.

WE have already seen that LESSONS or LECTIONS from Holy Scripture were first introduced into the office for Holy Communion (p. 155). Their use in the Daily Prayers or Choir Offices was originally confined chiefly to the Psalter, of which very large portions were employed. Lessons from other parts of Holy Scripture were indeed not wholly lacking but they were small in quantity, and were not selected on any regular plan. Our revised morning service, as already stated (p. 204), was formed on the basis of Matins, Lauds, and Prime, while the evening service was an adaptation of Vespers and Compline. Sometimes, as on Advent Sunday, there were three Old Testament Lessons in the unreformed Matins service, but they each consisted of only two verses from Isaiah.[1] A Lesson from the New Testament, called the "Little Chapter," generally taken on important days from the Epistle, formed part of the service of Lauds. We have here therefore the norm on which the revisers based their adoption of a First and Second Lesson, while greatly enlarging the amount. They adopted also a systematic method for the purpose, namely, the reading of the Old Testament through once, and the New Testament twice, in each year.

Though PROPER LESSONS were appointed in the First Book (1549) for a few Holy Days, it was not until the revision

---
[1] Is. i, 1-6.

of 1559 that a table of Old Testament Lessons for Sundays and Holy Days, with a few from the New Testament, was provided, and this Lectionary, with a few changes in 1662, remained in force in the English Church until 1871. At this latest revision of the English Book the principle was recognized that, while "all Scripture is given by inspiration of God, and is profitable for doctrine, for reproof, etc.,[1]" nevertheless all portions are not of equal value in this respect. Much of the Old Testament especially (e.g. Leviticus, the Song of Songs, and obscure chapters in the Prophets) is not adapted to the edification of modern congregations, though valuable in other ways, and there is probably still room for improvement in this direction. The principle of selection which we find in the Eucharistic Lections might well be applied to a large extent to the whole Lectionary.

In 1789 the American Church made many improvements in the Lectionary of 1662, which it had continued to use until then. Many chapters were divided, and less edifying passages omitted. All Sundays were given four Proper Lessons, different from those in the Calendar for the Daily Prayers. All Holy Days received Proper First Lessons, and some Holy Days Proper Second Lessons. A further revision of the American Lectionary was completed in 1883 when large omissions were made from the Old Testament, and nineteen days in November were supplied with Lessons from some of the most beautiful chapters of the Apocrypha. A table of optional Lessons for Lent was also provided. It is to be noted, moreover, that in the English and American Lectionaries alike the Old Testament is begun in January, and the book of Isaiah is read in Advent.[2]

---

[1] 2 Tim iii, 16

[2] The further revision of both the English and American Lectionaries is still under consideration by official bodies

LESSONS AND CANTICLES

The TE DEUM, which derives its name from the first words in Latin ("Thee, O God"), is really a poetical and precatory form of the Creed; "the Creed touched into music."[1] It is called in the Portuary, "The Canticle of Ambrose and Augustine," in allusion to the tradition that it was composed by these two Saints, and first used at the baptism of the latter by S. Ambrose at Milan on April 25, 387. Parts of it seem to have been known to S. Cyprian, the Bishop of Carthage, in 252. But "recent researches have discovered the real author in Niceta, missionary Bishop of Remesiana in Dacia at the end of the fourth century."[2] The rubric in the Sarum Portuary appointed it at Matins on Sundays and Festivals, except in Advent, and from Septuagesima to Easter. In the Book of 1549 it was ordered to be used every day except in Lent, when the *Benedicite* was to take its place.

The Hymn naturally divides itself into four parts. (1) An act of praise to God the Father (1–9). (2) A confession of faith in the three Persons of the Holy Trinity, beginning, "The Holy Church," etc. (10–13). (3) An act of adoration to our Lord for His Incarnation and Redemption (14–19). (4) A prayer addressed to Christ, and based on His work of love for men (20–end). The change in the last verse from the plural "we" to the singular "I" seems intended to give a personal touch to the hymn, bringing its appeal home as in the Creed ("I believe") to each and every worshipper. Or it may be meant to represent the pleading voice of the Church as the Bride of Christ, addressed to her Beloved.[3]

---

[1] Archbp Alexander on *The Psalms*, Lec VI
[2] P. and F., p 380
[3] As the Creed of this hymn of praise properly ends with the words "glory everlasting," permission to omit all that follows on festivals, including all Sundays, as suggested in *A Prayer Book Revised*, with Pref-

238 PRIMITIVE WORSHIP & THE PRAYER BOOK

The BENEDICITE gets its name from the Latin of its refrain, "Bless ye." It is the only canticle taken from the Apocrypha, where it is called the "Song of the Three Children," that is, Shadrach, Meshach, and Abednego, the Babylonian names of the three young Jews, Hananiah, Mishael, and Azariah, who were thrown into the fiery furnace for their refusal to worship the golden image of Nebuchadnezzar.[1] The *Benedicite* is part of the Greek addition to the third chapter of Daniel, as given in the Apocrypha, after the book of Baruch. It is a paraphrase of Psalm cxlviii, and was used as a hymn in the later Jewish Church. It was commonly sung in the Christian Church in the fourth century. In the ancient English use it was appointed for Lauds on Sundays.[2]

Though so simple in construction the Hymn is one of the most inspiring in all Jewish poetry. In the wide sweep of its outlook even the *Te Deum* does not excel it, including as it does "all the works of the Lord," the holy Angels, the Heavens, Nature animate and inanimate, the Children of Men, the Holy Church or spiritual Israel, the Priests of the Lord, and the Spirits and Souls of the Righteous in Paradise and Earth. In days when mere material views of the physical universe are so prevalent, it may well be said that the Hymn is most needful in lifting the soul above the beauty

---

ace by Bishop Gore, is deserving of serious consideration. The added verses, which form no part of the original, are taken from Psalms xxviii, 10, cxlv, 2, and lxxi, 1, together with an ancient antiphon, ' Vouchsafe etc.," and two *Kyries*, "Lord have mercy" Besides the inordinate length on ordinary occasions which a musical rendering involves, every Church musician knows the extreme difficulty of treating this great Hymn musically, ending as it does with a brief Litany, instead of a burst of praise as it began. "To be numbered with Thy saints" should be "to be rewarded, etc ;" *numerari* of the Latin text being an ancient miswriting or misprint for *munerari*, first found in the Breviary of 1491 (P. and F., p. 381).

[1] Dan. i, 6, 7, iii, 8, etc.   [2] Freeman, I, 288.

and grandeur of the world to Him who made it all, in the spirit of a noble passage of S. Augustine in his Confessions. "I asked the earth, and it answered me, 'I am not He'; and whatsoever are in it confessed the same. I asked the sea and the deeps, and they answered, 'We are not thy God, seek above us.' I asked the moving air, and the whole air with his inhabitants answered, 'Anaximenes was deceived, I am not God.' I asked the heavens, sun, moon, stars, 'Nor are we (say they) the God whom thou seekest.' And I replied unto all the things which encompass the door of my flesh; 'Ye have told me of my God, that ye are not He; tell me something of Him.' And they cried out with a loud voice, 'He made us!'"[1]

That too is the spirit of a modern Christian poet and philosopher in presence of "Sovran Blanc" : —

> "Who made you glorious as the gates of Heaven
> Beneath the keen full moon? Who bade the sun
> Clothe you with rainbows? Who, with living flowers
> Of loveliest blue, spread garlands at your feet?
> God! let the torrents, like a shout of nations,
> Answer! and let the ice-plains echo, God!
> God! sing ye meadow-streams with gladsome voice!
> Ye pine-groves, with your soft and soul-like sounds!
> And they too have a voice, yon piles of snow,
> And in their perilous fall shall thunder, God!"[2]

In the musical rendering of the canticle, with the approval of the Bishop of the Diocese, two or more of the invocations are sometimes united into a single strophe, the refrain, "Praise Him, etc.," being only repeated at the end of each. And as the hymn in its origin belongs to the Jewish Church, its Christian character is necessarily marked, as in the Psalter,

---

[1] Bk. X, vi, 9.
[2] Coleridge, *Hymn before Sunrise in the Vale of Chamouni.*

by the addition of the *Gloria Patri*.[1] In the first reformed Prayer Book it was ordered to be sung during Lent instead of the *Te Deum*, and though no direction is given in the present Book, it is a good custom to mark the penitential season by this change. It is to be remembered, however, that the Hymn is equally fitted for festal occasions, and was so used in the early Church.[2]

The BENEDICTUS (Latin for the first word of the hymn, "Blessed"), "The Song of the Prophet Zacharias" (S. Luke i, 68–80), is the most appropriate canticle to follow the second morning Lesson. As in the *Te Deum*, which follows the Old Testament Lesson, we declare that the promises made to the fathers were fulfilled in the Incarnation and Atoning Death and Resurrection of Jesus Christ, the Saviour, so, in the inspired words of the father of John the Baptist, we have, as the First Prayer Book describes it, a "Thanksgiving for the performance of God's promises" in the gift of His Son.

It was the canticle appointed in the old office of Lauds at the conclusion of the "Little Chapter," or Lesson from the New Testament. In the American Prayer Book permission is given to use only the first four verses, "save on the Sundays in Advent," when the whole canticle must be "sung or said."

The JUBILATE (Latin for "O be joyful"), the 100th Psalm, is the substitute for the Benedictus when that hymn is read in the Lesson for the day. This also occupies its old place

---

[1] The employment here of the ordinary form of the *Gloria* is contrary to ancient usage, and is a mistake both rhythmically and musically. It was first introduced in 1549 The ancient form is as follows: — "Let us bless the Father, and the Son, and the Holy Ghost; praise Him and magnify Him for ever Blessed art Thou, Lord, in the firmament of heaven, to be praised, and glorified, and magnified for ever. Amen." See Maskell, *Mon Rit*, II, p. 20.

[2] See Augustine, *Contra Don. ad Petit*, II, xcii, 211.

LESSONS AND CANTICLES

in the unreformed Office, being one of the appointed Psalms for Lauds.

Before speaking of the Evening Canticles it is well to call attention to the fact that the word EVENSONG, the shortened name for Evening Prayer, is peculiar to our reformed Prayer Book. It is first used in the Book of 1549 instead of the word Vespers of the Portuase or Breviary, and, together with Mattins (or Matins), it still retains its place in all books of the Anglican Communion except the American, from which it was unfortunately dropped in 1789. Though it had no place in the unreformed service books, it was evidently the popular name for Vespers long before the Revision, as evidenced by the familiar proverb: —

"Be the day short or never so long,
At length it ringeth to evensong."

The MAGNIFICAT, or "Song of the Blessed Virgin Mary,"[1] which closely resembles the song of Hannah, the mother of the prophet Samuel,[2] has been used at Vespers throughout the whole Western Church as long as the service can be traced. Its position, following the Lesson from the Old Testament containing God's promises of redemption, is a most fitting one. The whole Church finds in this glorious Hymn of the Mother of our Lord the very language which most truly expresses her adoration and thanksgiving for the mystery of the Incarnation, and all that flows from it of love and mercy and salvation. The Hymn has been called the "Marseillaise" of Christian democracy, in its confident prevision that He hath already "put down the mighty from their seat, and hath exalted the humble and meek. He hath filled the hungry with good things, and the rich He hath sent empty away."

---

[1] S Luke I, 46.   [2] 1 Sam. II, 1.

Concerning the *composition* of this great Hymn of the Incarnation it is to be observed that there is no suggestion in S. Luke that it was improvised at the moment of meeting Elizabeth. It was evidently the ripe fruit of prolonged and profound meditation in the heart of one who was "blessed above women," as already bearing within her the sacred Body of the Son of God, gifted, moreover, with spiritual and prophetic genius, and a mind saturated with the poetry of her ancestor David. Its framework and its spirit she found in the beautiful Hymn of Hannah, composed under circumstances similar, though infinitely inferior to her own.

Concerning the *time* of the composition of the *Magnificat*, as well as of the Songs of Zacharias and Simeon,[1] it is noteworthy how accurately this is in accord with the "dayspring from on high"[2] in which it was spoken. If inconceivable earlier, it is more inconceivable later. "Such sunlit mountain-tops in the distance," writes Archbishop Alexander, "with such mists over the paths that lead to them, such a firm grasp upon salvation and redemption, such a clear view of its character as consisting 'in the remission of sins,' yet such silence as to its details, can only belong to the thin border-line of a period, which was neither quite Jewish, nor quite Christian. A little less, and these songs would be purely Jewish; a little more, and they would be purely Christian."[3]

Concerning the *place* of the *Magnificat*, Dr. Liddon has said: —

"There is no mistaking the prominence assigned in the English Prayer-Book, as in many older Prayer-books of the Christian Church, to the Hymn of Mary. It is the centre and heart of our Evening Service. All else leads up to it, or

---

[1] S. Luke i, 68, sq; ii, 29, sq.   [2] *Ibid.* i, 78.
[3] *Leading Ideas of the Gospel*, p. 107.

expands it, or radiates from it. We mount upwards to it by successive steps; by confession of the sins which disqualify the soul of man for true communion with God; by the great prayer which makes all communion with God easy and natural; by Psalms which express the longings of the human heart for some nearer contact with God, or which sadly deplore whatever may hinder it, or which joyfully anticipate its realization. . . . Thus we approach the Hymn which proclaims that all for which Psalmists and Prophets have yearned has in very truth and deed come to be. Mary might seem evening by evening to stand in the Church of her Divine Son, while she celebrates an event compared with which all else in human history is insignificant indeed. As from her thankful heart the incense of praise ascends to the Eternal Throne, first in one and then another incense-wreath, each having its own beauty of tint and form, we reflect that the hardest questions of man's mind have been answered, and that the deepest yearnings of his heart have been satisfied."[1]

The CANTATE DOMINO ("O sing unto the Lord"), Psalm xcviii, was appointed as an alternative Canticle in the Book of 1552. Its appropriateness for this purpose, as being also a song of thanksgiving for the fulfilment of God's promises in the Old Testament, is manifest. The American Prayer Book has still another alternative Canticle, the BONUM EST ("It is a good thing"), consisting of the first four verses of Psalm xcii.

---

[1] *The Magnificat*, pp 3, 4. For some unaccountable reason both the *Magnificat* and the *Nunc Dimittis* were omitted from the American Prayer Book in 1789. In a body of men who adopted in substance the Eucharistic Prayer of Consecration in the Book of 1549, this could scarcely have been from sympathy with the absurdly inconsistent objections of the Puritans to the hymns of the New Testament while they accepted those of the Old. See Hooker, *Eccl Pol.*, V, xl. It may have been owing, however, to an equally absurd notion that in some way the great Hymn of the Blessed Virgin was Romish! Happily both hymns were restored in the revision of 1892.

244 PRIMITIVE WORSHIP & THE PRAYER BOOK

The NUNC DIMITTIS ("Now lettest Thou depart"), the "Song of Simeon,"[1] which follows the New Testament Lesson for Evensong, has been used as an evening Canticle from the very earliest days of the Christian Church. Equally with the *Magnificat*, its position is most appropriate after the Second Lesson telling of the actual fulfilment of God's promises in that salvation which is "a light to lighten the Gentiles, and the glory of His people Israel." In addition to this fitness to the Lesson, this "swan-song" of the aged Simeon, with this thought of "the Light that never was on sea or land," and of the joyful close of his own earthly life, is most appropriate to the close of another day, suggesting as it does the "rest" that "remaineth to the people of God,"[2] of which every night gives us the type and foreshadowing in our sleep.

The DEUS MISEREATUR ("God be merciful"), Psalm lxvii, was first appointed in the Book of 1552 as an alternative Canticle for the *Nunc Dimittis*. The American Prayer Book has still another alternative, the BENEDIC ANIMA MEA, ("Praise the Lord, O my Soul"), consisting of the first four and the last three verses of Psalm ciii.

---

[1] S. Luke II, 29.   [2] Heb. IV, 9.

CHAPTER XXIV
THE CREED

"*The man who has been wandering on the mountains does not recall and describe with a gladder heart the first glimpse which dawn gave him of the track he had lost, than that with which one who has found or recovered his faith in the divine government of the world, and its perfect manifestation in Christ, recites, if he can, the words, 'God of God, Light of Light, very God of very God' . . The recitation of the Creed is an act of intellectual adoration in a day when the intellect is the source of the deepest of our troubles.*" — R. H. HUTTON

WE speak of three Creeds or Confessions of Faith, Apostles', Nicene, and Athanasian, but the Church has in reality only "one Faith," as she has only "one Lord." [1] The three Creeds are but concentric circles around one central point, namely, belief in Jesus Christ, either as confessed by S. Peter when he said, "Thou art the Christ, the Son of the Living God," [2] or by the Ethiopian Treasurer, "I believe that Jesus Christ is the Son of God." [3] The so-called "three Creeds" add nothing to this confession, but only bring out with increasing fulness, when heretical attacks, or ignorance, have made it necessary, the meaning of that pregnant germ of "the one Faith." [4]

It is important to remember that the CREED (named from *credo*, its first word in the Latin, "I believe") is not a composition of human wit and ingenuity, the result of deep

---

[1] Eph. iv, 5.   [2] S. Matt. xvi, 16.   [3] Acts viii, 37.
[4] The Greek name is *sumbolon* or symbol, which means "a proof of authenticity, or a mark of recognition, as a seal-ring, a watch-word, — the proof of orthodoxy" (Procter). It was also called *canon*, that is, the short measure or rule, by which to test all other truths.

thought and research concerning the nature of God, and adopted by the votes of a committee of learned men. It is first a "trust" and then a "tradition," that is, a thing which has been "delivered once for all," [1] and then handed on from age to age, from person to person, from teacher to scholar, from parent to child. It is concerning this trust of the Catholic Faith or Creed that S. Paul writes to his son Timothy, "Hold fast the form of sound words which thou hast heard of me," and then adds, "That good thing which was committed unto thee [not which thou hast reasoned out for thyself] keep by the Holy Ghost which dwelleth in us." [2]

Unlike modern theological "platforms," and "confessions," and "articles," the Church's Creed is marked also by great brevity, conciseness, and simplicity.[3] It is a chart such as one needs on the wide ocean of human opinions, a map, and not a brilliantly colored picture, which would be of little value to a voyager.

As the salvation of Christ was meant for all, "the common salvation," as S. Jude calls it, so the formulary in which the Faith was summed up was suited to all capacities. The Gospel was not an abstract system intended for philosophers or even theologians, but a simple statement of fundamental facts of which the Person of our Lord, and belief in what He

---

[1] 1 Tim. i, 11, vi, 20; S. Jude 3, Rev. Ver.

[2] 2 Tim. i, 13, 14.

[3] The Augsburg Confession of Faith, the standard of Lutheranism, composed by a committee of divines in Augsburg in 1530, contains 28 chapters. The Westminster Confession, the standard of Presbyterianism, was framed by the Assembly of Scotch and English Puritans in Westminster in 1645, and consists of 33 chapters. The "Thirty Nine Articles" of the Church of England, adopted by Convocation in 1562, are not for the most part articles of Faith but of "Religion," dealing with controversies of the day. Though usually bound up with the Prayer Book, they form no necessary part of it, having a separate title page.

THE CREED

is and did and taught and commanded, was the living core and centre. And so, before a word of the New Testament was written, we find these essentials of a Christian's belief gathered by the Church into a brief "form of sound words," or "form of doctrine" in which every believer, no matter how unlearned, possessed the whole Gospel, the whole substance of "the Faith" which he was bidden to "hold fast," in which he must "stand fast," and for which he must "earnestly contend." [1]

Holding fast this simple Creed everything else becomes plain. Difficulties about Holy Scripture, and theories of inspiration, disappear. Believing in a *Person*, as the first Apostles learnt to do, and not merely in a system of religious opinions, the Christian necessarily believes in all He teaches concerning His Father, and the Holy Ghost who "proceedeth from the Father." [2] Like Mary of Bethany, he "sits at Jesus' feet, and hears His word." [3] And so, this "good confession," as S. Paul seems to call it, [4] naturally followed the order or took the form of that three-fold "Name" of Father, Son, and Holy Ghost, "into" which our Lord gave commandment that every believer in Him should be baptized. [5]

Such a simple Creed as this was plainly necessary before the New Testament was written. Even after the New Testament was completed (about the year 96), it still remained a necessity, for the vast majority of believers could not possibly possess a copy of these Scriptures, or read them if they had them, until the invention of printing and cheap paper fourteen hundred years later. It is a necessity even today if children, and those multitudes who always remain children in intelligence, are to have some brief compact statement

---

[1] 2 Tim, i, 13; Rom. vi, 17; xvi, 17; 1 Cor xvi, 13; Jude 3.
[2] S John x, 15; xv, 26, xvi, 28.   [4] 1 Tim. vi, 13.
[3] S. Luke x, 39.   [5] S. Matt. xxviii, 19.

248 PRIMITIVE WORSHIP & THE PRAYER BOOK

of those essential truths which every "Christian ought to know and believe to his soul's health."[1]

It is for this reason also that the Creed has been called the "Rule of Faith" (*Regula Fidei*), for the proper understanding of Holy Scripture, and in its due "proportion,"[2] with Christ as its "Alpha and Omega," its "beginning and ending,"[3] thus escaping those dangers of exaggeration or distortion to which all heresies, ancient and modern alike, invariably tend. The practical wisdom of the Church from the beginning, as well as her motherly care,[4] is seen here in providing for her children a brief "form of sound words" easily learnt, understood, and remembered. Unlike the ever-lengthening creeds and confessions that are buried one after another in dusty volumes, the Creed of the Church has lived upon the lips, and moulded the lives of little children in the weakness of youth, and men in the strength of manhood, in every generation from the first. It is the living voice of the living Church, a hymn of praise like the *Te Deum*, as well as a declaration of faith, which has ever resounded, and will keep on resounding all the days, not only on earth, but, we may well believe, even in Paradise.[5]

Still another most practical and useful purpose of the Creed is thus described by a very thoughtful writer: — "A man who gazes on the Alps for the solitary time in his life feels it fortify his soul to know that they will continue to stand in all their silent grandeur, when he can no longer see them, and long after his own body is part of the dust of the earth. Precisely of the same kind is the effect of the recital of their Creed on those who believe it. It arrays before their minds in all their grandeur and solemnity the great facts on

---
[1] The Baptismal Office.
[2] *Analogia*, Rom. xii, 6.
[3] Rev. i, 8.
[4] "The mother of us all," Gal. iv, 26.
[5] Compare Rev. v, 12; xv, 3.

THE CREED

which their faith is based, and reminds them that those facts are so, whether their attention be drawn to them or not, — are so, behind the clouds of dust in which the world's worries envelop them, as much as in the transparent moments of devotion, — in short, that their faith is the consequence of the *existence* of these great realities, and that these are in no degree the dream of their faith." [1]

Two striking illustrations of the power of the Creed to uphold one's faith are worth recording here. One is that of Lieutenant De Long of the United States Navy, the brave Arctic explorer and a Churchman, who in October 1881 stood amid his dying or dead companions, soon to sink down in death absolutely alone, and surrounded with a seemingly endless desolation of ice and snow. It was then that he and they found their greatest comfort and strength (so the last entry in his diary tells us) in standing up under that awful sky and reciting the simple Creed of their childhood. The other is that of a little child, a true story told by the late Primate of the Church of Ireland: — "A dying boy began to feel the very touch of death. He feared the great change, the dread unknown, 'what dreams may come' in the seeming sleep. Father and mother, friend and nurse, said their little word — hymn and text and prayer. The child asked to be propped upon the pillow and whispered, 'Let me say my Creed.' He said it from 'I believe in God the Father Almighty' down to 'the life everlasting,' and then smiled, and breathed out these words, 'Now I am not afraid to die.'" [2]

---

[1] R H. Hutton, *Aspects of Religious and Scientific Thought*, pp. 5, 6.

[2] *Primary Convictions*, p. 21. It is related of Mrs. Tait, the gifted wife of the Archbishop of Canterbury, that, after being obliged to listen to the loose opinions often expressed by intellectual guests of her husband, she would retire to her room and very slowly and solemnly recite the Creed.

CHAPTER XXV
THE THREE CREEDS

"*It seems to me by every true meaning of the word, by every true thought of the idea, a 'liberal faith' is a faith that believes much, and not a faith that believes little. The more a man believes, the more he sends forth his intelligence into the mysteries of God, the more he understands those things which God chooses to reveal to His creatures*" — PHILLIPS BROOKS.

"*To complain of the Creed as an interference with liberty is to imitate the savage who had to walk across London at night, and who remarked that the lamp-posts were an obstruction to traffic*" — LIDDON.

THE various steps by which the simple confession, "I believe that Jesus Christ is the Son of God" gradually developed into that which we call the APOSTLES' CREED cannot of course be accurately traced. The legend that the Apostles, before they separated at Jerusalem to enter on their world-wide work, compiled the Creed which is called by their name, each of the twelve contributing a clause, cannot be regarded seriously. Nevertheless, there is here a certain element of truth, namely, that it was not composed by any process of discussion or human reasoning, as modern creeds and confessions are made, but these fundamental truths were "committed" or "delivered" to believers as a sacred "trust" by those who were "witnesses" to Christ, who was Himself the chief Creedmaker, "the Faithful and True Witness," as He is called in the book of Revelation.[1] They were the great facts concerning His life, and those things undiscoverable by human wisdom which He had revealed to them.

---

[1] Rev. i, 5, iii, 14; and compare S Luke xxiv, 48, Acts i, 8; ii, 32; iii, 15; v, 32, x, 39, 41, xiii, 31; Rom. vi, 17, 2 Tim i, 13, 14; S. Jude 3.

THE THREE CREEDS 251

Though the substance of these early Creeds was the same in all, nevertheless, in the "form of sound words" setting forth these essential truths (the only ones required for the reception of Holy Baptism), a diocese or province often differed from its neighbor in its exact mode of expressing them. But in course of time the form which prevailed in the diocese of Aquileia, in the north of Italy, became the norm of universal adoption in the Western Church.[1]

The recitation of the Apostles' Creed was part of Prime, the third division of the old Morning Office (Matins, Lauds, and Prime), out of which the reformed Matin service was formed. In the old Evening Offices of Vespers and Compline, from which our Evensong was composed, the Apostles' Creed formed part of the latter Office. As the united confession of our faith it comes most fittingly after the instruction of Psalm and Lesson, and this has been its place from primitive days. In the earliest Greek Offices, as in the English, both old and new, it always appears in this position, and is followed by the Lord's Prayer.[2]

---
[1] The Creed of Aquileia, among other things in which it differed from that of Rome, had the clause "He descended into hell," which was lacking in the other Creed. The American Church allows the words, "He went into the place of departed spirits," to be substituted for the article; adding, "which are considered as words of the same meaning in the Creed." It is certainly very unfortunate that the English language employs the same word to describe two distinct and wholly dissimilar ideas, Hades and Gehenna.

[2] The Lord's Prayer and the three-fold *Kyrie* ("Lord, have mercy etc.") were omitted at the American revision in 1789, and have not been restored. At the same time the Nicene Creed was made an alternate for the Apostles' in the Daily Prayers. Its use in the Eucharistic Office was not made obligatory until 1892, and only on Christmas-day, Easter, Ascension, Whitsunday, and Trinity. The prevailing custom, however, is to use it at every celebration In the Roman Church to this day the Nicene Creed is not said at every Eucharist It was introduced into the

During the ages of persecution, when it was thought necessary to guard these summaries of Christian belief and devotion from the unbelieving, the Creed and Lord's Prayer were not said aloud but secretly and silently. This seems to be the explanation of the custom which continued in the Western Offices long after the reason for it had disappeared.[1]

The history of THE NICENE FORM OF THE CREED is more easily traced than that of the other two. Its original was some form of the Apostles' or baptismal Creed familiar to all the three hundred and eighteen Bishops who gathered from every quarter of the Christian world at the city of Nicæa in Asia Minor at the call of the Emperor Constantine in A.D. 325.[2] The particular Creed which formed its basis seems to have been that of the Mother Church of Jerusalem, and of the neighboring Diocese of Cæsarea. A new heresy had been broached in the Church affecting its very foundation. Arius, a Priest and Rector in Alexandria, a popular preacher, and jealous of his Bishop, Alexander, attempted to foist a new meaning on the words of the old Creed. While

---

Office of the Eastern Church in 471, into the Gallican Church in 589, and somewhat later into the English. It was not adopted into the Roman Liturgy until 1014, and then only "under external pressure, in order to assimilate the use of Rome with that of France and Spain." P. and F., pp. 388–9.

[1] Freeman, *Prin. Div. Ser.*, I, 97, 98.

[2] From the number of Bishops, 318, represented in Greek by the three letters, τιη, tié, the assembly was known as the Tee-ay Council. The Bishop presiding was not the Bishop of Rome, but the venerable Hosius of Cordova in Spain, a striking illustration of the different way in which that Church was regarded in the fourth century. In fact, at not one of the six General Councils did the Bishop of Rome preside either in person or by proxy The British Bishops were represented at Nicæa by two Priests of that Church. All the proceedings, moreover, were recorded in Greek, and not in Latin.

THE THREE CREEDS

still calling Christ "the Son of God," he declared that there was a time when He was not.[1] He denied His eternity, and therefore His true Godhead. And it was to combat this heresy, which had spread rapidly among wordly and unthinking Christians, that this first of the six great Ecumenical or General Councils of the Church was called.

It is important to remember that this Council was not convened to discuss subtle questions of metaphysics, but to declare what had been the belief of the Church "from the beginning."[2] It was not to make a new Creed, but to reaffirm the true meaning of the old, which had been "delivered once for all" to the Church three hundred years before, and whose identity was a matter of human and credible testimony. The doctrine of Arius was a novelty, unknown to the Church till he propounded it. "Who ever heard such doctrine?" Athanasius, the Deacon, and afterwards the successor, of Bishop Alexander, demanded, "Whence, from whom did they gain it? Who thus expounded to them when they were at school?"[3]

The chief question before the Council was how best to express the truth of our Lord's Godhead, so as to guard against future misinterpretation. The discussion centred on a single Greek word, in fact on a single letter. This word was *homoousion*, "of one substance," while the Arians were only willing to say that He was *homoiousion*, "of like substance." It was but the difference of an *iota* ("jot"), or *i*, the smallest letter in the Greek alphabet, but it signified all the difference between the Creator and the creature, truth and falsehood. Christ was either God, or else He was only a creation of God, therefore infinitely below Him, and

---
[1] See Hooker, *Ecc. Pol*, V, xlii.
[2] 1 S. John II. 7; 2 S John 5
[3] Newman, *The Arians of the Fourth Century*, 3rd Ed., p. 260, note.

one who could be no object of divine worship, or an infallible guide. There was no middle position possible.[1]

The original of the Creed uses the plural "We" throughout, instead of the singular "I," but in public worship "I" is the use of both East and West. The form adopted by the Council, all the three hundred and eighteen Bishops signing, was in substance that which we possess today, ending with "I believe in the Holy Ghost." The portion which follows was added at the Second General Council (Constantinople, A.D. 381), to meet the heresy of Macedonius who denied the Godhead of the Holy Ghost; and it was confirmed by the Third General Council (Ephesus, A.D. 431), and by the Fourth (Chalcedon, A.D. 451). "The Lord," after "the Holy Ghost, does not mean merely "the Lord of Life," but Jehovah, God, thus affirming His equality with the Father and the Son.

There is one exception to this statement which must be noted. The words "and from the Son," in Latin, FILIOQUE, describing the procession of the Holy Ghost, have never been admitted into the Creed as used by the Eastern Church. They were first introduced probably as an additional protest against the Arian denial of the perfect Godhead of the Son, at the great Council of Toledo in Spain in 589, or, according to Bingham, at the still earlier Council of Bracara in 411. Through the influence of the Emperor Charlemagne, the reputed author of the Hymn, *Veni Creator Spiritus* ("Come Holy Ghost"), it was adopted throughout France and Germany, and later in Rome, about 850. In 1054, together with

---

[1] It should be observed that the phrase "God of God," etc., is not the genitive of possession, but signifies "God *proceeding from* God," etc., as the use of the preposition *ek*, "out of," implies. "Of" should therefore be slightly emphasized in recitation. "Very" is of course an adjective as used here, signifying "true" or "real."

THE THREE CREEDS

the insolent assumptions of the Roman See, it became a chief cause of the separation of the Eastern and Western Churches which continues to this day.

The Eastern Church did not object so much to the doctrine involved, which, as held by the West, does not materially, if at all, differ from that of the East, as it did to the fact that the addition was made by a local and then unlettered Church, and especially that it was enforced by the Roman See by way of asserting its claim of dominion over the Faith of the whole Church. At the English Reformation the question was not raised, and so the clause was retained. As, however, the Western interpretation does not really differ from the doctrine as held by the great Eastern Churches (Russian, Greek, etc.), it is to be hoped that this cause of continued separation may be removed in time by mutual agreement.[1]

The work of the first great Council of the Church has been well summed in the words of the late Primate of the Church of Ireland: —

"Within six weeks three hundred and eighteen men, most of them unknown to one another, speaking many languages, and brought from the ends of the world, could give a formula which told of the Divine Nature, of the origin of the world, of the destinies of man; which answers the eternal questions — What am I? From whence do I come? Where am I going? — in a shape at once lofty and concise; at once so noble that it almost seems to touch the *Gloria in Excelsis*, and so precise that philosophy and legislation can show

---

[1] The Old Catholics have removed the offending *Filioque* clause from the Creed, while they retain it in their manuals of instruction As a result of their negotiations with the Eastern Church a commission of the Holy Synod adopted three propositions on the subject, the third of which seems to admit of the retention of the clause in the sense of "*through the Son*," as a theological "speculation " (W. J. Birkbeck, *Lec on the Russian Church*, pp. 39, 40, S. P. C. K., 1916).

nothing superior. It has crossed every sea, and outlived every generation."[1]

The third form of the Creed, "commonly called THE CREED OF S. ATHANASIUS," was named after that great defender of the faith (who died A.D. 373), as containing an accurate statement of what he and the true Catholics of his day believed. Many writers speak of it as a Hymn, or Psalm, placing it in the same list as the *Te Deum*, which is also a Creed in the form of a Hymn. It has been variously attributed to Hilary, Bishop of Arles in 429, and to Victricius, Bishop of Rouen in 401, as intended to meet the spread of Arianism in the French Church.[2] The title, *Quicunque vult*, is the Latin for the first two words, "Whosoever will." "In Rome the *Quicunque* does not seem to have been regarded as one of the Creeds before the days of Pope Innocent III (A.D. 1198–1216), and its acceptance in the Greek Church was probably somewhat later."[3]

The first two verses and the last are not, strictly speaking, part of the Hymn, or at least are not part of the Faith which the Hymn contains. They form a kind of preface and conclusion to the Creed proper.[4] Of this, Part I declares the Catholic doctrine of the Trinity, and Part II the doctrine of the Incarnation.

The words, "Whosoever *will* be saved," mean "Whosoever *willeth* (that is, desireth) to be saved." Neither they nor the

---

[1] *Primary Convictions*, p 20

[2] See Waterland, *Critical His of Athn Creed*, Harvey, *His and Theology of the Three Creeds*, p. 580, and Ommaney, *Critical Dissertation on the Athn. Creed*.

[3] J R. Lumby, *Prayer Book Commentary*, p. 82.

[4] The Nicene Creed, as adopted by the great Council, had a similar "damnatory clause," or anathema, appended to it, but it forms no part of the Creed, and has never been recited in the worship of the Church. For the words of the Athanasian Creed see pp. 258, sq.

THE THREE CREEDS

words in the second verse pronounce judgment upon any who have not the opportunity of knowing the truth. In fact, they express no more than our Lord's own words, "He that believeth and is baptized shall be saved; but he that disbelieveth shall be condemned"[1] Moreover, it is very certain that they who live holy lives, and who, through no fault of their own, do *not* while on earth "hold the Catholick faith," will have it made clear to them, and *will* hold it in Paradise ere the fulness of salvation is reached in the "life everlasting" of Heaven.

It is of this Creed that Keble wrote: —

"The Psalm that gathers in one glorious lay
All chants that e'er from heaven to earth found way:
  Majestic march! as meet to guide and time
  Man's wandering path in life's ungenial clime,
As Aaron's trump for the dread Ark's array.
Creed of the Saints, and Anthem of the Blest,
And calm-breathed warning of the kindliest love
That ever heaved a wakeful mother's breast,
(True love is bold, and gravely dares reprove,)
Who knows but myriads owe their endless rest
To thy recalling, tempted else to rove?"
                     — *Lyra Apostolica.*

All three forms of the Creed were used in the early English Offices. The Nicene had its place in that for Holy Communion, while the Apostles', and the Athanasian were appointed in the Daily Prayers. The latter was sung daily at Prime, whereas in the Roman Breviary it is ordered to be used only on Sundays.

In 1549 the Apostles' Creed was appointed for ordinary use, both morning and evening, but the Athanasian was to be said in its stead at Matins upon the six festivals of Christmas, Epiphany, Easter, Ascension, Pentecost, and Trinity.

---
[1] S. Mark xvi, 16, R.V.

In 1552 seven Saints' Days were added, so that the Creed might be said at intervals of a month throughout the year. This is still the rule of the English Book. The Church of Ireland at the revision of 1877 retained the Creed in its customary place after Evening Prayer, and continued to declare it, in her eighth Article of Religion, to be of equal authority with the other two Creeds, but the rubric providing for its public use was omitted. The American Church in 1789 unfortunately omitted the Creed itself, as well as any reference to it in the eighth Article, but she implicitly accepts it in the Preface to the Prayer Book, where she declares that "this Church is far from intending to depart from the Church of England in any essential point of doctrine, discipline, or worship; or further than local circumstances require."

Appendix to Chapter XXV
THE CREED OF SAINT ATHANASIUS
(COMMONLY SO-CALLED)
QUICUNQUE VULT

Whosoever will be saved: before all things it is necessary that he hold the Catholick Faith.

Which Faith except everyone do keep whole and undefiled: without doubt he shall perish everlastingly.

1. And the Catholick Faith is this: That we worship one God in Trinity, and Trinity in Unity.

Neither confounding the Persons: nor dividing the Substance.

For there is one Person of the Father, another of the Son: and another of the Holy Ghost.

But the Godhead of the Father, of the Son, and of the Holy Ghost, is all one: the Glory equal, the Majesty co-eternal.

Such as the Father is, such is the Son: and such is the Holy Ghost.

THE THREE CREEDS

The Father uncreate, the Son uncreate: and the Holy Ghost uncreate.

The Father incomprehensible, the Son incomprehensible: and the Holy Ghost incomprehensible.

The Father eternal, the Son eternal: and the Holy Ghost eternal.

And yet they are not three eternals: but one eternal.

As also there are not three incomprehensibles, nor three uncreated: but one uncreated, and one incomprehensible.

So likewise the Father is Almighty, the Son Almighty: and the Holy Ghost Almighty.

And yet they are not three Almighties: but one Almighty.

So the Father is God, the Son is God: and the Holy Ghost is God.

And yet they are not three Gods: but one God.

So likewise the Father is Lord, the Son Lord: and the Holy Ghost Lord.

And yet not three Lords: but one Lord.

For like as we are compelled by the Christian verity: to acknowledge every Person by himself to be God and Lord;

So are we forbidden by the Catholick Religion: to say, There be three Gods, or three Lords.

The Father is made of none: neither created nor begotten.

The Son is of the Father alone: not made, nor created, but begotten.

The Holy Ghost is of the Father and of the Son: neither made, nor created, nor begotten, but proceeding.

So there is one Father, not three Fathers; one Son, not three Sons: one Holy Ghost, not three Holy Ghosts.

And in this Trinity none is afore, or after other: none is greater, or less than another:

But the whole three Persons are co-eternal together: and co-equal.

So that in all things, as is aforesaid: the Unity in Trinity and the Trinity in Unity is to be worshipped.

He therefore that will be saved: must thus think of the Trinity.

2. Furthermore, it is necessary to everlasting salvation: that he also believe rightly the Incarnation of our Lord Jesus Christ.

For the right Faith is, that we believe and confess: that our Lord Jesus Christ, the Son of God, is God and Man.

God, of the Substance of the Father, begotten before the worlds: and Man, of the Substance of his Mother, born in the world;

Perfect God, and perfect Man: of a reasonable soul and human flesh subsisting.

Equal to the Father, as touching his Godhead: and inferior to the Father, as touching his Manhood.

Who although he be God and Man; yet he is not two, but one Christ;

One; not by conversion of the Godhead into flesh: but by taking of the Manhood into God;

One altogether, not by confusion of Substance: but by unity of Person.

For as the reasonable soul and flesh is one man: so God and Man is one Christ;

Who suffered for our salvation: descended into hell, rose again the third day from the dead.

He ascended into heaven, he sitteth on the right hand of the Father, God Almighty: from whence he shall come to judge the quick and the dead.

At whose coming all men shall rise again with their bodies: and shall give account for their own works.

And they that have done good shall go into life everlasting: and they that have done evil, into everlasting fire.

This is the Catholick Faith, which except a man believe faithfully he cannot be saved.

Glory be to the Father, etc.

CHAPTER XXVI

THE PRAYERS, LITANY, AND OCCASIONAL PRAYERS

"*Non vox sed votum; non chordula musica sed cor; non cantans sed amans cantat in aure Dei*" (*Not the word but the wish; not the harpstring but the heart; not the singing but the loving, sings in the ear of God*)
— S AUGUSTINE.

WE come now to the fourth and final division of the Daily Offices. The recitation of the Creed in the old service, as well as in the new, is followed in the English Book by what is called the "MUTUAL SALUTATION," or "Benediction" of Priest and People ("The Lord be with you," etc.), which is incidentally a witness to the priestly character of both Priests and People, each blessing the other according to their position as "Ministers," or else as Members of the "Royal Priesthood" to which every baptized and confirmed believer is admitted.[1] This Salutation, "which is of primitive if not Apostolic origin,"[2] marks the transition here from the service of Praise to that of Prayer.

The "LESSER LITANY," addressed to each Person of the Holy Trinity, "Lord, have mercy upon us; *Christ, have mercy upon us;* Lord, have mercy upon us," precedes the Lord's Prayer. Following the ancient custom, "the Priest," as he is now called, is directed in the English Book to stand up during the recitation of the six versicles and responses which are taken from the old service books, all save the fifth being found in the Psalter.[3]

---
[1] See 1 Peter ii, 9, Rev i, 6, v, 10, and compare the mutual Confession and Absolution, chap xvii, p 167.
[2] Proctor and Frere, p 393
[3] Ps lxxxv, 7, xx, 9, cxxxii, 9, xxviii, 9, li, 10, 11.

In the American Book the Lesser Litany and Lord's Prayer are omitted here. The word "Priest" is retained, but there is no direction for him to stand, as in the English Book. The Salutation also is followed directly in the American Book by the six VERSICLES, beginning "O Lord, show Thy mercy, etc."; but only the first and the last versicle are said at Matins. The others, which had been omitted in 1789, were restored to Evensong in 1892; "O Lord, save the State" being substituted for "O Lord, save the King." The response to "Give peace, etc.," "Because there is none other that fighteth for us but only Thou, O God," was also changed to, "For it is Thou, Lord, only, that makest us dwell in safety." The English form implies a state of frequent wars, the common experience of earlier days, and, alas, one that is not yet banished from the earth.

THE COLLECT FOR THE DAY, which follows first, is a link between the Daily Offices and that for Holy Communion. It is intended to carry forward the special teaching of the previous Sunday or other Festival, like

"Healthful founts in Elim green,
Casting a freshness o'er the week."[1]

THE MORNING AND EVENING COLLECTS "For Peace," "For Grace," and "For Aid against Perils," and the "Prayer for Clergy and People,"[2] are translations from the old Salisbury Use, and are found in the Sacramentaries of Gelasius and Gregory. The terse and beautiful phrase, "Whose service is perfect freedom," has a still more epigrammatic form in the Latin original, *Cui servire regnare est*, "Whom to

---

[1] Isaac Williams, *The Cathedral*, and see Ex. xv, 27.
[2] The phrase in this prayer, "Who alone workest great marvels" (Ps. lxxxvi, 8), was changed in the American Book of 1789 to "From whom cometh every good and perfect gift."

serve is to reign." It is not too much to claim, however, that the English version, while preserving the strength of the Latin, is more graceful, and at the same time suggestive of a great truth dear to English ears.

THE PRAYER OF S. CHRYSOSTOM, which brings the service to a happy close, is probably not the composition of this great Bishop. It does not occur in the old English Offices, but is taken directly word for word from the Liturgy of the Eastern Church which was originally revised by Basil and Chrysostom (370–397) and where it is called the "Prayer of the Third Antiphon".[1] Its position at the end of the Office may sometimes suggest to us the humiliating memory of wandering thoughts, and bid us ask, Have we indeed made "our common supplications" to God? It was first used at the end of the Litany in 1544. In 1637 it received its present place in the Scottish Prayer Book, and in 1662 in the English.

We have already seen the early beginnings of the use of a LITANY. The word has a Greek origin, and in its primary meaning denotes supplication or petition in general. In the *Testament of our Lord* (fourth century), and the *Apostolic Constitutions*, there is a form of supplication of the kind which we now call a Litany.[2] The Deacon names the subjects of petition, and the people answer to each, "Lord, have mercy"; the words, "Let us pray," being frequently introduced.

Sometime in the fourth century the Litany in the Eastern Church [3] assumed the form of a solemn street processional, as in Constantinople, for an offset against the Arian methods

---

[1] Neale, *Prim Lit*, p. 95.
[2] Maclean, *Recent Discoveries*, p. 33
[3] Called the *Ectené*, from the word *ektenesteron*, "more earnestly," describing our Lord's prayer in Gethsemane, S. Luke xxii, 44.

in 398. It was joined in by clergy and people, and hymns were employed in it also.[1] From the fact that the *Kyrie, eleison,* "Lord, have mercy," formed so large a part of the Litany, this alone came to be called the Litany, and the name with this signification lingers in that three-fold *Kyrie,* "Lord, have mercy — Christ, have mercy — Lord, have mercy," which is still called the *Lesser Litany.*

The use of Litanies in the West is clearly associated with the Rogation Days, the three fasts preceding the Feast of the Ascension.[2] Their use in the Church of France, about A.D. 460, on the occasion of grievous calamities in the diocese of Vienne, seems to be the first appointment of Litanies for fixed days of the year. At the close of the next century, under Gregory the Great of Rome, the custom was further developed, and we find S. Augustine with his company of missionaries, whom Gregory sent to convert the Angles and Saxons, entering the kingdom of Kent, and the old city of Canterbury, chanting such a Litany (A.D. 597). In course of time Psalms and even anthems were added in the solemn processions, which were usually headed with a cross, and collects were said at certain stations along the way. Besides the Rogation Days, Litanies were accustomed to be said in the early English Church during Lent also, and on special occasions.

THE LITANY as we have it today is said to have been arranged by Archbishop Cranmer, and the remarkable beauty and rhythm of its language seem to justify the praise of Hooker, himself a great stylist, when he speaks of it as "a work, the absolute perfection whereof upbraideth with error, or something worse, them whom in all parts it doth not

---

[1] P. & F, p 405.

[2] For the origin of these days see *The Christian Year; Its Purpose and Its History,* p 121.

satisfy." Defending it against the carping objections of the Puritans he writes: —

"As therefore Litanies have been of longer continuance than that we should make either Gregory or Mamercus the author of them, so they are of more permanent use than that now the Church should think it needeth them not. What dangers at any time are imminent, what evils hang over our heads, God doth know and not we. We find by daily experience that those calamities may be nearest at hand, readiest to break in suddenly upon us, which we in regard of times or circumstances may imagine to be furthest off. Or if they do not indeed approach, yet such miseries as being present all men are apt to bewail with tears, the wise by their prayers should rather prevent. Finally, if we for ourselves had a privilege of immunity, doth not true Christian charity require that whatsoever any part of the world, yea, any one of all our brethren elsewhere, doth either suffer or fear, the same we account as our own burden? What one petition is there found in the whole Litany, whereof we shall ever be able at any time to say that no man living needeth the grace or benefit therein craved at God's hands? I am not able to express how much it doth grieve me, that things of principal excellency should be thus bitten at, by men whom God hath endued with graces both of wit and learning for better purposes." [1]

Most of the petitions of our present Litany have been in use in the English Church for more than a thousand years. There were English versions of the Litany in the Prymers, or Prayer Books of the People, and in common use as early as the fourteenth century.[2] The present form was put forth in 1544, and was called the *Common Prayer of Procession*. With the exception of the Creed, Lord's Prayer, and the Decalogue, which were issued in English in 1536, it was the

---

[1] *Ecc Pol*, V, xli, 3, 4
[2] See Maskell, *Mon Rit*, II, pp 217, 223, for examples.

first part of the Prayer Book that appeared in the "tongue understanded of the people."

The rubric at this time directed the Litany to be "sung," as had been the custom hitherto. In 1549 it was ordered "said or sung" on Wednesdays and Fridays. In 1552 there was added "Sundays, and at other times." At the last revision in 1662, the order was changed to "sung or said," as in both English and Irish Books of today. In accordance with the Injunctions of Edward VI and Elizabeth the place where it was to be said was "in the midst of the church," that is, on the floor of the nave, at the entrance to the choir, and a "faldstool," or folding-stool, was usually provided for this purpose.[1]

It will add to the intelligent and reverent use of the Litany to note its several divisions, each distinct of its kind. There are in all five of these, namely, (1) the INVOCATIONS, "O God the Father," etc.; (2) the DEPRECATIONS (preceded by the prayer, "Remember not," etc.), "From all evil," etc.; (3) the OBSECRATIONS, "By the mystery," etc.; (4) the SUPPLICATIONS, "We sinners do beseech Thee," etc.; (5) the VERSICLES AND PRAYERS.[2]

In the mediæval Litanies numerous saints were invoked by name, beginning with the Blessed Virgin, angels and archangels, patriarchs, and apostles, each followed by the

---

[1] Compare Joel ii, 17, "between the porch and the altar." Bp. Doane of Albany used to say that the reason for this place for the Litany was that the Priest might be down among "the other miserable sinners."

[2] "Father of Heaven" (*Pater de coelis*) is of course the equivalent of "Heavenly Father" It is a common error in reciting the response, "Have mercy upon us miserable sinners," to emphasize the word "upon" as if it were of chief importance, and to make a pause after "us" A little thought will show that the emphatic word is "mercy," and that "us" and "miserable sinners," being in apposition, should be spoken, as they are printed, without any pause

PRAYERS, LITANY &c 267

response, "Pray for us" (*Ora pro nobis*). Following the revision of the offices made by Hermann, Archbishop of Cologne, these invocations were all omitted in the English revision of 1549.[1] The fifth deprecation at this time read, "From all sedition and privy conspiracy; from the tyranny of the Bishop of Rome, and all his detestable enormities; from all false doctrine and heresy; from hardness of heart, and contempt of Thy word and commandment, *Good Lord, deliver us.*" This reference to the Bishop of Rome was omitted in Elizabeth's reign (1559). The absence of the word "schism" in both Books is very noteworthy, as it was not until 1568 that the first Protestant sect, that of the Congregationalists or Independents, was formed; and not until 1570 that the Roman Bishop, Pius V, finding that he could not bring the English Catholic Church back into his obedience, sent foreign Priests into the country, who drew away members of the Church from their ancient parish churches, and their lawful English Priests and Bishops. This was the beginning of the Roman sect or schism in England. Up to this time there never had been any such body known, either to the ecclesiastical or the civil law, as the "Roman Catholic Church" in England.[2]

---

[1] On the general question of the Invocation of Saints, see chap xiv.
[2] It was not until 1623 that this Roman sect received its first Bishop, and it was not until more than two hundred years later, namely, in 1850, that it ventured to claim for itself any local jurisdiction in the land, or to adopt local titles for its Bishops, such as Westminster, Salford, etc , sees unknown hitherto in English history Up to that year they were merely Bishops *in partibus infidelium*, that is, with titles taken from heathen lands The first Presbyterian societies came into existence in 1572, and in 1633 the Baptists separated from the Congregationalists, since which time the "Dissidence of Dissent" has gone on increasing, so that in the beginning of the twentieth century there were nearly two hundred sects "professing and calling themselves Christians " in England alone.

It is to be observed that all the petitions of the Litany proper, with the exception of three (to the Father, the Holy Ghost, and the Holy Trinity), are addressed to the Lord Jesus. The appropriateness of this appeal to Him "who was in all points tempted like as we are," and can therefore be "touched with the feeling of our infirmities,"[1] is especially evident in the Deprecations from bodily and spiritual evils.

The American Church in 1789 necessarily omitted all mention of the King, the royal family, and the Council and Nobility, and changed the petition so as to read, "That it may please Thee to bless and preserve all Christian Rulers and Magistrates." The petition, "From fornication, and all other deadly sin" was changed to "From all inordinate and sinful affections." It was also ordered that after "O Lamb of God, etc.," the Minister may, at his discretion, omit all that followeth, to the Prayer, "We humbly beseech Thee, O Father, etc." In the American revision of 1892, after the petition, "That it may please Thee to illuminate all Bishops, etc.," there was added, "That it may please Thee to send forth labourers into Thy harvest." In the Preface, "Concerning the Service of the Church," it was declared that "The order for Morning Prayer, the Litany, and the Order for the Administration of the Lord's Supper or Holy Communion, are distinct services, and may be used either separately or together, Provided, that no one of these Services be habitually disused."

It will be observed that the beautiful Collect following the Versicle, "O Lord, deal not with us after [that is, as in the American Book, *according to*] our sins,"[2] does not end with the usual *Amen*, because the Versicles that follow carry on the thoughts there expressed. "This portion of the

---
[1] Heb IV, 15.   [2] Compare Ps, CIII, 10.

Litany was taken from the mediæval Litany sung on Rogation Monday, and the first clause, 'O Lord, arise, help us, and deliver us, for Thy Name's sake,' is adopted from Ps. xliv, 26, while the words of Ps. xliv, 1 supply the verse in which we seek to remind the Most High of the noble works declared unto us as wrought by Him in those days, and in the old time before them."[1] The introduction of the *Gloria* here is also very fitting as an act of praise and thanksgiving to the Holy Trinity for all that God has done for us in the past, is doing for us now, and we trust will do for us through all eternity.

The Versicles that follow the *Gloria*, "From our enemies, etc." are particularly appropriate to times of war and public sorrow, or of private trial and affliction. The final collect is an adaptation from one appointed in the old Sarum Office for All Saints' Day. The American Church placed the General Thanksgiving here before the Prayer of S. Chrysostom.

The prayers following those for Peace, Grace, and Aid against Perils at Matins and Evensong, and the Occasional Prayers and Thanksgivings (with one exception), were composed by Cranmer, Cosin, Gunning, Reynolds, and others. In this they only did what Basil, Chrysostom, Leo, Gelasius, and Gregory did a thousand years or more before. The one exception is the beautiful Collect in the Occasional Prayers, "O God whose nature and property is ever to have mercy and to forgive," etc., which had its place in the English Prymer from the earliest times, and may be traced to the Sacramentary of S. Gregory (A.D. 590). For some strange reason this prayer was omitted from the American Book in 1789, but was restored in 1892, and placed in the Penitential Office for Ash Wednesday.

---

[1] Maclear, *Pr. Bk Comm*, p. 55.

THE OCCASIONAL PRAYERS AND THANKSGIVINGS were given their present place in the Prayer Book in 1662. Of the two prayers for the Ember Days, the former was composed by Bp. Cosin, and the second is taken from the Ordination Service.[1] The Prayer for the High Court of Parliament was probably composed by Archbishop Laud in 1625, for that body which, "by a strange irony of history, some twenty years later, sent him to the block, as the first man in England condemned to death by Parliament," [2] that is, by attainder, and not by due process of law. In the American Prayer Book this became, with the necessary changes, "A Prayer for Congress." The "Collect or Prayer for All Conditions of Men,[3] to be used at such times when the Litany is not appointed to be said," was at the same time transferred, together with the General Thanksgiving, to the end of Morning and Evening Prayer, as being in that place more convenient for use.

The Thanksgivings for Rain, Fair Weather, Plenty, Peace, Deliverance from Enemies, and from Sickness, date from 1604. That for Restoring Peace at Home was appropriately inserted in 1662 after the Restoration of Charles II in 1660, when the Church was once more given her liberty, and the free use of her church buildings and her Prayer Book, after being forbidden to do so by the usurping Parliament for fifteen years. It owes its origin to Bishop Wren, perse-

---

[1] For the derivation of the word Ember, and the occasion of the appointment of the Ember Days, see *The Christian Year: Its Purpose and its History*, pp. 120, 121.

[2] Dr. Samuel Hart, *The Book of Common Prayer*, p. 109.

[3] The petition "that all who profess and call themselves Christians may be led into the way of truth" evidently referred to the Puritans, and is therefore peculiarly applicable today to those many sects which are an almost direct result of this earliest separation from the ancient branch of the Catholic Church in England.

PRAYERS, LITANY &c

cuted by the Puritans, and a prisoner in the Tower for eighteen years.

Prayers to be used at the Meetings of Convention (General or Diocesan), and for Persons going to Sea, also Thanksgivings for a Recovery from Sickness, and for a Safe Return from Sea, were added to the American Book in 1789. In 1892 there were added prayers for "The Unity of God's People" (taken from the English service for the Anniversary of the Accession of a Sovereign); for Missions, for Fruitful Seasons (two forms, for the Rogation Days, the former taken from the proposed English revision of 1689), and a Thanksgiving for a Child's Recovery from Sickness.[1]

---

[1] There is a confessed need, both in England and America, for additional prayers for special occasions. Some, however, are of the opinion that this can be better attained by the authorization of a separate Book of Offices, which would not be subject to the rigid rules necessarily controlling the Book of Common Prayer, and in which such prayers could be tested by actual use.

Canon Bright's *Ancient Collects*, containing translations from Eastern as well as Western Sacramentaries, is a rich mine of devotions which might well, nay must be, largely drawn upon for such a book as the Church needs.

CHAPTER XXVII
ORNAMENTS OF THE CHURCH, AND OF THE MINISTERS THEREOF

"Every particular or national Church hath authority to ordain, change, and abolish, Ceremonies or Rites of the Church ordained only by man's authority, so that all things be done to edifying." — ARTICLES OF RELIGION.

IN the revised Books of 1549 and 1552 few specific directions were given as to the externals of Divine Service. These were left, as is the case in our present Book, almost entirely to ancient custom. During the ten unquiet and reactionary years between 1549 and 1559, however, great diversity and gross irregularities had grown up in the Church, chiefly among the Puritans, and it became necessary in the latter year, when Elizabeth was on the throne, to adopt some definite rule on the subject. This was done in the form of a rubric substantially the same as that in the present English Book, which received its final shape in 1662. This is popularly called "THE ORNAMENTS RUBRIC," preceding the Order for Morning Prayer, and is as follows: — "The Morning and Evening Prayer shall be used in the accustomed place of the Church, Chapel, or Chancel; except it shall be otherwise determined by the Ordinary of the Place. And the Chancels shall remain as they have done in times past.

"And here is to be noted, that such Ornaments of the Church, and of the Ministers thereof, at all times of their Ministration, shall be retained, and be in use, as were in this Church of England, by the Authority of Parliament, in the Second Year of the Reign of King Edward the Sixth." (Jan. 28, 1547–8, to Jan. 27, 1548–9.)

ORNAMENTS OF THE CHURCH &c 273

Between 1559 and 1662 certain other directions were issued, namely: (1) Royal Injunctions in 1559, (2) Royal Advertisements in 1564-5; (3) Canons in 1603-4; and (4) Canons in 1640. It is important to remember, however, that all these were only either explanations of the rubric and statute, or else attempts to secure uniformity and decency in the conduct of Divine Service. Rubric and statute, as the highest laws of the Church and State in England, remained, and still remain, unaffected by them.

It is to be observed also that the word "ORNAMENTS" as used in the rubric has a wider meaning than that in ordinary use. In 1857 the Final Court of Appeal in Ecclesiastical Causes in England, namely, the Judicial Committee of the Privy Council, consisting of five lay Judges with the Archbishop of Canterbury, and the Bishop of London, decided that "the term 'Ornaments' in Ecclesiastical law is not confined, as by modern usage, to articles of decoration or embellishment, but it is used in the larger sense of the word 'ornamentum.' All the several articles used in the performance of Services and Rites of the Church are 'Ornaments.' Vestments, Books, Cloths, Chalices, and Patens, are amongst Church Ornaments." Then, after examining the "Advertisements," "Injunctions," Canons, etc., they decide that "they all obviously mean the same thing, that the same dresses and the same utensils, or articles, which were used under the first Prayer Book of Edward the Sixth may still be used."

"THE ORNAMENTS OF THE MINISTER" here referred to are as follows: — Cope (a large cloak or cape (*capa*) fastened at the neck in front), Vestment (that is, a chasuble), Tunicle (a short plain surplice), Albe (a long plain surplice with tight sleeves), Surplice, Hood (especially in preaching), with

Pastoral Staffe and Rochette (an albe with full sleeves) for Bishops.[1]

"There is nothing mysterious about Christian liturgical dress or sacred vestments. They are simply the adaptation to religious use of the ordinary dress of civil, and particularly of official, life in the Roman Empire in the first centuries of our era. Whatever value they possess comes from two considerations, first their beauty, dignity, and seemliness, and secondly their historical associations." These words are from the *Report of a Sub-committee of the Upper House of the Convocation of Canterbury, on the Ornaments of the Church and its Ministers*.[2] The same report describes the chimere as a sleeveless overcoat, and, "like cope and chasuble, an out-door dress"; a cassock, "a sleeveless under-chimere or tabard." "Cranmer is represented in a dark green chimere in his portrait by Gerbicus Flicius, now in the National Portrait Gallery, dated 1546, perhaps as a Doctor of Divinity."[3]

In the Office for the Consecration of a Bishop in all branches of the Anglican Communion the only portion of a Bishop's official dress that is named is the "rochet." The "chimere," as the vestment of satin in ordinary use today is called, is not mentioned there, the only direction given being the general one concerning "the rest of the Episcopal habit," which, according to the rubric of the First Prayer Book of Edward, was "a cope or vestment." In fact the origin of the chimere seems to be as follows. In the reign of Henry VIII and Edward VI the scarlet habit of a Doctor of Divinity

---

[1] See Blunt, *Ann Pr. Book*, pp. lxx–lxxiv. It is a curious fact that the "black gown," once so common in the pulpit, was probably a survival of the rule that if the preacher was a "regular," that is, a monk, "he was to continue clothed in the habit of his order only." Scudamore, 333.

[2] S. P. C. K, 1908, p. 5.

[3] *Ibid.* p. 32; P. and F., p. 361.

ORNAMENTS OF THE CHURCH &c 275

(sometimes called a chimere) over the rochet was substituted for the cope or vestment, but without any authority, and late in Elizabeth's reign the color was changed to black, probably in deference to Puritan prejudice. It is to be remembered therefore that the name chimere belongs only to the Doctor's satin robe, the lawn sleeves being properly a part of the sleeveless rochet, but now attached, as a matter of convenience, to the chimere.[1]

The Prayer Book contains no direction for the vestments to be worn by Priests or Deacons. The only provision is that they shall be "decently habited" at their ordination. For what this means we must look elsewhere. The story of Goldsmith presenting himself for ordination in a scarlet riding coat may illustrate this lack of definiteness in our ritual law.

"THE ORNAMENTS OF THE CHURCH" expressed or implied in the Book of 1549, though the rubric undoubtedly includes others, are as follows: — The Altar, Lord's Table, or God's Board, a Corporal, or "Corporas" (linen cloth for the bread), Paten, Chalice, and Cruets, a Credence Table, Poor men's Box, Font, Pulpit, and Chair for the Bishop.[2]

Though all these Ornaments, and others not here specified, are undoubtedly lawful for English Churchmen, it does not

---

[1] Blunt, 574, note. It is an interesting fact that the first American Bishops, Seabury, of Connecticut (consecrated in 1784), and Claggett of Maryland (in 1792) wore mitres That of Bishop Seabury is preserved in the Library of Trinity College, Hartford, Connecticut. In a note to his *Christian Ballad* Bishop Coxe says that the Rector of Litchfield said to him in 1847, in answer to the Bishop's enquiry, "Yes, in 1785, at the first ordination in this country, I saw him [Seabury] wearing his scarlet hood and that mitre; and though I was then a Dissenter, his stately figure and solemn manner impressed me very much. He was a remarkable looking man" (p. 216).

[2] *Ibid* pp. lxxii, lxxiii.

follow that where disuse has been of long standing, it would be advisable for any Incumbent of a Parish, under all circumstances, to introduce them. Even in ritual matters, as in more personal relations, the apostolic rule holds good, "All things are lawful unto me, but all things are not expedient." [1]

It is important to enquire also in this connection what authority, if any, this rubric has beyond the bounds of the Church of England. It is plain that no mere interpretation by an English court, even the highest, since 1776, or latest, 1784, can have any legal force in the American Church. But as a witness to the tradition, custom, and law inherited from the Church that gave her her Orders, and her independent national existence, the rubric must be regarded, unless formally repealed, as still the law of the Church in the United States.[2] Like the Church of England the Church in the United States, by her adoption of the "Articles of Religion," claims for herself as "a national Church, authority to ordain, change, and abolish, Ceremonies or Rites of the Church ordained only by man's authority."[3] This authority, so far as the Ornaments of the Church or of her Ministers are concerned, she has not seen fit to exercise either "to ordain, change," or "abolish," leaving all, or almost all, to inherited custom or tradition. She has declared, however, that she "is far from intending to depart from the Church of England in any essential point of doctrine, discipline, or worship." Moreover, she has laid down the rule that "what cannot be clearly determined to belong to Doctrine must be referred to Discipline."[4] It would seem

---

[1] 1 Cor vi, 12.

[2] For a full statement of this well-settled principle, with numerous high American authorities, see E A White D C.L , *Church Law*, New York, 1898, pp 92 sq.

[3] Art. XXXIV.   [4] Preface to the American Prayer Book.

ORNAMENTS OF THE CHURCH &c 277

to follow, therefore, that, inasmuch as she has neither by rubric or canon, "altered, abridged, enlarged, amended, or otherwise disposed of" the Ornaments prescribed in the English Book, the law by which she was bound from her first settlement at Jamestown, Virginia, in 1607, to the year 1776, necessarily remains her law today.[1]

Some account of the use of INCENSE may be given here as connected with the "Ornaments" of the church. Its use in the Church of Israel may be seen from many passages in the Old Testament.[2] Under the old dispensation incense was a symbol of acceptable prayer, giving its imagery to the Psalmist's petition, "Let my prayer be set forth in Thy sight as incense."[3] Like all ceremonial acts, however, it was subject to abuse, and in the later degenerate days of the nation as

---

[1] *Pr. Bk.* p. v. During the prolonged Ritual discussions in the General Conventions of 1868 and 1871, it was proposed by the House of Bishops, among other things, to prohibit the wearing by Priests and Deacons of any vestment except a white surplice, black or white stole, a cassock, "not reaching below the ankles," a black gown, and "bands" The use of incense, carrying a cross in procession, the ritual use of lights on the altar, the mixing of water with the wine of Holy Communion, the ablution of the vessels in presence of the congregation, surpliced choirs, choral service, without the consent of the Vestry and Bishop, cottas or short surplices for choristers, etc, were also to be forbidden In 1871 this attempt to legislate on ritual was finally abandoned. This was done by the adoption with practical unanimity of a resolution declaring that only "ceremonies, observances, and practices which are fitted to express a doctrine foreign to that set forth in the authorized standards of this Church" are to be condemned. For the "suppression of all that is irregular and unseemly, the paternal counsel and advice of the Bishops" was declared to be "sufficient" No ritual legislation has since been attempted in the American Church, and trials for ritual practices involving false doctrine have been almost unknown.

[2] Ex xxx, 8; xxxvii, 29; xl, 5; Lev. x, 1; Deut. xxxiii, 10, and other places.

[3] Ps. cxli, 2.

offered on heathen altars, or in impenitence or mere formality, it had become "an abomination."[1] Nevertheless, Malachi, speaking in the Name of God, foretells the time when "in every place incense," whether as typifying prayer, or else the material symbol itself, "shall be offered unto His Name," even among the heathen.[2] It is noteworthy, moreover, in this connection that it was "at the time of incense" in the Temple, when "the whole multitude of the people were praying," that the first startling message proclaiming the immediate coming of Christ came to Zacharias, the priest, the father of the Baptist, when "he went into the Temple of the Lord to burn incense."[3]

With such examples before them through more than a thousand years it would seem natural that the first Christians would not hesitate to use incense as a symbol of prayer in their worship. It was certainly much in their thoughts. S. John in his vision of heavenly things tells of an angel "having a golden censer, offering much incense with the prayers of all saints upon the golden altar which is before the throne,"[4] and some have seen in this a suggestion that the aged Apostle took his imagery from the custom of the Church in his own day. But this does not seem at all probable considering the condition of the Christians under persecution, compelled often to worship in secret, where the use of incense would at once expose them to danger. Duchesne is of opinion that as late as the ninth century "the portable censer was used at Rome only in processions," the route being thus "made sweet-smelling by incense." "As for censing the altar," he adds, "or the church, or the clergy, or

---

[1] Is. i, 13; Jer. xi, 17; xlviii, 35.
[2] Mal. i, 11.
[3] S. Luke i, 5, sq.
[4] Rev. viii, 3.

ORNAMENTS OF THE CHURCH &c   279

congregation, such a thing is never mentioned" in the liturgical books of that day.¹

However this may be, we know that the custom prevailed both in the Eastern and the Western Church after the ninth century, and still prevails. "There is reason to think that [in England] it was in practice burnt only on high festivals, down to the period of the Reformation." ² Associated as it was with solitary Eucharists, and doubtless overdone at other times, it was largely given up, though not forbidden, at the Reformation in England. At the same time it should be remembered that in itself it is as free from false doctrinal significance as sweet-smelling flowers, or the fragrant rosemary once scattered on the chancel floor, or the box or balsam for decoration of the church at Christmas. It was doubtless in use in many or most of the parish churches and cathedrals in "the Second Year of the Reign of King Edward the Sixth", and as late as 1662, in spite of the Puritan persecution of the previous years, incense was used in the cathedrals of Durham and Ely as well as in other places.³ Neither the English nor the American Church, since the Reformation, has formally either authorized or forbidden the ritual use of incense, though it is undoubtedly within the scope of their authority to do so.

The two EUCHARISTIC LIGHTS probably owe their origin to necessity in the first instance, and came to have a symbolical meaning attached to them later, as representing Christ as the Light of the World, or else as symbolizing His

---

¹ *Christian Worship*, p. 163, note. Compare Bingham, *Ant* VIII, vi 21, and Burbidge, *Lit and Off* , p 94, note.

² Scudamore, pp. 142–156.

³ See Wakeman, *His. Ch. Eng.*, p. 404; Baring-Gould, *Ch. Revival*, p. 37. Herbert's Country Parson sees that the church at great festivals is "perfumed with incense."

two Natures as God and Man. Equally with flowers, they are devoid of all doctrinal significance, and in the judgment of a purely ecclesiastical court, namely that of the Archbishop of Canterbury (Benson) in the trial of Bishop King of Lincoln in 1890, the two altar lights were pronounced legal.

CHAPTER XXVIII
THE BAPTISMAL OFFICES

"Where is it mothers learn their love?
In every Church a fountain springs,
O'er which the Eternal Dove
Hovers on softest wings.

"What sparkles in that lucid flood
Is water, by gross mortals eyed:
But seen by faith, 'tis blood
Out of a dear Friend's side." — KEBLE.

THE concluding portion of the Prayer Book represents what were known in the mediæval period of the English Church as the MANUAL and the PONTIFICAL. The Manual contained the Occasional Offices used by Parish Priests, and the Pontifical those pertaining to the Bishop.

The administration of HOLY BAPTISM TO INFANTS according to the Sarum Use had become a very complicated affair. The water was consecrated beforehand at a special service, with many ceremonies, including a Litany, and the addition of wax and oil, and the font was not changed as long as the water remained pure and clean. The ceremonies at the Baptism itself included the placing of salt in the mouth of the child, signing with the Cross, prayers for the exorcism of evil spirits, the recitation of the Lord's Prayer, "Hail Mary," and the Creed. All this was done at the Church door. At the font the child was anointed with oil (type of the Holy Spirit), then baptized, clothed in a chrisom, or white baptismal robe, and a lighted taper placed in its hand, in imitation of the Wise Virgins going forth to meet their Lord. If the Bishop was present, the child was at once confirmed.

These ceremonies had become so elaborate that in the popular mind they obscured the act of Baptism itself, of which the only essential part is that ordained by our Lord, namely, the application of water in the Name of the Father, and of the Son, and of the Holy Ghost.[1] In the First Reformed Book (1549) the only non-essential ceremonies retained were the benediction of the water (to be "changed every month once at the least"), the sign of the Cross, the anointing of the head, and the use of "the white vesture, commonly called the Crisome." This last was to be put upon the child with these words: — "Take this white vesture for a token of the innocency which, by God's grace in the holy Sacrament of Baptism, is given unto thee: and for a sign whereby thou art admonished, so long as thou shalt live, to give thyself to innocency of living, that, after this transitory life, thou mayest be partaker of the life everlasting." In the act of baptizing the Priest was required to dip the child in the water thrice: "First, dipping the right side; second, the left side; the third time dipping the face toward the Font: so it be discreetly and warily done; saying, etc." "And if the child be weak, it shall suffice to pour water upon it, saying, etc."[2]

In later revisions the only non-essential ceremonies retained were the BENEDICTION OF THE WATER at every Baptism, and THE SIGNING OF THE CROSS upon the forehead. The former was omitted in 1552 on the objection of Bucer, a foreigner, who had been made Regius Professor of Divinity

---

[1] S. John III, 5, S Matt xxviii, 19

[2] Concerning the wisdom of omitting these "adventitious ceremonies," see Sadler, *Ch. Doc.*, etc., p. 115 note.

at Cambridge,[1] but it was restored in 1662, being taken from its former place at the end of the Office for Private Baptism in the First Book, and made part of the Public Office. Both of these are so fitting to such an august Sacrament as that which admits one to "the Kingdom of God,"[2] and being "neither dark nor dumb ceremonies, but so set forth that every man may understand what they do mean, and to what use they do serve,"[3] that one can only wonder at the narrowness and perversity of those Puritans who objected to them.

Concerning the use of the sign of the Cross in Baptism the English Book, in the last rubric of the Public Office, refers to the 30th Canon of 1604 for "the just reasons for the retaining of it." Among these are the following: — "The honour and dignity of the name of the Cross begat a reverend estimation even in the Apostles' times (for aught that is known to the contrary) of the sign of the Cross, which the Christians shortly after used in all their actions; thereby making an outward show and profession even to the astonishment of the Jews, that they were not ashamed to acknowledge Him for their Lord and Saviour who died for them upon the Cross." "It must be confessed," the Canon adds, "that in process of time the sign of the Cross was greatly abused in the Church of Rome. . . . But the abuse of a thing doth not take away the lawful use of it. Nay, so far was it from the purpose of the Church of England to forsake

---

[1] Bucer was one of eight Lutheran divines who gave Philip of Hesse a dispensation to commit bigamy, requesting him, however, to conceal his second marriage. See Hare's *Mission of the Comforter*, p. 834, and Mozley's *Essays* I, 401–404.

[2] S John III, 5

[3] Present English Prayer Book, *Of Ceremonies*. Compare Rev. vii, 3; xiv, 1, Gal. vi, 14.

and reject the Churches of Italy, France, Spain, Germany, or any such like Churches, in all things which they held and practised, that it doth with reverence retain these ceremonies."[1]

A proper reverence suggests that the water, after use in Holy Baptism, should be emptied, and not used for any other purpose.

The first prayer in the Office is found in substance in the revised service of Hermann, Archbishop of Cologne. The second is a translation from that in the old Sarum Office. The Gospel in the old Office (Christ blessing little children) was taken from S. Matthew (xix). In the revised Office the more extended and more touching account of the same event was taken from S. Mark (x). Only two sponsors were required in the old Service; three are required in the new. The American Book has the same rule but adds, "when they can be had," and provides that "Parents shall be admitted as Sponsors, if it be desired."

The beautiful address to the Sponsors, "Beloved, ye hear, etc," and the prayer, and address following, were composed in 1549, being framed on a similar portion of the revised Service of Archbishop Hermann. The first three questions to the Sponsors are taken, with slight change, from the old Use of Sarum, and are identical with those in the Roman Service of Gelasius and Gregory in the fifth and sixth centuries. The fourth, "Wilt thou then obediently keep, etc.," was added in 1662. We have strong evidence in the New Testament that some such form of interrogation always

---

[1] Compare the Puritan objection to bowing at the Name of Jesus. It was a lingering Puritanism that caused the American Church in 1789 to allow the sign of the Cross in Baptism to be omitted if so desired, "although the Church knoweth no worthy cause of scruple concerning the same."

THE BAPTISMAL OFFICES 285

preceded Baptism. See Acts viii, 37; 1 Tim. vi, 12; 1 Pet. iii, 21.[1]

The four short prayers preceding the Prayer of benediction of the water are framed on similar prayers in the Gallican Ritual for Holy Baptism. They resemble also the Litany which begins the Eastern Baptismal Office.[2]

As to the METHOD OF BAPTIZING it is important to note that the Church has always recognized two ways of administering the Sacrament, namely, "dipping in the water," and "pouring water upon" the person.[3] Though total immersion of the body, as a ceremonial or ritual act, was a very ancient custom, and still continues in many parts of the Church Catholic, especially in the East, and in warm countries, it has never been regarded as essential. "Sacraments are means or instruments, and not mere figures. They depend, therefore, for their efficacy, not on exactness of likeness, or on quantity of matter, but on God's power and promise in the use of appointed means. A basin serves as well as a river; one crumb of bread and one drop of wine are as efficacious as a hundred loaves and a whole vintage. Were this not so, the Holy Communion ought to be made a meal for supplying the body, for in proportion as it did so, it would be an exact figure of satisfying the soul."[4] "In fact, total

---

[1] The American Book does not require the recitation of the Creed in the second question, but asks, "Dost thou believe all the articles of the Christian Faith, as contained in the Apostles' Creed?"

[2] See Blunt, *Ann. Pr Bk*, pp. 224, 225.

[3] The American Prayer Book, in the last rubric of the Office for the "Baptism of those of Riper Years," uses also the word "immersion" "Sprinkling" does not occur in any Prayer Book of the English-speaking Church.

[4] *The Gospel in the Church*, by the Author, pp. 263, 264   See S. John xiii, 10. This is a saying of our Lord that is applicable to all sacramental acts.

immersion of the body would seem to have been an impossibility on the Day of Pentecost. Three thousand persons were baptized on that day, not by a river side, but on a steep hill in the heart of a large city, where the religion of Christ was hated by those in power, and the Lord Himself had been publicly crucified a few days before." [1]

Another reason for not confining the method of baptizing to immersion is that the word translated baptize (Βαπτίζω, baptizo) does not necessarily mean to dip, or plunge under. In the following passages, where the word is translated "wash," namely, S. Mark vii, 4, and S. Luke xi, 38, it plainly does not mean to immerse. Moreover, the account of our Lord's Baptism in the Jordan,[2] and the rude sculptures of the second century in the Catacombs, seem to agree in representing our Lord and the Baptist as standing in the water, and S. John pouring water on His head. The promised "Baptism with the Holy Ghost" is also described as a "pouring-out," and not an immersion.[3]

It is therefore fully within the right of any candidate for Holy Baptism to demand for himself or for his child that the Sacrament should be administered by dipping, that is, by immersion, as the Church provides. It would, moreover, prove to be a wholesome custom, as meeting the contention of the modern Baptists, if a Baptistery for this purpose should be constructed in every large church, or cathedral, at the least.[4] In England in the sixteenth century immersion was

---

[1] *The Gospel in the Church*, p. 262. Compare the Baptism of the jailer and his family at Philippi (Acts xvi, 33)

[2] S. Matt iii, 16   [3] Joel ii, 28, 29; S. Matt. iii, 11; Acts ii, 16, x, 45.

[4] It is noteworthy that Archbishop Benson had such a Baptistery built in the parish church of Lambeth. The writer was glad to have the opportunity, some years ago, of exemplifying publicly the Church's rule, in compliance with the request of a man brought up among Baptists, by baptizing him with trine immersion in the Mohawk river.

still the custom as well as the law. But when whole nations had become Christian, "and rarely any were offered to the fonts but infants, whose tender bodies would not well endure it, this custom in the Western Church especially was discontinued, and aspersion [that is, pouring] only used."[1]

The Ministrant of Baptism differs from that of the other great Sacrament in that he is not necessarily a Priest. The evident reason for this is that Baptism is the Sacrament only of initiation into the Church, and that it requires for its completion the Laying on of the Hands of the Bishop in Confirmation. In the "Ordering of Deacons" it is declared that "It appertaineth to the office of a Deacon . . . in the absence of the Priest to baptize infants." In the days of the first Apostles, to baptize was one of the functions of Deacons, as seen in the case of Philip.[2]

Even baptism by a layman in case of emergency, provided it has been done with water in the Name of the Holy Trinity, was recognized in the early Church as valid, though irregular. This was the view held by Tertullian in the third century, and by S. Augustine in the fourth.[3] Concerning this Hooker makes the emphatic statement, "Yea 'Baptism by any man in case of necessity' was the voice of the whole world heretofore."[4] This was the rule laid down in the ancient Sarum Office, and it has never been reversed in the various revisions. As further proof of this it is pointed out that "although there were supposed to be about 300,000 persons in England who had been baptized by laymen [that is, by Puritan ministers who had not received Holy Orders] at the time when the clergy were restored to their duties in 1661, no public

---

[1] L'Estrange, *Alliance of the Divine Offices*, p. 365.
[2] Acts viii, 12, 38
[3] Ter. de Bapt., xvii; Aug de Bapt., vii, 102; cont. Parmen., ii, 13.
[4] *Ecc Pol* V lvi, 3. See also Bingham, *Antiq*. xvi. 1. 4.

provision was made by the Church for rebaptizing them, nor does it appear that any doubt whatever was thrown upon the validity of their baptism by those who revised our Offices."[1]

THE ADDRESS AND PRAYERS FOLLOWING leave us in no doubt as to what the Church holds in regard to the effect of Baptism. These were added in the Second Prayer Book, concerning which Canon Bright has said, "We generally associate the revision of 1552 with such changes as it wrought in our Sacramental services. It is well to remember that, if it took away much, it gave us a new and emphatic assertion of the regeneration of baptized infants."[2] Regeneration means literally a "new birth," and is taken from Tit. iii, 5 ("through the washing of regeneration," διὰ λουτροῦ παλιγγενεσίας), where S. Paul has in mind our Lord's words concerning Baptism in S. John iii, 5. Though the Puritans, following Calvin, persisted in regarding regeneration, or the new birth, and conversion as convertible terms, the Church has kept faithfully to the teaching of Holy Scripture, and of the Church Catholic through all her history, that the two things are wholly distinct. The new birth, like natural birth, is "the gift of God,"[3] which may be abused or forfeited, as in the case of the Prodigal, yet is still "without repentance" on God's part. Conversion is man's work, under God, whereby the Prodigal "comes to himself," and "converts," that is, turns his footsteps homeward to his Father.[4]

---

[1] Blunt, *Ann. Bk. Comm. Pr*, p. 213.

[2] *Ancient Collects*, p. 230, note.

[3] Rom xi, 29

[4] S. Luke xv, 18; and comp Is vi, 10. It is to be noted that the Greek word for convert (στρέφω), even in the passive voice, has always a reflexive meaning ("turn one's self"), and is so translated in the Rev. Ver in S. Matt. xiii, 15, xviii, 3, S. Mark iv, 12, S. Luke xxii, 32, Acts iii, 19, and elsewhere.

THE BAPTISMAL OFFICES   289

That is the very first thought presented to every Christian child in the Church Catechism as the foundation of all its duty, and the encouragement of all its efforts. It is taught to say, "In Baptism I was made a member of Christ, the child of God, and an inheritor of the kingdom of heaven." In spite of many shortcomings it is God's "dear child." [1] When the Eternal Son of God came into the world, "He took not on Him the nature of angels," [2] that is, He did not come as a mere spiritual being. He "was made flesh." [3] He took the body, soul, and spirit of man, and one purpose of this was that He might bring every man who would into union with Himself in body as well as in soul. Holy Baptism is the means by which this union with Christ is brought about, and we are made "members of His body, of His flesh, and of His bones," "partakers of the Divine Nature." [4] And if we are thus made "members of Christ," we also must be "the children of God." We are regenerated, "born again" into a new family, the family and "kingdom of God." [5] Here is our highest incentive to holy living. Here also is our warning against falling away. And so, Baptism has been called "the Sacrament of responsibility," for though our "names are now written in heaven," nevertheless, they may be "blotted out of the book of life" [6] by our unfaithfulness, unless we repent and amend.

THE RIGHT OF INFANTS TO BE BAPTIZED was never called in question in the Church until the rise of the Anabaptist sect in the sixteenth century. All Jewish children, including John the Baptist, the Apostles, and our Lord Himself, were made members of the Church of Israel by divine command

---
[1] Eph. v, 1.
[2] Heb ii, 16.
[3] S. John i, 14.
[4] Eph. v, 30; 2 Pet. i, 4.
[5] S. John iii, 5.
[6] Rev. xii, 23; iii, 5.

when eight days old.¹ It could, therefore, never have occurred to the Apostles, whom Christ had commanded to "feed His Lambs" as well as "His sheep,"² that the Church of Him who had bidden the children to come to Him for blessing, ignorant though they were of what He was doing to them, could have any less blessing for infant children than that older Church which was its shadow.

This fact of Baptism being the successor and the substitute of Circumcision, as the Holy Communion was the successor and the substitute of the Passover, is put beyond a question when we find S. Paul speaking of Baptism as "the circumcision of Christ," or Christian circumcision.³ S. Peter also, in his sermon on the very first day of the Christian Church, tells the people that "the promise of remission of sins," and "the gift of the Holy Ghost," by means of their baptism, are for their "children" as well as for themselves.⁴ So too, our Lord's final command to His Apostles to "make disciples of all nations, baptizing them, etc.,"⁵ necessarily included, not only men and women, but children and so we find the Apostles baptizing whole "households," where it would be unreasonable in the extreme to suppose that they contained no children.⁶

Moreover, leaving Holy Scripture, we find the earliest Christian writers in the first four centuries, Justin Martyr, Irenaeus, Clement of Alexandria, Tertullian, Cyprian, Augustine, Jerome, and others, all testifying to the custom

---

[1] Gen xvii, 1–15, S. Luke i, 59; ii, 21. [3] Col. ii, 11, 12.
[2] S. John xxi, 15. [4] Acts. ii, 38, 39.
[5] S. Matt. xxviii, 19, 20, Rev Ver
[6] Acts xvi, 15, 33, 1 Cor. i, 16. Wall, in his treatise on *Infant Baptism*, Intro , p. 21, in further proof that the Apostles could have had no doubt as to our Lord's intention, points out that the Jews, when they received proselytes from the heathen, in preparation for their circumcision, baptized not only the adults, but even the infant children.

THE BAPTISMAL OFFICES 291

of the Church in their day as to baptizing infant children, and taking the pledge of sponsors in their name for their future training in the Christian faith.[1]

The proclamation of the full reception of the child by its baptism "into the congregation of Christ's flock," and the touching words accompanying the sign of the Cross, are peculiar to the English Book, having been substituted in 1552 for the bestowing of the crisome, and the anointing, which were prescribed here in the Book of 1549. The Address to the congregation, "Seeing now, etc.," with its unequivocal statement that "this child is regenerate," the Lord's Prayer, and the Thanksgiving following, were also added in 1552. In the Prayer Book of 1549 the requirement to "bring this child to the Bishop to be confirmed" was only in the form of a rubric. In 1662 it was changed to its present form as an address, doubtless because many of the clergy had failed to bring the duty home to the parents and godparents.[2]

The Office for PRIVATE BAPTISM OF CHILDREN differs only from that for Public Baptism in the permission to omit all that is not essential to the valid administration of the Sacrament. It provides, however, that the People are to be "often admonished that they defer not the Baptism of their Children longer than the first or second Sunday, etc., unless upon a

---

[1] See Wall, *Infant Baptism*, chaps I-XV.

[2] The English Office declares that children baptized and "dying before they commit actual sin, are undoubtedly saved " The spirit of the Puritans' opposition to the Prayer Book is well illustrated by Baxter's declaration in regard to this rubric in 1662· "If only that rubric were continued, yet they could not conform" (Proctor and Frere, p. 20). When an eccentric American Priest, on the other hand, was once asked the question concerning the condition of unbaptized children, he replied that while the Church had made no pronouncement on the subject, his own private opinion was that they would be saved, but that he had grave doubts about the future condition of their parents!

great and reasonable cause." And the wonder is that Christian parents should so often have so little regard for their children's being "brought unto Christ," and into union with Him, that, from mere carelessness or indifference, they postpone their Baptism for months, or even years.

Another admonition which the Church requires her clergy to give is that children should not be baptized at home "without great cause and necessity," by which is meant primarily and chiefly the dangerous illness of the child, though there may also be other reasons which are justifiable, especially in missionary lands. Mere convenience, however, or the desire to make the event a social function cannot be one. There are strong reasons for this insistence on the Sacrament being administered ordinarily in the church. First there is the great dignity of the Sacrament, which must needs be guarded by the most reverent surroundings possible; again there is the blessing which must come from the united prayers of a congregation on the child's behalf; and finally there is the blessing which the people themselves may receive by being constantly reminded of the privileges and responsibilities which their own Baptism bestowed and imposed upon them.

It is to be observed that the phrase "lawful minister" is used throughout the service. This does not necessarily imply that, in case of extreme necessity, Baptism by a lay person would not be permissible. It is only meant to show that the Church does not, under ordinary circumstances, countenance any departure from the divine law which makes her ordained ministers the "stewards of the mysteries of God."[1]

Though "the Child so baptized is lawfully and sufficiently baptized, and ought not to be baptized again, . . . nevertheless," the Church declares, "if the Child do afterward

---
[1] 1 Cor iv, 1.

THE BAPTISMAL OFFICES 293

live, it is expedient that it be brought into the Church," etc., but only for the purpose of public certification of the fact, and for the saying of the remaining portion of the service for Public Baptism beginning with the Gospel, omitting only the act of Baptism itself.[1] In case of uncertainty as to whether a Baptism has been validly administered, and "all things done as they ought to be," a hypothetical form of baptizing is provided, beginning, "If thou art not already baptized, etc."

It is not surprising that there was no separate OFFICE FOR THE BAPTISM OF ADULTS either in the ancient English books, or in the revised Book of 1549. Ever since England had ceased to be a heathen country, all her people had been baptized in infancy. It was not until 1662 that the Office for "*Baptism of Such as are of Riper Years*" was added, and the reason given in the Preface to the Prayer Book is, first, "the growth of Anabaptism, through the licentiousness of the late times crept in amongst us," which had "forbidden little children to come" to Christ in the very way of His appointment; and, second, the extension of the British Empire in the colonies or "plantations" of the New World, where the Office would be "always useful for the baptizing of natives, and others converted to the faith." It was framed by a committee of Bishops and other Clergy appointed by Convocation, of which the Bishop of Salisbury was chairman.

The Office differs only in necessary things from that for Children; a different Gospel, and appropriate Exhortations.

---

[1] In the American Book, the clause of the certification in the English Book, beginning, "Who being born in original sin, etc ," down to "everlasting life," is changed to "Who is now by Baptism incorporated into the Christian Church," and this, together with what follows, is added to the first form of certification.

The catechumens, as they were called in the early Church, and as they are still called in heathen lands, are first to be "sufficiently instructed in the principles of the Christian Religion," and "exhorted to prepare themselves with prayer and fasting [according to primitive custom] for the receiving of this holy Sacrament." They answer the questions for themselves, their Godfathers and Godmothers being only "their chosen witnesses," whose duty it is to remind them of their "solemn vow, promise, and profession." They are also to be confirmed by the Bishop "as soon as conveniently may be; that so they may be admitted to the Holy Communion." It should be needless to say that any one who is fitted to receive the Holy Sacrament of Baptism as an adult must necessarily be fitted to receive Confirmation, and the Holy Communion, though some special preparation may be necessary after the person is baptized.

CHAPTER XXIX
THE CATECHISM

*"Oh! say not, dream not, heavenly notes
To childish ears are vain,
That the young mind at random floats,
And cannot reach the strain.*

*"Dim or unheard, the words may fall,
And yet the heaven-taught mind
May learn the sacred air, and all
The harmony unwind."* — KEBLE.

"Catechesis, the teaching of children in the presence of their elders the mysteries of the Kingdom of God, is the wisest of Church restorations."
— ARCHBISHOP BENSON.

THE WORD CATECHIZE is derived from the Greek word ἠχέω (echeo), which signifies to repeat, like an *echo*. It is used only twice in the New Testament. In the preface to S. Luke's Gospel he tells his friend Theophilus that his purpose in writing is, "that thou mightest know the certainty concerning the things wherein thou hast instructed (literally, *catechized*)"; or, as the margin has it, "taught by word of mouth."[1]

That the Jews had a similar method of instruction seems to be illustrated in the case of the Child Jesus tarrying behind in Jerusalem, and "sitting in the midst of the doctors, both hearing them, and asking them questions."[2]

In the primitive Church a person preparing for Holy Baptism was called for this reason a catechumen, though the instruction was by no means confined to questioning. In

---

[1] S. Luke i, 4, Rev. Ver.; see also 1 Cor. xiv, 19, where "instruct" is the same in the Greek.
[2] S. Luke ii, 46.

the Church of Alexandria in Egypt, founded by S. Mark, there was a famous Catechetical School, so-called, where the teaching of the elements of Christianity seems rather to have been carried on by means of lectures, though doubtless the strict catechetical method followed this instruction, just as it does today in our schools and colleges in order to test and deepen the effect of the direct teaching. Clemens (A.D. 150–215), one of the celebrated teachers in this school, the instructor of Origen, has left us a series of his Catechetical Lectures. Cyril, Bishop of Jerusalem, while still a Priest in that city, has given us a similar series of eighteen lectures addressed to catechumens before their baptism, in Lent, 347 or 348, followed by five others after Easter, in preparation for Holy Communion.[1]

S. Augustine also, in a letter to a young Deacon, Deogratias, in the year 400, gives us, in what is really a treatise on Catechizing, a lifelike account, and many valuable practical hints, as to the best method of teaching the first principles of the Christian faith and life. In his preface to this book he writes: "You have told me, brother Deogratias, that at Carthage, where you are a Deacon, persons are often brought to you to be instructed in the rudiments of the Christian faith, in consequence of your reputation for possessing great resource and power in catechizing, on account of your knowledge of the faith, and your happy way of expressing yourself; but that you yourself always experience a painful difficulty in deciding how to set forth with profit to your hearers that very truth, by believing which we are Christians." "Many a modern clergyman," writes Canon Liddon, "has shared the perplexity of Deogratias, and has wished, perchance, that he had an Augustine to instruct him in the difficult art of catechizing the unlearned. For that it is difficult, — more

---

[1] *Cat Lect.*, Oxford, 1838.

THE CATECHISM

difficult to most men than effective preaching, — no one who has tried his hand at it can well doubt."[1]

It was to aid in this work of rudimentary instruction that the Catechism of the Prayer Book was composed. It was not, however, something wholly new in England, except so far as the interrogatory method was employed throughout. The Creed, Lord's Prayer, and Ten Commandments formed the core round which it was constructed, and from the earliest period of English history we find injunctions of Bishops and synods requiring the clergy to teach and explain these in English to the children and people generally committed to their care. As early as A.D. 740 Egbert, Archbishop of York, directs "that every Priest do with great exactness instil the Lord's Prayer, and the Creed, into the people committed to him, and shew them to endeavour after the knowledge of the whole of religion, and the practice of Christianity." Two centuries later a canon of Aelfric, Archbishop of Canterbury, enjoins the clergy to "speak the sense of the Gospel to the people in English, and of the *Pater Noster*, and the Creed as oft as he can." Similar injunctions are found in the canons of many diocesan synods throughout the whole mediæval period.[2]

---

[1] Dupanloup, the great Bishop of Orleans, probably did more than any other man in the nineteenth century to keep alive the Christian faith among the people of France, and this chiefly by his marvellous work and example as a catechist In his judgment this was no easy matter. "A good Catechetical Instruction," he writes, "demands of the most skilful four, five, or six hours of preparation. I have sometimes had two or three days of continuous work, sometimes a whole week, in preparation for certain very difficult or very special Instructions" (*Ministry of Catechizing*, II. 3.)

[2] See Johnson's *English Canons*, I pp 186, 248, 398. It is to be remembered in this connection that for a long period, beginning with the Roman occupation in the first century, and continuing even as late as the fourteenth, England was more or less a bilingual country, as India under the British, and the Philippines and Porto Rico under the United States,

298 PRIMITIVE WORSHIP & THE PRAYER BOOK

It is important to note the great practical necessity of such a summary of Christian faith, doctrine, and practice as is found in the Church Catechism, especially in days when a different method of instruction of the young is being attempted. According to the mind of the Church, the child is not directed primarily to the vast store of history, poetry, prophecy, philosophy, biography, and doctrine contained in the Divine Library of sixty-six books, the religious literature of a nation, written in more than one language, and which we know today as "the Bible," that is, "the Book." The remarkable practical wisdom of the Church is seen in her setting before the young the great essential truths, which they have neither time nor ability to discover for themselves in the Bible, but only for the "certainty" and illustration of which, they are to "search the Scriptures."[1] In pursuing this course she is only exercising her divinely given authority to "teach" as well as to "preach" or proclaim the good news of the Gospel. In this she is in fact following exactly the rule expressed by S. Luke in the preface to his Gospel; the Church to teach, the Scripture to give "the certainty."

As further evidence of the Church's wisdom we can point also to the remarkable brevity of the Catechism, containing as it does only twenty-two questions and answers in addition to the Creed, the Lord's Prayer, and the Commandments.[2]

---

are today. In the earlier period the upper classes spoke Latin, and after the Norman Conquest French was the ordinary language of the rulers for several centuries. As late as 1362 "an act of Parliament was passed enjoining all schoolmasters to teach their scholars to translate into English instead of into French" (Blunt, *Ann. Pr. Bk*, xxiii., note).

[1] S John v, 39.

[2] In contrast with this the "Larger Catechism" adopted by the Puritan Assembly at Westminster in 1647, like those of the Continental Reformers, is very long. It contains 196 questions, and the "Shorter Catechism"

THE CATECHISM

In the first revised Prayer Book (1549) the Catechism ended with the question on the Lord's Prayer. The latter portion on the Sacraments was added in 1604 after the Hampton Court Conference, and, with two slight verbal emendations, was afterwards confirmed by Convocation and Parliament in 1662. It was composed by Overall then Dean of S. Paul's and Prolocutor of Convocation, afterwards Bishop of Norwich (1618–19).

Though the Catechism is so admirable as it is, it is felt by many that some further addition is needed concerning the nature of the Church and the Ministry. To meet this need in the spirit of the earlier portion, the following questions and answers, chiefly in the words of the Prayer Book itself, and without any change or addition of doctrine, were adopted by the Lower House of the Convocation of Canterbury in 1887. Inasmuch, however, as they had not originated in the Upper House, a privilege claimed by the Bishops in matters of doctrine, the approval of that House was withheld.

QUESTIONS AND ANSWERS ON THE CHURCH, SUPPLEMENTARY TO THE CATECHISM

I. *Q.* What meanest thou by the Church? — *A.* I mean the Body of which JESUS CHRIST is the Head, and of which I was made a member in my Baptism.

II. *Q.* How is the Church described in the Creeds? — *A.* It is described as One, Holy, Catholic, and Apostolic.

III. *Q.* What meanest thou by each of these words? — *A.* I mean that the Church is One, as being One Body under the One Head; Holy, because the HOLY SPIRIT dwells in it, and sanctifies its Members; Catholic, because it is for all nations and all times; and Apostolic, because it continues stedfastly in the Apostles' doctrine and fellowship.

---

has no less than 107, besides the Creed, Lord's Prayer, and Commandments. The Roman Catechism of the Reforming Council of Trent (1545–63) is a formidable volume by itself, but it was meant for the instruction of the clergy, and not for children.

IV. *Q.* We learn from Holy Scripture that in the Church the evil are mingled with the good. Will it always be so? — *A.* No; when our LORD comes again, He will cast the evil out of His kingdom; will make His faithful servants perfect both in body and soul; and will present His whole Church to Himself without spot, and blameless.

V. *Q.* What is the Office and Work of the Church on earth? — *A.* The office and work of the Church on earth is to maintain and teach everywhere the true Faith of CHRIST, and to be His instrument for conveying Grace to men, by the power of the HOLY GHOST.

VI. *Q.* How did our LORD provide for the government and continuance of the Church? — *A.* He gave authority to His Apostles to rule the Church; to minister His Word and Sacraments; and to ordain faithful men for the continuance of this Ministry until His coming again.

VII. *Q.* What Orders of Ministers have there been in the Church from the Apostles' time? — *A.* Bishops, Priests, and Deacons.

VIII. *Q.* What is the office of a Bishop? — *A.* The office of a Bishop is to be a chief Pastor and Ruler of the Church; to confer Holy Orders; to administer Confirmation; and to take the chief part in the ministry of the Word and Sacraments.

IX. *Q.* What is the office of a Priest? — *A.* The office of a Priest is to preach the Word of GOD; to baptize; to celebrate the Holy Communion; to pronounce Absolution and Blessing in GOD's Name; and to feed the flock committed by the Bishop to his charge.

X. *Q.* What is the office of a Deacon? — *A.* The office of a Deacon is to assist the Priest in Divine Service, and specially at the Holy Communion; to baptize infants in the absence of the Priest; to catechize; to preach, if authorized by the Bishop; and to search for the sick and the poor.

XI. *Q.* What is required of members of the Church? — *A.* To endeavor, by God's help, to fulfil their baptismal vows; to make full use of the means of grace; to remain stedfast in the communion of the Church; and to forward the work of the Church at home and abroad.

THE CATECHISM 301

XII. *Q.* Why is it our duty to belong to the Church of England? — *A.* Because the Church of England has inherited and retains the Doctrine and Ministry of the One Catholic and Apostolic Church, and is that part of the Church which has been settled from early times in our country.

"N or M" in the first question is probably the usual abbreviation of the Latin words *Nomen* and *Nomina*, "Name or Names." The translation of the Commandments both here and in the Eucharistic Office is taken from the "Great Bible" of 1539. It had become so familiar to the people that, together with the Psalter and the "Comfortable Words," it was not changed when the so-called Authorized Version was made in 1611.

A MOST IMPORTANT BUT MUCH NEGLECTED RUBRIC requires that "The Curate [that is, the Priest who has the *cure* of souls, be he Rector, Vicar, or 'Minister,' as in the American Book] shall diligently upon Sundays and Holy-days, after the second Lesson at Evening Prayer, openly in the Church instruct and examine so many Children of his Parish sent unto him, as he shall think convenient, in some part of this Catechism." In the next rubric the duty of sending the children is definitely laid on Fathers, Mothers, etc. The Irish and the American Books make some slight verbal changes here, and the Irish adds concerning the Catechizing "openly in the Church" the words, "with the approval of the Ordinary," that is, the Bishop of the Diocese. The American Church is still more explicit, having further provided by canon as follows: —

"It shall be the duty of Ministers of this Church who have charge of Parishes or Cures to be diligent in instructing the children in the Catechism, and from time to time to examine them in the same publicly before the Congregation. They shall also, by stated catechetical lectures and instruction, inform the youth and others in the Doctrines, Polity, History, and Liturgy of the Church."[1]

Concerning this "instruction and examination openly in the Church" it is plain that, as the present writer has said elsewhere, "Neither the law of our Lord nor of His Church will allow any priest with a cure of souls to release himself from that grave responsibility towards the children. He cannot even plead unfitness. It is his plain duty to make himself fit. Sunday School teachers and officers may help him, but they cannot take his place. By his ordination vow, by the rubrics and canons of the Church, but above all by the express command of our Lord Himself, this duty of teaching the young as well as the old is imperative. Christ's first command to His Apostles is 'Feed My lambs'; His second, 'Feed My sheep.' But our Lord's estimate of the two kinds of work is seen in the conditions which He imposes for each. For while for the second He puts the question, 'Lovest thou Me?' for the first He asks, 'Lovest thou Me more than these?' Surely then we are justified in claiming for the art of teaching the young a position equal, if not superior, to the art of preaching to their elders."[2]

---

[1] Canon 16, Sec. ii.

[2] *The Gospel in the Church*, p. x. The most serious defect in the elaborate organization of the modern Sunday School is the failure to have the children take part with their elders every Sunday in the regular services of the Church, and to acquire the use of the Prayer Book. One of the saddest sights today is the stream of young people on Sunday morning hastening homeward at the very hour when the actual worship of the Church is about to begin. It seems to be largely forgotten that the greatest and most enduring influence in a child's life is that acquired by the habit of church-going, reverent worship, and example. Divine Service, with its wealth of Psalm and Lesson, Epistle and Gospel, Creed, and Sermon, and Sacrament, provides the most effective teaching, not merely for the brief two hundred and fifty hours of the average child's life in Sunday School, but for the *whole* life in the Church.

CHAPTER XXX
CONFIRMATION

*"Draw, Holy Ghost, Thy seven-fold veil
Between us and the fires of youth;
Breathe, Holy Ghost, Thy freshening gale,
Our fevered brow in age to soothe.*

*"And oft as sin and sorrow tire,
The hallowed hour do Thou renew,
When beckoned up the awful choir
By pastoral hands, toward Thee we drew."* — KEBLE.

CONFIRMATION is not one of the "Sacraments generally [*generaliter*, that is, universally] necessary to salvation," nevertheless, the teaching of the New Testament (as we shall see later), combined with the universal custom of the Church from the earliest ages, testifies plainly that it was "ordained by Christ Himself as a means whereby we receive . . . the gift of the Holy Ghost"[1] though its "visible sign or ceremony" is not expressly said in the Gospel to have been ordained by Him. In mediæval days in the English Church it was "commonly called a Sacrament."[2] But in ancient usage very many religious ceremonies were called Sacraments. S. Augustine speaks of "the Sacrament of the Creed, which they ought to believe; the Sacrament of the Lord's Prayer, how they ought to ask."[3] The Greek word for Sacrament was "Mystery" (μυστήριον). "The Word made flesh" was in fact the source and pattern of all Sacraments or Mysteries in the Church, corresponding to the

---
[1] *Catechism* and Acts ii, 38   [3] *Sermon*, 228.
[2] See the XXV Article of Religion.

definition of the Catechism, in that He was outwardly the "visible sign" of God to men, and inwardly "full of grace and truth."[1] Christianity, being such as this, is necessarily full of Sacraments or Mysteries.[2] In this wide sense of the word, therefore Confirmation may be called a Sacrament, for it has unquestionably an "outward visible sign," and an "inward spiritual grace," nothing less in fact than "the gift of the Holy Ghost."[3]

The assertion of the XXV Article of Religion that "Confirmation and Orders," among other rites named, "have not any visible sign or ceremony ordained of God," can only be accepted as meaning that no "visible sign" is specified by our Lord in so many recorded words.[4] But this would apply equally against Holy Baptism being a Sacrament, inasmuch as the "visible sign" of Baptism, which the Church Catechism declares to be "water" is not named at all by our Lord in the only two places in the Gospel where He is recorded as "ordaining" the Sacrament.[5] The use of water can only be *inferred* from the mystical words of our Lord to Nicodemus, a year before He instituted Holy Baptism: "Except a man be born of water and the Spirit, he cannot enter into the kingdom of God,"[6] taken in connection with the universal custom of the Church from the beginning. And it is this selfsame process of inference and universal custom

---

[1] S John i, 14; 1 Tim. ii, 16.
[2] 1 Cor. iv, 1.
[3] Acts ii, 38, viii, 17, xix, 6
[4] It is not to be wondered at that Bishop Forbes in his *Explanation of the Thirty Nine Articles*, p 453, should say of Article XXV, "The language of the Article is unfortunate, not in that it raised two Sacraments above the rest, but in tending to obscure the sacramental character of the other five rites by undue disparagement"
[5] S Matt xxviii, 19; S. Mark xvi, 16.
[6] S John iii, 5

CONFIRMATION

which requires us to class Confirmation and Ordination as sacramental rites, "ordained by Christ Himself," though not in the first rank as "generally necessary to salvation."[1]

In proof of the divine origin of Confirmation we have, first, the distinct assertion of the author of the Epistle to the Hebrews that "the Laying on of Hands" is one of six "principles of Christ's Doctrine" or teaching, which form, he says, "the foundation" of the Christian religion.[2] No orthodox Christian can doubt that the other five "principles," namely, repentance, faith, baptism,[3] the resurrection of the dead, and eternal judgment, are such "foundation" truths. These, it will be observed, are all given in their natural order. What then is "the Laying on of Hands?" If mentioned elsewhere, it might mean ordination to the sacred Ministry. Here this is all but impossible. Such ordination is not a necessity for all, and these six "principles" are unquestionably necessary for all. It follows therefore that the Laying on of Hands can mean nothing else than that ordination to the universal Christian priesthood which we learn from the New Testament elsewhere, and from Primitive Church writers, to have been the custom of the Church from the beginning.

This is put beyond a doubt when we find, in the first year of the Church's existence, that two chief Apostles make a special journey to a city which they once despised, in

---

[1] It is to be observed moreover that "the laying on of hands" in Ordination, as well as in Confirmation, has no recorded authority of our Lord. In this respect the Ordinations of the clergyman and the layman stand on exactly the same footing.

[2] Heb vi, 2

[3] The word used here is "baptisms," not "baptism." The reason for this is found in the fact that these Hebrew Christians had to be taught, like those in Ephesus (Acts xix, 4, 5), the distinction between a mere Jewish ceremonial washing and a Christian Sacrament

order to lay hands, with prayer for the Holy Ghost, on certain Samaritans who had confessed their faith in Christ. They had been baptized by Philip the Deacon, but it is added significantly "that they had *only* been baptized."[1] Twenty years later, in the great heathen city of Ephesus, this scene is almost exactly reproduced.[2] Here S. Paul, also an Apostle or Bishop, asks some Jewish believers, "Have ye received the Holy Ghost since ye believed?" and finding that they had only received the Jewish Baptism of S. John the Baptist, proceeds to give them the Baptism of Christ, and then imitates the action of S. Peter and S. John by laying his hands upon them, "and the Holy Ghost came on them."[3]

Interpreted in the light of these two examples of apostolic custom, "written for our learning," it is evident that the assertion by the writer of the Epistle to the Hebrews that "the Laying on of Hands" was one of six "first principles," or "foundation truths, of "Christ's teaching," can only mean that it was delivered to His Church by Christ Himself. "It is plain that no Apostle, nor even the whole 'company of the Apostles,' could *invent* a 'principle of the doctrine of Christ.' Indeed, there is scarcely room for doubt that it was given among those *unwritten* 'commandments' of His to His Apostles, which He Himself speaks of when He bids them 'make disciples (*margin*) of all nations, teaching them to observe *all* things whatsoever I have commanded you,' the giving of which, S. Luke tells us,[1] was one of the chief objects of His stay on earth for forty days after His resurrection."[4]

Besides these definite testimonies to Confirmation in the Acts, as an ordinance of our Lord for the conveyance

---

[1] Acts viii, 16.   [2] Acts xix, 1–8.   [3] Acts viii, 15; xix, 2, 6.
[4] Acts i, 2, 3, *Confirmation and the Way of Life*, by the Author, p. 128.

CONFIRMATION 307

of the Holy Ghost to penitent, believing, and baptized Christians, there are many allusions to the sacramental rite in the Epistles. Some of these appear under the name of "The Seal," or "The Sealing," the name by which the Oriental Church, so conservative of Scriptural language, still calls it.[1] It is also referred to frequently as "Unction," or "Anointing." As our Lord Himself is the Anointed One, or the Christ, so also Christians are "anointed with the Holy Ghost, and with power." [2]

And when we come to the days succeeding those of the first Apostles, we find no different practice from that which we learn from Holy Scripture. In his treatise concerning Baptism Tertullian (A.D. 150–220) writes: — "After this, having come out from the bath [that is, the baptismal font] we are anointed thoroughly with a blessed unction. . . . Next to this, the hand is laid upon us, calling upon and inviting the Holy Spirit, through the blessing." [3] S. Cyprian in the same century writes: — "Anointed also must be of necessity he who is baptized, that having received the chrism, that is, unction, he may be anointed of God, and have within him the grace of Christ." [4] Expounding the Confirmation of the Samaritans by S. Peter and S. John, he says: — "Which now also is done among us, those baptized in the Church being brought to the Bishops of the Church, and by our prayer, and laying on of hands, they

---

[1] See Eph. i, 13, 14; 2 Cor. i, 21; 2 Tim, ii, 19; and compare S. John vi. 27.

[2] Acts iv, 27; x, 38; 2 Cor. i, 21; and compare 1 S. John ii, 20, 27. S. Paul's reminder to Timothy, now Bishop of the Ephesians, concerning "the gift of God, which is in thee by the putting on of my hands," when taken in connection with the preceding words, and with what is said of him in Acts xvi, 1, 2, 3, seems to have reference to his Confirmation, rather than his Ordination.

[3] *De Bapt*, vii, viii.   [4] *Ep*. lxx, 3.

308   PRIMITIVE WORSHIP & THE PRAYER BOOK

receive the Holy Ghost, and are perfected with the seal of the Lord." [1]

THE PURPOSE AND THE EFFECT OF CONFIRMATION are most definitely stated for us in the question of S. Paul to the twelve believers in Ephesus: — "Have ye received the Holy Ghost since ye believed?" [2] It may be enquired concerning this "gift of the Holy Ghost," Does not every one who repents and believes in Christ, or who is baptized, receive the Holy Ghost? And the answer to this question is that His gifts are as manifold as men's needs. Isaiah, with his imperfect knowledge of God, enumerates seven such gifts, and this thought has been incorporated into the chief prayer of the office, but only as the number seven may stand for countless other gifts which He has to bestow. S. Paul tells us that "No man can say that Jesus is the Lord but by the Holy Ghost." [3] And as it is with our belief, so is it with every other holy act or thought.

>"Every virtue we possess,
> And every victory won,
> And every thought of holiness
> Are His alone."

The special purpose which God has for us in Confirmation is best expressed in the word itself, namely, to make *firm*

---

[1] *Ep* lxxiii, 8. Our own service for Confirmation itself testifies to the continuous use of the rite "from the Apostles' time," and therefore to its divine origin   The phrase, "after the example of Thy holy Apostles," in the last Collect but one, shows also that the Church claims to do exactly what the Apostles did, and nothing less or different. For the present Office is nothing new in the Church, but is simply a revision of that which, for a thousand years or more before 1549, has been said in England over all her children. The very words of the prayer used by our Bishops today, "Almighty and Everlasting God, who hast vouchsafed, etc ," have been used through all the centuries from the time of Gelasius, Bishop of Rome, in the year 492, and probably from a much earlier period.

[2] Acts xix, 2.   [3] 1 Cor. xii, 3.

CONFIRMATION 309

or strong; or, as S. Peter puts it, to "stablish, strengthen, settle" the Christian in his faith and love.¹ It is plainly then a very low and unscriptural view of Confirmation to regard it as merely an opportunity for the confirming of one's baptismal vows in a public and solemn way. This in fact is done every time a child answers the question in the Catechism, "Dost thou not think that thou art bound to believe, and to do, as they [thy sponsors] have promised for thee?" and the child replies, "Yes, verily; and by God's help so I will." If this were all that Confirmation meant, there would be no need for any further service, and the person or child would not be asked, "Have you *been* confirmed?" but "Have you *confirmed?*" (that is, your baptismal vows), which is a totally different matter; proper in itself indeed, but only a condition of the "unspeakable Gift,"² which is promised in "the Laying on of Hands."³

This thought of "the manifold gifts" of the Holy Ghost is one that is sadly overlooked in practice among us. It has its full expression in the great mediæval hymn to the Holy Ghost, the *Veni Creator Spiritus*, sometimes attributed to Charlemagne, and which is still used as the Office Hymn in our Ordination Service. It is also beautifully set forth in the following passage from a Book of Homilies written before the Reformation; and preserved in York Minster Library: —

---

¹ Pet v, 10.   ² 2 Cor ix, 15.

³ This very common error in regard to Confirmation has received much encouragement from the phrase, "ratify and *confirm*," which now forms part of the opening address It was "ratify and *confess*" in the Book of 1549, where it formed part of one of the rubrics. The change was made under vicious foreign influences in the illegal revision of 1552. When the last revision was accomplished in 1662, the rubric took the form of an address, and the misleading word was unfortunately left unchanged.

"In Baptism he was born spiritually to live, in Confirmation he is made bold to fight. There he received remission of sin, here he receiveth increase of grace. There the Spirit of God did make him a new man, here the same Spirit doth defend him in his dangerous conflict. There he was washed and made clean, here he is nourished and made strong. In Baptism he was chosen to be God's son, and an inheritor of His heavenly kingdom; in Confirmation God will give him His Holy Spirit to be his Mentor, to instruct him and perfect him, that he lose not by his folly that inheritance which he is called unto."

It may be urged by way of objection to the continued use of Confirmation that, in both the cases recorded in the Acts,[1] miraculous powers followed on the gift of the Holy Ghost. How then, it may be asked, do we know that the Holy Ghost is given in Confirmation now? In reply I would say, as I have said elsewhere, — "The miraculous powers were granted at the first to establish once for all, by outward signs, the certainty of an invisible fact. This was indeed the purpose of all miracles, 'for a sign, not to them that believe, but to them that believe not,'[2] and when they had fulfilled their purpose, they passed away. To argue that because miraculous gifts do not attend Confirmation now would indeed prove too much. Our Lord promised that miraculous 'signs' would follow *them that believe*.[3] Yet I am sure that no one will assert that there is therefore no true *belief* in the world, because the miraculous signs are absent. It is indeed a low view of God's spiritual gifts to men to suppose that the power of speaking different languages, or of healing men's bodies, is greater than that of purifying the soul, nerving it for holy works, strengthening it against temptations, and driving back the tide of sin and corruption in the heart. . . . To enable

---
[1] Chapters viii and xix.   [2] 1 Cor. xiv, 22.   [3] S Mark xvi, 17.

CONFIRMATION

the soul to do these 'greater works,' as our Lord calls them,[1] is then the true purpose of the Holy Spirit being given in Confirmation."[2]

It is evident from all this that Confirmation should occupy a very high place in the life of every Christian. It has much of the character of Ordination of the Clergy. In fact it is a very real act of Ordination to that "royal priesthood" which is the privilege of *every* Christian.[3] It is a consecration to a life of service to Christ and our fellowmen just as genuine in its sphere of duty as that of the ministerial priesthood, and as indelible as Holy Orders.[4] Taken together with Holy Baptism, of which it is but the complement, it may well be named "The Sacrament of Responsibility for the priestly Layman." The two kinds of Priests are not opposed, but "are members one of another."[5]

There is no stated address or questioning of the candidates, either in the ancient Use of Salisbury, or in the first revised Book. In the latter the Catechism was not printed separately, but formed the beginning of the service, and the Bishop was left to his discretion to ask such questions as he saw fit. The service then proceeded with the versicles beginning, "Our help is in the Name of the Lord," etc., with the prayer for the seven-fold gifts.

---

[1] S John xiv, 12.

[2] *Confirmation and the Way of Life*, pp. 131-133. Compare 1 Cor. xiii, 1, 2, 3, 13, and Gal v, 22, 23. S. Chrysostom thus explains the withdrawal of miracles: — "The blossom faded because the fruit appeared."

[3] 1 Pet ii, 5, 9; Rev. i, 6, v, 10

[4] It is for this reason that Confirmation may not be repeated when once validly administered. The Upper House of Convocation of Canterbury in 1714 prepared "A Form for admitting Converts from the Church of Rome" who had already been confirmed. This was amended by the same House of Bishops in 1890, and is published by the S. P. C. K.

[5] See pp 180-184 for a full consideration of this subject.

312 PRIMITIVE WORSHIP & THE PRAYER BOOK

The beautiful prayer, "Defend, O Lord," etc., which accompanies the Laying on of Hands, was added by the Revisers in 1549, taking the place of the mere declaration of the old Latin rite which read, "N [naming the person], I sign thee with the sign of the Cross, and confirm thee with the ointment of salvation. In the Name," etc. All that follows down to the Blessing, which is found also in the Salisbury Office, was the work of the Revisers in 1549; the Lord's Prayer, and the second of the two Collects being added in 1662.

In regard to the MINISTER OF CONFIRMATION, we read in the New Testament that only Apostles or Bishops administered the Laying on of Hands. This was usually done in apostolic days immediately after Baptism, as seen in the case of the Confirmation in Ephesus, and it was the primitive rule even as regards infants,[1] who also received the Holy Communion. In later days authority to administer Confirmation was extended to Priests. In this, however, the Priest acts only as the Bishop's deputy, and with holy oil, the symbol of the Holy Spirit, blessed by him, for the anointing. "Together with this unction they usually joined the sign of the Cross. For this ceremony they used on all occasions, and therefore could not omit it in this solemn act of Confirmation."[2]

This custom of the Priest acting as the vicar of the Bishop seems to have grown up in the East on account of the increased size of Dioceses after the days when, as we know, each city and large country district had its own Bishop. In the Western Church the administration of the rite continued to be restricted to Bishops exclusively, and consequently Confirmation was postponed until the child had reached the age of discretion. Thus East and West solved the problem of larger Dioceses in opposite ways; the East

---

[1] Bingham, *Antiq.* XII, i, 2. [2] Bingham, *Antiq.* XII, iii, 4.

CONFIRMATION

not ignoring the authority of the Bishop, but recognizing him as the chief Pastor, and the centre of unity, by requiring the use of oil specially set apart and blessed by him; the West postponing the Confirmation to a later date, thus separating the time of the *two* gifts spoken of by S. Peter in his sermon on the Day of Pentecost.[1]

The result of this postponement has not always been so satisfactory as it would seem. In mediæval days there was much carelessness and neglect on the part of both Bishops and Parish Priests, as witnessed by the injunction issued by Archbishop Peckham of Canterbury in 1281, which says: — "We ordain that no one shall be admitted to the Sacrament of the Body and Blood of the Lord, except in peril of death, unless he shall have been confirmed, or unless he be reasonably prevented from receiving Confirmation." [2] Bishop Cosin has a note which shows that a loose practice of mediæval days prevailed even in the seventeenth century, Bishops sometimes confirming "children in the streets, in the highways, and in the common fields, without any sacred solemnity." [3] The present rubric excluding unconfirmed persons from the Holy Communion is almost an exact reproduction of the injunction of Archbishop Peckham.

This rubric and its original have lately been used in the most paradoxical way as an argument for *admitting* unconfirmed persons to the Holy Communion. This is done on the curious plea that the Church's laws are only meant for her own children, and that others who do not recognize her authority may have privileges which are denied to her own! It seems to be overlooked that a rule like this would allow any unbaptized persons, Quaker or otherwise, to be admitted to the Holy Communion, provided they were

---

[1] Acts ii, 38.   [2] *Constit* iv.   [3] Works v, 522.

only sincere in their belief. It is admitted of course that Confirmation is not "generally necessary to salvation," as Baptism and the Holy Communion are. During the first 180 years in all the American colonies, no one could be confirmed unless he made a dangerous voyage to England, as every candidate for Holy Orders was obliged to do. Two thirds of the signers of the American Declaration of Independence were Churchmen, and many of the leaders in the Revolution, including Washington and others, were communicants, yet they were not confirmed. But this was only because of physical impossibility. They were, however, "ready and desirous to be confirmed," as the rubric provides, and therefore were rightly admitted to the blessings of full communion at the altar.

So also, in missionary lands, and in new countries like the United States, Canada, and Australia, there are exceptional cases known to every loyal Priest where, as a result of honest misunderstanding, family tradition, or early prejudice, devout Christian parents who are regular worshipers in the Church, and even bringing up their children in it, should not be repelled from the Holy Communion, though not yet "ready and desirous to be confirmed." This is especially true of persons who have received so-called Confirmation at the hands of a Lutheran Minister, and who are unable to understand wherein this differs from the Laying on of Hands by a Bishop in the Holy Catholic Church. These are cases deserving of very tender consideration. Such persons cannot certainly be regarded as regular communicants. They cannot be formally invited to come unconfirmed, but a wise charity would hope that the grace of the Holy Sacrament, whose "cup runneth over over,"[1] would in process of time enable them to see their

---

[1] Ps. xxiii, 5.

CONFIRMATION 315

error, oftenest one of the head, and not of the heart. In seeking to persuade them, moreover, it is well to impress upon them the fact that they are not thereby casting any slight on the grace which has been already given them through their earlier training and spiritual experience, but are only coming to receive a new gift which God has had in store for them all along though they knew it not. "For all these worketh that one and the self-same Spirit."[1]

As to METHODS OF CONFIRMING, the rule is not the same everywhere. Both the Oriental and the Roman Churches retain the ancient custom of anointing, and signing with the sign of the Cross, but these are only ceremonial accessories. The essential "visible sign" is plainly specified by the scriptural name of "The Laying on of Hands," accompanied by prayer for the Holy Ghost. In the mediæval Church of England, as in the Roman Church today, the Bishop was accustomed to touch only the cheek of the candidate. This undoubtedly constitutes a valid Confirmation, but the rule of the Prayer Book, which requires that the Bishop "lay his hand [*hands* in the American Book] upon the head of every one severally," is not only more in keeping with Holy Scripture and primitive custom, but is also much more impressive. Many Bishops, moreover, still continue the ancient practice of signing with the Cross, as was already done in Holy Baptism.[2]

---

[1] 1 Cor. xii, 11 See also the note at the end of chap. xvi, p. 166, and the anecdote told there of Bishop Wilberforce.

[2] The Scottish Book makes special provision for this, leaving its use, however, to the discretion of the Bishop. The form is as follows· "N, I sign thee with the sign of the cross [*here the Bishop shall sign the person with the sign of the cross on the forehead*] and I lay my hands [*or* hand] upon thee, in the Name of the Father, and of the Son, and of the Holy Ghost." The prayer, "Defend, O Lord," follows immediately.

In regard to THE PROPER AGE OF CANDIDATES, the Church of England in her 112th canon requires that all persons shall become communicants before the age of sixteen. The American Church has no rule as to age, nor can any definite age be prescribed for receiving this gift of the Holy Ghost. It would seem, however, as if the age of twelve, when the Holy Child Jesus was admitted by a species of Jewish Confirmation to the full privileges of the Church,[1] should be the constant aim of both parents and clergy. It is not really a question of years (some are too young at seventy), but of fitness and desire. It should be noted however that, in the Office for the Baptism of Infants, the Church lays down the rule that "this child shall be *brought* to the Bishop," not merely left to itself to come. It is plain also from the smallness of her demand concerning religious knowledge that she has here in mind a very tender age. There is to be no delay, but "*so soon* as he can say the Creed, the Lord's Prayer and the Ten Commandments, and be further instructed in the Church Catechism set forth for that purpose."

The following words of one who knew and loved children are worth pondering in this connection: —

"Do you not judge the religion of young people by a harsher standard than you do your own? Do you not often expect more from them than you ask of yourselves? Do grown people never fall away afterward? I believe it will be found that the proportion is not so great in the case of the children as in the case of grown people. [This was also the remarkable confession of the late Mr. Spurgeon in his later years.] I am sure, if they do fall away, for evermore with a voice of increasing entreaty, the grace that came with their early Communion will plead with them, and knock at the door of their hearts, until, like him of old, they will

---
[1] S. Luke ii, 42.

CONFIRMATION 317

rise and go to their Father, and say, 'Father, I have sinned against Heaven and before Thee, and am no more worthy to be called Thy son.'"[1]

In the revision of 1892 the American Church provided the following form of presenting the candidates for Confirmation to the Bishop: — "Reverend Father in God, I present unto you these children (*or* these persons) to receive the Laying on of Hands." This is followed by the following rubric and Lesson: — "*Then the Bishop, or some Minister appointed by him, may say,*

"Hear the words of the Evangelist Saint Luke, in the eighth Chapter of the Book of the *Acts of the Apostles*" (Verses 14–18). After the final rubric of the original Office this also was added: — "The Minister shall not omit earnestly to move the Persons confirmed to come, without delay, to the Lord's Supper."[2]

---

[1] Dr. James de Koven What is said here about the early Confirmation and Communion of children generally is especially true of boys, who, if allowed to grow up and go away from home unconfirmed, find decision, preparation, and formal confession of Christ a formidable barrier in later life, much more so than girls under similar circumstances

[2] In "An Alternative Order for the Ministration of Confirmation, as Canonically Sanctioned in the Scottish Church," provision is made for "candidates who had not godfathers and godmothers at their baptism." Here the vows are asked separately.

CHAPTER XXXI
SOLEMNIZATION OF MATRIMONY — MARRIAGE AND DIVORCE

"While divorce of any kind impairs the integrity of the family, divorce with remarriage destroys it root and branch" — GLADSTONE.

IT is important to observe the title of this Office. It is only "The Form for the *Solemnization* of Matrimony," that is, the Church's solemn sanction and blessing upon the entrance on what is in itself a divinely ordained estate or condition of life. Without that blessing, the union of an unmarried man and an unmarried woman would still be marriage. For marriage, first of all, is a *natural* state of life, "instituted of God in the time of man's innocency," for this threefold purpose, (1) the continuance of the human race, in "a godly seed;" (2) "for a remedy against sin;" (3) "for mutual society, help, and comfort."[1] As thus ordained by God at "the beginning of the creation," and as sanctioned afterwards by our Lord, marriage is the union of one man and one woman so that they are no longer "twain," each independent of the other, but "one flesh."[2] It necessarily follows that marriage, once freely entered into and consummated by cohabitation, is indissoluble. To allow that the sin of one, or of both parties, could destroy the bond, would be to make marriage a mere contract to be dissolved at pleasure, and not a "holy estate." Moreover, being a natural union, "one flesh," it is no more possible for either the Church or the State to dissolve the bond than it

---

[1] Gen. i, 28, ii, 18, etc.; Mal. ii, 15; and the opening address in the English Office.

[2] Gen. ii, 24; S. Matt. xix, 5, S. Mark x, 6, 8.

is possible for them to dissolve the natural bond that binds the child to its parents, or a brother to a sister. "What God hath joined together" man cannot in reality "put asunder," for "they twain are one flesh." [1]

This original law of marriage was grievously abused and broken by the Jews. The effort of Moses in dealing with the question is the first of which we have any record in history, and it was rather in the way of restriction of inevitable evils, "because of the hardness of their hearts," [2] than of a return to first principles. Only the weightiest causes were admitted, and no divorce was allowed except from bed and board, *a mensa et thoro*. Divorce from the bond, *a vinculo*, had no recognition whatever.[3] The only prescription in the case of adultery was the death of the adulteress.[4] Moses' work undoubtedly produced beneficent results, but scribes and rabbis, like their modern representatives, the divorce lawyers, found or made plenty of loopholes whereby, fifteen hundred years later, they obtained for their clients divorces "for every cause." [5]

It was then in face of this condition that WE FIND OUR LORD RESTATING IN UNMISTAKABLE LANGUAGE THE LAW AS IT WAS "FROM THE BEGINNING." [6] His complete and unqualified teaching is summed up in the sayings as given by S. Mark and S. Luke: "Whosoever shall put away his wife, and marry another, committeth adultery against her. And if a woman shall put away her husband, and be married to another, she committeth adultery;" and "Whosoever marrieth her that is put away from her husband

---

[1] S Matt. xix, 5, 6.
[2] Deut xxiv, 1, S Matt xix, 8, cf Acts xvii, 30
[3] See a discussion of this in Luckock's *History of Marriage*, 30, *sq*.
[4] Lev. xx, 10
[5] S. Matt. xix, 3.   [6] S. Matt. xix, 8.

committeth adultery."[1] It is hard to conceive of words more definite than these.

In S. Matthew alone we find an allowance to put away a wife, but this only "for the cause of fornication."[2] The genuineness of this exception has been called in question by scholars. Moreover, the meaning of the word, as not being adultery (μοιχεία) but prenuptial sin (which, according to the Jewish law, made the marriage void, that is, no marriage at all) has also been a subject of much controversy. But putting these arguments aside as non-essential or inconclusive, the one supreme fact that stands out as strongly and clearly in S. Matthew as in S. Mark and S. Luke is that "whosoever shall marry *any woman* that is divorced" (a single word in the Greek, ἀπολελυμένην), whether for fornication or any other cause, "committeth adultery."[3]

But if the bond is *really* broken by adultery, fornication, or any other cause, it follows logically that *both* parties are free. In that case however a difficulty arises as to why our Lord should forbid remarriage to the guilty party, as He does, while He allows it by His silence, as some would contend, to the innocent. The only possible explanation of this apparent inconsistency is that the inference from His silence is wrong. The bond is *not* broken, but only profaned; neither party is free, and the prohibition applies equally to both innocent and guilty.[4]

---

[1] S Mark x, 11, 12, S. Luke xvi, 18.

[2] πορνεία, S. Matt v, 32, xix, 9

[3] Bishop Middleton on *The Greek Article* calls attention to the fact that in both passages of S Matthew, and in S. Luke xvi, 18, the article before "her that is divorced" is absent, so that "her" should rather be "any woman"

[4] The words of Dr Döllinger, the great Old Catholic theologian, and historian, are well worth quoting here. Referring to the assumption that

In dealing with this passage it is constantly overlooked that while the chief thought in the minds of our Lord's questioners is concerning "putting away," the thought uppermost in His mind and on His lips is the unlawfulness of remarriage. "Whoso marrieth any woman that is put away committeth adultery," is His unqualified assertion, not only here but in every instance where He speaks of divorce. The exception which He makes in this solitary passage, on the face of it refers only to "putting away." and not to remarriage. Mr. Gladstone has forcibly illustrated this by a parallel case. "Suppose," he says, "we found this precept: 'Whosoever shall flog his son, except it be for disobedience, and put him to death, shall be punished by law.' What should we think of the interpreter who founded upon this sentence the position that a father might, for disobedience, flog his son to death? . . . But if the exceptive words give a permission, as we contend, only for putting away, and not for remarriage, everything becomes at once clear and simple." [1]

That this was also the view taken by S. Paul is evident from such passages as the following: "The woman which hath a husband is bound by the law to her husband as long

adultery *ipso facto* destroys the very essence of marriage, and that remarriage in that case is allowable, he says, "This interpretation of the words of Christ goes against language, history and logic." According to this assumption, "the married person would know from the first, and all along, that however firm his own determination, it lay in the power of the other party to dissolve the tie And if Christ taught that marriage could be dissolved by adultery, S Mark, S Luke, and S Paul withheld this important fact from their readers, and misled them by misrepresenting the case; so that the Churches had first to learn the truth from the Greek translation of S. Matthew" (*The First Age of the the Church*, Eng Trans., II, 266, 267, 268). Dollinger's treatment of the whole question of Marriage and Divorce from the point of Scripture alone is worthy of careful study.

[1] *London Quarterly Review*, in article on the English Divorce Act of 1857.

322 PRIMITIVE WORSHIP & THE PRAYER BOOK

as he liveth. . . . If, while her husband liveth, she is married to another man, she shall be called an adulteress." "Unto the married I command, yet not I, but the Lord [Jesus], Let not the wife depart from her husband: but if she depart, let her remain unmarried, or be reconciled to her husband."[1] These last words about possible reconciliation suggest to us one other fundamental reason for the indissoluble character of marriage. Such a view is alone consistent with our Lord's great law of forgiveness "until seventy times seven,"[2] and with His word to the adulterous woman, "Neither do I condemn thee: go, and sin no more."[3] If remarriage were allowable to either party, the door of forgiveness and reconciliation would be for ever shut. In the *Shepherd*, a book dating from about A.D. 75, and of such weight in sub-Apostolic times that it was read in the services of the Church as Holy Scripture, Hermas declares concerning a penitent who is put away by her husband, "If the husband do not take her back, he sins, and brings a great sin upon himself; for he ought to take back the sinner who has repented. . . . But if he put away his wife and marry another he also commits adultery."[4]

WHEN WE PASS ON FROM THE NEW TESTAMENT and sub-Apostolic period to the following age, we find no variation from this teaching. "It is most significant that the testimony of the first three centuries affords no single instance

---

[1] Rom. vii, 2, 3; 1 Cor vii, 10, 11. In this latter passage the apostle speaks in the name of Christ, and is laying down His law for Christians In speaking of marriage with or among heathen people, which is still a difficult problem for our missionaries in pagan lands, he speaks less decisively, "I, not the Lord Jesus", but this only brings out with greater emphasis the authoritative and absolute character of his previous statement, "*Not* I, but the Lord."

[2] S. Matt. xviii, 22.

[3] S. John viii, 11.   [4] Book II, Commandment iv, chap. 1.

MARRIAGE AND DIVORCE 323

of a writer who approves remarriage after divorce in any case during the lifetime of the separated partner, while there are repeated and most decided assertions of the principle that such marriages are unlawful. . . . No writer of the first three centuries is found to advocate or admit the remarriage of the innocent husband. . . . If the voice of the earliest Church is to be heard, Christian marriage is altogether indissoluble." [1]

But it may be asked, How then does it happen that the great Eastern Church ever since the fourth century has departed from this primitive rule, while the whole Western Church with one exception, and that our own, has held it fast? When the Roman Empire became nominally Christian in the fourth century, the effect of the Church's teaching on civil legislation, as we might expect, could only be gradual. In 331 Constantine by edict restricted the right of divorce to five grounds, namely, murder, sorcery, breaking up of graves, acting as a procuress or pimp, and adultery.[2] The laws of Justianian (A.D. 534) effected other improvements in the civil law, but so low did the popular feeling on the subject remain that it was most difficult for the Church in the East to maintain her standard. The overshadowing influence of the court, which was now transferred from Old to New Rome (that is, Constantinople), was the chief cause of this state of affairs, and the practical result is seen even today in the loose marriage laws of the Oriental Churches.

IN THE WESTERN PORTION OF THE EMPIRE things were different. Here, after the removal of the seat of empire,

---

[1] *Holy Matrimony*, by Oscar D. Watkins, M A., pp. 222, 225. Macmillan and Co , 1895. This treatise is doubtless the ablest and most complete discussion of the subject in the English language.
[2] Luckock, *History of Marriage*, p. 114.

the Churches of Italy, Gaul, and Spain were left in comparative freedom from state interference, and the high views of Scripture in regard to marriage were more easily enforced, so that in 789 Charlemagne, who nearly twenty years before divorced his wife and married another, had lived to repent of his mistake, and enacted laws which brought the civil code into accordance with that of the Church.[1]

This was especially true of that part of the West which concerns us most closely. England and its Church had always occupied a peculiar position in Europe. Within a century after the Empire became nominally Christian (A.D. 321), the country ceased to be a part of the Empire, and the Church had not to contend against imperial influence. The battle, however, against the low pagan customs of our British and Anglo-Saxon forefathers was not an easy one, and it was not until the beginning of the eleventh century that the New Testament rule concerning marriage was fully accepted by the *civil* power. Parliament had no existence yet for two hundred years, but Councils of the Church were the parents of parliaments and became their models. The national Council of the whole English Church, summoned by King Ethelred at Eanham in 1009, and "composed not only of Bishops and Abbots, but also of lay representatives," enacted that "it should never be allowed for a Christian to marry a divorced woman, or to have more wives than one, but that he should be bound to her only as long as she lived." Thus it became part of the civil code of England.

During the years that followed, the Bishop of Rome claimed with various degrees of success to exercise an overlordship in the Church of England. Dispensations were from time to time sought and obtained from that quarter,

---
[1] Luckock, *History of Marriage*, p. 157.

but always in direct opposition to the civil and ecclesiastical law of the land. But no change was made in the national law itself from the Norman Conquest until the year 1857, a period of 800 years. In the sixteenth century foreign reformers who had taken refuge in England, following Luther's low teaching and practice, were strong advocates for lowering the tone of the marriage laws, though in vain. Under the Commonwealth, Selden and Milton, the latter for interested reasons, pleaded for laxity, but again in vain. It was in fact the refusal of the Presbyterian Assembly to grant Milton their sanction for a divorce, even according to the already debased standard of the Westminster Confession of that body, which occasioned his famous epigram that "New presbyter was only old priest writ large."[1] In the sixteenth century however the custom was introduced of obtaining private acts of Parliament for dissolution of marriage, irrespective of the law of the Church and of God, and this continued with increased frequency down to 1857. Then a new civil court was established "for Divorce and Matrimonial Causes," but the Church's law remained unchanged. Thus for the first time in the history of Christian England divorce for adultery, incest, and other unnatural crimes, was freely allowed by the State. A divorce granted for these reasons gave each party, guilty and innocent alike, the right to marry again.[2]

The matrimonial law of England at the time of the American Revolution was the common law of the Colonies, but immediately after that event it became subject to rapid and most radical modification. A lower tone in the religious teaching concerning marriage, and the abandonment

---

[1] He cited as a proper cause for divorce "inability for fit and matchable conversation."
[2] Luckock, *History of Marriage*, pp. 173-178.

largely of the old reverent marriage ceremonial among American Protestants, had much to do with this change. With one most honorable exception (South Carolina, which grants no divorce *a vinculo*), all the States of the American Union have "very far gone" (*quam longissime*) from the "original righteousness" of God's law of marriage.[1] Meanwhile the supreme law of the English, the American, the Scottish, and the Irish Churches as set forth in their Books of Prayer, remains true to our Lord's teaching, as it has done from the beginning. Here it is still declared in the Name and with the authority of Christ, that marriage is indissoluble "until death them do part," and that "what God hath joined no man must put asunder." Whatever departures from this strict law have been made throughout the ages by national Churches, or local councils, or individual Bishops, under secular influences, or by civil legislatures, *the whole Catholic Church has never sanctioned any theory of the indissolubility of the marriage bond.*

---

[1] Canon 40 of the American Church, in flat contradiction of the supreme law of her Prayer Book and of the whole Anglican Communion, presumes to allow "the innocent party in a divorce for adultery" to remarry, though only after careful scrutiny of the facts by the Bishop, under legal advice; and any Minister of the Church may decline to officiate This exception of "the innocent party" was first made by a resolution of the General Convention of 1808, which consisted of only two Bishops, fourteen clerical and thirteen lay deputies! It was not until a later Convention that it was incorporated in the Canons. Various efforts with increasing prospect of success have been made in General Convention to remove this blot on the American code, and the Commission of five Bishops, five Priests, and five Laymen, appointed in 1913, presented a report, with but one dissentient voice, to the General Convention of 1916 recommending its repeal This was carried by a large majority in the clerical order, but was rejected by a narrow majority of only three and three-quarters in the vote by lay diocesan deputations. It was again, however, referred to a new commission to report in 1919.

MARRIAGE AND DIVORCE 327

Reason and experience, moreover, as well as Holy Scripture, testify with unmistakable voice to the divine character of this law of marriage as it was "from the beginning." The law of pagan Rome in its earliest days declared that "Marriage is the union of a man and woman, including an inseparable association in their life,"[1] and for five hundred years, it is said, no divorce was granted in ancient Rome. But when the high religious sanction of the primitive pagan age was withdrawn in the later Roman Empire, divorce "for every cause," or none, came in like a flood, and was one of the chief sources of its political downfall.[2]

We find the same moral decadence taking place today among Protestant peoples especially, and with swiftly accelerating descent, as the direct result of the same abandonment of religious principle in regard to marriage. Luther was one of the earliest opponents of the Scriptural and Catholic doctrine of marriage. In his famous, or rather infamous, sermon at Wittenberg in 1522 he openly advocated adultery under certain circumstances, and advised Henry VIII not to divorce his wife but to take a second. Luther and the Wittenberg divines, Melancthon, Bucer, and five others, signed a dispensation giving Philip of Hesse permission to commit bigamy, and this "marriage" actu-

---

[1] Justinian's *Institutes*, I, ix, 1; qu. by Dr. John Fulton in *The Laws of Marriage*, p. 19.

[2] Seneca tells us that "there were women who reckoned their years rather by their husbands than by the consuls... Martial speaks of a woman who had already arrived at her tenth husband.... But the most extraordinary recorded instance of this kind is related by S. Jerome, who assures us that there existed at Rome a wife who was married to her twenty-third husband, she herself being his twenty-first wife." Lecky, *European Morals*, II, 306-7.

ally took place in presence of two of the signers.[1] Among English Puritans, Milton, in his work on *Doctrine and Discipline of Divorce*, allowed divorce by mutual consent, or even by the desire for divorce of *either* party, and the "Westminster Confession of Faith," [2] the standard of Presbyterianism, declares wilful desertion as well as adultery to be "cause sufficient of dissolving the bond of marriage." All this was the evil seed that has brought forth such an abundance of bitter fruit, especially in countries where Protestantism prevails.[3]

Thus a hard experience is giving proof to men and nations who would not listen to the teaching of God's Word and Church, that there is no logical or possible stopping place

---

[1] See Prof Mozley's *Essays*, I, 401-404; Hare's *Mission of the Comforter*, p. 834; and Wirgman's *Foreign Protestantism within the Church of England*, pp. 25, sq.

[2] Chap xxiv, v, vi

[3] The following facts taken from the latest Report on Marriage and Divorce (1909) by the United States Government (Part I, pp 12, 13 and Chapter V) tell a sadly eloquent story. In England and Wales there were in 1867 and 1906 respectively, 130 and 670 divorces; in Scotland, 32 and 202, in Ireland, 1 and 6, in Canada, 4 and 42, in the United States, 9,937 and 72,062, while in the German Empire the number more than trebled between 1881, the first year of record, and 1906, that is, from 3,942 to 12,180. In the United States the increase is at the fearful rate of 30 per cent every five years. Only two or three countries give statistics on the religion of the divorced In Russia in 1866-1885 there was 1 divorce to 642 marriages among the Orthodox; 1 to 152 among those of the Evangelical Augsburg confession, and 1 to 70 among those of the Evangelical Reformed. In Poland the ratio was 1 to 1258 among Roman Catholics; 1 to 142 among the Evangelical Reformed; 1 to 309 among the Russian Orthodox, and 1 to 4 among those of the Jewish faith In 1877-1886 the Jews had 80.9 per cent of all the divorces in Poland. The ratio among the Jews of Algeria is one divorce to 18 marriages.

in the downward grade, once the indissolubility of marriage as taught by our Lord is abandoned. Marriage becomes sooner or later a mere social contract, "a scrap of paper," to be kept or broken at will by either party. The only practicable stopping place is where our Lord put it. To allow even adultery as ground for remarriage is only to encourage men and women to sin. The inevitable result is what has been aptly termed "tandem polygamy." It is a principle of the common law that "no man can take advantage of his own wrongdoing." Yet according to much modern legislation, adultery, or even some lesser offence, is all that is necessary in order to live in so-called "honorable marriage" with another. This is the *reductio ad absurdum* to which rejection of the high Scriptural doctrine of marriage inevitably leads. It is as if one party to some business contract had only to rob his partner in order to be free from every legal and moral obligation to him.

It follows also that divorce with the right to remarry is A GRIEVOUS ACT OF CRUELTY to the greatest number, and those who are wholly innocent. It is often assumed that power to separate is a right possessed by those who have made rash, foolish, or unfortunate marriages. It is cruel, it is said, not to release them from their evil plight. But it is forgotten that in releasing those who are alone responsible, greater cruelty is practised against vastly greater numbers of persons who are *not* responsible, parents, children, brothers, sisters, and other relatives, even against the nation at large, by means of the shame and sorrow, the breaking up of families, the encouragement to wrong-doing, and the general lowering of the moral standard. On the other hand experience shows that where no divorce *a vinculo* is permitted, as in the State of South Carolina, or where it is made most difficult, as in the Dominion of Canada, there is greater, and not less, domestic happiness.[1]

On the other hand the assertion is frequently made that where the strict law of Christ is enforced "a general dissolution of manners follows." But even granting that secret licentiousness may exist in such lands, it is not to be compared for a moment with the open licentiousness and the cruelty practised and encouraged by the "tandem polygamy" of the 72,062 divorces granted in the year 1906 alone in the United States, an increase, according to the latest government report, of 30 per cent every five years. It seems to be overlooked by those who make this objection that the secret licentiousness which is kept in check by law, and dares not show its face in the open, is a very different condition from that which is condoned by the law, and smiled upon by "society," and by the indifferent or anti-Christian multitude. Regarded then from the purely practical or "pragmatic" point of view, divorce with the right to remarry is a grievous blunder as well as a breach of the law of Christ. The sacrifice of the few for the good of the many is a primary principle of patriotism as well as of Christianity, and to make the many suffer for the few is a reversion to the selfishness of paganism. Moreover, the statistics of every land show that the allowance of remarriage to the so-called "innocent party" is but the entering wedge which eventually permits divorce and

---

[1] It is true that after the Civil War, during the period of "Reconstruction" (1865–1878), when the State was under the control of ignorant negroes, and white politicians from the North called "carpet-baggers," laws were passed permitting divorce But when the white people of the State obtained control in 1878 all this legislation was annulled, just as the Acts of the Commonwealth Parliament were annulled at the restoration of Charles II in 1660.

MARRIAGE AND DIVORCE 331

remarriage "for every cause," and undermines the whole fabric of society.

> "It is the little rift within the lute,
> That by and by will make the music mute,
> And ever widening slowly silence all." [1]

In view, therefore, of the terrible facts which the statistics of the divorce courts present to us it has been well said: — "Because of 'the hardness of men's hearts' today, it becomes more and more needful to erect the barrier of stern legislation *against* [instead of formerly and at present in encouragement of] the corrupting tide of this degrading tendency." [2]

The clear testimony of Holy Scripture on this subject may be summed up as follows: — (1) The exceptive precept of S. Matt. v, 32 and xix, 9 is solitary, and, according to many modern scholars, of doubtful genuineness. In any case it is absolutely the only passage that even *seems* to allow divorce or remarriage for either party. *Every other passage in the New Testament condemns remarriage*

---

[1] Tennyson, *Vivien*.
[2] Bishop Doane of Albany. "One whose labors in the divorce court make his statements upon all questions pertaining to them of great weight tells us that in some hundreds of cases that he has known there has not been one instance when the woman has procured the divorce that she has not almost immediately married again, and but very few cases in which the man procured it that he has not done the same" (Laica in *The Outlook*, New York, Feb. 22, 1902). A pregnant illustration of this was told lately to the writer by a member of his own family. Two well dressed women on a train were overheard by her discussing a recent engagement. After enlarging on the many virtues of the prospective bridegroom, the woman who made the announcement remarked in the most casual manner that there was only one unfortunate circumstance. The man had not yet procured his divorce!

during the lifetime of the other party, without any qualification whatever.[1] (2) Granting that the genuineness of the present text with the exceptive clause was recognized by the Church in the first three centuries, this fact makes it all the more striking that the Church in those early days saw in it, as she did, only an allowance for "putting away," and stern condemnation of marriage with the guilty, *but no sanction whatever of marriage with the innocent* — a most pregnant silence in a matter of such vast importance.

---

[1] S. Mark x, 11, 12; S. Luke xvi, 18; Rom. vii, 2, 3; 1 Cor vii, 10, 11.

CHAPTER XXXII
SOLEMNIZATION OF MATRIMONY — THE OFFICE

"*They are no more twain, but one flesh. What therefore God hath joined together, let not man put asunder*" — OUR LORD.

WE come now to the consideration of the Office itself. From the earliest days of the Church marriage has always been solemnized with religious rites. Being an occasion of rejoicing, since the fourth century it has been forbidden during Lent, but there is no law in the Anglican Communion requiring this except that of natural propriety. In every respect, however, this Prayer Book Office differs less than any other from that of the ancient Office.

The publication of Banns on three successive Sundays in the Parish church was required by the Sarum Manual, as it is still in the present Book, the object being to guard against clandestine or unlawful unions. The form in all the Books, English, Irish, Scottish, and American, is the same. If the Banns are not published, a licence is required in England from the Bishop, or his representative.[1] The English law as to licence, time, and place, is very strict. The 62d Canon forbids a clergyman under penalty of three years' suspension, to marry any persons either by Banns or licence of the Bishop, except between the hours of 8 and 12 in the morning, and in the church. Special licences, however, may be granted by the Archbishop of Canter-

---

[1] Bann is derived from a barbarous Latin word, *bannum*, signifying an edict, or proclamation.

bury, which are not subject to these restrictions of time and place.[1]

THE PLACE FOR THE BEGINNING OF THE SERVICE in the ancient rubric was "before the door of the church" (*ante ostium ecclesiae*), by which was meant the porch, and not the outside of the church.[2] This was changed to "the body of the church," that is, the nave, as at present. The beginning of the service differs very little from the Sarum Office either in rubrics or address. What was originally a fourth and final publication of the Banns ("If any of you can shew just cause or impediment, etc.," and "I require and charge you both," etc.) is now lengthened into an instruction as to the meaning and solemnity of the occasion. In the American Book that portion of the address which states the three "causes for which Matrimony was ordained" has been omitted. In the Scottish an alternative form is provided giving two "chief causes" as follows: "It was ordained for the increase of mankind according to the will of God, and that children might be brought up in the fear and nurture of the Lord, and to the praise of His holy Name. It was also ordained for the mutual society, help, and comfort that the one ought to have of the other, both in prosperity and adversity."[3]

---

[1] "These Special Licences were originally a privilege of the Archbishop of Canterbury as 'Legatus natus' of the Pope. The right to grant them is confirmed by the Marriage Act of 1836." Blunt, *Ann. Pr. Bk.*, p. 262, note.

[2] "Housbondes at the chirche-dore have I hadde fyve." Chaucer, *Prologue to the Wife of Bath's Tale.*

[3] Some of the impediments to marriage, in addition to that of a previous marriage undissolved by death, are relationship within the prohibited degrees of "kindred and affinity," imbecility, sexual impotence, nonage, absence of consent, etc , as prescribed by Church and State alike While the American Church has never formally adopted the English Table of Prohibited Degrees in her Prayer Book, the House of Bishops in 1808

SOLEMNIZATION OF MARRIAGE 335

The first portion of the service down to "the giving away" of the bride, when the father relinquishes his *patria potestas* into the hands of the Church, that she in her turn may give the bride to her husband, is called the ESPOUSALS, that is, the solemn renewal of the "engagement" ("I will") which has already been made in private. This is now usually said in the nave, at the entrance to the choir.[1] That which follows is called the NUPTIALS, or BETROTHAL, the actual "plighting" and giving of the "troth" each to the other, as a pledge of fidelity and "truth." This is the marriage proper, and is said at the chancel rail.

The rubric directs that the Man shall be "on the right hand, and the Woman on the left," which is somewhat ambiguous. The ancient Sarum rubric, however, from which this is taken, makes the rule plain, namely, that the Man shall be on the Woman's right (*vir a dextris mulieris, et mulier a sinistris viri*), and not on the right of the Priest. This rule is usually and fittingly reversed in returning from the altar, as suggested by the words of the beautiful Marriage Psalm of Solomon, "Upon thy right hand did stand the queen in a vesture of gold," which is prophetical of "the mystical union that is betwixt Christ and His Church," "as a bride adorned for her husband."[2]

---

declared that "they consider that table as now obligatory on this Church" There is a distinction between impediments, some being *diriment*, that is, being contrary to the law of nature and the law of God. "They are such as not merely to forbid a marriage, but also to make it null and void, however solemnly contracted" (John Fulton, *The Laws of Marriage*, p. 27) There is much difference in practice, however, about many impediments which are created only by civil or ecclesiastical law. Marriage according to these may be forbidden and irregular, and yet be entirely valid

[1] As late as the time of Charles I there is evidence that these Espousals, or "engagement," and the actual Nuptials were sometimes separated by years. See Blunt, p. 267, note.

[2] Opening Address in Marriage Office, Ps. xlv, 10, and Rev. xxi, 2.

In the Vows the Letter "M" is a printer's mistaken emendation for "N." The letter "N" stands for the Christian name both of the Man and the Woman, and is so printed in the old books. But the best authority is for using only so much of the baptismal name as is commonly employed.[1] A reference to the original form of the Vows, which were of course necessarily in the "tongue understanded of the people," throws much light on the much criticised word "obey." The ancient form in the Salisbury Manual is "to be bonour and buxum," that is, gentle (as in *debonnaire*) and bough-some, or pliable.[2]

THE GIVING OF A RING to the bride was probably in use long before the Christian era. We seem to find a suggestion of it in the gift of "a golden earring and bracelets" to Rebekah on behalf of Isaac;[3] and Tertullian speaks of the custom of a Roman husband "placing the pledge of the nuptial ring on one finger."[4] The symbolism of the

---

[1] The late Queen of England and her Consort were married as Victoria and Albert (Dean Hart, *The Book of Common Prayer*, p. 245).

[2] In the York Manual the word "buxum" does not occur at all, and some Manuals added "in all lawful places." See Blunt, p. 267. It is to be remembered, moreover, that each party promises undivided allegiance and love, and where these exist submission to the "headship" of the husband (Eph. v. 23) can never prove irksome.

"Yet the light of a whole life dies
When love is done " — F. W BOURDILLON.

Bishop Jeremy Taylor has well pointed out that nothing is said in the man's part of the vow about "ruling," and he sums up the whole matter in a single sentence: "The man's authority is love, and the woman's love is obedience." (Sermon on *The Marriage Ring*) On the only occasion in the present writer's experience when the bride objected to the word "obey," she was divorced within a year!

[3] Gen xxiv, 22

[4] *Apol.* vi; *De Idol*, xvi.

SOLEMNIZATION OF MARRIAGE 337

ring, as having neither beginning nor ending, is plainly that of eternity and constancy, yet this most natural emblem was vigorously objected to by the Puritans with "scornful cavil," for what good reason it would be difficult to say.[1] The English Book makes it plain as to the way in which "the Man shall give unto the Woman" the ring by directing him to "*lay the same on the book* with the accustomed duty [that is, the fee] to the Priest and Clerk." Though no form is now provided for the benediction of the ring, it is most seemly that at least a silent blessing should be said over it at the altar. The following beautiful prayer is a literal translation of the ancient Latin form in the Sarum Use: "Bless, O Lord, this Ring which we bless in Thy Name, that she who wears it may abide in Thy peace, continue in Thy favor, live, go on, and grow old in Thy Love, and may be increased with length of days; through Jesus Christ our Lord."[2] In the English Office, at the placing of the ring, the phrase, "With my body I thee worship," was also much objected to by the Puritans, and at the Revision of 1662 it was agreed that "honour," the word used for "worship" in the York and Hereford Uses, should be substituted, but either by accident, or for some other reason, the old Salisbury word was allowed to remain. The two words had originally the same meaning, as they still have in the words "worshipful" and "honor-

---

[1] See Hooker, *Ecc. Pol* v, lxxiii, 6

[2] It was the ancient custom to place the ring on the thumb while saying, "In the Name of the Father," on the second finger while saying, "and of the Son," on the third while saying, "and of the Holy Ghost," and on the fourth at "Amen" This seems to be one reason why the fourth has been made the ring finger. A rubric in the Sarum Office gives an additional reason, namely, that a vein runs from the fourth finger to the heart, and while the physiology may not be exact, the sentiment is undoubtedly sound

able," and in the expressions, "Your worship" and "Your honour," addressed to magistrates. The phrase has been omitted from the American Prayer Book. The root meaning of "worship" is of course *worth-ship*.

The American Book inserts the Lord's Prayer here before the prayer, "O Eternal God, Creator," etc., which is formed from the two prayers formerly said at the blessing of the ring. It may seem strange that Isaac and Rebecca should be chosen as examples for the newly married. The reason evidently is that, under the old dispensation, they were almost the only pair who most nearly fulfilled the Christian ideal of marriage, most of the patriarchs in those early ages being polygamists. Chaucer in 1388 alludes to this prayer in the Merchant's Tale: —

> "But finally y-comen is the day
> That to the churchè bothè be they went,
> For to receive the holy sacrament.
> Forth came the priest with stole about his neck,
> And bade her be like Sarah and Rebecc,
> In wisdom and in truth of marriáge."

THE NUPTIALS in all the Books of the Anglican Communion end with the Joining of Hands of the couple by the Priest, as he says our Lord's words, "Those whom God hath joined together," etc., the Declaration ("I pronounce," etc.), and the Blessing. This last is almost word for word the same as that in the ancient Sarum Use.

The American Church has omitted the remaining portion of the service in the English Book. Concerning the right of a Deacon in this Church to read the service, Dean Hart has this to say: — "The law of the land recognizes the Deacons of our Church as 'Ministers of the Gospel,' and permits them to marry; and our service uses the word 'Minister' throughout, and that intentionally, as the English

SOLEMNIZATION OF MARRIAGE 339

Book has confusedly 'Priest,' Curate,' and 'Minister.' But the Benediction is priestly, and evidently ought not to be said by a Deacon. It would seem, therefore, that a Deacon may use the Marriage Service, in any place where he has the Bishop's or Priest's authority to minister; but that he should substitute 'The grace of our Lord,' or some other prayer, for the Benediction." [1]

In the English, Scottish, and Irish Books appropriate prayers, mainly from the ancient Office, with Ps. cxxviii, or lxvii, and a formal Address to all present ("if there be no sermon") [2] are intended to lead on to the Holy Communion, "the Minister or Clerks going to the Lord's Table" (Rubric). The Book of 1549 had the rubric, "The new-married persons, the same day of their Marriage, must receive the Holy Communion." This was wisely changed in 1661 to "It is convenient [that is, fit or seemly] that the new-married persons should receive the Holy Communion at the time of their Marriage, or at the first opportunity after their Marriage."

Concerning this rule of the Church Hooker has these wise words:—"To end the public solemnity of marriage with receiving the blessed Sacrament is a custom so religious and so holy, that if the Church of England be blameable in this respect it is not for suffering it to be so much, but rather for not providing that it may be more put in ure [that is, in use]. The laws of Romulus concerning marriage are therefore extolled above the rest amongst the heathens which were before, in that they established the use of certain special solemnities, whereby the minds of men were drawn to make the greater conscience of wed-

---

[1] *The Book of Common Prayer*, p 248.
[2] It is in reference to the last word in this Address that Dickens makes Captain Cuttle say that the service ends with "amazement."

lock, and to esteem the bond thereof a thing which could not be without impiety dissolved. If there be anything in Christian religion strong and effectual to like purpose it is the Sacrament of the Holy Eucharist, in regard of the force whereof Tertullian breaketh out into these words concerning matrimony therewith sealed; 'I know not which way I should be able to shew the happiness of that wedlock the knot whereof the Church doth fasten, and the Sacrament of the Church confirm.'" [1]

The Scottish Church alone has provided a special Collect, Epistle, and Gospel for a Marriage Eucharist. The Collect, taken chiefly from the final blessing of the ancient service, is as follows: — "O Heavenly Father who didst join together in marriage our first parents, Adam and Eve: Sanctify and bless these Thy servants; and grant that those whom Thou by matrimony dost make one, may stedfastly keep the covenant betwixt them made, and ever remain in perfect love and peace together; through Jesus Christ our Lord." The Epistle is Eph. v, 25 to the end; the Gospel, S. Matt. xix, 4, 5, 6.

[1] *Ecc. Pol.* V, lxxiii, 8.

CHAPTER XXXIII
VISITATION AND COMMUNION OF THE SICK

"*Then spreads she there an altar lone,*
Her priest, to bless and break, is there,
And angels, radiant from the throne,
Come winging round the scene of prayer." — BISHOP COXE.

THE VISITATION OF THE SICK, being an essential duty of all who have the cure of souls, as declared in their ordination vow, scarcely needs the specific authority of Holy Scripture. Such authority, however, is found, not only in the example of our Lord and His Apostles,[1] but also in the express injunction of S. James.[2] The service as we possess it today is mainly taken from that of the old Sarum Use. The ancient Office prescribed the seven penitential Psalms to be said by the Priest on his way to the sick man's house. Then followed the salutation, "Peace be to this house," etc., as in our present Office, for which we have the express authority of our Lord.[3] The rubric does not seem to make it necessary that this should be said immediately on entering the house, but it should never be omitted in beginning the Office, or any portion of it. Its utterance makes it known in the most modest, yet most impressive way to the ears of both sick and well, that this is no mere friendly or neighborly visit, but that of one who comes as the ambassador of Him who of old went about healing the sick, and manifesting Himself as the God of peace and the

---

[1] S. Mark vi, 7–14; xvi, 18; Acts v, 15, 16; ix, 17; xxviii, 8.
[2] v, 14, 15.   [3] S. Luke x, 5, 6.

Lord of all life. Though not prescribed, it is a most fitting custom to raise the right hand as in the act of benediction while reciting the salutation.

The versicles and the two prayers following are translations, with slight changes, from the ancient Office. So also are the exhortations, the examination in regard to belief, the confession and absolution. The rubric, and the form of absolution in the English Book following the rubric about being "liberal to the poor," are as follows: —

"*Here shall the sick person be moved to make a special confession of his sins, if he feel his conscience troubled with any weighty matter. After which Confession, the Priest shall absolve him (if he humbly and heartily desire it) after this sort.*"

" Our Lord Jesus Christ, who hath left power to his Church to absolve all sinners who truly repent and believe in Him, of His great mercy forgive thee thine offences: And by His authority committed to me, I absolve thee from all thy sins, In the Name of the Father, and of the Son, and of the Holy Ghost. Amen."

It will be observed that all this is voluntary on the part of the sick person, and is in full accordance with what is prescribed for the well in the first Exhortation in the Communion Office. The indicative form of absolution in the English Office ("I absolve thee") was the custom of the mediæval Church, but is without primitive precedent. It was not used in fact before the 12th or 13th century.[1] While acknowledging its late use, Bingham says concerning this indicative form, "It must needs be of considerable weight and moment towards the satisfaction and comfort of an afflicted, or a doubting and despondent soul, to have the declara-

---

[1] See Bingham, *Antiq.* XIX, ii, 5, 6; Hooker, *Ecc. Pol.* VI, iv, 15.

VISITATION OF THE SICK 343

tion of a skillful physician to rely upon; and to have one, who by his office is qualified to be a proper judge in such cases, to pronounce his absolution."[1] The collect that follows, "O most merciful God," has been in use in the Church since the days of Gelasius (5th century). This is followed in the English Book by Psalm lxxi, with its Antiphon, "O Saviour of the world," etc., "The Almighty Lord, who is a most strong tower," etc., and the Aaronic benediction," "Unto God's gracious mercy," etc.[2]

It is at this point in the Book of 1549 that provision is made for THE ANOINTING OF THE SICK in the following rubric and prayer —

"*If the sick person desire to be anointed, then shall the Priest anoint him upon the forehead or breast only, making the sign of the Cross, saying thus,*

"As with this visible oil thy body outwardly is anointed, so our heavenly Father, Almighty God, grant of infinite goodness that thy soul inwardly may be anointed with the Holy Ghost, who is the Spirit of all strength, comfort, relief, and gladness. And vouchsafe for His great mercy (if it be His blessed will) to restore unto thee thy bodily health and strength, to serve Him; and send thee release of all thy pains, troubles, and diseases, both in body and mind. And howsoever His goodness (by His divine and unsearchable Providence) shall dispose of thee; we His unworthy Ministers and servants, humbly beseech the eternal Majesty to do with thee according to the multitude of His innumerable mercies, and to pardon thee all thy sins and offences committed by all thy bodily senses, passions, and carnal affec-

---

[1] *Antiq , Appendix, Sermon I.*

[2] Num vi, 24, 25, 26 "This Antiphon is extremely interesting as being the only one retained in the Book of Common Prayer; and as still showing the manner in which Antiphons were formerly appended to Psalms for the purpose of drawing out their spiritual meaning, or giving them the turn required for the special occasion on which they were used." Blunt, *Ann. Pr. Bk.*, p. 286.

tions; who also vouchsafe mercifully to grant unto thee ghostly strength, by His Holy Spirit, to withstand and overcome all temptations and assaults of thine adversary, that in no wise he prevail against thee; but that thou mayest have perfect victory and triumph against the devil, sin, and death; through Christ our Lord: who by His death hath overcome the prince of death; and with the Father and the Holy Ghost evermore liveth and reigneth God, world without end. Amen."

The Office of 1549 closed with Psalm xiii, "How long wilt Thou forget me?" This service for the Unction of the sick was omitted in 1552, and four special prayers were added in later revisions.[1]

In view of the fact that the Apostles, under our Lord's direction, "anointed with oil many that were sick,"[2] and that S. James gives the specific injunction to "the Presbyters of the Church" to pray over the sick, "anointing him with oil in the Name of the Lord,"[3] it seems passing strange that this service, so simple and so thoroughly scriptural, should never have been restored in later revisions. Probably the omission in 1552 under foreign Protestant influence was largely owing to their unreasoning prejudice against anything that seemed at all sacramental, and also because of the perversion of the primitive custom which had come to be used only at the imminent approach of death, and for that reason was called, as it is still in the Roman communion, *Extreme* Unction. But such rejection of what is plainly an Apostolic practice for restoration of health to body and soul alike, can have no ground in reason. It is to be feared moreover that its omission has had some-

---

[1] The mediæval office for the Anointing of the Sick was a much more elaborate one See Maskell, I, 83–103.
[2] S. Mark vi, 13.   [3] v, 14.

VISITATION OF THE SICK 345

thing to do, by reaction, with the rise of such modern fanaticisms as "Christian Science," and "Faith Healing."

The true balance between the spiritual and the bodily physician is beautifully and accurately expressed by the wise author of Ecclesiasticus: — "My son, in thy sickness be not negligent; but pray unto the Lord, and He will make thee whole. . . . Then give place to the physician, for the Lord hath created him."[1] Many eminent physicians have of late borne witness to the wonderful influence of prayer merely as a mental sedative, in the restoration of bodily health. This is doubtless part, though by no means all, of what is claimed by S. James when he says, "The prayer of faith shall save the sick."[2] Nothing is said about any *miraculous* effect of the oil. It is only an appropriate symbol meant to aid the faith of the patient. To many in the Church today it seems that the only rubric required for its use is this very definite one of S. James. The Book of 1549 gives a suitable Office for the purpose, though it may be regarded as capable of improvement.[3]

THE AMERICAN OFFICE FOR VISITATION OF THE SICK is the same as the English with the following exceptions: (1) The omission of the rubric providing for "a special confession," and the indicative form of absolution following; (2) the substitution of Ps. cxxx, for Ps. lxxi; (3) the addition of two rubrics in regard to the use of other prayers in the Book: (4) and the addition of three new prayers, (a) "On behalf of all present," the beautiful prayer of Bishop Jeremy Taylor, "O God, whose days are without end,"

---

[1] xxxviii, 9, 12.   [2] v, 15.
[3] The Lambeth Conference of 1908 decided not to recommend the Unction of the Sick, but to allow its use, expressing the hope that the other apostolic act for helping the sick, the Laying on of Hands, might be used as an accompaniment to prayer.

(b) "In case of immediate danger," (c) "Thanksgiving for the beginning of a recovery."

THE SCOTTISH OFFICE differs from the English only in the addition of a brief prayer "for the recovery of a sick person." THE IRISH OFFICE, as revised in 1877, differs only from the English in changing the rubric concerning "a special confession" so as to read, "Here, if the sick person feel his conscience troubled with any weighty matter, he shall be moved to open his grief, after which (if he humbly and heartily desire it) the Minister shall say thus": namely, the Absolution in the Office for Holy Communion.

While it is undoubtedly well to have a set form as a guide for the Visitation of the Sick, and occasionally to follow it with tolerable accuracy, much liberty must be left to each physician of souls, dealing necessarily with most diverse cases and circumstances. The use of a collection of other prayers, and even of extemporaneous prayer, will sometimes be found a necessity. There is no Office in the Prayer Book which so tests and shows the character of the true, fatherly, and sympathetic Priest as this.[1] Quietness, gentleness, and reverence are some of the outward signs that must never be absent. It is probably the lack of such qualities in many that has caused some physicians to tell relatives of the sick person not to allow a clergyman to see the patient.

THE OFFICE FOR THE COMMUNION OF THE SICK in the American, Scottish, and Irish Books varies in no material point from the English. The slight differences to be noted in the American Book are (1) the use of "Minister" for "Priest," as it is frequently used in other parts of all the Books to indicate the Priest who has the charge of a parish.

---
[1] See 2 Cor. vi, 6.

VISITATION OF THE SICK

(2) The permission, "*In the times of contagious sickness or disease, or when extreme weakness renders it expedient,*" to abbreviate the service by using only "*The Confession and the Absolution;* Lift up your hearts, etc., *through the* Sanctus; *The Prayer of Consecration, ending with these words,* partakers of His most blessed Body and Blood; *The Communion: The Lord's Prayer; The Blessing.*" (3) Permission to use "*with aged and bedridden persons, or such as are not able to attend the public Ministration in Church,*" the Collect, Epistle, and Gospel for the Day, instead of those appointed in the Office. The Irish Book gives practically the same permission as in the last two cases. Concerning reservation of the Sacrament for the sick see chap. xx, pp. 197 sq.

Some things worthy of note in all the Books are (1) that the Clergy "shall diligently from time to time exhort their parishioners to the often receiving of the Holy Communion of the Body and Blood of our Saviour Christ." It is to be feared that this injunction is not always obeyed as it ought to be. The monthly use of the long Exhortation can scarcely be said to be a compliance with it, inasmuch as, in accordance with a common and unauthorized custom, the people who really need it have already left the Church. (2) The use of the word "communicate," and the total absence of the word "commune" which expresses the thought of a mere mental act, and not that oneness wrought by a faithful reception whereby "we dwell in Christ, and He in us."[1]

The Office for a private celebration in the Book of 1549 begins with the 117th Psalm, the three-fold Kyrie, "The Lord be with you," etc., and the Collect, Epistle, and Gospel, as in our present service. The rubrics of the present

---
[1] Prayer of Humble Access.

Book, with the exception of that for reservation, are taken almost without change from this first revised Book.[1]

---

[1] If any one should infer from the rubric concerning what is to be said to those who "by reason of extremity of sickness, or other just impediment, do not receive the Sacrament of Christ's Body and Blood," that actual reception is of only minor importance, he must remember that exactly the same direction existed in the ancient Sarum and York Offices. In each of these, when the highest views were held concerning the necessity of the Sacrament, the words of S. Augustine are directed to be said to every such penitent, "Only believe, and thou hast eaten" (*Tantum crede, et manducasti*). Compare 2 Cor. viii, 12 for the principle involved.

CHAPTER XXXIV
BURIAL OF THE DEAD

"Our mother the Church hath never a child
To honor before the rest,
But she singeth the same for mighty kings
And the veriest babe on her breast;
And the Bishop goes down to his narrow bed
As the ploughman's child is laid,
And alike she blesseth the dark-browed serf
And the chief in his robe arrayed."
— BISHOP A. C. COXE, *Christian Ballads.*

THE custom of the Christian Church from the beginning in regard to BURIAL OF THE DEAD has been the same as that of God's ancient Church, which was her shadow. The Patriarchs and the Jewish people through all their history had reverently buried their dead in the earth, or in a sepulchre like that in Joseph's garden where our Lord was laid. The heathen around them frequently burnt their dead bodies. The Christian Church has, above Jew or heathen, a special reason for treating the bodies of her dead with great care and respect, for she knows that the body has been redeemed as well as the soul,[1] and that the body of every Christian was grafted into the sacred Body of Christ, made a "member of His Body, of His Flesh, and of His Bones." [2] Even the bodies of Christians who have died in sin, as Ananias and Sapphira, are reverently carried to a grave and buried.[3]

---
[1] Eph. v, 23, 1 Thess v, 23
[2] Eph v, 30.
[3] Acts v, 10; and see Bingham, *Antiq* XXIII, chaps. 2 and 3.

It does not follow, however, that cremation or incineration must necessarily be regarded as un-Christian. By some the utmost reverence may be felt for one whose body, thus united to Christ, is returned to its native dust by a more rapid process. By others the process may be felt to be unnatural and shocking. No question of principle is involved. The power of Christ to raise the dead body remains the same in either case. It is natural, however, that the preference of the Church should always remain for that method which is most like her Lord's.[1]

The mediæval services for burial were very elaborate. They included (1) the *Commendation*, consisting largely of prayers for the departed, said at the house, and on the way to the church, or the grave; (2) the *Inhumation*, or *Burial;* (3) the *Mass for the Dead;* (4) the *Dirge* and *Placebo*, the office used throughout the month.[2]

A simplification of these many and elaborate services became a great necessity, especially as regards the prayers. In all the ancient Liturgies prayers for the faithful departed were for their peace and rest in Paradise, and for a joyful resurrection. [See pp. 65 and 163.] In the mediæval Offices they had become prayers for deliverance from a Purgatory which only differed from the final Gehenna in that its pains were not eternal. In 1549 these complicated services were reduced to the following: —

---

[1] In view of the reverent custom of the Church in all ages, it is passing strange to find the Puritans in the seventeenth century forbidding the use of any kind of service at the burial of the dead.

[2] The former word, applied to the Matins of the Office, was derived from the first word of the Latin Antiphon, *Dirige in conspectu tuo viam meam,* "Make my way plain," etc., from the Psalm used in this service (v, 8). The Vespers was called *Placebo* for a similar reason, *Placebo Domino,* "I will walk before the Lord," etc , from Ps. cxvi, 9, but in the Vulgate, Psalm cxiv, 9.

BURIAL OF THE DEAD

(1) The same sentences as in the present Book, "said or sung," on the way from "the Church stile," either to the grave or to the church.

(2) If to the Church, Psalms cxvi, cxxxix, and cxlvi follow.

(3) The Lesson from 1 Cor. xv.

(4) The Minor Litany, "Lord, have mercy," etc., and the Lord's Prayer.

(5) Four Versicles with their Responses, beginning with, "Enter not into judgment," etc., followed by the present prayer, "O Lord, with whom do live," etc., down to "joy and felicity," petitions for the departed that his sins "be not imputed unto him," that he "may ever dwell in the region of light," and at the general Resurrection he may hear those "most sweet and comfortable words; 'Come unto Me, ye blessed,'" etc., as in our present concluding prayer; then "The grace," etc.

(6) The service at the grave, which may be said either before or after the service in church, consists of the sentences, "said or sung," beginning, "Man that is born," etc., the Committal substantially as at present, but commencing with "I commend thy soul to God, the Father Almighty, and thy body to the ground"; "I heard a voice," etc., ending with two prayers.

Though changes were made in 1552, the service did not reach its present form until the revision of 1662, when Psalms xxxix, and xc, were substituted for cxvi, cxxxix, and cxlvi. The last two prayers of the Office are new, but the great bulk of the service is found in the ancient Use. This is true of the two opening sentences, "I am the Resurrection," etc., and "I know that my Redeemer," etc.; the Lesson from 1 Cor. xv; the noble Anthem or Sequence, *Media vita*, beginning, "Man that is born," etc.;[1] the Com-

---

[1] It should be noted that the Anthem, "Man that is born," etc, is directed to be said, not *when*, but "*while* the corpse is made ready," etc., and with a definite purpose. This is the moment most trying to natural

mittal; "I heard a voice," etc.; the Minor Litany, and the Lord's Prayer. The custom of casting earth upon the body, which the ancient rubric required should be done *ad modum crucis*, in the form of a cross, was continued. The most marked difference is the absence of any direct prayer for the faithful departed, such as is found in all the ancient Liturgies.

"The original composition of the *Media Vita* is traced back to Notker, to whom that of the *Dies Irae* can be traced, and who was a monk of S. Gall, in Switzerland, at the close of the ninth century. It is said to have been suggested to him by a circumstance similar to that which gave birth to a noble passage in Shakespeare.[1] As our English poet watched the samphire gatherers on the cliffs at Dover, so did Notker watch those on the rocks at S. Gall. And as he watched them at their 'dreadful trade,' he sang, 'In the midst of life we are in death,' moulding his awful hymn to that familiar form of the Trisagion, 'Holy God, Holy and Mighty, Holy and Immortal, have mercy upon us,' which is found in the primitive Liturgies. In the Middle Ages it was adopted as a Dirge on all melancholy occasions in Germany: armies used it as a battle song; and superstitious ideas of its miraculous power rose to such a height, that, in the year 1316, the Synod of Cologne forbad the people to sing it at all except on such occasions as were allowed by their Bishop." [2]

---

affection, when the body is to be laid in the grave, and the slowly uttered words of this Sequence are most needed for the comfort and support of the mourners.

[1] *Lear* iv, 6.

[2] Blunt, *Ann. Pr Bk.*, p. 297, note. While we have in the *Media Vita* a needful reminder of "the shortness and uncertainty of human life," by the reversal of the order of the words we get a most consoling Christian truth. It is said that the late Archbishop Benson of Canterbury placed

BURIAL OF THE DEAD

THE AMERICAN OFFICE throughout is almost identical with the English except in the following minor points: — In the first rubric, "any that die unbaptized" is changed to "any unbaptized adults"; the two Psalms, xxxix, and xc, have been abbreviated; in the Committal, "dear brother" becomes "deceased brother"; and "in sure and certain hope of the Resurrection to eternal life, through, etc., who shall change," etc., becomes "looking for the general Resurrection in the last day, and the life of the world to come, through our Lord Jesus Christ, at whose second coming in glorious majesty to judge the world, the earth and the sea shall give up their dead; and the corruptible bodies of those who sleep in Him shall be changed, and made like," etc. There are also a few verbal changes in the last two prayers, and the words of the Committal when the burial is at sea are printed here. Three prayers were added in 1892 for occasional use, the last being part of the prayer "for the whole state of Christ's Church" in the Book of 1549.

THE IRISH OFFICE of 1877 permits an abbreviated service for unbaptized Infants, and others who, "at the time of their death, were prepared for or desirous of Baptism." It also changes the English rubric about those "who have laid violent hands on themselves" to read, "in whose case a verdict shall have been found of *felo de se*."

THE SCOTTISH OFFICE, as revised by the Bishops in 1912, is identical with the English down to the end of the Lesson from I Cor. xv, except that it permits, "with the sanction of the Bishop," the omission of verses 27–40 inclusive. It

---

upon the grave of a beloved daughter this inscription, "In the midst of death we are in life." It is also worthy of note that the use of the Sequence at Burials is peculiar to the Anglican Communion, alike in its ancient and its modern Office. It never had a place in the Roman.

also provides seven other brief Lessons which may be substituted for the first, as follows: — S. John v, 24–28; vi, 37–41; xi, 21–28; 2 Cor. iv, 16 to v, 11; 1 Thess. iv, 13 to end; Rev. vii, 9 to end; and xxi, 3–6.

After the Lesson it provides for the use "of one or more of these prayers;" the Collects for Advent Sunday, Palm Sunday, Easter Eve, Twenty-first Sunday after Trinity; "Almighty God, the fountain," etc., at the end of the Communion Office; "We humbly beseech Thee, O Father," etc. at the end of the Litany; a prayer entitled "Commemoration of the Faithful Departed," and "A Prayer for those in sorrow." An alternative form of Committal is provided which is almost identical with that of the American Office, with the single exception of using the Revised Version of Phil. iii, 21 instead of "who shall change our vile body," etc., as in the Auth. Ver.

AT THE BURIAL OF BAPTIZED CHILDREN it is permitted to use among the opening sentences, "Jesus said, Suffer the little children to come unto Me," etc., and to substitute for the Psalms and the Lesson, Psalm xxiii, and S. Matt. xviii, 1–11. Three special prayers are also provided as follows: —

"O Heavenly Father, whose face the angels of the little ones do always behold in heaven: Grant us stedfastly to believe that this little child hath been taken into the safe keeping of Thy eternal love; through Jesus Christ our Lord. *Amen.*

"O Lord Jesu Christ, who didst take little children into Thine arms and bless them: Open Thou our eyes, we beseech Thee, that we may perceive that Thou hast now taken this child into the arms of Thy Love, and hast bestowed upon *him* the blessings of Thy gracious favour; who livest and reignest with the Father and the Holy Spirit, one God, world without end. *Amen.*

BURIAL OF THE DEAD

"We yield Thee hearty thanks, most merciful Father, that it hath pleased Thee to regenerate this child with Thy Holy Spirit, to receive *him* for Thine own by adoption, and to incorporate *him* into Thy Holy Church. And humbly we beseech Thee to grant that, as he is made partaker of the death of Thy Son, *he* may also be partaker of His resurrection; so that finally, with the residue of Thy Holy Church, *he* may be an inheritor of Thy everlasting kingdom; through Christ our Lord. *Amen.*"

A Prayer for the BENEDICTION OF A GRAVE in unconsecrated ground is provided as follows: —

"O Lord Jesu Christ, who wast laid in the new tomb of Joseph, and didst thereby sanctify the grave to be a bed of hope to Thy people: Vouchsafe, we beseech Thee, to bless, hallow, and consecrate this grave, that it may be a resting-place, peaceful and secure, for the body of Thy servant which we are about to commit to Thy gracious keeping, who art the Resurrection and the Life, and who livest and reignest with the Father and the Holy Ghost, one God, world without end. *Amen.*"

THE CELEBRATION OF THE HOLY COMMUNION WHEN THERE IS A BURIAL OF THE DEAD was provided for in the Book of 1549 as follows: — For the Introit, Psalm xlii; the Collect is the same as that in the present Book preceding "The grace," etc., down to "the life of righteousness," after which it reads, "that, when we shall depart this life, we may sleep in Him (as our hope is this our brother doth); and at the general Resurrection at the last Day, both we, and this our brother departed, receiving again our bodies, and rising again in Thy most gracious favor, may, with all Thine elect Saints, obtain eternal joy. Grant this, O Lord God, by the means of our Advocate Jesus Christ; which, with Thee and the Holy Ghost, liveth and reigneth one God for ever. Amen." The Epistle, 1 Thess. iv, 13 to end; The Gospel, S. John vi, 37–41.

CHAPTER XXXV
OTHER OCCASIONAL OFFICES, CHURCHING OF WOMEN, ETC.

"*Is there, in bowers of endless spring,*
  One known from all the seraph band
By softer voice, by smile and wing,
  More exquisitely bland?
Here let him speed: today this hallowed air
Is fragrant with a mother's first and fondest prayer." — KEBLE.

THE THANKSGIVING OF WOMEN AFTER CHILDBIRTH, commonly called *The Churching of Women*, varies little in any of the revised Books from the mediæval Use, or from the Book of 1549, the chief difference being the appointed Psalms. In this latter Book, as in the ancient Office, the title was *The Order of the Purification of Women*, in allusion to the Jewish rite scrupulously observed by the Mother of the Holy Child, and prescribed by the ancient law.[1] The mediæval Use required the Office to begin in the church porch (*ante ostium*), as in the Marriage service, and after the prayers the woman was sprinkled with holy water, and the Priest led her by the right hand into the church (*per manum dextram in ecclesiam*). It is for this reason that the Office acquired the popular name of *Churching*. The Book of 1549 prescribes "some convenient place nigh unto the Quire door," and begins with the present brief address, adding as an additional cause for thanksgiving (after the word "deliverance"), "and your child Baptism." "Decently apparelled" means or includes the wearing of a veil, according to the ancient custom.

---
[1] S. Luke ii, 22, etc., and Lev. xii, 2, etc.

CHURCHING OF WOMEN, &c. 357

The mediæval Office had Psalms cxxi, and cxxviii. The Book of 1549 had omitted the latter. The present English, Irish, and Scottish Books have Psalm cxvi, or cxxvii; while the American has a "hymn" or cento composed of verses 1, 2, 4, 5, 11, 12, 13 of Psalm cxvi. The American Book also permits the use of "the concluding prayer alone as it stands among the Occasional Prayers and Thanksgivings." The Irish Book adds the Aaronic benediction, "The Lord bless thee," etc. To the requirement of "accustomed offerings," as in the present Books, the First Revised Book directed that the woman shall "offer her Crisome," that is, the white dress put upon her child at Baptism. It is surely much to be regretted that gratitude for deliverance in "the great danger of childbirth," the gift from God of the soul and body of a child, and its admission into the Church by Baptism, should not compel every Christian mother to welcome the use of such an Office as this, and to fulfil its final requirement by receiving the Holy Communion in further token of her thankfulness and of her need.

A COMMINATION, OR, DENOUNCING OF GOD'S ANGER AND JUDGMENTS AGAINST SINNERS, WITH CERTAIN PRAYERS, ETC. This is the title of the special penitential Office for "the first day of Lent, and other times, as the Ordinary shall appoint." The title in the Book of 1549 was simply, "The First Day of Lent, commonly called Ash Wednesday." The present title was adopted in 1662. The service is practically identical with that of the mediæval Use. This prescribed that an address should be made by the Priest at the beginning, but no form was given, as is done in the present Book. The seven penitential Psalms formed part of the ancient Office, and these are still prescribed for the day; vi, xxxii, and xxxviii, at Matins; li, in the Commination; and cii, cxxx, and cxliii, at Evensong. The blessing and distribution of ashes took place before the prayer, "O Most Mighty God," the beginning of which is taken from the Benediction of the Ashes (*Benedictio Cinerum*), and the remainder from one of the preceding collects. The General Supplication, said by people and priest, is formed from portions of the ancient service, and occupies the place of the Procession, or Litany.

The American Church omitted in 1789 the whole of this Office, justly feeling that a service so largely composed of Malediction (cursing), or Commination (threatening), was not in keeping with the spirit of the New Testament. Mr. Blunt writes of these "awful Judaic maledictions": "The form in which these are used is singularly out of character with the general tone of the Prayer Book; denunciation of sin ordinarily taking the form of a Litany, not of an exhortation, under the Christian dispensation. . . . Persons 'convicted of notorious sin' are now otherwise punished; and an aspiration after the revival of an 'open penance' [as in the 'godly discipline of the Primitive Church'] which is utterly impossible, is apt to lead the thoughts away from the restoration of a discipline and penance which is both possible and desirable."[1] In 1892 the American Church restored the whole of the supplicatory portion of the Office, beginning with the 51st Psalm, under the title, "A Penetential Office for Ash Wednesday," and introduced the beautiful fifth century collect from the Gelasian Sacramentary, "O God, whose nature and property," immediately before the final prayer of benediction.

FORMS OF PRAYER TO BE USED AT SEA are not a substitute for the ordinary Offices, but are only a collection of prayers suited to various occasions. There are prayers for use in storm and before a fight, and thanksgivings after

---

[1] *Ann. Pr Bk.*, p 309.

CHURCHING OF WOMEN, &c. 359

a storm or a victory. It seems to be in keeping, however, with the traditions of the English-speaking race that, as has been ingeniously remarked, "the compiler does not seem to have in mind the possibilities of a defeat."[1] These prayers were composed and inserted in the revision of 1662, and are said to have been the work of Bishop Sanderson of Lincoln. The need of them was doubtless forced on the attention of the revisers by the wonderful growth of British commerce, colonies, and sea power, which began to receive its vast expansion in "the spacious times of great Elizabeth."

The American Office for THE VISITATION OF PRISONERS was taken by the revisers of 1789 from the Irish Prayer Book, as "treated upon by the Archbishops and Bishops, and the rest of the Clergy of Ireland, in their Synod, holden at Dublin, in the year 1711." Some slight changes were made in the service by the Irish Synod in 1877. The Office provides a special Collect, Epistle (1 S. John i, 9), and Gospel (S. John v, 24), for a celebration of the Holy Communion. There is no service corresponding to this in the English and Scottish Books.

The American and the Irish Prayer Books alone contain Offices for HARVEST THANKSGIVING. In the early days of New England the old English custom of Harvest Home had been retained by the colonists, and it had become an established rule that the Governors should appoint each autumn a day of public thanksgiving and prayer. The custom spread to other States, but was not observed in the South until the Church in 1789 adopted the present "FORM OF PRAYER AND THANKSGIVING TO ALMIGHTY GOD, For the Fruits of the Earth, and all the other Blessings of His merciful Providence." At first the date appointed by the different

[1] Dr. Samuel Hart.

360 PRIMITIVE WORSHIP & THE PRAYER BOOK

Governors varied, and so the Church prescribed "the first Thursday in November, or such other day as shall be appointed by the Civil Authority." As no day was appointed by the Governors in the South, Churchmen there naturally observed the first Thursday, while in the North the day varied in each State according to the proclamation of the Governor. It was only during the Civil War (1861–1865) that the President of the United States appointed a Day of National Thanksgiving, and since then the custom has been universally observed, the day being fixed, though not necessarily, for the last Thursday in November.

The form provided for the day is not an Office by itself but consists of certain additions to and substitutions for the ordinary services. Among the opening sentences are passages from Prov. iii, 9, 10, 19, 20; and Deut. xxiii, 27; xxviii, 28, 29. The *Venite* is replaced by a "cento" consisting of vv. 1, 2, 3, 7, 8, 9, 12, 13, 14 of Psalm cxlvii. A portion of the Psalms is left "to the discretion of the Minister." The Lessons are Deut. viii, and 1 Thess v, ver. 12 to 24. A special thanksgiving is said after the General Thanksgiving, and a special Collect, to take the place of that for the day. The Epistle is S. James i, 16 to end; the Gospel, S. Matt. v, 43 to end. This is the only service that was taken from the "Proposed Prayer Book" of 1786. The Irish "Form of Thanksgiving for the Blessings of Harvest" (adopted in 1877) follows the same general lines as the American. It gives a larger choice of Lessons, and provides two Collects, two Epistles, and two Gospels.

The two "FORMS OF PRAYER TO BE USED IN FAMILIES" (for Morning and Evening), placed in the American Book in 1789, had already been much used in the Colonies. They were composed by Edward Gibson, Bishop of London

CHURCHING OF WOMEN, &c. 361

(1724-1748), in whose jurisdiction all the Churches in the Colonies had been placed by royal patent.

The English Book, "until the year 1859, contained four services for special days of the year which were commonly called 'STATE SERVICES,' because they commemorated certain public events connected with the political history of the country." [1] These were drawn up by Bishops, or by Convocation, but had no joint authority of Convocation and Parliament such as that of the Book of 1662. The four services are, (1) FOR THE FIFTH OF NOVEMBER, in commemoration of the discovery of the Powder Plot to destroy the King and the two Houses of Parliament at the opening session of 1605; (2) FOR THE THIRTIETH OF JANUARY, "as a day of fasting and humiliation" for the anniversary of the death of "King Charles the Martyr" in 1649; (3) FOR THE TWENTY-NINTH OF MAY, with thanksgivings, for a double reason, as being the birthday of Charles II as well as the day of his Restoration; (4) FOR THE ACCESSION OF THE REIGNING SOVEREIGN, which, in its original form, was issued in 1578, to be used on Nov. 17th, the anniversary of the accession of Queen Elizabeth (in 1558). In 1859 a "Warrant" was issued by Queen Victoria, at the request of Convocation and Parliament, for the discontinuance of the first three of these services.

THE "ACCESSION SERVICE," for use on the anniversary day of the Accession of the reigning Sovereign, is very similar in the three English, Scottish, and Irish Books. The two latter have given up the use of the "Anthem," or cento composed of verses of various Psalms, to be said or sung antiphonally by priest and people, in place of the *Venite*. The other changes in these Books are chiefly in the prayers. The Scottish has two new prayers, and pro-

---
[1] Blunt, *Ann. Pr Bk*, pp. 578, 579.

vides a short additional service which "may also be used on the same day at any convenient time." This begins with the Te Deum, which is here divided into its three natural strophes, (1) "We praise Thee," to "the Comforter"; (2) "Thou art the King," to "glory everlasting"; (3) "O Lord, save," to end. All the Books have the "Prayer for Unity," "O God, Father of our Lord Jesus Christ."

CHAPTER XXXVI

The Ordinal — The Witness of Holy Scripture

"*Who is God's chosen priest?*
He who on Christ stands waiting day and night,
Who traced His holy steps, nor ever ceased,
From Jordan's banks to Bethphage height:

"*Who hath learned lowliness*
From His Lord's cradle, patience from His Cross;
Whom poor men's eyes and hearts consent to bless;
To whom, for Christ, the world is loss." — KEBLE.

THE Revisers of 1549 made a bold and uncompromising statement in the Preface to the Ordinal which the whole Anglican Communion has never since modified, much less withdrawn. "It is evident," they said, "unto all men, diligently reading Holy Scripture and ancient Authors, that from the Apostles' time there have been these Orders of Ministers in Christ's Church, — BISHOPS, PRIESTS, AND DEACONS." And then they add this inference or corollary, "No man shall be accounted or taken to be a lawful Bishop, Priest, or Deacon, in the Church ('of England,' or 'Ireland,' *or* 'this [American] Church') . . . except he be admitted thereunto, according to the Form hereafter following, or hath had formerly Episcopal Consecration or Ordination." It is important, therefore, at the outset to enquire concerning the accuracy of this declaration by accepting the challenge to "read," and that "diligently, Holy Scripture and ancient Authors" with this object in view.

It must never be forgotten that our Lord was a loyal Jew, accustomed from childhood to a strict order of Divine appointment, not only of worship and festival and fast, but also of Ministry.[1] He Himself tells us He came "Not to destroy but to fulfil" the old law of God,[2] which S. Paul tells us was the shadow and similitude of that which was to come.[3] To this ancient Ministry of High Priest, Priest, and Levite He was ever obedient, and required others to be obedient, even though many of its members were utterly unworthy of their office, and even though the chief rulers of the Church were they who actually sent Him to the Cross.[4] In Him the great High Priest,[5] all the offices of the ancient threefold Ministry were fulfilled, and at His death ceased to be, while henceforth He became the greater Aaron, or rather the new source and fountain of the Ministry which was to continue to speak and act in His name "unto the end of the world."[6]

It is most important, therefore, to observe the way in which our Lord set about the preparation and establishment of His "Kingdom," or, as He also calls it, His "Church."[7] He does not begin by preaching to the multitudes in great cities. Though possessed of the powers and the infinite love of the Incarnate Godhead, and knowing the fearful need of His message, not only by His countrymen the Jews, but by the great Roman and Greek world, and the vast "barbarian" world beyond its borders, we find Him,

---

[1] See *The Christian Year, Its Purpose, etc.*, chaps. v and vii.
[2] S. Matt. v, 17.
[3] Col. ii, 17; Heb. x, 1.
[4] See S Matt. viii, 4, S. Mark i, 44; S Luke xvii, 14; S. Matt. xxiii, 2.
[5] Heb. ii, 17, iii, 1; v, 5, ix, 11.
[6] S Matt xxviii, 20.
[7] S Matt xvi, 18, xviii, 17. For the reasons for the frequent use of "Kingdom" and the infrequent use of "Church" in the Gospels, while in the Acts, Epistles, and Revelation "Kingdom" occurs only 25 times, and "the Church" 111 times, see the author's *Christian Year*, pp. 30, 31, note.

with marvellous self-control, living His secluded life as a carpenter in the little village of Nazareth until His thirtieth year, when the commission and consecration of His Father came to Him at His baptism.[1] It is to this wonderful self-abnegation and "call" that S. Paul refers when he declares that even "Christ glorified not Himself to be made an high priest; but He that said unto Him, Thou art a priest for ever after the order of Melchisedec."[2] Thereafter, without further delay than the solemn preparatory fast in the wilderness, He proceeds at once to His brief but transcendently fruitful work of the three remaining years of His earthly life. He does indeed preach to the multitudes, though He finds them fickle and uncertain. He teaches also in the quieter atmosphere of the synagogues, and by the lonely lake-side, and in private houses. But His first and constant work is the preparation of the men who are to be, not only the founders but, in themselves and those whom they should appoint and send, His "ministers" and "ambassadors."[3]

Before teaching the multitudes He chooses one by one the twelve men, most of them already drawn to the ranks of the Baptist by his trumpet-call to repentance.[4] The choice was no random one. "He knew what was in man."[5] This was the stuff whereof the founders of His Church were to be moulded and made, plain men of "the common people," "whose hearts God had touched."[6] To these twelve, whose names are afterwards four times carefully recorded, after a night of lonely prayer on the mountain top, He gives their first commission and the title of "APOSTLES." He keeps them very close to His person that He

---

[1] S Luke III, 21, 22, 23.
[2] Heb. v, 5
[3] 1 Cor IV, 1; 2 Cor. v, 20.
[4] S John I, 35 to end.
[5] S John II, 25
[6] S Mark XII, 37; 1 Samuel x, 26

may train and teach them by signs and words and example.[1] And in addition to these twelve He had "seventy others" in this training school for His future Ministry.[2]

It is not until after His resurrection, when "all power is given unto Him in heaven and in earth,"[3] that the Apostles receive their full commission. On the first Easter Day, fifty days before His gift to the Church at large, He gives the Holy Ghost to His "chosen" ones,[4] and with It the power of "the keys," which He had only *promised* them during the early days of their schooling. This He bestows by the sacramental act of "breathing on them," and by the use of words which are still claimed and used by the successors of these same Apostles to this day, in the ordaining of both Priests and Bishops. To the Apostles *alone* also, during the great forty days that follow, He gives, not only the authority to teach and govern His Church, but also special "commandments" and directions as to how the vast enterprise of establishing "the Kingdom of God" in the earth — especially difficult to men of their race, and social and intellectual rank — is to be accomplished.[5]

It is true that only a few of these "commandments" have come down to us in words, but most of them we know by means of *acts*, and this is the chief value of the book which we call "The Acts of the Apostles." We learn from them, and from other acts related in the apostolic letters addressed to fully organized branches of "the Church" in Rome, Galatia, Corinth, etc., or to other Apostles as Timothy and Titus, the things which Christ commanded them to do. Among these unwritten commandments are

---

[1] S. Matt. x, and xi, 1; S. Mark iii, 14; S. Luke vi, 13; xxii, 29, 30; Acts i, 13.
[2] S. Luke x, 1, 17. [3] S. Matt. xxviii, 18. [4] S. John xx, 22.
[5] S. Matt. xvi, 19; xviii, 18, S. John xx, 21–23; Acts i, 1, 2, 3.

THE ORDINAL AND SCRIPTURE 367

such things as the observance of the first day of the week, instead of Saturday, as "the Lord's Day"; the celebration of the Holy Communion as the chief act of the Church's worship; the practice of Confirmation, the baptism of infants as well as adults, liturgic worship, the observance of a ritual year corresponding to that of the ancient Church of Israel, etc.[1]

But what concerns us here is those "Acts of Apostles" which tell us "the mind of Christ"[2] in regard to the sacred Ministry. We have already seen that the very first thing our Lord did was to choose, train, and commission a select number from out of the larger body of His "disciples" or followers to be the future ministers and rulers of His Church. Were these men to be only the first preachers and heralds of His Gosepl of good news, or were they to be a permanent "order" of ministers, "as was that of Aaron?"[3] Our Lord's final words to the eleven faithful Apostles plainly show that their commission was not for themselves alone, during their own brief life, but for that perpetual succession which He foresaw and foreordained for "all the world," "every creature," "all nations," and "unto the end of the world."[4]

The recorded "acts" or doings of the first Apostles leave us in no doubt on this subject. The utmost care is taken at once to fill the place of the traitor Judas, and as the work extends, and the earlier Apostles die, new Apostles are added. Matthias takes the place of Judas by the direct commission of our Lord from heaven.[5] S. Paul and S. Barnabas become the fourteenth and fifteenth in the great Succession.[6] In the case of the former he too claims

---

[1] See *The Christian Year*, chap. vii.   [2] 1 Cor ii, 16.
[3] Heb. v, 4.   [4] S. Mark xvi, 15; S. Matt. xxviii, 19, 20.
[5] Acts i, 25, 26.   [6] Acts xiv, 14.

that he received his commission as well as his complete instruction in the Gospel directly from our Lord,[1] though he is not allowed to exercise it in its fulness until the Holy Ghost, as in the case of the eleven original Apostles, endued both him and Barnabas with "power" through the hands of the "prophets and teachers" of the Church.[2]

It is thus plain that the number of the Apostles is not to be confined to the original twelve. These first indeed were to be witnesses of Christ's actual Resurrection from the dead, and to lay foundations, but other Apostles were no less needful for the "edifying," that is, the building up, of the Church until the fabric is complete.[3] Hence we find S. Paul himself ordaining Titus to be the Apostolic Bishop in charge of the Church in the island of Crete.[4] Here is a sixteenth Apostle. Again, he consecrates Timothy and Silas to the same high office, a seventeenth and eighteenth.[5] Andronicus and Junias, James, "the Lord's brother," and Epaphroditus make twenty-two, all of whom are distinctly called or described as Apostles.[6]

To these twenty-two Apostles must be added "the angels of the seven Churches in Asia," who, according to the only intelligible interpretation of the book of Revelation, and the witness of all early history, were the chief ministers of the

---

[1] Acts xxvi, 16, 17, 18, Gal i, 1, 11, 12.

[2] Acts xiii, 1, 2, 3, 2 Cor. xi, 5, and see Gore, *Orders and Unity*, pp. 95, 96.

[3] Eph. iv, 11, 12, 13.

[4] Titus i, 5.

[5] 1 Thess i, 1 and ii, 6.

[6] Rom xvi, 7, Gal i, 19, Phil ii, 25 In this last passage the word "messenger" in the original is "Apostle," which, taken in immediate connection with the context, "the Bishops [that is, Presbyters in pastoral charge of congregations] and Deacons," seems to imply an official rank of one temporarily absent, and not that of an ordinary "messenger."

THE ORDINAL AND SCRIPTURE 369

Church in that Roman province of which S. John had the supreme oversight.[1] In fact so numerous did the Apostles become, as the Church spread rapidly throughout the Roman world that, as early as the year 60, or thereabouts, S. Paul finds it necessary to warn the Corinthian Church against "false apostles,"[2] and at the close of the first century we see the aged S. John commending the "Angel" or Apostle of the Church in Ephesus because he had "tried them which say they are Apostles, and are not, and had found them liars."[3] It is surely a clear inference from these facts of the New Testament that the office of Apostles or chief rulers of the Church was never intended by our Lord to die out, but was to be continued in unending succession "unto the end of the world."

And as we find this highest order of Apostles continued by the laying on of hands and prayer of other Apostles, so we find them ordaining a second order of ELDERS, or, as it is in the Greek, PRESBYTERS, or PRIESTS (Priest being simply a triple abbreviation of the Greek word *presbuteros* — presbyter, prester, priest), who seem to be the successors of the Seventy Disciples, as the Apostles were of the Twelve.[4]

---

[1] Rev i, ii, iii. Angel and Apostle have the same meaning in Greek, both words signifying *one sent*.

[2] 2 Cor xi, 13

[3] Rev ii, 2.

[4] See Acts iv, 5; xi, 30; xiv, 23; xv, 4, 6, 23; xvi, 4; xx, 17; 1 Tim. v, 17; Tit i, 5; James v, 14 It will be observed here that, while in the consecration or ordaining of an Apostle or Bishop, Apostles alone take part, at the ordination of a Presbyter other Presbyters present join with the Bishop in the act, a custom still continued in the Church. See the rubric in the Ordering of Priests, and compare 2 Tim i, 6, "*by* the putting on of *my* hands," in evident ordination to the Apostleship, and 1 Tim. iv, 14, "*with* the laying on of the hands *of the presbytery*," to the order of Priesthood.

This perhaps is the best place to observe that, while the name now given universally to a successor of the Apostles since the beginning of the second century, has been BISHOP, it is only used once with that meaning in the New Testament,[1] though S. Peter applies it to our Lord as the Apostle of the Father — "the Shepherd and Bishop of your souls."[2] The word is a corruption of the Greek *Episkopos*, literally Overseer or Superintendent, and like the word Pastor or Shepherd, it was at first applied to both orders, Apostle and Presbyter.[3] It was probably at the close of the first century, or the beginning of the second, when the first generation of the Apostles had died, that the word Apostle was usually (though not universally) restricted to them as a token of special honor. The original word had a distinctly missionary signification, and when the Church began to assume its normal and more settled condition, and the general missionary idea became less prominent, the Episcopacy, that is, the overseeing of many congregations united in a single Diocese, became the chief thought. Henceforth Bishop, that is, *Episkopos* or Overseer, became the word in common use for the Apostle, while the *Episkopoi* or Overseers of *single* congregations were known only as Presbyters. Only the name was changed, while the office remained the same.[4]

The third order of the Ministry, DEACONS, corresponding to the Levites in the older Church, while it doubtless existed in our Lord's original plan, seems to have had its actual beginning in the Ordination of the Seven, when the

---

[1] Acts i, 20.   [2] 1 Peter ii, 25.
[3] See Acts xx, 17, 28, Rev. Ver , 1 Tim iii, 1, 2; Tit. i, 5, 6, 7, Phil. i, 1.
[4] Bishop Pearson sums up his argument on this point thus: — "Therefore an Apostle is an extraordinary Bishop; a Bishop is an ordinary Apostle." *Minor Theol. Works*, 284.

THE ORDINAL AND SCRIPTURE 371

need of an additional class of helpers was forced upon the Apostles in the first year of the Church's existence.[1] Later we see them form an integral part of the three-fold Ministry.[2] We see, therefore, that even during the lifetime of the first Apostles, who "had the mind of Christ," and knew His will,[3] the Christian Ministry took the settled form of three sacred Orders, Apostle or Bishop, Presbyter or Priest, and Deacon; and "stedfast continuance in the Apostles' fellowship,"[4] as represented by this three-fold order, remained as at first one of the four tests of faithful membership in "the congregation of Christ's Flock." Thus the challenge of the Preface to the Ordinal, so far as the New Testament is concerned, is seen to be well grounded: "It is evident unto all men, diligently reading Holy Scripture, that from the Apostles' time there have been these Orders of Ministers in Christ's Church, —Bishops, Priests, and Deacons." In the following chapter we shall examine the witness of "Ancient Authors."

[1] Acts vi, 1–7.
[2] Phil i, 1, 1 Tim. iii, 8, 10, 12.
[3] 1 Cor. ii, 16.
[4] Acts ii, 42.

CHAPTER XXXVII

THE ORDINAL — THE WITNESS OF ANCIENT AUTHORS

"*Other doctrines develop slowly, this of Apostolic Succession starts forth at once Other doctrines find their first formal statements in Fathers removed by a century or even more from apostolic times, this is enunciated and enforced in the most emphatic words by those who had been taught by the Apostles themselves. Other doctrines have been disputed from time to time; this one held undisputed possession of men's beliefs throughout the Church for fifteen hundred years*" — A W. HADDAN.

"*Let preachers take heed that they deliver nothing from the pulpit to be religiously held and believed by the people, but that which is agreeable to the Old and New Testaments, and such as the Catholic Fathers and ancient Bishops have collected therefrom*" — Canon of the Convocation which adopted the Articles of Religion in 1571

WITH the testimony of Holy Scripture in regard to the three sacred Orders of the Christian Ministry, ALL THE WRITERS OF THE FIRST THREE CENTURIES who have dealt at all with the subject are in complete agreement. During all this period not one voice is raised against the three-fold Ministry of Bishops, Priests, and Deacons, as of Divine authority. Clement the Bishop of Rome who, some thirty years before, had been a valued "fellow laborer" with S. Paul in that city,[1] wrote a letter to the Church in Corinth, not later than A.D. 97, in regard to such irregularities there as the Apostle himself had done his best to check.[2] Ignatius, born about A.D. 30, Bishop of Antioch and all Syria in A.D. 69, the disciple of S. John, and the "little child" to whom tradition has assigned the honor of being "set in

---

[1] Phil. iv, 3 [2] I Cor chaps. iii and xii, especially.

THE ORDINAL AND ANCIENT AUTHORS

the midst" of the Apostles as an example of humility,[1] wrote six letters to the Churches through which he passed on his way to Rome as a prisoner and a martyr, and one to Polycarp, another friend of S. John, who was probably "the angel of the Church in Smyrna," to whom our Lord by that Apostle sent one of His most comforting messages from heaven.[2] Polycarp also (born about A.D. 65), who followed Ignatius to martyrdom about A.D. 150, has left us one letter of undoubted authenticity, addressed to "the Church of God sojourning in Philippi." And in all these letters of pupils of the Apostles we have the same testimony in regard to the Ministry as that which we have found in the New Testament itself.

Clement, the former of these authors, dealing with the sectarian divisions in Corinth, writes: "Let us then, men and brethren, with all energy act the part of soldiers, in accordance with His holy commandments. Let us consider those who serve under our generals. . . . All are not prefects, nor commanders of a thousand, nor of a hundred, nor of fifty." He refers them to the example of the ancient priesthood in its three divinely ordained orders. "His own peculiar services are assigned to the high priest," he says, "and their own proper place is prescribed to the priests, and their own special ministrations devolve on the Levites. The layman is bound by the laws that pertain to laymen." He writes also, "Our Apostles knew, through our Lord Jesus Christ, that there would be strife on account of the office of the episcopate. For this reason, therefore, inasmuch as they had obtained a perfect foreknowledge of this, they appointed those [ministers] already mentioned, and afterwards gave instructions, that when these should fall

---

[1] S. Matt. xviii, 2.
[2] Rev. ii, 8–12.

asleep, other approved men should succeed them in their ministry."[1]

THE SEVEN LETTERS OF IGNATIUS in their shorter form are pronounced by the best critics to be genuine and authentic.[2] Condemned as a Christian Bishop about A.D. 110 to be killed by wild beasts in the amphitheatre at Rome, he was led thither under guard of ten Roman soldiers, whom for their harshness he calls "ten leopards." As he passes through the cities of Asia Minor he receives deputations of fellow Christians who make his progress a triumph. From Smyrna, the city of Polycarp, he writes letters to the Churches of the Ephesians, Magnesians, Trallians, and to the Church in Rome. Farther on, at Troas, he writes to the Churches in Philadelphia, and Smyrna, and to Polycarp. These letters of a man who was now of a great age are of extraordinary interest. "They are full of a passionate holiness and a rich theology of the incarnation."[3] But their special historical value is in their witness to the primitive character of the Christian Ministry. A few extracts out of many will show the nature of this evidence.

To the Trallians he writes: — "When ye are obedient to the Bishop as to Jesus Christ, it is evident to me that ye are living not after men but after Jesus Christ. . . . It is therefore necessary, even as your wont is, that ye should do nothing without the Bishop; but be ye obedient also to the Presbytery, as to the Apostles. . . . In like manner let

---

[1] *Ep. to the Corinthians*, Edinburgh edition, chaps. xxxvii, xl, xliv. Likewise S. Jerome, in the fourth century, writes in his *Ep. ad Ev.:* — "What Aaron and his sons and the Levites were in the Temple, that let the Bishops, and Presbyters, and Deacons claim to be in the Church."

[2] See Bp. Lightfoot, *Apostolic Fathers;* Harnack in *Expositor*, Jan, 1886, who says their genuineness is "certain;" and Gore, *The Christian Ministry*, 289.

[3] Bp. Gore, *Orders and Unity*, p. 119.

THE ORDINAL AND ANCIENT AUTHORS 375

all men respect the Deacons, etc. . . . Apart from these there is not even the name of a Church."[1] To the Philadelphians: — "There is one altar, as there is one Bishop, together with the Presbytery and the Deacons my fellow-servants."[2] To the Church in Smyrna: — "Let no man do aught of things pertaining to the Church apart from the Bishop. Let that be a valid Eucharist which is under the Bishop, together with the Presbytery and the Deacons my fellow-servants, or one to whom he shall have committed it."[3]

Bishop Gore sums up the chief points of the testimony of Ignatius as follows: —

"1. He has an intensely clear perception that the mind of God for man's salvation has expressed itself not in a doctrine only, but in an ordered society with an authoritative hierarchy.

"2. He regards this hierarchy as essentially threefold — a ministry of Bishops, Presbyters, and Deacons. 'Without these three orders,' so Dr. Lightfoot renders the words cited above, 'no Church has a title to the name.'

"3. He presents the monarchical episcopate as 'firmly rooted' and 'completely beyond dispute.'[4] He bases its authority on 'the ordinances of the Apostles.'

"4. He regards episcopacy as coextensive with the Church. He speaks of the Bishops as established 'in the farthest part of the earth.' He knows, therefore, of no non-episcopal area.

"5. He does not speak of the Presbyters as if they could supply the place of the Bishop when he is gone — that is to say, as sharing essentially the same office."[5]

---
[1] Chaps ii, iii.   [2] Chap. iv.   [3] Chap. iii.
[4] Harnack, *Expositor*, Jan., 1886, p 16.
[5] *Orders and Unity*, pp. 122, 123. See also his *Christian Ministry*, chap. vi, iii. Other references to the Ministry in the letters of Ignatius will be found as follows: — To the *Ephesians*, ii, iii, iv, v, vi; to the *Magnesians*, ii, iii, vi, vii, xiii, to the *Romans*, ii, ix; to *Polycarp*, iv, vi.

Polycarp, Bishop of Smyrna (born about A.D. 65), the youthful friend of S. John and of Ignatius, to whom the latter addressed one of his seven letters, has also left us a letter of undoubted authenticity addressed to "the Church of God sojourning in Philippi." Irenæus (born about 130), Bishop of Lyons, and a pupil of Polycarp, writes concerning him: — "I could describe the very place in which the blessed Polycarp sat and taught; his going out and coming in; the whole tenor of his life; his personal appearance; how he would speak of the conversation he had with John and with others who had seen the Lord." And he adds: — "Polycarp was not only instructed by Apostles, and conversed with many who had seen Christ, but was also, by Apostles in Asia, appointed Bishop of the Church in Smyrna, whom I also saw in my early youth, for he tarried [on earth] a very long time, and, when a very old man, gloriously and most nobly suffering martyrdom [about 150], departed this life, having always taught the things which he had learned from the Apostles, and which the Church has handed down, and which alone are true. . . . There is also a very powerful Epistle of Polycarp written to the Philippians, from which those who choose to do so, and are anxious about their salvation, can learn the character of his faith." [1]

This letter of Polycarp's is full of the gentle spirit of his master, S. John, but its chief value in relation to the Christian Ministry is found in the seal of approval which he sets to the teachings of his friend Ignatius. "The Epistles of Ignatius," he says, "written by him to us, and all the rest [of his Epistles] which we have by us, we have sent to you, as you requested. They are subjoined to this Epistle and by them ye may be greatly profited; for they treat of

---

[1] *Against Heresies*, Book III, chap. iii, 3, Edin. Ed.

faith and patience, and all things that tend to edification in our Lord."[1] In Ignatius' Epistle to Polycarp he writes: — "My soul be for theirs who are subject to the Bishop, and the Presbyters, and the Deacons."[2]

"When Hegesippus, 'the father of Church history,' visited the West about A.D. 167," writes Bishop Gore, "he found a 'succession' of Bishops in each city, and made a list of the Bishops for the purpose of his history at Rome. When Irenæus, the great representative of tradition, writes against the Gnostics about A.D. 180, he regards episcopacy, as among the first principles of the Church, and as the supreme safeguard of the orthodox faith. Tertullian, about A.D. 200, uses the same language, and confronts the Gnostic 'churches' with the requirement of the succession."[3] Bishop Lightfoot asserts that "the institution of the episcopate must be placed as far back as the closing years of the first century, and that it cannot, without violence to historical testimony, be dissevered from the name of S. John." "The threefold ministry can be traced to Apostolic direction; and short of an express statement we can possess no better assurance of a Divine appointment, or at least a Divine sanction." In the sixth edition of this book, referring to "a rumor that he had found reason to abandon the main opinions" on the Ministry expressed in earlier editions, the Bishop "disclaims any change in his opinions," while attributing the erroneous report to the fact that he was "scrupulously anxious not to overstate the evidence in any case." "The result has been," he says, "a confirmation of the statement in the English Ordinal, 'It is evident

---

[1] *Ep to the Philippians*, chap. xiii
[2] Chap. vi.
[3] *Orders and Unity*, p. 127; and see Eusebius, *His Ecc* iv, 22; Irenæus against Heresies, chaps. iii, iv, v.

unto all men reading Holy Scripture and ancient Authors, that from the Apostles' time there have been these orders of Ministers in Christ's Church, Bishops, Priests, and Deacons.'"[1]

With such witnesses from the earliest and purest days of the Church, interpreting and confirming the witness of the New Testament, it is needless to do more than refer to the hostile judgment of Gibbon, the skeptical historian of *The Decline and Fall of the Roman Empire*, in what he calls "the fifth cause of the progress of the Christian religion." He is compelled to admit that "this episcopal form of government appears to have been introduced before the close of the first century"; that "Bishops, under the name of Angels, were already instituted in the seven cities of Asia"; that "*Nulla Ecclesia sine Episcopo* [No Church without a Bishop] has been a fact as well as a maxim since the time of Tertullian and Irenaeus"; and that "after we have passed the difficulties of the first century, we find the episcopal form of government universally established, until it was interrupted by the republican genius of the Swiss and German reformers." In a later chapter he writes, "The Bishops alone possessed the faculty of *spiritual* generation," that is, of giving Holy Orders.[2]

It is in view of all these facts that Hooker, in his great defence of the "Ecclesiastical Polity" of the Church of England, published in 1594, made this challenge to the learned among the Puritans, in their adoption of the novel scheme of government first proposed by Calvin, and forced by him on the Protestants of Geneva: — "A very strange thing sure it were, that such a discipline as ye speak of should

---

[1] *The Epistle to the Philippians* — Dissertation on the Christian Ministry, pp 234, 267, and Preface, p. x.

[2] Chap. xv, and notes 110, 111, 112, also chap. xx, 2.

be taught by Christ and His Apostles in the Word of God, and no Church ever have found it out, nor received it till this present time; contrariwise, the government against which ye bend yourselves be observed everywhere throughout all generations and ages of the Christian world, no Church ever perceiving the Word of God to be against it. *We require you to find out but one Church upon the face of the whole earth, that hath been ordered by your discipline, or hath not been ordered by ours, that is to say, by episcopal regiment, sithence the time that the blessed Apostles were here conversant.*" [1]

Archbishop Bancroft, in his Sermon at S. Paul's Cross, in 1589, made the same challenge in almost the same words. "A very strange matter if it were true, that Christ should erect a form of government for the ruling of His Church, to continue from His departure out of the world until His coming again; and that the same should never be once thought of or put in practice for the space of 1500 years." [2]

It is here to be noted that the question of DIOCESAN EPISCOPACY, so far as it means only the organization of the Church into Dioceses, each with its single Bishop as head, must be clearly distinguished from the question of APOSTOLIC SUCCESSION, that is, of the Bishop being the successor, and possessor of the ordinary spiritual gifts and authority, of the original Apostles, with the sole power of ordaining men to the three orders of the Ministry. It is plain from the necessities of the case that at the first, and for many years later, there should be no clearly defined limits for the work of any one Apostle, though we find S. Paul, with his thoughtful and courteous consideration of others, careful "not to preach the Gospel where Christ

---
[1] Preface, chap IV, sec. 1.
[2] Qu. by Keble in his ed. of Hooker, p. 193, note.

was [already] named, lest he should build on another man's foundation."[1] The first Apostles and their many successors, up to the close of the first century, were missionaries at large, and it was only by slow degrees, and by a natural process of evolution, the result of experience, and with the example of the orderly civil government of the Roman Empire before them, that the jurisdiction of their successors was confined to particular districts, in the system which we call Diocesan Episcopacy.[2] We seem to see its beginning in the selection of "James the Lord's brother,"[3] as the first Bishop with jurisdiction over "the mother of all Churches," as the local Church of Jerusalem was called by the Fifth General Council. For the sake of proper organization mon-episcopacy, or the setting of one *Apostle*-Bishop as overseer over the *Presbyter*-Bishops of each city, and of the surrounding country and village parishes, became a necessity, and early writers attribute its rapid development to the work of S. John in "the seven Churches of Asia."

Even in the sixth century in Ireland and the Scottish Highlands, neither of which had ever been brought under the military power of Rome, Apostle-Bishops retained much of their original missionary character. Lacking the discipline of the Empire, the Celtic character was not strong in the direction of organization, and Bishops were not always found in charge of settled Dioceses. "The Church was intensely monastic in all its arrangements," writes Prof. Stokes. "Its monasteries were always ruled by abbots who were sometimes Bishops, but most usually

---

[1] Rom. xv, 20.

[2] It is to be remembered that the words, Diocese and Province, were both designations long in use for departments of the Roman Empire, and were simply taken over by the Church for her own use.

[3] Gal. i, 19; ii, 12; Acts xv, 13; xxi, 18.

Presbyters. This does not prove that they were Presbyterians in Church government; for, if not themselves Bishops, the abbots kept a Bishop on the premises for the purpose of conferring Holy Orders. The abbot was the ruler of the monastery, . . . but recognized his own inferiority in ecclesiastical matters whether in celebrating the Eucharist, or in conferring Holy Orders, — a function which appertained to the Bishop alone." [1]

[1] *Ireland and the Celtic Church*, p 104 See also Gore, *The Church and the Ministry*, p. 162, note, Todd, *S Patrick*, and Reeves, *Ecc Antiquities*. Prof. Stokes adds in a note, p. 105; — "Wasserschleben, in his Introduction to the second edition of *Die Irische Kanonensammlung* (Leipzig: 1885), p. xlii, has shown that the custom of monasteries having their own Bishop under the government of an abbot, was not peculiar to the Irish Church, but was spread as far as Mount Sinai." The Professor of Poetry at Oxford, J C Shairp, himself a Scotsman and a Presbyterian, writes concerning S Columba's famous monastery on the island of Iona, from whose organization inferences have been drawn unfavorable to the principle of the threefold Ministry — "It may be safely asserted that the first taste Iona had of Presbyterian Church polity was when the redoubtable presbytery of Argyll in one day hurled its 360 crosses into the sea " *Sketches in History and Poetry.*

These cases throw light on the solitary statement of S Jerome (in the fourth century) that at Alexandria, down to about A D 230, there was a certain equality between the Bishop and the Presbyters, so that when the ruling Bishop dies, one of these Presbyters succeeded by mere election without any further ordination In view of what we have seen in the New Testament and what was clearly the universal practice of the first and second centuries, the most natural explanation of the statement would be that these clergy "were in the same position as the Presbyters of any modern Diocese would be in, if they were all, in modern phrase, in episcopal orders" (Gore, p. 131). Compare the declaration of S Peter who, though an Apostle, tells the Presbyters of his flock that he is "also a Presbyter," and S. Paul, who speaks of himself and other Apostles again and again as also "Ministers" (literally *diakonoi*, or Deacons), the lower offices being necessarily implied in the higher (1 Pet v, 1, 1 Cor iii, 5, 2 Cor iii, 6; vi, 4, xi, 23; Eph. iii, 7; Col. i, 23, 25, 1 Thess. iii, 2)

Moreover, as a matter of fact, a succession through Presbyters never had any formal recognition whatever by council or otherwise. Until the sixteenth century the Bishop, as the successor of the first Apostles, was alone recognized as the rightful source of Holy Orders. The question, moreover, is purely an academical one today. Succession through Presbyters is occasionally broached as a theory, but is wholly disregarded in practice. Only two theories exist now in regard to the Christian Ministry. One is the theory of practically all the 150 or more Protestant communions that, one after another, have separated from the historic Catholic Church, reformed or unreformed, or else from one another. This is, in effect, that an inward call of the Holy Spirit, and a certain fitness or success as preacher or pastor, combined usually with a form of setting apart by some one already recognized as a Christian minister, or else by the representatives of a congregation (as in the case of all Independent or Congregational bodies, including all Baptists), constitute all that is necessary for a valid commission. This was the theory preached and practised by Luther, Calvin, Zwingli, Knox, and other intemperate reformers in the sixteenth century. The only other theory in existence today is that of the whole Catholic Church, East and West, Greek, Roman, Anglican, Armenian, Syrian, Coptic, etc., recognized and practised everywhere "from the Apostles' days," and which is known as the rule of Apostolic Succession. It is this theory which is expressed in the Preface to the Ordinal when it declares that "no man shall be accounted or taken to be a lawful Bishop, Priest, or Deacon in the Church of England [or this Church], or suffered to execute any of the said Functions, except he hath had Episcopal Consecration or Ordination."

THE ORDINAL AND ANCIENT AUTHORS 383

It is this, and this only, which is the clear and unmistakable teaching of the whole Catholic Church. It has been also the constant practice of the whole Anglican Communion, in spite of occasional irregularities in England during the unsettled days of the Puritan revolution, when some who had received Presbyterian or other form of Protestant ordination in Holland or elsewhere, were appointed to the charge of parishes by the Puritan government, but were obliged to resign them when the Church regained her authority, and they refused to submit to ordination by a Bishop. It does not follow, however, that all who fail to recognize the threefold Apostolic Ministry ordained by Christ are outside the Christian pale. All the baptized are members of Christ and therefore of His Holy Catholic Church, even though they are not in the enjoyment of all its grace and benefits. We must not judge them; we cannot. To their own Master they stand or fall. They will be judged according to their light and their faithfulness to Him, and we believe that His word, "According to your faith be it unto you," [1] will be fulfilled in them, though they miss the fulness of blessing which He has provided for them.

But we are now dealing, not with individual Christians, but with a system. Apart from the witness of "Holy Scripture and Ancient Authors," this system has shown its unsoundness by its endless divisions, "the dissidence of Dissent," where Christ demanded perfect unity, and by that "down grade" in doctrine lamented by the late Mr. Spurgeon amongst English Nonconformists. This has reached its utmost depth in many quarters already, particularly in Germany and Switzerland, in complete rejection of the Faith; a condition which finds no single example

[1] S Matt. ix, 29.

among those who, with all their shortcomings, hold to the ancient Ministry of Apostolical Succession.¹

---

¹ "It took one thousand years to corrupt primitive Christianity, with its sacramental teaching, into Popery, whereas it did not take one hundred years to corrupt Puritanism, or ultra-Protestantism, with its anti-sacramental teaching, into the rankest Socinianism — a Socinianism utterly denying all that makes Christ and His doctrine of value to lost souls. Within a half a century from the time of the Reformation, the evil was fully developed, and in less than two centuries (that is, by about 1750) the evil spirit of unbelief had subdued, or all but subdued, to itself the Reformed communions in Poland, in France, in Holland, in Switzerland" (Sadler, *Church Doctrine, Bible, Truth*, p. 344, where details are given concerning these countries). In 1874 when the population of Berlin was 700,000, the accommodation in all places of worship put together was for only 40,000. "With a nominal Protestant population of 2,060,000, a record kept last February [1914] on a Sunday when numerous confirmations were to take place, showed a total attendance at the various State Protestant churches of only 35,000" (New York *Churchman*, Aug 8, 1914). It is needless to point out the bearing of these facts upon the bold and open teaching of such men as Bernhardi and Treitschke among the Germans, that "the end-all and be-all of a State is power," that "the State cannot be judged by the standard of individual morality," and that war "is not only a biological law, but a moral obligation, and, as such, an indispensable factor in civilization."

CHAPTER XXXVIII
THE ORDINAL — IMAGINED DIFFICULTIES IN THE SUCCESSION

"It is as impossible for an impartial man to doubt whether there was a succession of Bishops from the Apostles, as it would be to call in question the succession of the Roman Emperors from Julius Cæsar, or the succession of Kings in any other country." — ARCHBISHOP POTTER (*Canterbury*).

BEFORE proceeding to an examination of the Ordinal itself it will be well to speak here of TWO COMMON OBJECTIONS to the principle of any succession in the Ministry by means of ordination.

(1) The former of these is the seeming impossibility, or at least uncertainty, concerning the fact of an actual succession "from the Apostles' time." It is assumed that there is but a single series of links in this succession, and if one of these should, at any time, be broken, as for instance in the "Dark Ages," all that follows is rendered void. But this is based on an entirely mistaken idea of what constitutes Apostolic Succession. On the contrary it is exactly analogous to what is going on continually in all orderly civil government. Kings, presidents, governors, sheriffs, judges, and other officers of state, never form a single chain of separate links, but a complete concatenation or net-work, so that it is practically impossible for any one to force his way into an office to which he has not been lawfully appointed. In the Church even greater care has been taken in every age that there shall be no failure in this respect. The consecration of Bishops to vacant sees must be made only by the joint action of the Diocese, or neighboring

Dioceses affected, and must be accomplished by at least three Bishops uniting their hands and prayers in the act, and all other Bishops of the Province must at least be notified.

This has been the rule of the Church ever since the first great General Council which met at Nice in Asia Minor in 325, and in adopting this rule the Council was doubtless only giving formal sanction to what had been the ordinary rule of the Church from the beginning. It will be readily seen, therefore, that in such a case the assumption of authority by "false apostles"[1] is practically impossible. And even though, in one or more cases, such an unlikely thing should occur, this could not affect the whole body of the Ministry any more than the cutting of many strands of an electrified network could prevent the current from flowing freely into every other part.[2]

In fact the succession in the Ministry "from the Apostles' time" is much more surely attested than that of the succession of our Bibles, dependent as that was in early days upon the accuracy and honesty of thousands of individual copyists, on the correctness of translations, on the preservation of manuscripts, and, in these last centuries, on the care of printers. The Ministry, as the New Testament and all ancient history testify, necessarily existed before a word of the New Testament was written. It was not an institution growing out of the teaching of the New Testament (which was not completed until two generations after the

---

[1] 2 Cor xi, 13; Rev. ii, 2.

[2] It has been mathematically calculated that, even if we make the absurd supposition of one consecrator in every twenty being *at all times* without valid consecration, the chances *against* a Bishop consecrated under such circumstances are as one to 512,000 millions! See Gladstone, *Church Principles*, pp. 235, 236.

Church's birth), but, on the contrary, every writer of these sacred Scriptures was a member of that Ministry. Moreover, it is upon the continuous witness of their successors, and of the whole Church which they ruled and fed, that we believe these Scriptures to be indeed the Word of God.[1]

(2) A second objection, formerly made by the Puritans, and one that is still common, is that referred to and refuted in the 26th Article of Religion, concerning "the unworthiness of the Ministers." This perhaps is "the main obstacle which any theory of ministerial authority and commission, officially transmitted, has to encounter," and "which has so often in history prejudiced the minds of men against the very idea of their office."

It is concerning this objection that Bishop Gore has further said: — "Our Lord, more perhaps than any other teacher of men, had under observation the failure of priesthoods and offices of trust, in temporal things and spiritual. He was subject to no illusions about human trustworthiness. He knew all the misuse of the office of stewardship, 'the power of the keys.' He knew the desolating havoc that has been wrought by those who misused their trust, — who 'took away the key of knowledge.' . . . And yet, on reconstituting the people of God on a new basis, in founding the new Israel, He deliberately again commits to men the powers which He knew to be so liable to abuse. He contemplates in the stewards of His household, after He was gone, violence and debauchery and apathy and unfaithfulness. He contemplates failure of faith on the largest scale.[2] And yet He made men stewards of His household. He gave them, according to one report, the keys of the Kingdom, not of earth only, but of heaven,

---
[1] See the 6th and the 20th Articles of Religion.
[2] S. Matt. xxiv, 48, 49; xxv, 26; S. Luke xii, 45, xviii, 8.

the binding and loosing power, with a heavenly sanction, over their fellow men, and, according to another report, the power to forgive and retain their sins. . . . It was with the weakness of the human instrument full in view that Jesus Christ entrusted to men the spiritual charge over their fellows." [1]

From what has been already said it is plain that the revisers of the ancient Ordinal of the Church of England in 1550 were only stating the simplest and most unassailable of historic facts, when they declared in the Preface of our present Office: — "It is evident unto all men, diligently reading Holy Scripture and ancient Authors, that from the Apostles' time there have been these Orders of Ministers in Christ's Church, — Bishops, Priests, and Deacons"; and that a necessary inference from this was the rule that "no man shall be accounted or taken to be a lawful Bishop, Priest, or Deacon in the Church of England [or, as it is in the Scottish and American books, *this Church*], or suffered to execute any of the said Functions, except he be called, tried, examined, and admitted thereunto, according to the Form hereafter following, or hath had Episcopal Consecration or Ordination."

This was a declaration which the wild theories of such intemperate reformers as Luther, Calvin, Zwingli, Knox, and others forced from the Church, and which is even more needful in our day when the ripe fruit of their revolutionary and anarchistic theories is seen in nearly 200 sects in the British Empire and the United States alone, and in the most widespread loss of faith in the very fundamental truths of Christianity, especially in their original centres, Germany and Switzerland.

It is, moreover, a strange, forced, and unnatural inter-

---

[1] *Orders and Unity*, pp. 17, 18.

THE ORDINAL AND THE SUCCESSION 389

pretation that would make the words "in the Church of England," or "in this Church," to mean "this Church *only*"; and that, outside of "this Church," persons who have *not* received "Episcopal Consecration or Ordination" may be just as really and as fully the commissioned Ministers of Christ as those who have! This is surely a strange logic, which every branch of the Anglican Communion is so far from accepting that, while Bishops, Priests, and Deacons coming to it from the Roman, Greek, or other branches of the ancient Catholic Church are received without any reordination, nevertheless, the most learned and eminent minister of any of the Protestant denominations must be both confirmed and ordained like any layman among ourselves desirous of Holy Orders.

It does not follow, however, that God does not bless the zealous labors of men whose only authority comes from the choice and act of their fellow men, in some self-constituted society of believers. All this is freely granted, and we may "rejoice" with S. Paul that "in every way, whether in pretence or in truth, Christ is preached."[1] God never refuses His blessing to any word or effort spoken or made "out of an honest and good heart" in His Name. His cup "runneth over." But this fact does not in the least affect or diminish our own duty to use for ourselves only that ministry which bears the test of S. John's great law that it has been "from the beginning"[2] and therefore has necessarily the authority of Christ, and of the Holy Spirit which He gave to guide His Church into all truth. That much good comes from these individual efforts of men or organizations must not blind us to the fact of the fearful losses, and positive evils, the criminal waste of men and of means, that *necessarily* result from those divisions which

---
[1] Phil 1, 18.   [2] 1 S. John ii, 7, iii, 11, 2 S. John 5.

our Lord warned and prayed against. Chief of these, as He foresaw, is the failure of the vast majority of "the world" to believe that the Father had sent Him to redeem it.[1]

THE REVISED ORDINAL was not published until 1550, nearly a year after the publication of the First Prayer Book. In this revision there was little or nothing new or different from the services which had preceded it, except that it was marked with great simplicity and directness of purpose in contrast with the earlier Office. The essential part of all ordinations, as seen in the New Testament in every case,[2] and in the primitive Liturgies, consisted in the laying on of the hands of the Apostle or Apostle-Bishop with prayer. But to these had been added in later days, in the English Church and elsewhere, such ceremonies as the anointing of the hands of the ordinands, and the presentation to Priests of the vessels for Holy Communion (*traditio* or *porrectio instrumentorum*), which so overlaid and obscured the essential action, removed as this was to the very end of the service, that it was almost completely lost to sight. In fact, this "tradition" or handing of the chalice and paten, accompanied by the words, "Receive power to offer sacrifice," etc., was held to be the real "mat-

---

[1] S. John xvii, 21. The Ordinal was not printed as a part of the first revised Book, nor is it properly speaking a part of the Book of Common Prayer today Though bound up with it and subject to the same conditions in regard to alteration, it forms a separate book for the use of Bishops, corresponding to what was known in the mediæval Church of England as the Pontifical; and to it are added, in the American Church, "The Form of Consecration of a Church or Chapel," and "An Office of Institution of Ministers into Parishes or Churches." In the Irish Book of 1877 there are also forms for "The Consecration of a Church," and of "a Churchyard or other Burial Ground" The Confirmation Service of course, belongs to this book for the use of Bishops

[2] Acts vi, 6, xiii, 3, xiv, 23, 1 Tim. iv, 14, v, 22, 2 Tim. i, 6

THE ORDINAL AND THE SUCCESSION

ter" of ordination of a Priest, though it is confessed by Roman writers that this was not the practice until the tenth century.[1]

The revision of 1550 was therefore simply a return to primitive practice as found in the New Testament and the ancient Ordinals. In the Ordination of Priests the giving into the hand of "the chalice or cuppe with the bread," was retained, but came after (and not before, as in the mediæval Office) the laying on of hands. The unction therefore was the principal ceremony lacking in the first revised Ordinal. The novel custom of giving the chalice or paten was abandoned in the Book of 1552, and has never been restored. The giving of a copy of the New Testament to the Deacon, and of the whole Bible to the Priest, immediately after ordination, was required in the Ordinal of 1550, and is still retained. It may well be regretted that one beautiful ceremonial act, incapable of superstitious interpretation, as permitted in the Book of 1550, namely, the putting into the hand of the newly consecrated Bishop "the pastorall staffe," was *not* retained. The touching words in bestowing it, however, "Be to the flock of Christ a shepherd," etc., were retained, and added on to the address at the giving of the Bible.

When it is considered, moreover, that the vast majority of the Christian world, probably 350 millions, still possess and hold fast the three sacred Orders which have come to them "from the Apostles' time," with all the sanction of divine authority, it is inconceivable, and would be most unreasonable and futile, that they should give up this sacred heritage in order to meet the widely divergent views of nearly two hundred different organizations of Christians

[1] See Lowndes, *Vindication of Anglican Orders*, vol i, pp 37, 38, 291, 295 [New York and London, 1897].

that have sprung into existence since the sixteenth century, and have it not.

These ancient Apostolic Churches may have much to learn about neglected truths from some of these separated bodies, but they have also much to give. It is for this reason, and not from any desire to "be lords over God's heritage,"[1] that the great assembly of Bishops of the whole Anglican Communion, assembled at Lambeth in 1888, adopted as their own, with a slight change of wording, the four fundamental principles formulated by the Bishops of the American Church in 1886, "as essential to the restoration of unity." These are: — (1) "The holy Scriptures of the Old and New Testaments as containing all things necessary to salvation, and as being the rule and ultimate standard of faith; (2) the Apostles' Creed as the Baptismal Symbol, and the Nicene Creed as the sufficient statement of the Christian Faith; (3) The two Sacraments ordained by Christ Himself — Baptism and the Supper of the Lord — administered with unfailing use of Christ's words of institution, and of the elements ordained by Him; (4) The historic Episcopate, locally adapted in the methods of its administration to the varying needs of the nations called of God into the unity of His Church."

In view, then, of what we have learnt from "Holy Scripture and Ancient Authors," as well as from other facts of history, it is evident that to give up this sacred trust of the Apostolic Succession in the Ministry would not be to advance the cause of unity among Christians, but to make it impossible.

---

[1] 1 Pet. v, 3.

CHAPTER XXXIX
ORDINALS, PRIMITIVE, MEDIÆVAL, AND MODERN

"*Nihil in hac vita est difficilius, laboriosius, periculosius, presbyteri vita*"
("*Nothing in this life is more difficult, more laborious, more fraught with peril than the life of a presbyter*") — S AUGUSTINE

THOUGH the ORDINAL is not an essential part of the Book of Common Prayer, as not in itself an Office of public worship, its place, according to all ancient custom, is found in the midst of the Church's highest act of devotion, the Holy Eucharist.[1] All the earliest Ordinals of which we have copies are so placed, and an examination of some of these which have only lately come to light testifies in the strongest way to the learning and wisdom of the Bishops and other Clergy who did the work of revision in the sixteenth century. Dr. Maclean, Bishop of Moray, Ross, and Caithness, in his lectures on "Recent Discoveries Illustrating Early Christian Worship" writes as follows: — "The last generation of the nineteenth century has been singularly fortunate in the discovery of literature which throws light on early Christian life and worship. . . . The light thrown on fourth century usage is very great; but some is also thrown on that of the third century, and even of the second." There are nine of these "Church Orders," as they are called, five of them recent discoveries, which treat especially of Ordination.[2]

---

[1] Compare Acts xiii, 2, where "as they ministered" [λειτουργούντων] is interpreted by some as referring to Holy Communion.

[2] S P. C. K. 1904, p 6 The latest discoveries are· — *Canons of Hippolytus* (A D 220), Latin trans , *Verona Latin Fragments*, part iii. (A.D. 340); *Testament of our Lord* (A D. 350, possibly re-edited about

394 PRIMITIVE WORSHIP & THE PRAYER BOOK

Speaking of the manner of ordaining to the ministry, as seen in the light of these Church Orders, Bishop Maclean writes: — "In the case of Bishops, Presbyters, and Deacons, the ordination consisted of a single prayer, with laying on of hands, or more generally the laying on of one hand. . . . The usage [in the ordination of a Bishop] is not quite the same in all the Church Orders. In some of them one Bishop, chosen by the rest, lays on his hand, and says the prayer of ordination, all the others being silent; in the *Ethiopic Church Order* all the Bishops lay on hands, and all say the prayer; in the *Egyptian Church Order* all lay on hands in silence, and then one of the Bishops again lays on hands and prays; in the *Testament of our Lord* and the *Arabic Didascalia* all the Bishops lay on hands and say a declaration, after which one Bishop lays on hands and says the prayer of ordination; in the *Apostolic Constitutions* three Bishops are selected, the rest praying in silence. . . . The prayer in all these authorities is practically the same; that is, a common original underlies them all. . . . If we put these prayers side by side, and leave out anything that is not common to them all, we shall doubtless arrive at a more or less accurate reconstruction of the original prayer of ordination, which will therefore take us back probably to the second century, to the time of Irenæus. . . . We get then the following: —

"'O God, Father of our Lord Jesus Christ, Father of mercies and God of all comfort, who dwellest in the heights and

---

A D 400), English trans; *Arabic Didascalia*, appendix (A D 380), German trans, *The Prayer Book of Sarapion* (A D. 350), English trans. The others are: — *Egyptian Church Order* (A D. 310), English trans.; *Ethiopic Church Order* (A D 335), Latin trans, *Constitutions through Hippolytus* (A D 375); *Apostolic Constitutions*, Book VIII. (A D 375), English trans.

lookest on humble things, who knowest all things before they are, who hast constituted the bounds of the Church, by whose power it is that there should remain a just race which is from Abraham, who hast constituted prelacies and principalities, give [to Thy servant] Thy power and effectual [or princely] Spirit, whom Thou gavest through our Lord Jesus Christ, Thy only Son, to the holy Apostles, who founded the Church in every place to the honor and glory of Thy holy Name. Forasmuch as Thou knowest the heart of each one, grant him to be worthy to feed Thy great and holy flock, and receive his prayers and offerings which he shall offer to Thee day and night, and may they be to Thee a sweet savour. Give also to him, O Lord, the episcopate and a mild spirit and power to forgive sins; and give him the ability to loose all bonds, through our Lord Jesus Christ, by whom be glory to Thee, with Him, and the Holy Ghost, for ever. Amen.'"[1]

In the ordination of a Presbyter the oldest manuals direct that the same prayer is to be used, except that the word Presbyter is to be substituted for Bishop. In most of these Church Orders no priestly function is specified in the prayer. "I mention this," writes Dr. Maclean, "to show how unwarranted is the objection in the Papal Bull on Anglican Orders,[2] that the words used at the laying on of hands in our Ordinal do not refer to priestly or sacrificial functions." "The custom of Presbyters assisting at the ordination of a Presbyter by laying on of hands," he adds, "or by 'touching' the ordained, is very ancient. . . . On the other hand, the Bishop acts alone in ordaining a Deacon."[3] In the setting apart of lower orders, subdeacon, etc., there was no laying on of hands.

---

[1] Maclean, *Recent Discoveries*, etc , pp 108-110.
[2] *Apostolicæ Curæ*, by Leo XIII, 1896   [3] *Ibid*. p. 111.

396 PRIMITIVE WORSHIP & THE PRAYER BOOK

We are now in a position to see how intelligently the revisers of 1550, even with much less light from "ancient Authors" and Liturgies than is possessed by us, did their work. They found both the old English Sarum and the Roman Ordinals so overlaid by mediæval ceremonies, borrowed from feudal customs, and in such confused order, that the essential part of the service as seen in the New Testament, and in these early Ordinals, was so obscured as to be almost completely lost to sight. This was particularly true of the ordination to the Priesthood, where, according to the mediæval doctrine, the real ordination was effected by the giving of the instruments (*traditio*, or *porrectio, instrumentorum*), that is, the putting of the chalice and paten, with unconsecrated wine and wafers, into the hands of the ordinand, accompanied by the words; "Take the power of offering sacrifice in the Church for the living and the dead: In the Name," etc.[1] This, in fact, was held to be the real "matter" and "form" of ordination of a Priest, though it is confessed by Roman writers that it was not the custom until the tenth century, and many modern authors of that Communion have expressed grave doubts as to its propriety. The present Roman Pontifical still makes the *traditio instrumentorum* the central part of the service.[2] Other ceremonies preceding this are the anointing of the hands of the candidate, the placing of the hands of the Bishop on his head without saying anything (*nihil dicens*), after which he is still called *ordinandus*, or a candidate, and it is not until the very end of the Office

---

[1] "It was of the essence of feudalism that all power was conveyed by the delivery into the hands of the appointee of something significant of the power conveyed — the keys of a fortress or of a city gate, a sod of earth, a few grains of corn," etc. (Lowndes, *Vindication of Anglican Orders*, I, 209 [Rivingtons, London, Gorham, N Y., 1897]).

[2] *Ibid.* I, pp. 37, 38, 179–197, 291, 295.

when all the "Priests," including the candidates, have communicated, that the Bishop lays his hands on his head saying, "Receive the Holy Ghost, whose sins thou shalt remit," etc. [1]

These are some of the defects and inconsistencies of the Roman Ordinal, and in a measure of the mediæval English as well. Concerning the former a Jesuit writer is compelled to say: — "It is certain that the subject of the ceremony, who was not a Priest at the beginning, is a Priest at the end, but the difficulty is to tell at what part of the ceremony he became a Priest." [2] Concerning the two Ordinals Dr. Lowndes has well said: — "A candid comparison of the Roman with the Edwardine Ordinal will show that the prayers in the former do not set forth the dignity and office of the Priesthood as weightily as the Edwardine. That the Roman contains no special Epistle or Gospel. That the solemn priestly vows of the Edwardine are completely lacking in the Roman. That the scattered allusions in the various prayers to the power of the candidate to celebrate Mass are not equal in force to the one simple expression of authoritative power said to the Anglican Priest at the indisputable moment of his ordination, 'Be thou a faithful dispenser of the Word of God and of His Holy Sacraments.'" And again: — "In all Christendom it may be boldly affirmed that no Church has been as jealous as the Church of England, and the Churches in communion with her, in upholding the honor and dignity of the Christian Priesthood in relation to its gift of forgiveness and retention of sins. No Church has ever in her Service Books given such a prominence to the remission of sins as is given in the Book of Common Prayer;

[1] Maskell, *Mon Ritualia Ecc Anglic*, III, 204, 219.
[2] Hunter, *Outlines of Dogmatic Theology*, III, 378

... the power of binding and loosing in Baptism, in the Holy Eucharist, by Word and Doctrine, by Prayer, by Absolution on Confession, by Remission of Ecclesiastical Censures. If her children have been neglectful of their responsibilities and of their privileges at any period of her history, it has been their fault, and not that of their Mother." [1]

It is not necessary to examine in detail the Ordinal as we possess it today. Though the first revised Book was published in 1549, the Ordinal did not appear until the following year, and few changes were made in 1552 and 1662. In this revision there was little or nothing new or different from the ancient Ordinals, except that it was marked with great simplicity and directness of purpose. The essential part of all ordinations, as seen in every case in the New Testament,[2] and in the primitive Liturgies, consisted in the laying on of the hands of the Apostle, or Apostle-Bishop, with prayer, and this, which had been sadly obscured in the mediæval Ordinals, was carefully restored. The primitive, and probably Apostolic rule of conferring Holy Orders during a celebration of the Holy Eucharist was continued.[3]

It is noteworthy, moreover, that in all the revisions the word Priest (*sacerdos*), which was the almost universal use

---

[1] *Vindication*, etc , I, pp 195, 351   Compare the 36th Art. of Religion. The present Roman Ordinal in English, compared with the ancient Roman ordinals of Leo, Gelasius, and Gregory [5th and 6th centuries], is given in full in *Ordinals Past and Present*, by J. B Smith [Parker, London, 1898]. It is also given by Dr Lowndes in Vol II, appendices V and VI.   The Sarum Ordinal in the original Latin is given by Maskell, *Mon Rit* III, 154-280   For the purpose of comparing our present Ordinal with this, of which it is a revision, an outline of the former will be found as an appendix to the present chapter

[2] Acts vi, 6, xiii, 3, xiv, 23, 1 Tim iv, 14, v, 22, 2 Tim i, 6.

[3] Maskell, III, 158, note.

ORDINALS, PRIMITIVE, &c 399

of the old English Office, as contrasted with the almost universal use of the word *presbyter* in the Roman, was retained, even in the Book of 1552, in spite of the constant opposition of the Puritan party.

The "FORM OF CONSECRATION OF A CHURCH OR CHAPEL," and an "OFFICE OF INSTITUTION OF MINISTERS INTO PARISHES OR CHURCHES," follow the Ordinal in the American Book, inasmuch as they belong to the special functions of a Bishop. The original of the Consecration service was an Office prepared by Bishop Andrewes of Winchester for the consecration of a chapel near Southampton in 1620, and was adopted in substance by the Convocation of Canterbury in 1712, though not made part of the Prayer Book. In 1799, with slight changes, it was incorporated into the American Book, and in 1877 into the Irish. In the latter there is added a brief form for "the Consecration of a Churchyard, or other Burial Ground."

The American Church provides by canon "that the building and the ground on which it is erected" must have been "fully paid for, and are free from lien or other encumbrance; and also that such building and ground are secured from the danger of alienation, either in whole or in part, from those who profess and practise the Doctrine, Discipline, and Worship of this Church."

The "OFFICE OF INSTITUTION OF MINISTERS," Dr. Samuel Hart, official Custodian of the American Prayer Book, says, "was drawn up in 1799 at the request of the Convention of the Diocese of Connecticut by the Rev. Dr. William Smith of Norwalk. It was formally accepted by the Diocesan Convention of Connecticut in 1804, but two years before that time it had been adopted by the Convention of the Diocese of New York. In 1804 it was adopted also by the General Convention, which four years later changed its title ['Induction'] to its present form, and made its use discretionary."[1] The Office consists of the Bishop's "Letter of Institution" giving "Licence and Authority to perform the Office of a Priest in the Parish [or Church] of E. . . . possessed of full power to perform every act of sacerdotal Function among the People of the same. . . . You are faithfully to feed that portion of the flock of Christ which is now entrusted to you; not as a man-pleaser, but as continually bearing in mind that you are accountable to us here, and to the Chief Bishop and Sovereign Judge of all, hereafter," etc.[2]

The Proper Psalms are 122, 132, and 133; the Lessons, Ezek. xxxiii to v. 10, and S. John x to v. 19. The Institution is followed by the Holy Communion, which is here called "the Holy Eucharist," and the words "altar" and "sacerdotal" are used several times. Another peculiarity is the use of the words "Senior" and "Junior" for designating the two Wardens, though the terms are unknown to canonical legislation both in America and England. "This Office of Institution," Dean Hart says, "has really no legal value either civil or ecclesiastical; but it has an educational and moral value."[3] As an integral part of the Prayer Book it has, nevertheless, the same authority as any other in the Book.[4]

---

[1] Dean Hart, *Book of Common Prayer*, p. 284.

[2] In 1820 the General Convention declared this Office "of equal authority with the Book of Common Prayer."

[3] *Ibid.* 285.

[4] The thirty-nine "ARTICLES OF RELIGION," though bound up as an appendix to the Prayer Book, form no essential part of it. It is to be observed that they are in no sense a substitute for the Catholic Creeds, nor a complete system of doctrine. They are "Articles of Religion," and not of Faith, though many of them, especially the first eight, deal with fundamental truths. Their purpose is well defined in the Royal Declara-

ORDINALS, PRIMITIVE, &c 401

APPENDIX TO CHAPTER XXXIX

THE SARUM ORDINAL, OR PONTIFICAL — *Celebratio Ordinum*, and *Consecratio electi in Episcopum*.
The text referred to is that given by Maskell, *Mon. Rit. Ecc. Anglic.*, III, 154–225 and 241–280. The first portion, pp. 154–185, deals with the ordination of doorkeepers (*ostiarii*), readers (*lectores*), exorcists (*exorcistae*), acolytes (*acolyti*), and subdeacons (*subdiaconi*). The second portion, pp. 185–225, gives the order for Deacons and Priests. The third, pp. 240–280, is the form for consecrating a Bishop. The second and third portions alone, with the preface to the first, are given here in outline.

1. Address (*sermo sub hac forma*) on Orders in general (pp. 154–157).

---

tion of 1562, where it is said that they are for the avoidance of "unnecessary Disputations, Altercations, or Questions which may nourish Faction both in the Church and Commonwealth" Their germ is found in the "Ten Articles" adopted by Convocation in 1536, followed by the "Thirteen Articles" in 1538, and later, by the reactionary "Bloody Statute of the Six Articles" In 1553 Convocation issued forty-two Articles prepared by Cranmer, but these were abrogated the same year In 1562 thirty-eight Articles were adopted by the Convocation of Canterbury, prepared by Archbishop Parker. In 1571 the final revision of the Articles, now thirty-nine, took place, being adopted by both Convocations, and by Parliament, and published both in Latin and in English. The American Church in 1801 adopted the Articles as a whole, but left out the reference to the Athanasian Creed in Article 8, and omitted Article 21 entirely, while it retained the old numbering. It provided also a special title-page Up to the year 1865 the clergy of the Church of England were required to "sign the Articles," but in that year this was abolished and the following declaration was substituted: — "I assent to the Thirty-nine Articles of Religion, and to the Book of Common Prayer," etc. The American Church requires only the general declaration "to conform" to the Church's "Doctrine, Discipline, and Worship." See Article VIII, of the Constitution.

2. Presentation of all candidates to Bishop, Bishop's caution (*Vide ut natura*, etc.), and address to people (*Si quis*) (pp. 160–162).

Ordination of Deacons

3. Presentation of candidates for Deacons' and Priests' Orders, followed by Litany (p. 185).

4. Admonition to the Deacon ordinands (p. 191).

5. Laying on of hand (*manum*) saying secretly (*dicens solus secrete*), "Receive the Holy Spirit" (*Accipe Spiritum Sanctum*), followed by prayer (pp. 192–197).

6. Placing of stole on left shoulder, and giving the book of the Gospels (*librum Evangeliorum*), with "authority to read it in the Church of God" (*Accipe potestatem legendi Evangelium in Ecclesia Dei*). "This rite of delivering the Gospels was for many ages peculiar to the English Church. . . . Martene says it is not to be found in any pontifical before the tenth century, those of the English use alone excepted." The original and earliest rubric, as it stands in the English pontificals of the eighth century, gives the words, "Receive, etc. Read, and understand, and hand on to others, and do thou fulfil it by thy work" (*et tu opere adimple*). (Pp. 199, 200, note.)

7. Giving of the dalmatic, a white vestment with short sleeves, and perpendicular ornamental stripes in the color of the season (not noticed in the Winchester Pontifical), followed by the reading of the Gospel (S. Luke iii, 1–7) by one of the Deacons (pp. 201, 202).

Ordination of Priests

8. Presentation by the Archdeacon of ordinands for the priesthood (*sacerdotes*),[1] and "Take heed, etc." (*Caveatur*, etc.), with address (short in Sarum, long in Winchester) by the Bishop.

9. Silent blessing by the Bishop, while he and all Presbyters present (*omnes presbyteri presentes*) hold their hands over

---

[1] The Roman Ordinal almost always uses *Presbyteri* instead of *Sacerdotes*. Its rubrics are always in the indicative also, instead of the imperative as in the English, both ancient and modern.

ORDINALS, PRIMITIVE, &c 403

the heads of the ordinands, the Bishop "with one hand touching," but "saying nothing" (*nihil eis dicente, et una manu tangente*—pp. 204, 205).

10. Brief address followed by prayers for candidates, after which the Bishop turns the stole as it hangs down the deacon's back, placing it over his right shoulder, and crossing it over his breast, while he says, "Receive the yoke of the Lord: for His yoke is easy, and His burden light. The Lord clothe thee with the robe (*stola*) of innocence" (pp. 207, 208).

11. Giving of chasuble with prayer, followed by the hymn, "Come, Holy Ghost" (*Veni Creator Spiritus*), the Bishop beginning (*incipiat*), and the benediction and anointing of the hands of the ordinands (pp. 209-213).

12. The giving of the paten and chalice containing unconsecrated bread and wine, with the words, "Receive power to offer sacrifice to God, and to celebrate Mass, as for the living so also for the dead. In the Name of the Lord Jesus Christ." "No mention is made of this rite before the eleventh century. Nor is it to be found in the early sacramentaries of Gelasius or Gregory: or in the often-quoted canons of the fourth Carthaginian council" (p. 214 and note).

13. The Eucharistic service then proceeds, the newly ordained "Priests" (*sacerdotes*) communicate (in one or both kinds is left uncertain), and not until then does the Bishop lay his hands on the head of each one separately (*singulorum*), saying, "Receive the Holy Ghost: whose sins thou shalt remit, they are remitted unto them: and whose sins thou shalt retain, they shall be retained." [1]

---

[1] Maskell has a very important note on this last laying-on of hands — "All the early pontificals omit this second imposition of hands, and explicit delivery of the power to remit or retain sins It is not in the early English MSS. of Egbert or Dunstan, or the Winchester Use. it is not in any of the foreign Orders, printed by Martene, before the 12th century; it is not in the old Sacramentaries of S Gregory, or Gelasius: nor lastly, does one of the ancient ritualists . . . allude to it in the most distant terms " He points out the "considerable difficulty" in which this places the

Consecration of a Bishop

14. Before Mass is celebrated, the Bishop-elect, vested as Priest, but with cope (*capa*) instead of chasuble (*casula*), is presented by two Bishops to the Metropolitan, who sits with his back to the high altar.

15. Examination of Elect by interrogatories as to teaching, and life, kindness to poor and strangers, belief in articles of the Creed, and in the Old and New Testament, with oath of obedience to Metropolitan.

16. Beginning of Mass.

17. Vesting of Elect with sandals, alb, stole, maniple, tunic, dalmatic, chasuble, followed by Litany with special suffrages.

18. Placing the Book of the Gospels on the neck of the Elect.

19. The Consecrator and other Bishops with their hands touch (*tangant*) the head of the Elect, while the Consecrator begins the hymn, *Veni Creator* ("Come, Holy Ghost"). The "essential form," "Receive the Holy Ghost," as declared by the Council of Trent, is lacking here, and in all other English Ordinals except that of Exeter. Here, therefore, is the same "considerable difficulty" for Roman authorities as we found in the ordination of Priests. The logical inference would be that all consecrations of Bishops according to the ancient Use of the Church of England before the Reformation, except in the Diocese of Exeter, were null and void!

10. Prayers, and unction of the head and hands of the Elect, giving of gloves (peculiar to Sarum), pastoral staff, ring, mitre, and book of the Gospels.

21. Eucharistic Office to end.[1]

Roman Church, which, by the Council of Trent has declared, according to Bellarmin, that this second imposition of hands with the accompanying words, is "*de essentia.*" If this be so, it would follow that for a thousand years the service for the ordination of Priests lacked *an essential* part! (pp. 220–221, note).

[1] Maskell, *Mon. Rit. Ecc. Ang*, III, pp. 241–280.

CHAPTER XL

CONCLUSION

"*O worship the Lord in the beauty of holiness*" — *Psalm xcvi, 9.*
"*The palace is not for man, but for the Lord God.*" — *I Chron. xxix, 1.*

WE have traced the stream of the Apostolic Liturgy as it issues with its four rivers, Judæan, Ephesine, Egyptian, Roman, from the one great spring and source of all Divine Worship in the Upper Room, until we find it today in the British Isles, in North America, Australia, in every land where the English tongue is spoken, and among races of men for whom it has been translated into more than one hundred other tongues.[1] Thus with all its original elements unchanged and undiminished, and with new features and enrichments added, it is yet the same great vehicle by means of which, as in a censer, the worship of one of the most powerful and gifted of "the nations" gathered into the kingdom of Christ has offered, and still offers, to God the worship which He has commanded. Many strains have entered into it in its passage through the centuries. It has been enriched by the gathered experiences of many souls in many lands, by their penitence, their longings after God, their sense of need, their gratitude, their ador-

---

[1] Besides Latin, Greek, Hebrew, Irish, Gaelic, Manx, Welsh, French, Spanish, German, Scandinavian, Italian, Portuguese, the English or American Book has been translated into many of the languages of Eastern Europe, India, the Far East, Australia, the Pacific Islands, Africa, Madagascar, and the Amerinds (American Indians) North and South See Muss-Arnoldt, *The Book of Common Prayer among the Nations*, S. P. C. K., 1910.

ing love. Jerusalem, Syria, Gaul, Rome, Milan, Celt, Saxon, Norman, have each brought their gifts. Martyrs, Confessors, Saints, holy men and women through nigh two thousand years have all had part in making the Book what it is today. It has had many revisers, Basil, Chrysostom, Leo, Gelasius, Gregory, Osmund, Cranmer, Cosin, and many another whose name has not come down to us, but whose impress has been left on the thought and language of its devotion.

Of Cranmer's part in the great work one can scarcely speak too highly. His difficulties were enormous, for unlike former revisions, this of the English Book was wrought out in the midst of enemies of many kinds, political, social, and ecclesiastical; fanatical adherents of Rome on one side, and equally fanatical Protestants on the other. Nevertheless, by the mercy and goodness of God the result was one for which to be most thankful. And to Archbishop Cranmer, with his mixture of great qualities and infirmities, more than to any other man, just as in earlier days in other national Churches, to Basil, and Chrysostom, and Gregory, the English-speaking world owes, under God, the rich heritage of its purified Offices of Prayer and Sacrament. A stronger man would have fallen before the domineering power of Henry, as Wolsey, Cromwell, and More fell. A weaker, less learned, and less conscientious man would have failed as Wicliffe failed.

To quote the well balanced language of Canon Mason: — "Cranmer's large mind and temper, while essentially conservative, was capable of taking in the new, and of going great lengths with it, and yet of coördinating it with the old, instead of substituting the one for the other. In this way he was able to preserve, by means of the Prayer Book, the Ordinal, and the Articles, a truly Catholic foot-

CONCLUSION 407

ing for the Church of England. If, instead of an ever narrowing sect of adherents to the Papacy, confronted by a Protestantism which drifts further and further away from the faith of the ancient Fathers, our country possesses a Church of unbroken lineage, true to the age-long inheritance in its framework of government, doctrine, and worship, yet open to every form of progress, and comprehensive enough to embrace every human being who confesses Christ, the thanks are due, under God, to the sagacity, the courage, the suppleness combined with firmness, of Archbishop Cranmer. The unparalleled splendour of his dying actions secured for ever to the Church of England what his life had gained." [1]

It may be well to sum up here in conclusion the many benefits we have seen in this latest revision of those Offices of Catholic worship which are the inheritance of a race whose numbers and extent of dominion already exceed that of every other in the history of the world.[2] Besides the restoration of primitive usage in regard to "a tongue understanded of the people," many manifest abuses in doctrine and practice were corrected. Ceremonies had abounded beyond measure.[3] The rubrics for the general govern-

---

[1] *Thomas Cranmer*, p 202. Something may be gathered concerning the vast extent of Cranmer's theological and liturgical learning from the partial list of MSS and printed books of his private library, now in the British Museum and elsewhere See Burbidge, *Liturgies and Offices of the Church*, pp. xvii–xxxvi

[2] Green the historian may not be over bold when he ventures the prediction that " English institutions [he is speaking of North America as well] English speech, English thoughts will become the main features of the political, the social, the intellectual life of mankind."

[3] The first rubric in the Office for the Consecration of a Bishop in the Sarum Use provided for no less than thirty-five separate articles necessary for the function!

ment of the services, which were contained in the Ordinale or Pie, had become so multiplied that the Revisers say of it: — "The number and hardness of the Rules called the Pie, and the manifold changings of the Service, was a cause, that to turn the Book only was so hard and intricate a matter, that many times there was more business to find out what should be read, than to read it when it was found out."[1]

Serious errors in doctrine also had crept into the mediæval Offices, especially in regard to the central act of worship. The true sacrificial aspect of the Holy Eucharist had become so distorted and exaggerated as to drive completely into the background its other equally important aspect as a Communion. For not only was the cup denied to the people contrary to our Lord's specific and prophetic command that "all" should drink of it, but actual reception of this Divine Food of the soul was restricted in the practice of the people to a single Communion in the year. Auricular confession to a Priest as an obligatory condition of Communion; the "Romish"(*Romanensium*) doctrine of a Purgatory of quasi material torment after death, and the related offering of the Holy Eucharist and prayers for the abbreviation of this suffering, which was a gross perversion of the undoubted primitive custom of Eucharistic prayers for the rest, and peace, and complete sanctification of the faithful departed; and prayers addressed directly or indirectly to the Blessed Virgin and other great saints, were all corruptions swept away in the new revision.

One other glory of the revised Prayer Book is the return to primitive usage in the large place it gives to the reading of Holy Scripture. In the mediæval Church the Lessons from the Bible were reduced to very small proportions,

---

[1] Preface to the English Book, *Concerning the Service of the Church.*

CONCLUSION 409

and in many cases, as stated in the Preface "Concerning the Service of the Church" in the English Book, their place was taken by "uncertain stories and legends"; while of the Psalms, which were from the beginning the very core of the Daily Offices of worship, "a few of them were daily said, and the rest utterly omitted." On the other hand an examination of the revised Book will show that three fifths of it is taken directly from Holy Scripture; one fifth consists of prayers, creeds, and canticles more than 800 years old, some reaching even to Apostolic times; and only one fifth consists of prayers and exhortations newly composed by the revisers.

Dr. Döllinger, the learned German Old-Catholic professor and historian, has said concerning this prominence given to Holy Scripture in modern England, due largely to the Prayer Book: — "I believe we may credit one great superiority in England over other countries to the circumstance that there the Holy Scripture is found in every house, as is the case nowhere else in the world." Puritans, in spite of all their defects in other ways, deserve credit along with Churchmen of that day for their zeal for "an open Bible." Strange to say, however, they attached such exaggerated importance to what they called "the preaching of the Word," that is, their own novel and strained interpretation of the Gospel of Christ, that the reading of the Bible in their services was reduced to almost mediæval proportions.[1]

But it is not only the contents, and the character, and the venerable associations of the Prayer Book that make it

---

[1] See Hooker, *Ecc. Pol*, V. xxi On the other hand, in a single service of Morning Prayer, with Holy Communion, in part or whole, at least four times as much of God's Word is read or sung (Psalms, Canticles, Old and New Testament Lessons, Epistle and Gospel) as is read in an ordinary service among our separated brethren even today.

worthy of our love and admiration. Cranmer, to whom we are perhaps chiefly indebted for this beauty of diction in both Bible and Prayer Book (for the "Great Bible" of 1539 was largely his work), was one of a number of great scholars in an age of revived and great scholarship. But great scholars are not always masters of prose as Cranmer was. Criticism and literary art are rarely wedded to each other. Liddon, himself a master of style, has said: — "For the English language the sixteenth century was the period of consummate excellence. . . . The English writers of the sixteenth century — and Archbishop Cranmer in particular — had an ear for English which has not been given even to the most gifted of their successors; and their work is unapproached in its simple and forcible vocabulary, and still more in the ordered beauty of its rhythm." [1]

Moreover both the Prayer Book and the Bible are translations from another tongue; the latter wholly, the former almost wholly. And good translation is no easy matter. Success in avoiding stiffness is rare, and smooth and melodious English is rarer still.[2] Yet the translators of both

---

[1] Preface to *Reflections on the Psalms*. Nevertheless, in a deeply interesting letter to King Henry in 1543, Cranmer confesses his inability to write verse. After telling of his "travail" to translate the ancient office hymn, *Salve festa dies*, into English verse, he writes, "But because mine English verses lack the grace and felicity that I would wish they had, your Majesty may cause some other to make them again, that can do the same in more pleasant English and phrase." It seems probable that the longer version of the *Veni Creator Spiritus* in the Ordinal is by Cranmer. If so he showed his excellent judgment in writing as he did above. See *Thomas Cranmer* by Canon Mason, pp. 141, 142, and Julian's *Dic. of Hymnology*, p. 1209

[2] Macaulay's description of translation in general was "champagne in decanter." Coleridge's translation of Schiller's *Piccolomini* and *Wallenstein* is probably the only example in English secular literature of which it has been said that the translation is superior to the original.

CONCLUSION 411

Prayer Book and Bible were successful, and both books have become English classics, in fact the greatest of them all. Lord Macaulay has said of the Prayer Book, "The essential qualities of devotion and eloquence, conciseness, majestic simplicity, pathetic earnestness of supplication, sobered by a profound reverence, are common between the translations and the originals. But in the subordinate graces of diction the originals must be allowed to be far inferior to the translations." And he adds, "The diction of our Book of Common Prayer has directly or indirectly contributed to form the diction of almost every great English writer."[1] What has been often written concerning the uncommon beauty and matchless English of our translation of the Bible is equally applicable to the Prayer Book. "It lives on the ear like a music that can never be forgotten. Its felicities often seem to be almost things rather than mere words. It is part of the national mind, and the anchor of the national seriousness. The memory of the dead passes into it. The potent traditions of childhood are stereotyped in its verses. The power of all the gifts and trials of a man is hidden beneath its words."[2] This is the judgment, not of an Anglican, but of a member of the Roman Communion.

That the Book is still capable of improvement, and, as in former revisions, requiring from time to time adaptation to the growing needs of a new age and new conditions, is unquestionable. If it were not so it would be on a level with "The Everlasting Gospel" itself, as contained in the writings of the New Testament. The fact remains, nevertheless, that it is a marvelous work as revised in the sixteenth and seventeenth centuries by the skill and wisdom of

---

[1] *Hist. of England*, III, p. 475.
[2] *The Dublin Review*, qu. by Neale in *Essays on Liturgiology*, p. 221.

many devoted men, through nearly 150 years of varied conflict, and as remarkable for what it has persistently retained of Catholic doctrine and practice, as for what it has left out of mediæval accretions and perversions. An eminent American layman has written concerning it: — "The Book of Common Prayer has been the study of the most acute and vigorous minds, not only of ecclesiastics, but of lawyers, statesmen, and scholars. A body of literature has been created as to its sources, meaning, and purposes which for learning, reasoning, and style is unsurpassed. Those who know it best love it best, and the very earnestness of their discussions as to its origin and meaning attests their devotion to it. It has profoundly influenced not only the moral, but also the intellectual and political, life of England, and of the world. . . . Its history is a part of the warp and woof of the history of the English people and nation which no one can fully understand who does not know its story."[1]

[1] J H. Benton, LL D., President of the Boston Library, in *The Book of Common Prayer, Its Origin and Growth*, pp. v. vi.

INDEX

Aaron, 71, 374
Aberdeen, 122
Ablutions, 197
Abraham, 178
Absolution, 113, 167-171, 206, 342
Abyssinia, 69, 207
Accession Service, 361
Acts of Apostles, 24, 366, 367
Administration of Holy Communion, 60, 112, 114, 195
Adultery, 319-332
"Advertisements," Royal, 273
Aelfred, King, 93
Aelfric, Archbp., 297
Agape, 32, 47, 191
Agnus Dei, 113, 196
Agricola, 71
"Air," 63
Alb, 405
Alban, S., 71
Albania, 75
Albany, Bp. of, 266
Alcuin, 84
Alexander, Archbp. of Alexandria, 252, 253
Alexander, Primate, 210-213, 215, 218, 222, 229, 237, 242, 249, 256
Alexandria, 57, 66, 157, 252, 381
All Saints, 269
Alps, 248
Altar, 40, 41, 44, 45, 54, 56, 112, 138, 139, 159, 275, 400
Ambrose, 66, 78, 98, 137, 221, 231, 234, 237
Amens, 140
American Prayer Book, 104, 112, 118, 120-134, 141, 150, 156, 169, 174, 177, 196, 205, 206, 208, 221, 233, 236, 243, 244, 251, 258, 267,
269, 270, 276, 279, 284, 285, 293, 301, 317, 326, 334, 338, 345, 346, 353, 357-361, 400, 401
American Presbyterians, 7
Amerinds, 406
Anabaptist, 289, 293
Anamnesis, 178, 179
Anaphora, 59, 62, 67, 140, 172-184
Anaximines, 239
Andrewes, Bp., 128, 164, 399
Angel, or Apostle, 369, 378
Angles, 74, 82
Anglican Chant, 232
Anointing, 307, 312, 343-345
Antioch, 58, 59, 62, 98, 157, 230, 372
Antiphon, 67, 100, 164, 218, 219, 263, 343, 350
Antoninus Pius, 48
Apocrypha, 116, 238
"Apostle" for Epistle, 155
Apostles' Creed, 245, 250, 392
Apostolic Constitutions, 54, 59, 61, 156, 263
Apostolicae Curae, 395
Apostolic Succession, 367, 379
Appeal, Final Court of, 273
Apulia, 73
Aquileia, 67, 251
Arabic, 80
Arius, 157, 252, 253, 263
Arles, 71, 256
Armagh, 76
Armenian Lit., 21, 141, 155
Armorica, 79
Arndt, Joh., 208
Articles of Religion, 185, 186, 189, 191, 246, 272, 276, 303, 304, 372, 387, 398, 400
Ash Wednesday, 269, 357

INDEX

Asterisk, 64
Athanasius, 59, 253
Athanasius, Creed of, 174, 245, 256–260, 401
Athos, Mt, 61
"Audible Voice," 143
Augsburg, Confession of, 246
Augustine of Canterbury, 74, 79, 82, 83, 88, 264
Augustine of Hippo, 33, 182, 208, 212, 221, 230–232, 237, 239, 240, 261, 287, 296, 303, 348, 393
Auricular Confession, 168, 206
Australia, 314
"Authentic Modes," 233
"Authorized Version," 117, 216, 217
Auxerre, 79

BANCROFT, ARCHBP, 379
Bangor, 86, 101
Banns, 333
Baptism, 59, 80, 113, 166, 169, 181, 281–294, 305, 311
Baptists, 267, 286, 382
Baring-Gould, 110, 142, 168, 279
Bartholomew's Day, S, 118
Basil, 35, 58, 98, 263, 269, 407
Basilica, 40
Baxter, 13, 45, 115, 146, 291
Bede, 71, 73, 74, 83, 93
Bellarmin, 404
Bema, 41, 55
Benedicite, 79, 217, 237, 238
"Benedictions, Eighteen," 173
Benedictus, 48, 240
Benedictus qui venit, 67, 113, 173
Benton, J H., 413
Berlin, 384
Bernhardi, 384
Benson, Archbp., 140, 280, 286, 295, 352
Betrothal, 335
Bible, 93, 95, 102. See also "Great Bible"
Bidding Prayer, 79, 158
Bingham, 33, 40, 42, 44, 51–53, 104, 143, 161, 185, 202, 203, 221, 222, 254, 279, 287, 312, 342, 349

Birkbeck, W J, 255
Bishop, 363, 368, 369, 404
"Black Gown," 274
"Black Rubric," 199
Blessing, The, 197
Blunt, J. H, 61, 86, 87, 96, 99, 145, 165, 168, 174, 186, 274, 275, 285, 288, 298, 334–336, 343, 352, 358
"Body of the Church," 138, 139, 334
Bohemia, 73
Book of Common Prayer, see American, Irish, etc, Prayer Book
"Book of Common Worship," 7
Book of the Gospels, Giving of, 403, 405
Bowing at the sacred Name, 116, 157, 158
"Bow in the Cloud," 179
Bracaria, Council of, 254
Bramhall, Archbp, 169
"Breaking of Bread," 31–39
Breviary, 87, 88, 96, 99 See also Portuary
Bright, Canon, 82, 85, 114, 146, 150–152, 160, 180, 271, 288
Brightman, 58
British Church, 69, 70–81
Brittany, 78
Brooks, Bp Phillips, 250
Brownell, Bp, viii, 170
Bryennios Philotheos, 51
Bucer, 110, 282, 283, 327
Bulgaria, 59
Burbidge, 279, 408
Burial, 349–355
Burke, Edmund, 127
Bury, Prof, 75
Butler, Bp, 213
"Buxum," 336
Byzantine, 57, 58

CAERLEON, 71
Caesarea, 58, 98, 252
Calabria, 73
Calpurnius, 75
Calvin, 10, 110, 114, 189, 288, 378, 382, 388

INDEX 415

Cambridge, 89, 283
Canada, 132, 228, 230, 314
Cancelli, 42
Canonical Hours, 203
Canon of Holy Communion, 140, 172-184
Canons, English, 273, 283, 316, 333, 372
Cantate, 243
Canterbury, 79, 83, 84, 86, 88, 89, 91, 95, 264, 333, 334, 352
Cantus Directus, 219
Capernaum, 35, 38
Capitals, Use of, 141
Capitula, 205
Carthage, 77, 237, 404
Catacombs, 40, 192
Catechetical School, 59, 296
Catechism, 295-302
Catechizing, 301
"Catholic Remainder," 6, 122
Caxton, 101
"Celebration," 140
Celtic, 72, 76, 84, 99, 380
Chalcedon, 59
Chalice, 54, 160, 275, 390
Chamouni, 239
Chancel, 138
Charlemagne, 84, 157, 254, 309, 324
Charles I, 121, 361
Charles II, 115, 121, 122, 271, 362
Chasuble, 403, 404, 405
Chaucer, 334, 338
Cheyne, Prof, 44
Chickely, 89
Chimere, 274
Choir Offices, 235
"Christian Science," 345
Christian Year, 7
Chrysostom, 35, 57, 58, 59, 62, 98, 128, 263, 269, 311
"Church" and "Kingdom," 364
Church, Dean, 55, 61, 145, 220, 222
Church Law, 276
Church Orders, 42
Church Buildings, 40-42, 54, 55, 56
Church Wardens, 139, 400

Churching of Women, 356
Claggett, Bp , 275
Clarendon, Council of, 91
Clarke, Sir Edw , 214, 216
Clemens of Alexandria, 296
Clement I of Rome, 49, 50, 62, 372, 373
Clement VII of Rome, 99, 205
Clementine Liturgy, 62, 165
Clovesho, Council of, 84
Clyde, 70, 75, 76
Coleridge, 179, 187, 239, 411
Colet, Dean, 89
Collects, 145-153, 262
Colman, Bp , 76
Cologne, 99, 101, 205, 352
Columba, 75, 120, 150, 381
Columbanus, 75, 76
Commandments, 140-142
Commination, 357
Compline, 203, 204
Commune and Communicate, 195, 347
Communion, Holy, 35, 59, 104, 135, 140, 191-199
Communion in both kinds, 104
Confession, 167, 168, 194, 206, 342
Confirmation, 59, 166, 181, 294, 303-317
Congregationalists, 10, 11, 267, 382
Confiteor, 167, 169, 206
"Comfortable Words," 171, 301
Consecration, Prayer of, 105, 112, 129-132, 175-184
Consecration of Church, 390, 399
Consecration of Churchyard, 400
Constantine, 54, 55, 252, 323
Constantinople, 78, 157, 254, 263, 323
Consubstantiation, 185
Consumption of Elements, 197
Convocation, 88, 94, 95, 98, 99, 101, 102, 109, 115, 117, 134, 193, 198, 246, 274, 293, 299, 311, 361, 372, 399, 401
Cope, 404
Corporal or Corporas, 275
Cornwall, 75, 79, 82

INDEX

Cosin, Bp., 128, 163, 269, 270, 313
Councils, English, Parents of Parliament, 324
Councils, General, 254
"Covenant, Solemn," 115
Coxe, Bp, 23, 120, 128, 163, 275, 341, 349
Cranmer, 95, 96, 107, 146, 149, 207, 216, 246, 269, 274, 407, 411
Credence, 162, 275
Creed, 156, 245–260
Cremation, 350
Crisome, 282
Cromwell, Oliver, 115
Cromwell, Thomas, 407
Cross, Sign of, 113, 282, 284, 312, 315
Cup, see Chalice
Curate, 301
Cyprian, 21, 33, 54, 237, 307
Cyril of Alexandria, 34, 36
Cyril of Jerusalem, 55, 59, 61, 194, 296

"DAILY BREAD," 195, 196
Dalmatic, 403, 405
Darwin, 230
Davison, W. T , 215
Deacons, 55, 363, 370, 402
Dead, Prayers for, see Departed
Dearmer, Percy, 156, 165
Decalogue, see Commandments
De Koven, Dr. J , 129, 317
De Long, Lieut., 249
Denison, Archdeacon, 110
Deosculatorium, 165
Departed, Faithful, 65–67, 163, 354
Deprecations, 266
Didache, 51
Didascalia, 54
Dies Irae, 352
Diocesan, see Episcopacy
Diocletian, 52, 71
"Directory," Presbyterian, 115
Dirge, 350, 352
" Disc," 64
"Discerning of Spirits," 171
Disciplina Arcani, 53

Dissenting Worship, 182
"Dissidence of Dissent," 267
"Divine Service," 5
Divorce, 318–332
Dix, Dr. Morgan, 111
Dixon, Canon, 110
Doane, Bp. W. C , 331
Dollinger, 11, 320, 410
Dorchester, Mass., 10
Doxology, 21, 196
Dublin, 359
Dublin Review, 412
Duchesne, 42, 45, 47, 50, 51, 53, 55, 59, 73, 77, 78, 83, 84, 112, 137, 141, 143, 147, 155, 157, 164, 176, 221, 278
Dumbarton, 75
Dunstan, Archbp , 404
Dupanloup, Bp , 230, 297
Durham, 279
Dykes, J B., 233

EADGAR, 85
Eanham, 324
Eastern Church, 59, 323
"Eastward Position," 181
Ectené, 263
Edersheim, Dr , 16, 19, 38, 160
Edinburgh, 121
Edward the Confessor, 85
Egbert, Archbp , 297, 404
Egbert, King, 84
Egyptian Lit., 57
Eleutherus, 73
Elizabeth, Queen, 113, 187, 361
Elizabeth, Saint, 242
Ely, 96, 279
Ember Days, 270
Emmaus, 32
Endowments, Church, 159
Engagement, 335
Engla-land, 85
English Church, 88, 91
English Titles to Psalms, 223–229
Ephesian Lit., 57, 66, 78, 80
Epiclesis, see Invocation
Episcopacy, 370, 379
Epistle and Gospel, 67, 141, 145, 154

INDEX 417

Espousals, 335
Ethelred, King, 324
Etheria, 55, 137
Ethiopia, 69
Eton, 89
Eucharist, 34, 47, 49, 51, 66, 172, 375, 393, 398, 400, 409
Eulogia, 36
Euphrates, 58
Eusebius, 42, 50, 55
Evensong, 200–207, 241
Excommunication, 138
Exeter, 405
Exhortations, 164, 165, 205, 206
Extempore Prayer, 4, 9, 46

FAITH HEALING, 345
Faldstool, 266
Family Prayers, 360
"Fan," 64
Farce, 219
Faroe, 76
Fasting Communion, 191–194
Ffoulkes, E. S., 176
Filioque, 157, 254, 255
First Pr. Book of Edward VI, 98–108, 179, 205
Florence, Council of, 104
Font, 275
Forbes, Bp., 304
Forms of Prayer, 8, 9, 10, 26–30
Fornication, 320
France, 264
Francis of Assisi, 92
Frankfort, 114
Fredericton, 194
Freeman, Archdeacon, 21, 25, 78, 80, 83, 87, 99, 137, 151, 189, 196, 201–205, 208, 218, 219, 238, 252
Frere, 46, 61, 86. See also P. and F.
Fridolin, 75
Froude, 110, 111, 127
Fulton, J., 327, 335

GAELIC, 71
Gall, Saint, 75, 352
Gallican Lit., 66, 77, 78, 82, 83, 162, 252, 285
Gallienus, 41

Garrick, 143
Gasquet and Bishop, 111
Gaul, 77, 78
Geddis, Jennie, 122
Gelasius, 82, 98, 151, 174, 185, 269, 284, 343, 358, 398, 404
Genealogy of English Lit., 133
General Convention, American, 112, 123, 125, 129, 175, 277, 326, 400
General Councils, 254
"General Thanksgiving," 141
Geneva, 114, 378
Georgia, 73
Germanus, 79
Germany, 383, 388
Gibbon, 378
Gibson, Bp., 92, 360
Gildas, 80
Gladstone, 4, 209, 318, 321, 386
Gloria in Excelsis, 48, 113, 196
Gloria Patri, 221, 240, 269
Gloria Tibi, 156
Gloves, 405
Goldsmith, Oliver, 275
Good Friday, Eucharist on, 145
Goodrich, Bp., 96
Gore, Bp., 177, 183, 184, 198, 214, 238, 374, 375, 377, 381, 387
Goulburn, Dean, 151
Gradual, 100, 101, 221
Grave, Benediction of, 355
"Great Bible," 102, 117, 301, 411
"Great Entrance," 67, 162
"Great Intercession," 162
Greek Lit., 57–59, 74, 77
Green, J. R., 85, 408
Gregorian Tones, see Plain Song
Gregory, Dean, 145
Gregory Nazianzen, 234
Gregory the Great, 74, 82, 89, 98, 152, 232, 264, 265, 269, 284, 398, 404
Gregory VII, 90, 99
Grove, Sir George, 233
Gutenberg, 101

HADDEN, A. W., 74, 372
Hallel, 37, 48, 228
Hampton Court Conference, 115, 299

INDEX

Hardwick, 107
Hare, Archdeacon, 283
Harmony, 230
Harnack, 374, 375
Hart, Samuel, 119, 270, 336, 359, 399, 400
Harvest, see Thanksgiving Day
Harvey, 256
Hatch, E, 183
Heber, Bp, 234
Hebrew Poetry, 215, 216
Hegesippus, 377
Helmore, 233
Henry VIII, 87, 96, 97, 411
Herbert, G, 279
Hereford, 86, 101, 337
Hermann, Archbp, 99, 101, 205, 267, 284
Hermas, 322
Higham Ferrers, 89
Hilary of Arles, 256
Hilary of Poictiers, 35, 79, 234
Hildebrand, see Gregory VII
Hippolytus, 34
Holland, 383, 384
Holland, Canon, 190
Holy Synod, 255
Homoiousion, Homoousion, 253
Homophony, 231
Hooker, 21, 33, 82, 185, 186, 188, 189, 222, 243, 253, 264, 287, 337, 339, 342, 378, 410
Hopkins, Prof, 7
Hore, 91
"Hours of Prayer," 201-204
How, Bp. W. W, 154
Humble Access, Prayer of, 67, 112, 175, 177
Huns, 150
Hunter, 397,
Huntington, W. R., 3, 12, 146, 200
Hutton, R. H, 245, 249
"Hymn" in Passover, 48
Hymns, 48, 207, 233, 334

Iceland, 76
Ignatius, 40, 221, 222, 230, 372, 374, 375

Immersion in Baptism, 285
Impediments to Marriage, 334
Imprecatory Psalms, 213-215
Incense, 277-279
Independents, 382
India, 70
"Induction," 400
Ingram, Bp, 163
"Injunctions," 266, 273
Innocent III, 256
Institution of Ministers, 390, 399, 400
"Intinction," 161
Introit, 100, 113
Invitation to Communion, 165
Invitatory Psalm, 208
Invocation of Saints, 148, 266
Invocation of the Holy Ghost, 60, 65, 104, 111, 123, 176, 177
Iona, 75, 84, 120, 381
Iota, 25, 31
Ipswich, 94
Irenæus, 40, 77, 78, 376, 378
Irish Church or Prayer Book, 70-81, 85, 103, 117, 120-134, 169, 258, 266, 301, 326, 339, 346, 353, 357-361, 380, 390, 400
Italics, Use of, 140
Italic Version, 217
Italy, 73

James I, 121
James, Lit of Saint, 57-66
Jamestown, 119, 277
Jerome, 79, 217, 374, 381
Jerusalem, 58, 59, 62, 69, 98, 252, 380
John, King, 91
John, Saint, 57, 66, 78, 187, 188, 376
Johnson, John, 141, 297
Joseph, Saint, 15
Jubilate, 240
Judea, 58
"Judicial Committee," 273
Julian, J, 411
Julius, 71
Justinian, 143, 323, 327

INDEX 419

Justin Martyr, 45, 47, 48, 51, 53
Juxon, Bp , 121

KEBLE, 33, 137, 167, 186, 191, 257, 281, 295, 303, 356, 363, 379
Kellner, Prof , 137
Kells, 76
Ken, Bp , 234
Kentigern, 150
King, Bp , 140, 145, 160, 280
"Kingdom" and "Church," 364, 366
Kingdon, Bp , 194
Kingsley, Charles, 148
"Kiss of Peace" or "Charity," 60, 67, 165
Kneeling at Holy Communion, 113
Knox, Alex , 145
Knox, John, 146, 382, 388
Korah, 183
Kyrie, 142, 264

LAMBETH CHURCH, 286
Lambeth Conference, 345, 392
Lambeth Judgment, 140
"Lamb of God," 178, 202
Langton, Archbp , 91
Late Comers to Church, 207
Lateran Council, 73
Latin Liturgy, 58, 71, 72
Laud, Archbp , 121, 128, 139, 270
Lauds, 203, 240
"Laying on of Hands," 181, 305, 315
Lecky, W E H , 327
Lectionary, 119, 236
Lections or Lessons, 141, 155, 235, 236
Lee, Archbp , 95
Legenda, 100
Leighton, Archbp , 182
Lent, 264, 333, 357
Leo the Great, 98, 151, 269, 398
Leo XIII, 395
L'Estrange, 176, 287
Levites, 221, 374
Lex orandi, viii, 11
Liddon, 145, 169, 177, 184, 216, 222, 229, 242, 250, 296, 411

Lightfoot, Bp , 374, 375, 377
Lincoln, 86, 101, 139, 140, 160, 192, 280, 359
Lingard, 84
Litany, 87, 96, 142, 261–269, 281, 405
"Little Chapter," 235
Littledale, 58, 59, 72, 177, 208, 220
"Little Entrance," 67, 162
Liturgic Worship, 8, 9, 26–30
Liturgies, 51, 52, 57
Liturgy, 32, 136
Lloyd, Julius, 6, 121
London, 71, 86, 360
Longland, Bp , 94
Lord's Prayer, 20, 140
Lord's Supper, 32, 47, 136
"Loud Voice," 143
Love Feast, see *Agape*
Lowell, J R , 98
Lowndes, 80, 391, 396–398
Lucius, King, 73
Luckock, Dean, 3, 73, 99, 116, 182, 214, 319, 323–325
Lumby, J R , 256
Lupus, Bp., 79
Luther, 114, 185, 325, 327, 382, 388
Lutheran Usages, 137, 162, 246, 314
Lutterworth, 93
Lyons, 77, 78
Lyra Apostolica, 109
Lyra Innocentium, 146

MACAULAY, 150, 411, 412
Macedonius, 157, 254
Maclean, Bp , 2, 54, 61, 142, 177, 181, 202, 207, 263, 393, 395
Maclear, G F , 114, 269
Magna Charta, 91
Magnificat, 48, 217, 241–243
Malabar, 57, 66, 69, 202
Malcolm, King, 85
Mamercus, Bp , 265
Maniple, 405
Manning, Archdeacon, 92
Manual, 85, 101, 281
Marbeck, 233
Margaret, Queen, 85, 150

Margaret, Church of Saint, 110, 115
Mark, Lit. of Saint, 57, 66
Marriage, 318–340
Married Clergy, 90
Martene, 403, 404
Martin, S , 79, 83
Martyr, Justin, see Justin
Martyr, Peter, 110
Mary, Queen, 113, 114
Mary, Virgin, 15, 241
Maskell, 99, 100, 156, 165, 200, 265, 344, 397, 398, 402, 404
Mason, Canon, 66, 148, 407, 411
Mass, 136, 137, 179, 184
Mass "of the Presanctified," 145
Massachusetts, 6, 10
Matins, 200–207, 241
Maundy Thursday, 145, 193
Media Vita, 352
Melancthon, 327
Melchizedek, 179, 365
Mendelssohn, Moses, 214
Metropolitan, 404
Middleton, Bp , 320
Milan, 66, 67, 78, 98, 137, 155, 221, 231, 233
"Militant, Church," 162, 163
Milton, 4, 325, 328
Ministry, see Ordinal
Missa Catechumenorum, 67
Missal, 85, 87, 101
Mitre, 405
Monasteries, 94, 203
Monica, 232
Monsell, J. S. B., ix
Montgomery, J , 234
Moravians, 126, 162
More, Sir Thomas, 407
Morning and Evening Prayer, 200–207
Moses, 319
"Mother of all Churches," 380
Moulton, R. G , 216
Mozarabic, 66, 80, 81, 133, 162
Mozley, J B., 283, 328
Musical Colon, 216
Music in the Church, 229
Muss-Arnoldt, 406

NAME OF AMERICAN CHURCH, 125–129
Name of Jesus, Bowing at, 284
Nave, 55, 138
Nazareth, 14, 15, 20
Neale, J. M., 27, 28, 58, 59, 65–67, 73, 78, 81, 177, 219, 220, 263, 412
Neander, 41
New England, 6
Newman, J. H , 172, 182, 253
Nice or Nicaea, 71, 80, 157, 252, 386
Nicene Creed, 251–256, 392
Niceta, 237
Ninian, 150
Nocturns, 203
Nones, 203, 204
Nonjurors, 122, 141
"N or M," 301, 336
Norman Conquest, 85, 298, 325
"North Side of the Table," 139, 140
"Notices," 165
Notker, 352
Nunc Dimittis, 48, 243, 244
Nuptials, 335, 338

"OBEY," 336
Oblation, 65, 67, 140, 143
Obsecration, 266
Occasional Prayers, 270
Odoacer, 150
Oesterley, W. O. E., 44
Offertory, 67, 159
Old Catholics, 255
"Old Learning," 97
Ommaney, 256
Orarion, 64
Ordinal, 62, 170, 363–405
Ordinale, see *Pica*
"Ordinary of the Mass," 140
Oriental Lit., 59
Origen, 54, 296
"Ornaments Rubric," 103, 114, 272–280
"Orthodox," 10
Osmund, Bp., 85, 86, 89, 99
Outlook (N. Y.), 331
Overall, Bp., 299

INDEX 421

Oxenham, 11
Oxford, 89, 92, 94, 234

PALESTRINA, 232
Pall, 76
Palmer, Wm., 58, 59, 62, 86, 104, 174
P and F., see Procter and Frere
Papacy, 74, 89, 91, 92
Paradise, 34, 163
Parent Liturgies, 56–69
Parker, Archbp , 401
Parliament, 5, 94, 102, 109, 115, 117, 119, 120, 126, 270, 298, 299, 324, 361, 401
Paschal, 79, 178, 190, 200
Passover, 36, 37, 160, 161
Pastoral Staff, 274, 391, 405
Paten, 64, 275, 390, 404
Patriarchine, 67
Patrick, S , 75, 76, 150
Paul, Saint, 58, 70, 75, 78
Paul's Cathedral, S , 86, 89, 96, 110, 111, 114, 379
Pax, 67
Pearson, Bp , 370
Peckham, Archbp , 166, 313
Penitential Office, 269
Penitential Psalms, Seven, 201
Pentecost, 38
Peregrinatio, 55, 137
Perry, Bp , 123, 124
Perry, Canon, 6, 95, 97
Persecution, 67, 71
Persian Lit , 57, 66
Peter, S , 58, 66
Pica or *Pie*, 100, 409
Picts, 71, 75
Pius IV, 114, 232
Pius V, 114, 267
Placebo, 350
Plain Song, 231–233
Pliny, 33, 47, 48, 230
Poictiers, 75, 234
Polycarp, 77, 373, 374, 376
Polyphony, 231
Pontifical, 101, 281, 390, 402
Poore, Bp , 86, 89, 99
Pope, see Rome, Bp. of

Portiforium, Portuisse, 85, 87, 96, 99, 100, 204. See also Breviary
Post-Communion, 196
Potter, Archbp , 385
Præmunire, 91
"Prayers, The," 23–29
Prayer Book of 1549, 87, 89, 98–108, 339, 343, 347
Prayers for Dead, see Departed
Prayers to Saints, 148
Prefaces, 158
Prefaces, Proper, 173
Preparation for Holy Communion, 140–144
Presbyter, see Priest
Presbyterians, 11, 115, 267, 381
Presence in Holy Communion, 185–190
Pressensé, 43
Priest, 363, 369, 399, 403
Priesthood, 180–184
Prime, 203, 204
Pro-Anaphora, 67, 140
"Processions," 96, 265, 358
Procter, 148, 205, 206, 245
Procter and Frere (P and F), 21, 34, 47, 61, 101, 103, 114, 141, 237, 238, 261, 264, 291
Prohibited Degrees in Marriage, 334
"Prophecy," 67, 141, 155
"Proposed Book," 124, 360
"Protestant Episcopal," 125–129
Protestants, Foreign, 40, 120, 127
Prothero, R. E , 222
Prothesis, 162
Province, 380, 386
Provisors, 91
Prymers, 87, 101, 142, 265, 269
Psalter, 43, 44, 48, 100, 117, 208, 234
Psalter, Method of Using, 219–222
Psalter, Music for, 230–233
Ptolemy, 70
Pullan, L , 81
Purgatory, 66, 163, 409
Puritans, 5, 114, 115, 138, 222, 246, 264, 270, 272, 275, 283, 284, 286, 288, 291, 298, 328, 337, 350, 378, 383
Pusey, 137, 142, 169, 194

INDEX

Quicunque vult, 256
Quignonez, 99, 101, 205

RAVENNA, COUNCIL OF, 167
Recent Discoveries, 393
"Reconciliation, Ministry of," 169
Reeves, Bp, 381
Reformation in England, 90
Religio licita and *illicita*, 41, 52, 56
Rémusat, 70
"Repulsion" from Holy Communion, 138
Reserved Sacrament, 197–199
Respond, 221
Reynolds, Bp, 269
"Right Side of Table," 140
Ring, 336, 337, 405
Ritual Discussion, 277
Robert, Bp, 95
Rochette, 274
Rogation Days, 264, 269
Roman Bishops in England, 91
Roman Church, 76, 91, 221, 256, 267, 311, 404
Roman Liturgy, 58, 66, 78, 80, 82, 84, 98, 162, 176, 196, 396
Rome, Bishop of, 252, 267, 334
Rouen, 79, 85, 256
Roumania, 59, 76
Rubrics, 79, 80, 100, 273, 301, 403. See also "Black Rubric"
Rule of Faith, 248
Russia, 66, 73

SABBATH AND SUNDAY, 142
Sacerdotal, 181–183, 399, 400, 403
Sacramentary, 82, 100, 174
Sacraments, Nature of, 185, 303
Sacrifice, 177–180
Sadler, Preb, viii, 170, 282, 384
Salisbury, 85–87, 99, 101, 174, 284, 293, 312, 337, 338, 348, 396, 402, 403, 408
Salutation, Mutual, 261
Sanctus, 60, 64, 67, 173, 352
Sandals, 405
Sanderson, Bp, 359
Sarapion, Bp., 58, 61, 394

Sarum, see Salisbury
Savoy Conference, 3, 115, 117, 118
Saxons, 74, 82
Schiller, 411
Schism, 267
Scotland and Scots, 70, 74, 75
Scottish Church, 6, 84, 120–134, 380
Scottish Prayer Book, 21, 35, 104, 120–134, 141, 150, 156, 158, 160, 163, 169, 174, 175, 177, 179, 196, 199, 220, 263, 315, 317, 326, 334, 339, 340, 346, 353, 357
Scudamore, 35, 139, 145, 155, 156, 167, 169, 197, 274, 279
Seabury, Bp, 6, 122–125, 176, 275
Seal and Sealing, 307
Secker, Archbp, 170
Second Prayer Book of Edward VI, 109–113
Secreta, 144
Selah, 16
Selden, 325
Self-examination, 142, 191
Seneca, 327
Sentences, 205
Sepulchre, Holy, 55
Septuagint, Greek, 27, 211, 217
Sequence, 351–353
Seraphic Hymn, 173
Sermon, 158
Sermon on Mount, 44, 159
Servia, 59
Seven Hours, 203, 204
Seven Words, 210
"Seventy Disciples," 366, 369
Severn, 75
Sext, 203, 204
Shairp, Prof, 381
Shakespeare, 127, 137, 352
Shaxton, Bp., 95, 96
Sheldon, Bp, 115
Shema, 16, 141
Sicily, 73
Silvia, or Etheria, 55, 137
Sinclair, Archdeacon, 110
Si quis, 402
Slavonic, 59, 73
Smith, J B, 398

INDEX 423

Smith, Dr Wm, 124
Smyrna, 374, 376
Socinian, 11, 384
Socrates, Historian, 221, 230
"Solemn League and Covenant," 115
Somerset, Duke of, 102, 109, 110
Song of Blessed Virgin Mary, 241
Song of Simeon, 242, 244
Song of Zacharias, 240
South Carolina, 226, 230
Spain, 70, 78
Spurgeon, 229, 383
Stanley, Dean, 214
State Services, 361
Sternhold and Hopkins, 233
Stigand, Archbp, 92
Stokes, Prof, George, 76, 380
Stole, 402, 403, 405
Stubbs, Bp, 40, 74, 90, 93
Succat, 75
Sunday, 48, 142
Supplications in Litany, 266
Sursum Corda, 60, 67, 171, 173
Symbol, 245
Synagogue, 8, 13, 14, 36, 41–45
Syrian Liturgy, 57, 58, 66
Switzerland, 383, 384, 388

TABLE, HOLY, 40, 54, 112, 125, 138
Table of Liturgies, 68, 133
Tacitus, 71
Taine, 220
Tait, Arcbp, 249
Tallis, 233
Talmud, 160
Tate and Brady, 233
Taylor, Bp Jeremy, 115, 128, 177, 336, 345
"*Tee-ay*" Council, 252
Te Deum, 237, 256, 362
Temple, 8, 13, 14, 15, 20, 24, 36, 39, 41–45, 141, 173, 200, 201, 278, 374
Tennyson, 148, 331
Tersanctus, see *Sanctus*
Tertullian, 47, 54, 287, 307, 336
Testament of our Lord, 263
Thanksgiving Day, 208, 359, 377, 378

Theodore, Archbp., 84
Theodoric, 150
Thomas, Lit. of Saint, 57, 66
Tierce, 203, 204
Tithes, 159
Titlepage, 4, 102, 125–129
Todd, Dr., 380
Toledo, 81, 254
"Tongue not understanded," 72, 73, 107, 167
Tonstal, Bp, 95
Traditio Instrumentorum, 390, 396
Traditores, 52
Trajan, 33, 47, 230
Transfiguration, 150
Translations, 93, 95, 146–148, 150
Transubstantiation, 123, 185
Treitschke, 384
Trent, Council of, 34, 232, 299, 404, 405
Triest, 67
Trisagion, see *Sanctus*
Triumphal Hymn, 67
Troperium, 100
Troyes, 79
Trypho, 45
"Tulchan" Bishops, 121
Tunic, 405
Tyre, 42
Twysden, 148

UNCTION, 307, 312, 343
Unitarian, 10, 11
United States Report on Marriage, 328
Unleavened Bread, 161, 162
"Unworthiness of Ministers," 387
"Upper Room," 38
"Use," 5

VANDALS, 150
Vedas, 220
"Veil," 64
Veni Creator Spiritus, 157, 207, 254, 309, 403, 405, 411
Venite, 208, 217, 360, 361
Vernacular, see Vulgar Tongue
Vespers, 200, 203, 241

INDEX

Vestments, 273–275
Vicar, 301
Victoria, Queen, 336, 361
Victricius, 79, 256
Vienne, 77, 264
Visitation of Sick, 341–348
Vulgar Tongue, 59, 71–74, 107
Vulgate, 93, 196, 217, 350

WAFER BREAD, SEE UNLEAVENED BREAD
Wakeman, H. O., 93, 118, 279
Wales, 71, 74, 79, 82, 85, 86, 103
Wall, Wm., 290, 291
Ward, W P., 201
Wardens, see Churchwardens
"Warnings," 164, 165
Warren, Canon, 19, 33, 42, 45, 54, 61, 71, 73, 76–78, 80, 85, 141, 157, 158, 162, 173
Washington, 125, 314
Wasserschleben, 381
Waterland, 256
Watkins, O D , 323
Watts, Dr., 234
Wesleys, 196, 234
Westminster, 110, 267
Westminster Assembly, 5, 115, 298

Westminster Confession, 246, 325, 328
Whitby, 76
White, Bp , 123–125, 176
White, Dr. E. A., 276
Whithern, 79
Wicliffe, 92, 93
Wilberforce, Bp , 166, 315
Wilfrid, Bp , 92
Wilkins, 95
Williams, Bp. John, 125
Williams, Isaac, 151, 235, 262
William the Conqueror, 85, 90
William III, 122, 126
Winchester, 89, 399, 403, 404
Wine in Holy Communion, 160
Wirgman, Archdeacon, 328
Wittenberg, 327
Wolsey, 94, 407
Wordsworth, Bp. Christopher, 45, 192
Wren, Bp , 121, 270
Wykeham, Bp , 89

YORK, 71, 84, 86, 95, 101, 309, 336, 337, 348

ZACHARIAS, 240, 278
Zwingli, 114, 186, 382, 388

www.ingramcontent.com/pod-product-compliance
Lightning Source LLC
Chambersburg PA
CBHW071138300426
44113CB00009B/1011